Planning and design of
library buildings

Planning and design of library buildings

Godfrey Thompson

The Architectural Press, London

TO DOREEN WITH LOVE

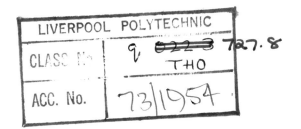
ISBN 0 85139 526 0
© Godfrey Thompson 1973
First published 1973
Printed in Great Britain
by Page Bros (Norwich) Ltd, Norwich

Contents

Preface

This book is meant for beginners: not only for students but also for those, however skilled and experienced in their own professions, who are approaching for the first time the fascinating and important task of creating a new library. Its theme is that few architects in such a situation know very much about libraries, and far fewer librarians know anything about architectural planning.

The literature on the subject is already large but it is dominated by a book so outstanding that any new one must appear to be presumptuous. No librarian needs to be told that the reference is to Keyes D. Metcalf's *Planning academic and research library buildings,* a book based on wide experience and considerable research.

The justifications for another book in the field are that Metcalf deals only with academic and research libraries, that the book was published seven years ago and that much has happened in the last seven years. Another reason is that Metcalf deals almost entirely with American practice; this book deals with British practice. One further point: Metcalf is an expert and he writes mainly for experts, dealing with problems (for example of construction) in a way which requires librarians to think in architectural terms. This may be the right approach to the specialist library building consultant, but the less experienced need guidance expressed in more general terms.

More new libraries have been built in Great Britain during the last ten years than in the previous thirty. The financial limitations of the 1930s, the second world war, and the inevitable building restrictions in the first post-war decade, created a backlog of building projects; the same period saw a steady growth in public demand for library services and a dawning, much slower in official quarters, that libraries were vital instruments of education at all levels. While British architects and librarians waited for the opportunity to build, they visited or studied the new library buildings of America and Scandinavia.

Now we have many new libraries and a considerable literature on them. Talent among architects and librarians is not lacking: those who had the task of creating our new libraries had time to prepare themselves and models on which to draw. A golden age of library building appeared to be imminent. Many of the libraries which arose were striking pieces of architectural design—adventurous, attractive, original. Some won prizes—architectural prizes: very few indeed would win prizes awarded by working librarians. The number of these striking and desirable pieces of architectural design which have proved unsatisfactory as libraries is high. A few, including work by some very distinguished architects, deserve enrolment in the record of monumental howlers. If an architect thinks I am biased, let him ask a librarian colleague for his views on some of these famous modern libraries: better still, let him ask the librarians who have to operate them.

Given all the talent available, the examples to study, an ample literature, an efficient library furniture industry, one must ask why the results should have been so disappointing. I believe that the answer lies in the lack of adequate co-operation between the two professionals most concerned—architect and librarian. Not that there is any lack of goodwill, but there is failure to understand the contribution each has to make, and certainly the importance of machinery of direct and regular communication. Perhaps more important, there is often a lack of knowledge of precisely what the other is trying to do; what the librarian really wants; how the architect plans to identify and meet this need.

The architect alone cannot build a library; many other specialists will be involved and will form part of a design team under his leadership. Some architects may be startled that the librarian is recorded in this book not only as the client but also as a member of that team; such a reaction indicates the seriousness of the problem. It is important that each of the professionals most deeply involved—architect and librarian—knows how the other works and what he is trying to achieve; equally important is a crystal clear understanding of their separate responsibilities and of the lines of demarcation. Nothing is to be gained, and a great deal lost, in goodwill if one tries to usurp the function of the other.

It may be said that no librarian is likely to interfere with an architect's job because he has not the training for it; it happens nevertheless when a librarian expresses his wishes in terms which prejudge the issue. On the other hand too many architects approach the problems of reader service from scratch and offer solutions of their own on matters which have been studied by the library profession for many years. The architect has to give a solution in spatial and concrete terms of a requirement which is in itself a solution of a problem: so much is clear but it is less clear who is to define the requirements and in what terms.

Not all library projects involve creation of a new building. Some may be conversions, others merely a transfer of an existing service to another area within an institution. For tasks such as these the procedures followed throughout this book will seem unnecessarily detailed and laborious but it is important that the librarian should have a sound grasp of the basic principles of library planning and design. It is perhaps even more important that he should know something of every factor involved when, as sometimes happens with a small scheme, he is not to have the benefit of an architect's help. For this reason alone it is worth going in some detail into matters which an architect would normally decide alone.

A study such as this, which emphasises so strongly the importance of close liaison between architect and librarian, may make its point more easily to a librarian than to an architect. To the latter a librarian, though no doubt a worthy fellow, is just another client. When the library building is completed the architect will go on to develop a relationship with the next client—butcher, baker, candlestick maker. In this matter, therefore, architects are much more professional in their approach than librarians and it is almost inevitable that it will be the librarian who presses for closer co-operation and the architect who is the wooed partner.

Those parts of this book which deal with the work of an architect will offer nothing new to a member of that profession but it is hoped that they will help a librarian to understand what the architect is doing at each stage of his work; similarly parts which deals with factors being considered by the librarian will tell the experienced librarian little that he does not already know, but may help an architect to understand what lies behind the librarian's stated requirements.

There is no separate section dealing with the design and planning of a school, college, university, public or any other type of library. Access to books and audio-visual materials in conditions of comfort and economy, efficiency and security are common to all. Because this book deals with libraries of many different types, and is intended for the beginner, not the expert, the recommendations must necessarily be less specific than they would in a more specialised study.

Although the subject is both planning and design, the latter element is considered only as it directly affects, and is affected by, the library's operational plan. Discussions of the interrelation between function and form have been avoided but there is undeniably an aspect of "appearance" which is entirely aesthetic and concerns only the architect; this subject has been ignored. The choice of photographs has been dictated entirely by the need to illustrate planning points: if an architect feels the need to obtain inspiration by looking at photographs of beautiful modern libraries, he will know where to find them.

Plans and statistics of four recent British university libraries have been used to illustrate how each architect has tackled a problem which, while basically similar to the others, is affected by its own peculiar constraints. Universities have been chosen because no other class of library serves communities so easily comparable; these particular libraries were chosen because they were erected as independent buildings and because they are all planned as cubes. Comparison with university buildings of a less conventional design (for example Glasgow University library) would not have shown the same parallels of purpose and variations of solution.

The relationship between architect and librarian in the field of library design has been a matter close to my heart for some time now and it would like here to record my indebtedness, for both education and friendship, to my colleagues on the Architect-Librarian Working Party set up by the Library Association which, under the chairmanship of Herbert Ward, has for some years given, and is still giving, a valuable lead in this field.

I am particularly indebted to two professionals for continuous advice and specialist help: Mrs N. E. Wilson BA, ALA, planning assistant of the City of London Libraries, and G. K. V. Tomlinson RIBA, AADip. For help on security matters I must thank K. G. Wright, security consultant to the Corporation of London.

I also thank all those librarians, architects and suppliers who have kindly allowed me to draw upon their work. In particular I am indebted to Peter J. Bassenet for allowing me to quote from an unpublished thesis, to the American Library Association for permission to use some most valuable drawings by the late F. J. McCarthy from *Planning library building for service*, and to the RIBA for permission to quote from its *Handbook of architectural practice and management*. Some of the plans, tables, diagrams and spatial analyses have already appeared in *The Architect's Journal*, which has kindly given me permission to use them. These buildings have in several cases grown since the analyses were written, but it has not been possible to prepare new studies.

1 Libraries

An architect is unlikely to design a satisfactory library building without first understanding clearly its function and the proposed methods of carrying out that function. The information he receives from the librarian will guide him in detail, but there is a danger that, in providing the information, the librarian will assume that the architect is familar with the type of library to be built. Different types of library have different spatial and environmental emphases and it is only too easy for an architect to assume that his experience in designing one type of library can be used, with only small adjustment, in designing another. The following paragraphs are meant for architects: they give a very general outline of the purposes of the main categories of library, but it must be emphasised that there can be enormous variations within each category. "Fundamentally a library is not a building but a service organisation"[1].

UNIVERSITY LIBRARIES

This term is taken to include polytechnics, but not the older universities (Oxford, Cambridge, London etc) which are collections of colleges and faculty buildings generally widely dispersed among alien surroundings. The central libraries in some of the older universities are so huge as to form a class of their own. Fully established British universities (other than the collegiate ones) average between 4000 and 6000 students, (while US universities average between 10 000 and 30 000); these numbers obviously affect both the scale of the library and the contribution it has to make.

A new university, given space in which to build, usually takes the form of a campus, with the library occupying a key site, easily accessible from the main thoroughfare and with all-weather approaches. The library may be associated with a bookshop, and as it is intended to accommodate readers for long periods at a time, will need auxiliary provisions in the way of restaurants, lavatories and perhaps meeting rooms. It may have to remain open far into the night and at least part of it may be open through twenty-four hours. Car parking can usually be ignored as it is the responsibility of the campus planners.

The present programme of transforming colleges into polytechnics and polytechnics into universities can mean that library has to be designed to serve those working in growing and often isolated buildings within a campus which is at the planning stage. In effect this means the expansion of college libraries on their existing sites or their transmutation into subject libraries in separate buildings until space and money can be found for a single library building large enough to serve the completed university.

Other universities may opt for permanent departmental libraries, physically separate from the central library building, or for a series of faculty libraries, each often large entities, but unless extra funds can be found, this will mean the weakening of the central collection and the duplication of book stocks, so the more common decision is to have central collections; the breaking of the barriers between the sciences and the growth of multi-disciplinary courses encourage this trend. On the other hand certain departmental libraries, particularly in institutes of education and medical schools, will have a full life of their own, with book consultation and borrowing facilities. For comment on the sublibrary, the departmental library, the class library and the institute library, see the Parry Report[2].

The main function of the university library is to store bibliographical and audio-visual materials and to make them available swiftly to students, faculty and research workers. A few years ago most universities would have assessed their main role as service to research, but today it is generally accepted that the library is an active participant in the teaching and learning programme at all levels. All university libraries have the duty to provide biblio-graphical tools necessary not only for subject interests but also for education and development of the whole university body as human beings. The library will serve as a tool to assist learning, teaching and research, and will offer hospitality in varying degrees to outsiders—visiting students, local industry and, to a limited extent, the general public. Because it is important to give first-year students a thorough appreciation of the library's services, lecture space may have to be provided within the library itself.

Almost the whole of the material will be open for readers to search, but rare and valuable books, and materials which require careful handling, may be locked away and accessible only through requests to the staff. Paradoxically books in short supply and in heavy demand by undergraduates may be kept off the open shelves and issued only for short periods and under stringent conditions.

Because the vast bulk of the book stock will be open to readers, seating will be needed near each section of the shelving. A large proportion of the books can be borrowed for use outside the library and so a control area for book issue and return will be a prominent feature. University libraries will tend to have a higher proportion of books *per reader* on issue at any one time than most other types of library; some impose no limit on the number that may be borrowed by faculty members.

Periodicals will be an important part of the storage and service problem: 5000 titles is a not unreasonable estimate. The evidence of SCONUL (Standing Conference of National and University Libraries) in the Parry Report[3] recommended 4000 volumes (plus extra multiple copies) for an established university with 3000 students. Universities which offer service to industrial research will need to hold large numbers of reports and pamphlets. As the stock will run into hundreds of thousands of volumes the library must either be spread over a vast area or have several floors; subject division of stock within the areas will be inevitable and may dictate different shelving and furniture requirements for different areas (maps, for example, are more difficult to house than classical texts).

The use of the building will vary very considerably at different times of the day or of the term. Entrances will have to handle large numbers at a time, yet provide security controls. Close to the entrance the area for issue and return of books will generate noise and movement that will have to be insulated both acoustically and visually from the main parts of the building where quiet study will prevail. Loan periods may be complicated: some items may be issued for whole terms while books in heavy demand may be loaned for as little as three hours, with very strict control on return times. The movement of readers (largely young and uninhibited) to their target areas will have to be shielded in order to minimise disturbance.

A main service area, easily accessible from all parts, will hold the common bibliographical tools; bibliographies and catalogues will take up considerable space and will be used heavily by both readers and library staff. Communications from this region to both shelving and book supply areas will need to be highly organised.

Although for the foreseeable future the main material will certainly be in the form of printed books, other forms already exist in great quantities and some will proliferate swiftly. Microfilms (roll microfilm, micro-opaque, Microcard, microprint, microfiche), tape (magnetic and video), disc (audio and possibly computer), all call not only for accommodation space but also for room for expansion; fortunately they are compact and simple to store. Providing for the use of such forms however presents a much more serious planning problem; to find space to seat a given number of readers with adequate room to read and write is one matter; it is quite another to provide a growing number, possibly even an equal number (working as individuals, not as classes) with the opportunity to use audio-visual materials. As part of the learning process, readers may need to use sophisticated apparatus to create their own media; research workers will certainly need to do so. The parallel is with the space and equipment requirements of the university's laboratories—a frightening one for planners.

The enormous runs of bound volumes of periodicals in older university libraries eat up a large proportion of the storage space so a decision by the librarian of a future university to use microforms for storage and retrieval of periodicals will have a very important influence upon stack, and therefore upon space planning.

In terms of numbers the greatest use of the library is by undergraduates who, while needing access to large holdings of books, make intensive demands upon a comparatively limited range of materials. The Parry report[4] discusses undergraduate collections, browsing rooms and libraries in halls of residence, all of which can affect the planning of the main library. There is as yet no separate undergraduate library in Great Britain (although there are several undergraduate collections), but at least one is being built and more may follow; such libraries, which have the helpful effect of freeing the main library from undergraduate pressure, have been the fashion in American libraries for the last twenty years and many more are being built. Even in America, however, doubts have been expressed about such libraries: unless they have very large stocks they may become holdings of non-loan runs of "set books", tending to encourage the undergraduate to limit his reading to recommended main texts, a tendency which is against the basic principles of modern university education. An extreme example of this is the recent American fashion for very large libraries solely for undergraduates, with a comparatively small book stock but with a space allocation and an atmosphere which encourages their use as a social meeting place for new students.

Special provisions of any kind for undergraduates would certainly free space in the main library for research workers who need carrels or other secluded seating arrangements. It can also enable the main library to spend more time on its very important creative activities—literature searches and compilation of bibliographies for researchers, production of current awareness bulletins and other direct contributions to the life of the university.

In order to do all this the university library must be a processing plant and to a lesser extent a factory. New books must be selected and ordered and will be delivered in quantity, passing along organised lines and through a processing sequence before taking their place on the shelves. Some volumes will need to be treated in a repair shop or bindery, either outside the library or as part of the flow-line itself. Business affairs and general accounting work generated by the library will have their spatial and service needs, and the usual arrangements have to be made for the staff, including food, recreation and lavatories.

For many years now university expansion has been both continuous and ubiquitous; for the future the views of the forecasters oscillate wildly but, given a fair measure of prosperity, continuation of the trend seems to be fairly certain.

Some new universities have begun with a few faculties and with the intention of adding more as the opportunity occurs: space for growth will therefore be essential, as will a high degree of flexibility. These will imply not only space for new sections but also allowances for enlarging the common staff service and bibliographical areas. Communications have to be planned between the pioneer elements and those future additions to the building which can at first be only dimly envisaged. New materials and communication systems, including those not yet invented, have to be allowed for: obvious examples are the developments of closed-circuit television, video-tape and computer-based retrieval systems.

Fortunately, most entirely new universities have space in which to plan; because they are usually built in open country, their buildings can be designed for expansion more easily than can those within cities. The upgrading of existing colleges within cities and their physical expansion presents a much more difficult planning problem and offers a task challenging enough to stimulate any architect.

COLLEGE LIBRARIES

Colleges vary enormously in size and function but most consist of a single large building of which the library occupies a floor or a wing. Colleges which have their own campus (some recently built colleges of education, for example) are best thought of as small universities even though at present they seldom serve more than 1000 students: they will grow.

The function of the college library will generally be similar to that of the university library but on a smaller scale; because colleges generally include fewer residential students then universities, there may be more emphasis on the issuing of books for use outside the building. The staff's bibliographical activities will include providing reading lists and bulletins to exploit the library's resources, both in association with the curriculum and for general cultural ends.

Some colleges make use of recreational literature to encourage reading among students who are not basically book-orientated. This means that there will be attractive browsing areas with paperback books, displays and other features more usually associated with the public library. Any special features the college may use in its educational programme (film theatres for example) will have repercussions on the library's activities and services.

All colleges will have an active programme of teaching directly associated with the use of the library: such a programme will be particularly extensive in colleges of education and will call for a large space allowance, possibly in adjoining lecture rooms. The requirements include facilities for efficient handling of large numbers of readers, easy access to books, quiet study conditions and encouragement of private reading. Because their subject range is limited (when compared with universities) and the emphasis is more directly on teaching, colleges may be particularly advanced in their use of non-book resource media. Because these media are in so many ways extensions of the book form, the librarian will probably be in charge of the entire work of the college in this field; he will therefore require both space to store these materials and workshops and laboratories where the forms may be prepared, processed and presented. Video-tape is an example; to the college librarian it will be not only a form of recorded information but also a way of using the many of the library's special resources in live teaching sessions.

In many modern colleges (as in many schools) the library has changed its identity[5] and is no longer merely a place where books are housed. The students' increasing involvement in its activities, and their participation in its work, make it a workshop for their creative self-education and an environment in which they can express themselves by using its materials and techniques. If the classroom is now where they are stimulated to use their minds, the library is a place where the resources can be found to follow up this approach and where they can create something unique to themselves; this act of creation is a fundamental part of the aim of education today.

Because colleges operate as independent entities, book intake and processing areas similar to those of university libraries will be needed. The basic difference between the institutions is that college library stocks will be neither so vast in number nor so comprehensive in range as those of universities and they will more directly echo the subject emphases and limitations of the college.

SCHOOL LIBRARIES

At one extreme will be the primary school library, which may be a few books housed centrally in an informal atmosphere and supplemented by collections in classrooms; at the other extreme— rather like a college library in miniature—will be the library in a senior school with a large pre-university group.

It is commonly said that the library is the heart of the school: this truism certainly has meaning if we apply it to the central position which it should occupy in the school's internal layout. Examples below from two very different schools—the American

Wreake Valley College: south-north and east-west sections

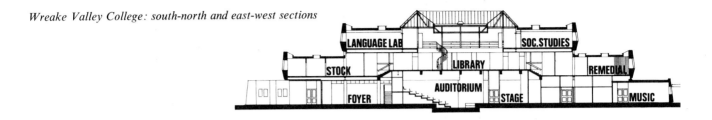

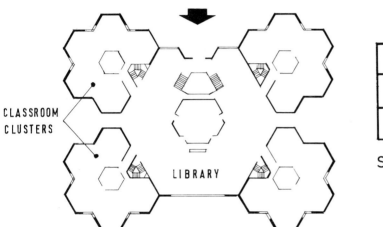

PLAN

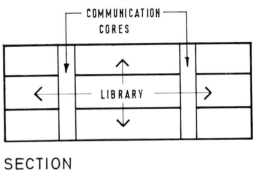

SECTION

The American School in London

School in London and Wreake Valley College in Leicestershire—show how the library holds a position which is both central and easily accessible from all parts of the school. Care is taken, of course, to prevent it being used as a passageway to and from other areas.

Because a school must be designed as a single entity, the architect will have limited freedom to display originality in designing the library. Encouragement of use must be the keynote, the comparatively small stock of books presenting few storage problems. In other ways also the traditional school library is easy to plan; much less space will be needed for preparing books for the shelves, particularly if, as is usually the case, the school is associated with a central supply organisation. Lavatory and other facilities for the library staff will be found in the provision made for the teaching staff. Because librarians and teachers will be in close contact with individual readers, control and security arrangements can be less stringent.

On the other hand, no institution is changing as fast as schools. Where classrooms have disappeared and individual learning takes place in flexible areas within open-plan rooms, the library will act as the centre in which all the resources of modern education are housed and from which they are supplied (and indeed created) for the whole school. It will be both the place to which children and staff come to choose and to read books and the learning materials resource centre; this term is already beginning to replace "school library" as its designation. Here are housed film reels, strips and loops, audio tapes and records, which can not only be used on the appropriate machines by children within the resources centre but can also be piped by sophisticated switching installations to both individuals and groups at the discretion of the teachers. It is also the duty of the resources centre to produce teaching and learning media for specific needs by drawing upon its own holdings and borrowing from other centres. Students themselves create such media within the centre.

As these alterations transform the traditional function of the school library, so they have repercussions in every aspect of its design. If the trend in school design is towards clusters of study areas of which audio-visual projectors and picture transmitters are the focal point, rooms will tend to become wedge-shaped, perhaps with sloping ceilings. The library, offering the same facilities, will also change shape to offer good viewing and listening positions. Lighting will need to be far more flexible when there are functions other than book-reading to be accommodated; the different lighting levels needed for various audio-visual conditions must be obtainable at the touch of a switch. Acoustic problems will be quite different from those of the past, while electrical outlets will need to be more numerous; conduits for remote control apparatus will be a normal provision.

The architect who has to plan a new school library will not necessarily find that his project is to create such a sophisticated entity. The education authority or the head teacher may have gone only a short distance along this road, but at the very least the switch of emphasis from teaching to learning will mean the need both for more space and for the more flexible use of the space, while the hospitality to advanced technological ideas and equipment will alter the conventional image of a school library.

Whether or not audio-visual materials are held in any quantity, the usual storage, study and browsing areas will be needed and locations where students can study individually. Where space is available these can be in the form of carrels; in other libraries they may be merely quiet areas within the perimeter of shelving. More and more schools feel the necessity for group viewing and listening rooms as well as seminar rooms, and because of the importance of having information materials to hand, they are being associated with the library. As the barriers within the schools come down the library is taking a focal position, its information resources used in all learning activities at all times. To an architect this can be an exciting challenge; it is also a very difficult one.

PUBLIC LIBRARIES

Extracts from the UNESCO *Public library manifesto* state the purpose of the public library in convincing terms:

"The public library is a practical demonstration of democracy's faith in universal education as a continuing and lifelong process, in the appreciation of the achievement of humanity in knowledge and culture. It is the principal means whereby the record of man's thoughts and ideals, and the expression of his creative imagination, are made freely available to all."

For the last fifty years the provision of public libraries in Britain has been in the hands of two different types of local government authority—municipal (borough and urban district) and county. The basic difference between their systems has been that one is designed to serve a single concentration of citizens while the other serves a larger region which may include several sizable towns but will also certainly include larger and more thinly populated country areas. The laws under which public libraries operate were consolidated and amended into the Public Libraries Act of 1964[6], but the local government reorganisation proposals of 1970–71, have altered the picture entirely and it is at the moment impossible to say with any certainty how the proposed new authorities will operate. There will certainly be fewer of them; their areas will usually be larger and they will operate services to both town and countryside within a single unit. How much autonomy will be given to large towns within the new county authorities is as yet undecided, but it is still possible to discern a functional difference between central libraries serving urban concentrations, branch libraries serving either suburbs of large towns or providing the whole service for small towns and villages, and headquarters which will provide the administration as well as the supply and support services for smaller branch libraries and run mobile library operations for rural areas. What is unresolved is the relationship between the central libraries and the headquarters within the new combined regions.

The coming of sophisticated new media and audio-visual techniques will certainly affect public library planning, but because the contribution is made to so large and disparate a clientele, the future is not easy to foresee.

Central libraries for towns and cities

These are extremely complex organisations; they may have to serve as all of the following:

—administration and distribution headquarters for a system of libraries for a large population with an infinite variety of needs (the building will have to deal with the intake and processing of up to 100 000 new books a year);

—book-lending and consultation point for the town centre as well as providing for the more advanced bibliographical requirements of the entire area;

—a collection of research libraries, housed together and used by a clientele basically similar to that of a university but with an even wider intellectual spectrum and including the needs of local industry and commerce.

Because of these very different functions the central library will need to be more sectionalised than other types. In addition to the divisions listed above there may be division by operation (lending, reference, children's etc) or by subject (art, science,

music etc): there are various alternative ways of organising the operations and the appropriate one will be explained by the librarian in the brief. In all cases there will be problems of control, security and economy of staffing.

The range of materials to be housed will be similar to that of a university library and may include large holdings of manuscripts and rare books for which special temperature and humidity conditions will be needed. A large part of the book stock will be housed in closed stack (non-public access) which will be economical in space but heavy on floor loading. An essential of the planning will be that all materials housed in this stack, often millions of volumes, must be so arranged that they can be easily and economically traced and conveyed to public service points.

Conditions of use of the materials will again be similar to those in university libraries except that pressure of demand will be greater at peak times of the day, if more evenly spread throughout the year. Technological advances in communication methods (eg microforms, Telex, video-tape, punched cards, computers) will influence this library at least as much as they will any other kind.

Architectural requirements for spatial expansion will perhaps be given less emphasis than in college and university libraries, not because demand is growing more slowly but because official backing and financial support usually get a lower priority than for educational projects. Developments such as the Open University will add to the pressure of demand for book loan and study facilities on such a scale that even central government will have to take notice. Integration with other social services, and advanced communications links with libraries of all kinds in future networks will be increasingly developed and their planning implications will be profound. A minor point, but one not to be overlooked, is that the lending of gramophone records and tapes, both audio and visual, is most highly developed in central public libraries.

Central libraries for counties

These will have some of the concentrated lending and reference features of the town central libraries; the extent will depend on the size of the town in which the library is situated and on whether that town also has its own municipal central library; this latter anomaly will no doubt be cleared up by the new legislation.

In addition the county central library will have to serve as the administration and distribution headquarters for the library services of the whole county, a region which may include small towns as well as villages and isolated communities. In future the scope may also include larger towns at present offering independent services. The greatest emphasis therefore will be upon acquisition, storage, distribution and communications; the latter element will include not only answering inquiries and sending books and information swiftly to individuals in all parts of the county but also running a service by van or mobile library to isolated areas which do not warrant the provision of a permanent library building. Library services to schools are a common feature, calling for large book stocks from which teachers and librarians may draw permanent as well as circulating collections. Even more than town central libraries, county libraries will run services to welfare homes, small hospitals and housebound readers. In general then design considerations will be dominated by the acquisition, storage and transport requirements of such a large undertaking but with these must be incorporated the town central library features.

Branch libraries

In both town and country, these exist chiefly to serve their immediate catchment areas, but in large systems there may be district or regional libraries which in addition act as parent libraries for the smaller, often part-time, libraries in surrounding areas. Branch libraries generally offer a service of books (and possibly of pictures, records, tapes and so on) for loan to people of all kinds and all ages; they also provide minor reference and study facilities for both adults and children. Branches which are open full-time will house between 6000 and 50 000 books, the vast majority on open access, that is, spread on shelves from which readers will help themselves; a smaller number of books will be kept in a quiet study area as a reference library, while others will necessarily be held in operational reserve. Where a full-time branch library cannot be justified because of the smallness of the immediate population, a part-time service may be given, but the bookstock should not in any case be less than 5000.

The primary design and siting requirements are that the building shall be very easily accessible for the general public and that they shall be attracted to use it. At peak times large numbers will do so, perhaps several hundred an hour. Again control and security arrangements are important features of the planning as is economy of staffing. Workrooms will be needed for staff, but the basic processing work on new books will have already been carried out centrally for the whole system. Of the two types of service which the branch library has to give—lending and reference—the former must have much the greater emphasis.

In the past there was always a separate reading room and a children's library but these are now much less often provided. Certainly newspapers and periodicals will be available but they are usually to be found within the general open area; children will certainly be catered for, often in large numbers, but the tendency is for barriers to be broken and a single integrated library designed, with areas for choosing books, for quiet study, for quick reference and for children's facilities, all separated only notionally by furniture and layout within a single open-plan room.

In branch libraries the attention given to children's reading needs are most important because children will use branch libraries more than central ones; all librarians recognise the importance of inducing young people to make the transition from reading as a child to reading as an adult. For this reason young adults' sections may be found; experiments in this direction have been made for many years now but most librarians are as yet unconvinced that such sections are a desirable feature.

The social contribution the library has to make in its own particular situation and to its own particular community may drastically influence both siting and design. Examples are the incorporation of the library in a shopping or community centre, an arts or an education complex. The social planning of an area—the creation of hypermarkets for example—can change the library's emphasis and even its opening hours. Car parking space may soon become a basic siting requirement rather than an amenity feature.

HOSPITAL AND WELFARE LIBRARIES

These are important because they serve people or communities who, for various reasons, cannot have access to other libraries. They vary in size from libraries in large hospitals (particularly mental hospitals) where they have some similarity to public branch libraries, to small reading and issuing rooms in old peoples' homes. The importance of libraries for hospital patients is being increasingly recognised as the value of reading as a practical therapy to alleviate worry and boredom is accepted. *Library service in hospitals* states:

"An efficient trolly service visiting each ward at sufficiently frequent intervals to enable the service to be used properly is required for patients who cannot leave the ward. Patients who can do so should be encouraged to visit the library and make their own selection from the shelves . . . The library service might also include the maintenance of a stock of gramophone records and the provision of sets of plays for play reading."

Quoting *Library service in hospitals*[8] again:

"The purpose of the staff library is to serve the needs of the hospital medical, dental, nursing and other professional and medical staff; and to provide a service for general practitioners, local authority doctors and other professional people who work in the National Health Service outside the hospital and who make use of the hospital's postgraduate training facilities."

Developments in the field have been rapid within the last few years; the latest revision of the Library Association's *Hospital Libraries*[9] deals separately with the needs of medical and professional libraries (including regional libraries, libraries in postgraduate medical centres, and libraries for nurses in training). After many years of comparative indifference, official support is at last being given to these important services. There is real scope therefore for the architect to design units which, while providing separate staff and patients' libraries of different degrees of complexity according to the nature of the hospital, can associate them together to make full use both of stock and of library staff time. If such a library complex can also serve the local general medical practitioners (and such schemes are already in action), the integrated service becomes of value to a wide range of people.

PRISON LIBRARIES

These libraries are doing a great deal towards the successful rehabilitation of those who are confined within prison walls. No other community consists of active people with so much time on their hands; in no community is there greater need for the opportunity to read a wide and inviting selection of books. The architect may think it unlikely that he will be asked to design such a library; so much the worse for us all, because a prison library—planned to attract and to look like a public library "outside"—could have a civilising influence in a world where the primitive too often rises to the surface. Pioneering work is being done; public libraries assist with book stocks and staff advice. Problems exist of course, and it would be absurd not to acknowledge them, but a well-designed library can make its own small contribution towards solving these problems.

SPECIAL LIBRARIES

This term is used to denote libraries which are *not* university, college, school, welfare or public libraries. Despite this negative description special libraries have some positive attributes in common. Their collections are usually limited in subject range but have great depth of coverage of their particular interests; they are perhaps the most positive libraries of all in that they are the least inclined to sit and wait for their clientele to approach them. They not only acquire source material but also produce it by scanning and abstracting to the exact requirements of the users. They serve as information centres for their parent institutions and because of their dynamic approach the planning of layout is less easily predictable.

Other functions may include catering for the educational and recreational needs of the members of the organisation but undoubtedly an efficient and up-to-the-moment information service is the very essence of much special library work.

Among the chief divisions of special libraries are:

Government bodies Here the service will be to the Government itself (usually to a special section of government), to the Civil Service sections concerned and, to a lesser degree, to the whole community when information relating to the speciality is needed. The latter function is a long-term one and may be inhibited by limitations imposed by official secrecy.

Nationalised industries These libraries will vary widely but can be very large indeed and some will need to provide an information service to vast complexes spread over the entire country; they may have central and branch libraries each with its own specialised or merely regional service.

Learned institutions and research associations Obviously the service to members is the main interest but again such a source of specialist knowledge will recognise its obligations to scholarship by co-operating with other libraries. The range of specialities here is very wide indeed, from pure art to applied science and technology.

Professional associations, societies, and trade unions The collecting of information in its own field for the use of its own members must take priority, but the library will co-operate with other libraries and may also do some public relations work for the parent body.

Commercial and industrial firms There is an enormous size range here from the library of a large manufacturing organisation to that of a small firm of lawyers, architects or stockbrokers. Collection of specialised information and speed of retrieval to serve the needs of the organisation itself are essential. If the firm is large enough to have its own training scheme, the library may contribute by supplying textbooks and other educational material to the trainees.

OTHER TYPES OF LIBRARY

Bodies ranging from private clubs to subscription societies may have their own libraries (indeed some subscription libraries, remnants of a once large class of institution, still function). They serve members according to the latters' wishes and to the funds available.

To lay down guide lines for planning libraries of such a wide variety is impossible; without knowing the specific purpose and function few comments can have value. To generalise, special libraries tend to be smaller than public or university libraries and seldom occupy separate buildings, but there are exceptions. Some, in large complexes of scientific establishments, may themselves have sublibraries, comparable to departmental libraries in universities. Siting problems are generally similar to those of school libraries: a central position easily accessible from all parts of the institution, preferably near the main (ground floor) entrance but not usable as a thoroughfare is desirable.

One factor which most special libraries have in common is that their interests are much less restricted to the bound book than other types of library. Some may have large collections of books (particularly in the older learned societies) but their chief interest will be current periodicals, pamphlets, parliamentary papers, reports and other more immediate forms of information. They are also more likely to prepare and circulate their own reports, abstracts, indexes and guides specifically tailored to the needs of the institution. The other factor in common between special libraries is their restricted clientele; on the whole they serve only their own, so the size of operations can be estimated quite easily and there is little need to plan for them to attract reluctant readers.

NATIONAL LIBRARIES

These, the largest of all libraries in book stock and reader seating, have been disregarded in this book because they are so rarely rebuilt. With both the British Museum and the Public Record Office in London at advanced stages of planning and rebuilding, it is felt that, for England at any rate, the problem is settled for many years. There are national libraries in the other countries of Great Britain, as well as the smaller libraries which are national in that they are provided by state funds (national museum libraries and so on) but the problems of planning are so very special that they can hardly be dealt with in a general survey of the field.

LIBRARIES OF THE FUTURE

Obviously a new library must be designed to operate with the materials and the techniques of the future rather than of the past. Libraries have always been associated with books and it is certainly with printed books (and periodicals) that the vast majority of libraries will continue to be concerned for very many years. The coming of microforms into libraries on a large scale (in the 1940s in Great Britain) added a new dimension and this has been increased by the arrival into normal library stock of film, audio disc, audio tape and video tape. The loan of paintings by a public library is now regarded as normal community service.

In whatever form information may be stored in the future, it will continue to be the business of the library to obtain, house and process it for readers. To plan for this without knowing what form it may take is a seemingly impossible task and this adds force to the well-known dictum that "long term planning is impossible". An example of the difficulty concerns video-tape; ten years ago no library planner could have imagined that libraries would be required to accommodate stocks of such materials and machines to run them on, but a machine which allows the playback of television programmes, as well as the recording and playing of specially generated materials, now has an important place in college and school libraries. How much such a machine will be used in public libraries is as yet impossible to predict.

Unfortunately it is by no means clear in what forms such material will be available. It could be disc or tape, cassette or cartridge, or possibly all these forms will be in use simultaneously. If the television camera is to be a familiar part of educational activities, it follows automatically that the library will have to make parallel advances. Libraries have for some time loaned photographs; some now lend ciné films; it may be that the next decade will see also a loan service of ciné projectors. University libraries already lend audio-playing machines.

Although the future is misty and more new materials and techniques arrive every year, each planning team will in practice tacitly accept a freeze date, planning according to what is available at that particular time and not according to what might one day become available. Nevertheless, as an attempt at flexibility certain allowances can be made for future changes which can be dimly discerned. One of these is the relative decrease in materials storage and a relative increase in the space required for the reader. All microfilms, for example, take up only a small fraction of the space needed for the same amount of information in book form but each reader using such a form needs his own machine; even if the material is used by a group, a projector, screen and viewing area will take up a great deal of space. Some libraries are being planned to hold the bulk of their information on microfilm (particularly on microfiche which is easily handled by the reader) and, however compact the microform reading machine may become in the future, the result will inevitably mean that a very much greater proportion of the library will be devoted to reading areas. A more generous provision of electrical outlets throughout the building is apparently called for—but can we even be sure that electricity will be the power source of the future?

Communications devices for staff use present less difficulty. Modern developments such as facsimile transmission, closed-circuit television, Telex (if a fifty-year-old method can be called modern), tape-typewriters and automatic catalogues are not in themselves difficult to house nor do they radically affect the operation of the library: space and electrical connection are all they require. The real importance is the relationship which they will make possible between networks of co-operating libraries and the consequent effects upon the acquisition of, and access to, materials.

Much the most important machine looming over libraries at present is the computer. The total contribution it will make in the library world cannot be known for many years. It can certainly relieve people of routine work in many fields; it can eliminate card catalogues, stock records and present issue methods in most libraries and this has already happened in many; but when, if ever, it will compete seriously with the book as a source of general information which can be retrieved for the reader is another matter. In small libraries it is unlikely to do so, in this century at any rate, but the views of Kemeny[10] are worth studying.

It may be that the only action the planner can take at this time is to arrange that all equipment which *might* be entirely superseded (card catalogues for example) should be freestanding, and to allow space for a possible systems department which might have to be installed to work parallel with the traditional administration section while conversion to full computer operation takes place. Because it seems unlikely at the moment that a library, other than a very large one, will house its own computer, there need be no alarm on the question of floor loading. The machines likely to be housed in a library will weigh less than books housed in mass: probably no more will be needed than the outlet points with which we are already familiar. The use of air-conditioning, however, may become more important, perhaps universal.

To provide extra space and electrical connections and hope for the best—even this unglamorous planning principle is not necessarily wise. A few years ago there was an enormous increase in the use of staff-operated photocopiers in libraries: who now can be sure that the use of do-it-yourself photocopying and the central provision of photocopies direct to the reader will not reverse the trend?

For an interesting discussion of the future effect and contribution of technological developments in library planning from an architect's viewpoint see Brawne[11]; it is questionable however whether his easy assumption that large portions of the bookstock can be microfilmed has much connection with the problems of existing libraries. In the long term this may be the answer, and the coming of ultramicrominiaturisation has increased the possibility: the whole of the Bible has now been produced on one 2 in $\times$ 2 in transparency[12].

The future contribution of the microfilm is more likely to be an active than an archival one. Computer output microform can open completely new fields; it may be that a single central library will hold vast quantities of microforms and that each will be swiftly retrievable at a terminal in any of thousands of satellite libraries. The result can appear on a screen or, by the use of a reader-printer, produce another microform version (not necessarily at the same reduction) which can become the property of the inquirer, to form part of his own collection and be read on a miniature reader. Such a "lap reader", already on the market, will enable 1000 pages to be read from a single small microform. Nevertheless the problem is not entirely a technological one: account has to be taken of the propensity of the human to prefer familar methods.

In an unpublished thesis, Bassenet[13] quotes two opposing views recorded from a conference of the Educational Facilities Laboratories of New York[14]:

"If it is a fact that in the future the bulk of knowledge will be stored on magnetic tapes or greatly reduced microforms and fed into computers; that information transactions will be negotiated through terminals located at home, in the dormitory, the classroom, the office, or in service stations remote from where information is stored; and that information will be transmitted to users over long distances, then indeed it is imprudent, if not illogical, to plan costly structures to house non-existent books and their readers."

Bassenet says[15]: "This is the essence of the problem and one that should be considered by any librarian planning a new central library, because his building will probably be functioning for the next fifty years, despite the twenty-year assessment of many authorities."

The other conclusion, reached by the conference participants who included top librarians, architects and computer specialists from the US and Canada was:

"In sum, it is the consensus of those who participated in the conference that for at least the next twenty years the book will remain an irreplaceable medium of information. The bulk of library negotiations will continue to be with books—although the science and technology sections will shrink. Remote retrieval of full texts in large amounts over long distances will not be generally feasible, and the continued use of a central library building will still be necessary."

"For at least the next twenty years." Any library planner must think very carefully about the implications of these statements. Future trends in co-operation between libraries, not only in more efficient interloan of books but also in providing the information itself by photographic and electronic methods, are likely to be the greatest influence on decisions relating to both the size and the space allocation of new libraries. The way ahead is hazy, as ever, but the librarian will know more about these trends and their application to his situation than will the architect and he will make the decisions that will be communicated in the brief. The need for flexibility is at least as important in the librarian's mind as in the architect's design.

LIBRARIAN AND ARCHITECT

Creation of a new library cannot be the work of one man, or one firm. It requires the co-operation of a whole team, each member with his own contribution to make. The constituents of the team and their relationships are dealt with elsewhere; here we are concerned with the people most directly and continuously involved, on whom the praise or odium of succeeding generations will fall: the librarian and the architect. Each will contribute his professional skills and the skill of his own staff and associates. Each profession knows, in a general way, something of the other's work. Because their working relationship is so vital to the success of the project it is worth giving some details of the background and training of each for the enlightenment of the other.

The librarian

The librarian in charge of a library, or potential library, will be a senior member of his profession and will be one of more than 12 000 chartered librarians. He will have been educated at a library school and will have passed examinations in a variety of subjects, some dealing with the basic principles of librarianship, others concerned more directly with the particular field in which he chooses to specialise. Some library schools prepare students for external examination by the Library Association but the trend is towards internal examining in the schools themselves to standards approved by the association, success giving exemption from its own examinations. The qualification obtained may be a degree, a higher degree or a diploma. There are considerable variations between schools although the Library Association's standards are applied in them all.

The course will have included both theoretical study and periods of working practice in different types of library. The title "chartered librarian" (ALA or FLA*) is awarded only after approved and supervised practical library service, following completion of the examinations. Because the library profession is highly organised (through the Library Association, its branches, groups and sections, and through other specialist bodies) the young librarian will almost certainly have spent a great deal of time visiting new libraries and studying new methods and future developments. Because his profession is information based, he will be better read in the practices and progress of his trade than many other professional men. The librarian who represents the client in library building projects is not always the chief librarian, although he will act with his chief's authority. In most small libraries, however, the chief librarian himself will have the job. If he is in the service of a large public body he will probably have become familiar with the work of his own colleague, the authority's architect. He may have worked with this architect on alterations and adaptations to his libraries. Nevertheless, he will have little knowledge of the architect's total contribution to a major project.

The architect

The architect will have been educated at a school of architecture, either full-time or part-time, although the trend is towards entirely full-time courses. A full-time student cannot qualify in less than seven years, of which four to five years are spent at a school of architecture. After passing parts 1 and 2 of the examinations at the school, or after part-time study, the student must undertake a minimum of two years' practical training (although one year of this may have been included in the school period)

---

* Fellowship of the Library Association is now awarded only as a higher qualification to experienced librarians who produce a thesis or similar contribution to advanced librarianship.

before passing the part 3 examination. The student is then qualified to become a corporate member of the RIBA and to registration as an architect under the Architect's Registration Acts 1931–8. Under these acts it is an offence for any person who is not registered to practice or carry on any business under any name, style or title containing the word architect.

There are therefore many parallels between the two professions, although the architects' is the large—over 20 000 architects against 12 000 librarians—and the training takes much longer.

An architect is not a builder; he is above all an artist, but in order that he may apply his designs and control the whole operation of erecting a building, he has to learn to understand fully the work of a great number of specialists who will be called into action. Although he may employ, or cause to be employed, experts in structural engineering, soil mechanics, electrical, ventilating and heating (among others), he will still himself be familiar with the work they perform. He will have a good knowledge of scientific management and will order his complicated procedures in a systematic way: his own technical field is well documented and his office will include an effective specialist information service[16]. He is an organiser and an entrepreneur, familiar with property values, commercial development possibilities and ways of financing building operations of all kinds. He must have the ability to work with, to persuade and be accepted by, the planning authorities on whose permission so much of his proposals depends.

The RIBA[17] distinguishes two functions of the architect: "(1) The management function—to ensure that the project as a whole is well run, and to co-ordinate the process of design. (2) The architect's function—to contribute particular architectural skills."

The complexities of his world are vast: he is responsible for the safety of the structure under all conditions, and for ensuring that it complies with all regulations and by-laws. He has an obligation to see that his client is given the best possible value for money but also that contractors and subcontractors are treated fairly. He is employed by the client but has to act as a judge in matters affecting both those who provide the money and those who receive it for work done. The legal implications of his work are considerable, not only in respect of his own direct responsibilities but also because of the maze of official permissions and rules which he, on behalf of his client, neglects to follow at his peril. In the vastly complicated world which he rules he is at great financial risk for every possible error and omission.

About half of the architects in the profession work in private offices; about two-fifths work in public offices (for local authorities, government departments); others are employed by industrial and commercial firms. The architect is both artist and technician but in his mind there can be no separation of his work into solely aesthetic and solely technical aspects. Because the result will depend so much on his own judgment he will wish at an early stage to make his own assessment of the problem facing him, and this he is trained to do. His design will attempt to meet the client's vision of function, not the client's idea of a new building; to satisfy not only the needs of which the client is aware but also those which he does not know a good design can satisfy. He is not, therefore, merely carrying out the client's orders; it may be claimed that as an artist and servant of the community he has a primary duty to the library's users and to the people at large. This may seem exaggerated but it has an element of truth: the RIBA *Handbook* is worth consulting on this point. For further information see *Working with your architect*[18] and *Your architect*[19].

The library situation

When designing a library the architect is forwarding a service whose rationale is not easy to assess. There is no easily defined "purpose of a library"; the contribution a library has to make to the community reflects something special in the nature of that community and in the particular direction of development which the library, among other instruments, exist to further. It cannot be assumed that the public library is basically a collection of books made conveniently available; its role is much more sophisticated,

more dependent upon and involved in certain trends in the community's unconscious aims—"self-improvement in an atmosphere of freedom". In an institution the purpose of the library cannot be understood without knowing both the purpose of the institution and the essential contribution, recorded or implied, which the library has to make in it.

It is small wonder that the library profession has acquired an approach for which professional training gives only a broad basis and in which much depends on experience and the vision of the individual. If an architect has to be taken on his own terms because he is an artist, then a librarian has a similar claim because of the essentially pragmatic nature of his craft. He can estimate the number of books he will need and the numbers of readers who will use them but these estimates can be based only on his experience of a relevant past and on his own beliefs. The future library will alter under the influence of social and educational trends whose direction he can only vaguely foresee; if the library is successful, its very popularity will create problems of growth and changing demand. Because of this he will call for "flexibility", for the opportunity to make alterations in the service at short notice. In doing so he will add enormously to the architect's design problems: flexibility is always an expensive stipulation. The architect can satisfy the needs only if he understands the reasoning behind them: the librarian can comment constructively on the designs only if he understands what the architect is trying to do. Mutual understanding trust, co-operation and patience are needed on both sides. It has been truly said that a good building requires a good client as well as a good architect.

REFERENCES

1 AMERICAN LIBRARY ASSOCIATION Minimum standards for public library services. ALA, Chicago, 1966

2 UNIVERSITY GRANTS COMMITTEE Report of the committee on libraries: the Parry report. HMSO, London, 1967, pp 98–104

3 The Parry report. Ibid, appendix 8, p 267

4 Ibid, pp 44–49

5 SHORES, LOUIS The library college idea. *In Library Journal*, 91:3871, 1 September 1966

6 Public Libraries and Museums Act 1964. CH. 75, HMSO

7 DEPARTMENT OF HEALTH AND SOCIAL SECURITY and WELSH OFFICE Library service in hospitals. HM(70), 23 April 1970

8 Ibid

9 LIBRARY ASSOCIATION Hospital libraries: recommended standards for libraries in hospitals. Library Association, London, 1972. (New standards will follow after the reorganisation of the health and local government services has taken place.)

10 KEMENY, JOHN G. A library for 2000 AD *In Management and the computer of the future*, editor Martin Greenberger. MIT Press and Wiley, Cambridge and New York, 1962, pp 133–178

11 BRAWNE, MICHAEL Libraries: architecture and equipment. Pall Mall Press, London 1970

12 THOMPSON, DONALD E. Form v function: architecture and the college library. *In Library Trends* v 18 no 1, July 1969, p 45

13 BASSENET, PETER J. Spatial and administrative relationships in large public libraries: an investigation into the planning of municipal libraries serving populations exceeding one hundred thousand. Thesis accepted by Library Association, 1970

14 EDUCATIONAL FACILITIES LABORATORIES The impact of technology on the library building. New York, 1967, p 6

15 BASSENET. Op cit

16 CALDERHEAD, PATRICIA (editor) Libraries for professional practices. Architectural Press, London, 1972

17 ROYAL INSTITUTE OF BRITISH ARCHITECTS, Handbook of architectural practice and management. RIBA, London, 1967 (loose-leaf), part 3.220.02

18 RIBA Working with your architect. RIBA, London 1954

19 SENIOR, DEREK Your architect. Hodder & Stoughton, London, 1964

2 Preparing the way

Even a librarian has to admit that the finished product, the new library, will show the influence of its architect far more strongly than that of its librarian, and that the architect is the more important of its creators. Although the architect's goal has a large element of visual satisfaction, no architect can be proud of a building that does not function effectively. He will try to create the perfect machine and it is of the greatest importance that he should fully understand the exact function which the library is being created to perform. Similarly no librarian can be content with a machine that works perfectly if it does so in an unattractive or unsuitable atmosphere. It is equally important therefore, that the librarian should understand the aesthetic objectives.

Given two competent professionals, the result should be a library satisfactory from both viewpoints, and even more important, satisfactory both aesthetically and practically to its users, but this is not always so. A look at libraries built in this country during the last half-century will show that somewhere along the line there has been a gap, a lack of understanding and co-operation. Over and over again the student of library architecture sees an attractive building which just does not work as a library, or an efficiently working library building which creates the wrong mood for those who use it.

The division of duties between librarian and architect seems quite clear; the librarian tells the architect by means of a brief (the American term is program), what the proposed library has to accommodate and what functions it has to perform; the architect creates a building which meets those requirements and will also be an acceptable piece of architecture. This division seems clear, but is it necessary? An architect is trained to assess needs and analyse problems in many fields of service; could he not write the brief himself? This would be most inadvisable: neither the architect, nor even the executive of the parent institution can define the exact need without having considerable working experience of libraries. The librarian, however experienced, will be able to do so only after consultation with his senior colleagues, with his maintenance staff and perhaps with his readers.

To leave an architect without an adequate brief is not to liberate his genius, but to limit his potential: an architect is a specialist in designing to meet client requirements, not in guessing what those requirements are, or should be. Collaboration at all stages, not least in preparing the brief, is the only way to utilise the entirely different skills of the two professionals.

The time will come when the architect has to explain his ideas to the librarian, so that functional solutions can be appreciated within the forward-looking and unfamiliar designs presented. Like all humans the librarian will have his blind spots and he will generally be less alive than the architect to the changes caused by technology in familiar mechanical problems. On the other hand experience may have taught him to suspect some "modern" solutions to old problems. From their many meetings, architect and librarian will learn to understand each other's aims and intentions. On some occasions the architect will bring one of his consultants to meet the librarian so that special problems—heating, acoustics, security—can be fully explained, the architect often acting as interpreter. At even the most informal of these meetings certain agreements will be reached, therefore it is absolutely essential that minutes are always kept. These should be drawn up by the architect and a copy sent to the librarian for confirmation. This may seem bureaucratic; in fact it is a sensible precaution because each member of a team may leave a meeting with a different view of what has been agreed. The minutes will form appendixes to the brief, can be referred to when required, and are the architect's authority for spending time and money in developing certain lines of action.

Each profession has its own jargon and this can be a source of misunderstanding. Librarians are aware of the common usage of such words as planning and design but in the architects' world their meaning is at once wider and more specific. For a librarian, planning begins with his assessment of the library's total contribution to the community, securing a viable fiscal base, establishing priorities and relationships with other social, cultural and education services and then turning to the detailed organisation of the library's resources, including in particular the siting of the various reader services. It can involve both regional and town planning, particularly in the case of public libraries, or the planning of the contribution of a special library to its parent organisation. Later each function of the library will need to be planned both for its own effectiveness and for its relationship with all the other operational activities.

Design has artistic implications; applied to library buildings it consists of devising a satisfactory environment in which the already planned series of operations is to take place. Design cannot begin until overall planning has been completed and will therefore start later in time; nevertheless the librarian's planning will not cease at the early stage but will have to be continued after he is able to consider the inevitable restraints which the proposed design will have on his original ideas. The definitions however are far from exact: the architect will refer to stages of his work as "outline planning", "detail planning" and so on, but these uses of the term refer to the organisation of his own concepts in order that he may arrive at the design which he has visualised. Generally then planning will begin the process but real planning, by both librarian and architect, will continue throughout the various stages of design. A major hazard is that the librarian may not be absolutely clear in his own mind when he puts a particular stipulation in the brief. If he is not himself quite sure what a particular functional problem is, the architect cannot be expected to provide the perfect solution. Take, for instance, the requirement for a room for occasional extra-library activities: the librarian may have in mind lectures, recitals and so on, but may not have worked out the exact range of activities which the room is to house, or have defined in his own mind the term "occasional". Would the occasions be daily, monthly or yearly? If the exact function and its frequency are not made specific, the space itself will be ill-conceived and spaces ancillary to it may be over- or under-provided. Very often the result is a room that is too lavish for a simple series of talks, having rudimentary stage fittings, lighting and projection apparatus, but not sufficiently equipped to be used for even the simplest stage presentation in costume. Many libraries have such rooms and find them an embarrassment.

The writing of a brief gives the librarian an incentive to take a long, hard, look at his present processes and procedures, to see whether they are adequately serving the real purpose of the library. It is the opportunity to use operations research methods which simulate activities and experiment with models to find the best possible procedures to use in the new library. This means that a team of experts will have to be employed: the expense can be justified because the circumstances may never recur. Systems analysis can be of great value in presenting an accurate picture of the structure and of the processes which it employs: if time and money permit, a systems evaluation can follow with a survey of how effectively the system now analysed is serving its purpose. The systems techniques are of course a much larger enterprise than operations research.

FIRST ACTIONS

The creation of a new library, for many of those involved and for many institutions, will be literally the event of a lifetime. It calls for the expenditure of a great deal of money—usually public money.

It is obvious that the initial cost will be high, less obvious that this cost is small compared with the running costs throughout the life of the building. It is only reasonable therefore to give the scheme the most careful study by the best available talent from the very moment of its inception.

It is horrifying that valid and binding decisions on a proposed library have often been taken before appropriate professional advice is obtained: many a library has been built before its librarian was appointed. The scale and position of a library in a college or school has often been fixed by spatial and positional allocations within the building long before thought has been given to the library's role, and before a librarian has been allowed to speak for its needs. It is easy to say that this should not ,be allowed to happen; it is less easy to prevent it. The key figure should be the architect; as he will certainly be involved in the discussions about the future building, he can point out that any library planning will be handicapped from the start without the contribution of a professional librarian.

Similarly, binding decisions have been taken by authorities on the suitability of a particular site without consulting an architect, who may later find valid objections to it on planning or design grounds. Each professional should insist on the presence of the other: the architect can act as a check on the personal preferences and prejudices of an individual librarian (who may not be the man who will eventually run the building). The librarian can exercise a similar influence on his architect.

Outside factors often override the early decisions; social, political, educational and financial considerations—in many cases the very factors which led to the creation of a new library—will inevitably take precedence. A new branch of the public library service in a previously unserved area is produced in the first place by the presence of a community of citizens who are aware of the cultural and educational advantages to be gained by having a library in the area; but it is only when these needs are interpreted and expressed through the machinery of the local council that they approach reality. Decisions by a commissioning authority are always needed to evaluate demand and to assign a place in the list of priorities among many projects, all of which require money. In such circumstances it may happen that the project acquires certain site associations, social emphasese or financial limits before any professional officer has been given the opportunity to express his views. This is not the ideal method of conception: we are not living in an ideal world.

There is no shortage of professional expertise available to an authority: what may be lacking is the decision at a very early stage to assemble a body of experts and to encourage them to work as a team, their proposals being submitted to the authority at each progressive stage. For a team to work effectively each member must appreciate the peculiar skills of the others and there must be a crystal clear understanding of the respective spheres of action and powers of decision. Lack of this understanding has been the greatest single cause of failure in the past.

The moment when the idea of a new library first begins to take shape is not always easy to identify. Some projects are statutory: a new secondary school *must* be provided with a library. Sometimes the need for a library is so obvious as to make the provision automatic: a new university certainly *will* have a main library and it *may* have secondary ones. But there will be many occasions when inclusion of a library among the facilities of a new project will not immediately occur to the planners: in the case of hospitals it has taken decades of persuasion by librarians to make hospital authorities take seriously the idea of a hospital library; many commercial firms have yet to be persuaded of the advantages of having an efficient library information service.

The project normally first acquires a form when it is drafted by a librarian: his proposals will be studied, and possibly drastically amended by his governing body—be it library committee, university council, local council, board of governors or board of directors—theirs is the decision and theirs the control at all stages. It is therefore in the librarian's mind as he first drafts proposals

for a new library, that we can recognise the moment of conception, but from this very first moment he will need specialist information and specialist advice. He will, in fact, be making a preliminary feasibility study and he will begin by drawing upon his own experience and on that of others who have solved similar problems. If we take the simplest example, provision of a branch library for a new housing estate, he can turn to published information on recently constructed libraries serving similar communities; initial costs can be ascertained and rough estimates made of running costs. In the same way librarians of hospitals, schools, colleges and universities can turn to their colleagues for guidance of this kind.

The librarian will soon find, however, that he is faced with hundreds of questions for which his experience, and that of his own profession, can produce no solution; for these he will need to consult legal, financial and other officers to help him to forecast whether it will be possible to create a suitable library under the powers of the institution and within its financial abilities. Because the project will usually be associated with some particular site, the librarian will have already made informal inquiries as to the availability and conditions of use of that site. This may have involved planning officers or surveyors who will make general comments on his ideas.

When he considers that he has sufficient relevant information, the librarian will report to his authority, summarising both the need and his recommended functional solution. He will, of course, explain the advantages which he believes a new library will bring. In the case of a commercial firm he will naturally emphasise the economic advantages the library would contribute to the efficient operation of the undertaking. Where such basic arguments are superfluous, for example in the building of a new university, he may give his views upon appropriate organisation—either central library facilities with close links to specialist schools, or a network of libraries within the campus. He will make no references to matters of design or structure, nor will he attempt more than the vaguest indication of possible costs.

Even if the authority looks favourably upon the proposal it is unlikely, at this point, to do more than give approval in principle. The librarian may have to satisfy it on points in doubt, or even prepare a second report, before the authority agrees to appoint an architect for the scheme. This is not always done in the same way. The authority may employ its own architect to make a feasibility study and, if this is acceptable, appoint a private architect to design a library within the financial and other limits recommended: this would be done in order to save professional fees and in the belief that the authority retains greater control over the project— an odd but prevalent notion. Other ways are to appoint an architect to prepare a feasibility scheme and then reappoint him to carry on with the scheme if the proposals appear to be satisfactory, or to appoint a private architect to design a library and produce all documents necessary for the building contractor and then leave the scene, the authority itself through its own architect inviting tenders and supervising the building process. Such alternatives are not common but they do happen. All are in varying degrees unsatisfactory, the latter particularly being unacceptable to many architects.

In the normal way an architect will be appointed with a written contract, either on the model approved by the RIBA, or on the authority's own pattern; if in private practice, he will be remunerated according to the published scale of professional fees, generally a percentage of the final total cost of the project. Whatever the method of appointment chosen, the architect will be tied to the authority by contract, and one of the obligations laid upon him will be to report at specified intervals upon his proposals and their financial implications.

The question of how the architect is chosen is not easy to answer. Unless the choice is already dictated by a decision to have the same architect for the whole of a campus or complex, it is most usual for the authority to survey past work done by architects who have been recommended to it. Who draws up the original short list? Possibly the authority's own architect; the RIBA may provide a list of suitable firms. Whichever method is used the principle is always to employ a firm of architects which has already done good work in a similar project. This seems hard on the newcomer but presumably he has to make his name with small jobs first.

Another much publicised method is to hold an architectural competition. Here schemes are invited from architects, the creator of the winning design being awarded the job. This is not an infrequent method for choosing both a design and its architect in the case of a prestige bulding; the RIBA *Directory* contains regulations for such competitions. However, even if the new library is to be a prestige building the method is highly dangerous. The brief for the competition will have to be drawn up in great detail by the librarian working in a vacuum, or alternatively with the assistance of an architect who will not be responsible for the design. There can, of course, be no previous satisfactory contact with the successful architect. The system is in fact the perfect example of how not to use the best available talent to create a solution.

In Great Britain the costs of the entire project will usually be met from one financial source, the authority's central funds. Large private donations for such projects are almost unknown because of a tax structure inhospitable to potential donors. This may deprive the librarian of "pump-priming" advantages but at least the architect is spared the task, common in American college library planning, of isolating, in cost and design, a section of the building so that it can be financially debited (and publicly credited) to a particular donor.

The total cost estimate will have to be broken into its major elements, not only so that the authority can assess the relative proportions of expenditure proposed, but also because official cost targets are often based on separate main divisions—site cost, building cost, services, loose furniture and so on. This is reasonable because it is obviously unfair to compare projects when costs can vary enormously with factors such as the availability of a free site or communal main services.

Although required to report on his proposed design and its financial implications and to await approval at every stage, the architect has now in fact become responsible for the end product, the completed building. He cannot bear this responsibility alone; the project must be the result of team-work, with the architect as both leader of the team and its spokesman.

THE DESIGN TEAM

In a large project the team will include experts from many different fields. Even with a large team, only a few will be actively engaged at any one time. Some will be brought in for consultation at very infrequent intervals; others may make their total contribution once and for all at a very early stage. The following cast-list of a design team is based on the requirements of a very large and complicated library. In most library projects the number involved will be very much smaller, but special knowledge will always be needed and must be at the team's service in some other way, many specialist professions being in fact represented by the architect.

Architect

Leader of the team. He, with his assistants, will visualise the future building both as a machine and as a aesthetic contribution to the life of the community. He will have overall responsibility for creating a suitable environment for the function, for the visual impact of the building and for its engineering efficiency. He carries a grave responsibility for the safety of all who will use it throughout its life.

He will not simply devise a library building according to instructions received but will review the whole project and its intentions; he may be able to bring forward fundamental and original proposals which can give the authority the opportunity to improve the impact, offer new amenities or obtain greater financial viability.

Librarian

He will not necessarily be the chief librarian but may be the professional member of the library staff appointed to act on his chief's behalf in this particular planning task. If he is responsible for all library developments within his library system he will, in time, develop an expertise which can be of great value to his employer in future projects. In small libraries he will perforce be the chief librarian, and will have to fit the task into an already busy working life.

He will act as the client, representing his authority in all day-to-day decisions, always in close contact with the scheme and keeping clearly before him the functional aims of the proposals. Because he represents the client, many architects cannot agree that he should himself be a member of the design team: I believe this to be a dangerous view and one which is among the causes of the gap which often develops between the two sides. The librarian is an expert in his own field and he has special knowledge of the peculiarities of his own library scene; if he is party to all discussions (other than the purely technical) he can make a most valuable contribution, if only in the negative way of finding functional flaws in proposals at an early stage and thus preventing waste of time in developing ideas which would produce unacceptable results. His positive reactions will be much more valuable as will the very fact that he is at hand to clear up queries or inconsistencies in the brief. If, as client, he is to remain outside the design team, then he must be represented by a library consultant.

Library consultant

This office is rarely found in this country (although the Parry report recommended its inclusion in university projects); in some countries it is so common as to be an accepted part of most large schemes. The consultant's great value is that he can bring to the scheme a wide experience of library planning that may be lacking in the team. Because of his knowledge of the architect's work, he will have a better grasp of what the architect needs to know and later in the programme he will be better equipped than the librarian to evaluate the plans and proposals. He will be an expert interpreter between two highly specialised professions. Not the least of his merits is that he will be able to devote to the project at every stage that attention to detail, from the librarian's point of view, which that officer is unable to give because he has other duties to perform; he can represent the librarian's interests in continuous discussion with the architect. The library consultant's fees will of course add a small percentage to the total cost of the project, but this may be covered many times over by the savings obtained and the elimination of possible mistakes.

Quantity surveyor

This specialist is a key figure; he is employed, ideally (and usually) on the recommendation of the architect, at an early stage. His link with the architect will be close and should be one formed in mutual knowledge and confidence. His main task is to estimate, from the architect's drawings at every stage, the probable cost of the work and to assist him in evaluating the various alternatives open at any time in different constructional systems, details and materials and even alternative types of contractual arrangements with the builders. He prepares the particulars necessary for obtaining competitive tenders by drawing up bills of quantity based on the architect's details which will accompany the drawings and form together the contract documents. The function of the bills of quantity is primarily to establish a quantitative basis for measuring and evaluating work in progress and for final assessment in settling its total value, taking into account any variations. His value will be apparent from the beginning in assisting with the first rough estimates of cost and will continue throughout every subsequent operation. He assesses the value of building work in progress and recommends the amount of interim payment on account. In carrying out his responsibilities he will work closely with all the various specialists concerned in the building operation to ensure an accurate valuation, both of proposals, and of work done. His appointment is usually by contract to the client and not to the architect.

Specialist consultants

There can be almost as many of these as there are problems to be solved. Soil surveys, structural design, heating, acoustics, electricity, ventilating, mechanical equipment, security, interior decoration—all these require expert attention. The architect will normally recommend to his client what specialists should be appointed and may suggest appropriate firms. His advice in this matter is valuable because these consultants will form with him the design team. If at all possible, his preferences should be followed. This is important because he will then have around him people in whom he has confidence and with whom he has probably worked before. The number appointed will depend on the complexity of the project and whether or not there are such experts on his own staff or on the staff of the authority: security officers are an example of the latter. Similarly, a heating and ventilating consultant may already have been retained for the campus of which the library is to form part.

Although the specialist's work is part of the architect's province it is normal for the consultants to be employed on a contract direct to the authority. In this way the architect will have at his disposal the expert advice of independent consultants, but the authority may, if it wishes, reject the advice and its implications. It is possible for the architect to offer an inclusive service by employing such experts himself but he will be taking a great risk in assuming the responsibility to advise the client on all these special matters. At the other extreme the authority may decide to require the consultants to report directly to it and independently of the architect: this is both tactless and ominous.

Clerk of works

The architect will generally advise the client authority as to whether or not the job merits the appointment of a clerk of works and the decision will depend largely on the size and complexity of the scheme. This officer is an inspector, constantly on the site, supervising the work on the client's behalf to see that the architect's intentions are followed in every detail. The architect's own appointment carries responsibility for general, but not constant supervision and it is this constant element which the clerk of works particularly provides. Thus, while he is employed by the client, his function is an extension of the architect's supervisory function. The clerk of works is, in fact, the counterpart of the builder's foreman or agent, and will work closely with him to ensure the smoother progress and the efficient, accurate construction of the building. He takes no part in design and become necessary only when building contracts have been allocated. For a full definition of the clerk of works' responsibilities see the RIBA *Handbook*[1].

The librarian will not be the authority's only representative involved in the project. Others are:

Chairman

—or other responsible member of the board. In an educational establishment this may be the principal, headmaster or his representative. He is unlikely to take part in regular teamwork but will be consulted, or kept informed, on all policy matters which do not need the authority's formal decision. To the inexperienced it is surprising how many policy decisions arise, particularly in a complex building project with some amenities and access routes common to more than one area.

Planning officer or surveyor

He will take the wider overall view of the area and make recommendations to the authority on space priorities in accordance with the needs of the community as a whole. His contribution may be completed at an early stage but in some cases he will be involved whenever proposed changes affect the preconceived use of the site. If he is also the local authority's planning officer he will certainly be involved throughout the project.

Finance officer

He will be called upon to comment upon the estimates and all financial proposals and will need to be kept fully in the picture so that he can arrange for payments to be made, even at quite early points in the programme. For example, trial bore holes may be required before a decision can be reached about the suitability of the site; throughout the programme he will be paying instalments of fees to the various consultants.

The authority's own architect

—(if such a post exists and if he is not also the architect to the scheme). He may be given specific duties at an early stage, such as advising on the possibility of a scheme or helping to write the brief. He may also be used as a watchdog to see that the project is proceeding satisfactorily, but this is a potential source of professional conflict and should not be necessary.

The authority's clerk or legal officer

He will be concerned throughout, both with the presentation of reports to the authority and in drawing up contracts; he may also be involved in approaches to outside powers (ministries particularly) for requisite consent.

Other officers of a local government authority

Several of these will have to comment on, and recommend for acceptance, various aspects of the proposals. They can include police, health, roads, fire and other officers but sometimes, and always in the case of non-local government libraries, some or all of them may be "outside powers". If they are officers of the library authority they can be represented directly on the controlling committee where contact will obviously be more direct and efficient.

Future users of the library

Users may be represented at some committee or discussion group by a readers' and/or a staff delegate. In universities and colleges this is a not uncommon arrangement because both staff and users are organised and identifiable. This applies to a lesser extent in hospitals (where democratic principles find less acceptance), while in public libraries only the staff are likely to be involved. This is because the council members are themselves elected to represent the views of the citizens—the potential users—and it is often held that direct reader-representation means that self-appointed pressure groups will exert undue influence.

The design team's proposals will be submitted to the authority but will seldom be considered in full detail by the council, board of governors or other ultimate power; in practice the proposals will go to a committee of the authority, either a special committee set up for the purpose of supervising this particular project, or to a standing committee. Where the project is to form part of a much larger venture, such as a new university or college campus, a building committee may already exist and have made overall decisions on planning and site allocation. Here matters concerning the new library will be only a small part of the committee's interests. Whatever form the committee takes, it will have at its service the librarian, the legal and financial officers and such other permanent officers as may be needed. The team will make periodic reports to this committee which will deal with matters of detail but decisions concerning principles and finance will usually require recommendations to the authority itself.

The architect, quantity surveyor and consultants may be required to deal directly with this committee and this can leave the librarian in a difficult position unless he and the architect have been working very closely together. It can even lead to disagreements between them being expressed at committee meetings—obviously most undesirable. It is recommended here, from long personal experience, that not only should the librarian represent the authority in its dealings with the design team but that where possible the architect and the librarian should submit joint reports to the committee until the project has reached the stage at which purely technical matters predominate.

In practice this means that the team's feasibility report (for example) will include a section written by the librarian explaining how the proposed library will operate. This may be a counsel of perfection and prove impossible in large projects or where an established building committee already exists; in this case the reports will be produced by the architect and all that the librarian can do is to secure absolute agreement beforehand on all vital matters so that architect and librarian can speak with one voice against objections which may be made by those unfamiliar with the design team's aims and intentions.

CHANNELS OF COMMUNICATION

From the outset it is vital that everyone concerned shall be absolutely clear as to the powers, responsibilities, progress procedure and methods of communication which shall apply. In a large project the procedures can be shown elaborately in a network diagram (see pages 22–23) but even in the smallest undertaking the principles should be recorded. Similarly nothing can be more chaotic than for an architect to be instructed by one person or committee and then be responsible for the results of his work to a different body; it must be arranged that there is a single line of communication with the architect and that this shall be via the librarian (or library consultant).

The relationship with specialists must also be defined clearly; normally they will work through the architect but if the authority already has its own consultant on a certain aspect, such as security, then it must be made clear whether the architect has access to him or whether this consultant is to report direct to the authority. In the latter case the librarian should act for the authority so that the architect is still dealing with a single representative of his client.

Four full reports from the architect may be needed; the feasibility report after a survey of the possibility of carrying out the required project; the outline planning report after an outline plan has been completed; a scheme report with sketch designs, and a final report when working drawings are produced. In each report a cost estimate will be given so that the authority can see whether the project is still acceptable financially. It is seldom, however, that absolute approval can be given by a single board; other consents will be needed. Statutory planning approval has to be obtained if a new building or substantial alterations to an existing one are proposed; a new educational building may require more specific sanctions from the Department of Education and Science or from the University Grants Committee: fire and office working conditions will involve other official bodies. Reference to the method of approach to such bodies will be made in subsequent chapters at the appropriate point in the programme.

When the architect wishes to tell the librarian what he proposes and to seek his concurrence, he will communicate not in words, but in plans, drawings, sketches and models. He will have to bear in mind that while these media are the common currency in his own world they are not as familiar to the librarian. The latter will be happy to study floor plans at $1:100$ (or $\frac{1}{8}$ in:1 ft) but will find elevations on section much more difficult to grasp. Detail from one-tenth up to full scale he will find very difficult indeed (especially joinery sections) and the spatial relationships between plan and section most complex of all. On the other hand he may be seduced by the charm of "artist's impressions" and isometric drawings, while failing to grasp the essential points which the architect is trying to show. Architectural models he will probably love, but these are always expensive.

This is not to suggest that the librarian is a dilettante, happy to play with the attractive fringe of another's world. The point is that it cannot be assumed, because the librarian has been supplied with a full set of plans, that he understands and accepts everything the architect is proposing. Teamwork involves understanding, and it will be necessary for the architect to spend time in patiently explaining the significance of the plans' features in order to be sure that they are fully understood. Because both professionals are busy men with other pressing duties, the best solution is to have a library consultant, who has the ability and the time to see that no dangerous gap develops between the ideas of architect and librarian.

The programme

To the architect the creation of a new library is just another job; he will set about it on a programme of operations familiar to him through his training and experience. To the librarian the experience will probably be new and it will be a great help to him to know exactly what the architect is doing at any one time. This will reassure him during the, inevitable, long periods in which he receives no communication from the architect. The programme and the time schedule of operations (which the architect will draw up and which will be referred to later) will keep him informed. The design programme has been expressed thus:[2]

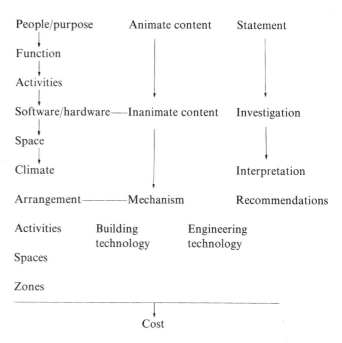

Although the architect will be free to set his own programme it will usually be based on the RIBA's "Plan of work for design team operators". This plan, and the *Handbook of architectural practice and management* of which it forms part, deals with the systematic planning of the design process in much greater detail than the librarian will ever need, but from it he can see the main sequence of activities.

From this point on, the arrangement of this book is based on a typical programme from a briefing guide[3], in order to make the librarian familiar with a likely sequence of events. In summary the programme is set out on page 24.

Those concerned with creating a very small library within a building, or with converting existing buildings to make a library, may find this an over-elaborate proposition but even in the most modest scheme the principles still apply, although it will be found in practice that some sections will require little or no attention. The great advantage of an agreed programme of this kind is that it reduces the likelihood of mistakes arising from the librarian's failure to communicate vital information, having assumed that the architect already knew about it. The oft-quoted example of the primary school provided with washbasins in every classroom (as requested in the brief) but not with a supply of water at these points (as it had not been requested in the brief) may be untrue but it draws attention to a real danger. If the librarian stipulates one need in great detail the architect is entitled to assume that his other needs have been similarly included. An agreed programme

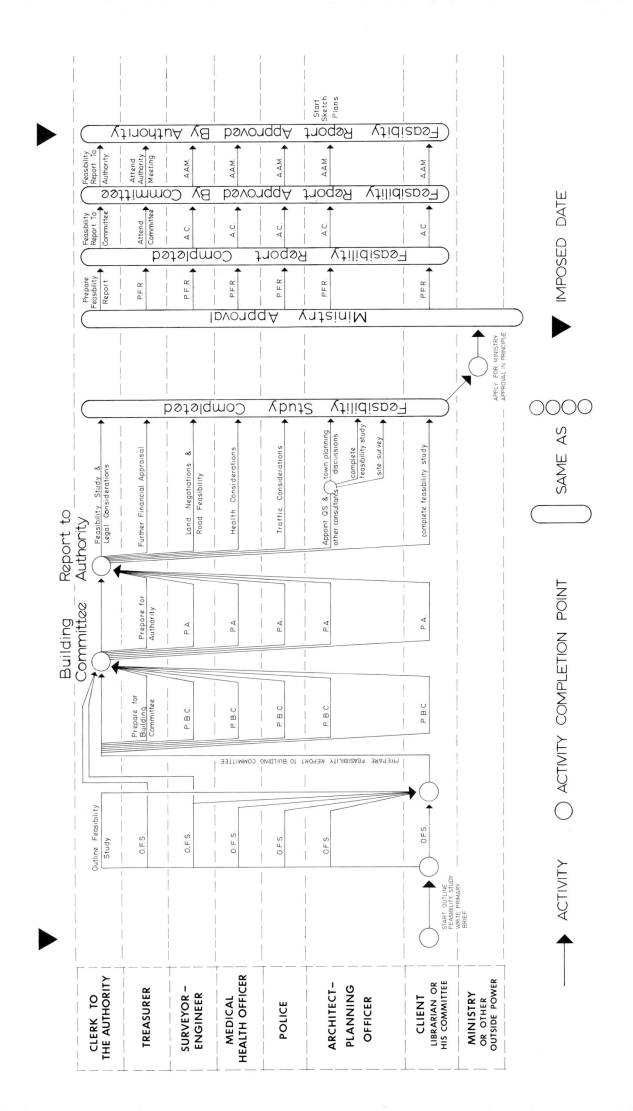

IMPOSED DATE

SAME AS

ACTIVITY COMPLETION POINT

ACTIVITY

ACTIVITY

22

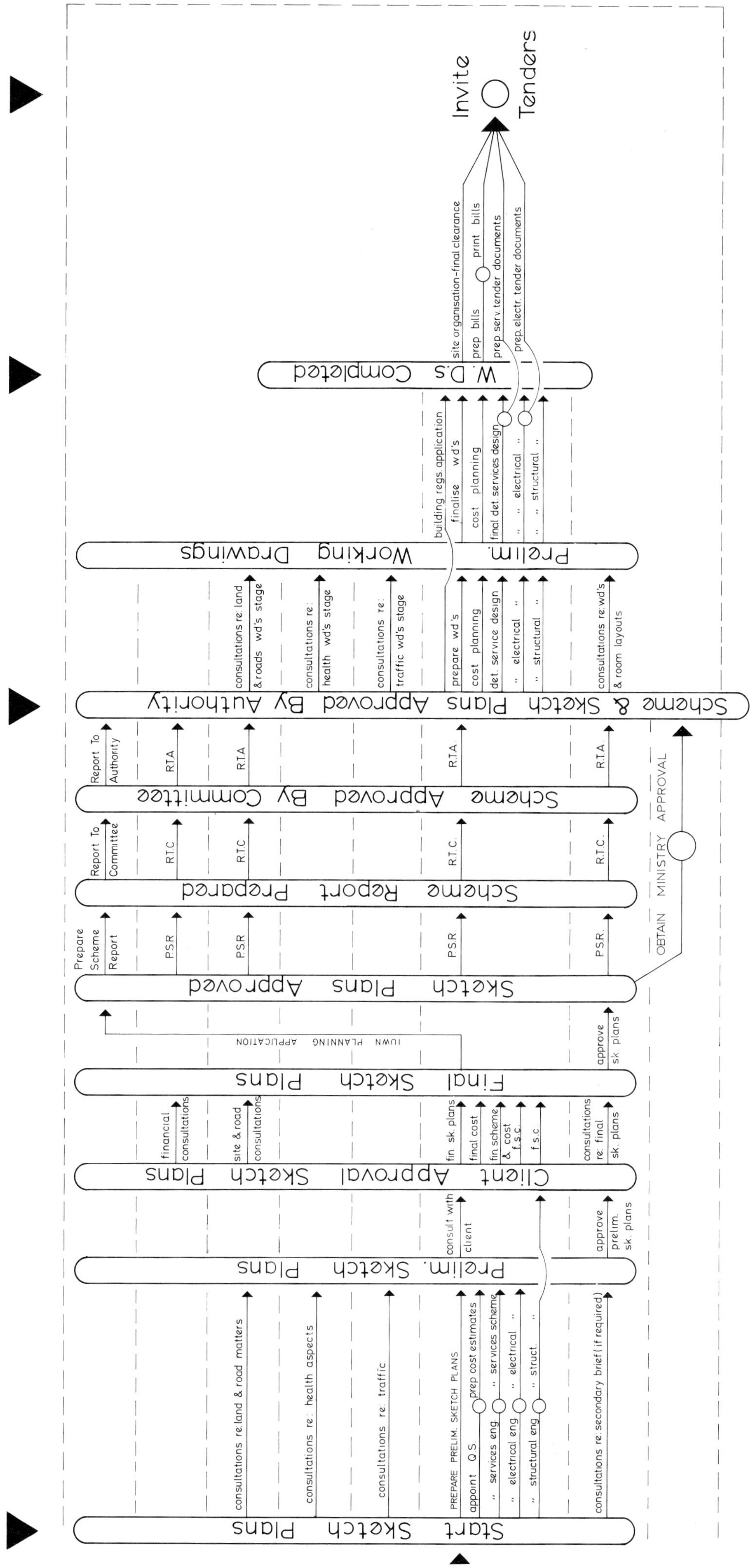

Invite

Tenders

W.D.s Completed

site organisation-final clearance
prep. bills   print bills
prep. serv. tender documents
prep. electr. tender documents

building regs application
finalise   wd's
cost   planning
final det. services design
electrical ::
structural ::

Working Drawings

Prelim.

consultations re land
& roads   wd's stage
consultations re:
health wd's stage
consultations re:
traffic wd's stage
prepare wd's
cost   planning
det. service design
electrical ::
structural ::
consultations re wd's
& room layouts

Scheme & Sketch Plans Approved By Authority

Report To Authority
R.T.A.
R.T.A.
R.T.A.
R.T.A.

Scheme Approved By Committee

Report To Committee
R.T.C.
R.T.C.
R.T.C.
R.T.C.

OBTAIN MINISTRY APPROVAL

Scheme Report Prepared

Prepare Scheme Report
P.S.R.
P.S.R.
P.S.R.
P.S.R.

Sketch Plans Approved

TOWN PLANNING APPLICATION

approve sk. plans

Final Sketch Plans

financial consultations
site & road consultations
fin. sk. plans
final cost
fin scheme & cost f.s.c.
f.s.c.
consultations re final sk. plans

Client Approval Sketch Plans

consult with client
approve prelim. sk. plans

Prelim. Sketch Plans

consultations re land & road matters
consultations re: health aspects
consultations re: traffic
PREPARE PRELIM. SKETCH PLANS
appoint Q.S.
" services eng.   prep cost estimates
" electrical eng.   services scheme
" structural eng.   electrical ::
                         struct ::
approve prelim. sk. plans
consultations re secondary brief (if required)

Start Sketch Plans

This page and opposite: procedural network

23

Inception of project
Setting up the design team
Primary brief:
      statement of aims
      contents to be accommodated
      activities and users
      life of building, flexibility and expansion requirements
      special physical requirements and conditions within the
          building
      site location and limitations
      security
      communications
      cost limits and controls
      consents
      time schedule (from client's viewpoint)
Feasibility study:
      use of site: site investigation
      space relationships
      structural implications of space relationships and physical
          requirements
      cost feasibility
      feasibility report
Secondary brief:
      pattern of operations
      verification and amplification of information
      contract policy: client nominees; proprietary libraries
          (where applicable)
      maintenance policy
Outline planning:
      planning principles redefined
      division into major areas: reader circulation
Scheme design:
      planning the structure:
      flexibility
      structural grid: columns
      floor loadings
      service equipment: stairways
      internal environment
      column sizes
      construction
      services
Detail design:
      layouts and critical sizes:
      book accommodation
      reader service areas
      staff areas
      non-assignable areas
      furniture and fittings
      floors
      circulation
      lighting
      enclosing elements and finishes
Security and protection
Physical conditions
Cost studies
Final report
Production information:
      drawings, schedules and specifications
      bills of quantity
      tender action
      project planning
      operation on site
      completion

has the further advantage that the architect can refer at the appropriate time to a known place in the brief for any specific details but it will not obviate the need for continual discussions or for amplification of detail. Indeed, it will be found that many subjects are dealt with at several different stages of the programme, for different reasons.

It is not only a matter of progressing through a sequence of actions known to all who are to be in any way concerned in it; the programme is a chain in which each link is dependent upon each other link, and in which one single omission can cause a complete breakdown. Approval for each step in the planning must be obtained, either from the authority itself or from an outside body, and without such approval all future actions will be impeded— indeed the whole programme can come to a costly standstill. With the list of actions by the design team therefore must be integrated the sequence of actions by all the powers and officers who will be concerned in the project; this can add up to a formidable list. To lay down a full and exact record of all actions which must be taken can be a daunting prospect; where such a building project is a regular occurrence, in the case of large university or local authorities for example, it is common for a network analysis of the operations to be undertaken (see pp 22–3, 174) so that all who are involved can be in no doubt as to what is the next step in the sequence and who is to take it.

The programme shown above sets out general principles, rather than a comprehensive recipe. The emphasis has to be varied according to the nature of the job. A typical example of a small design task, for instance, is that of making a library from a room, or group of rooms, which had previously been used for other purposes. Here, although the principles will be the same, some parts of the programme, and particularly of the brief, can be taken as read. A statement of aims and list of contents will be needed, but they will consist of a very few lines; most of the attention will be directed to the best possible use of the space at the disposal of the team (usually just the librarian and the architect, or even the librarian and the head of a works section). The essential information will be that necessary to decide the treatment to be given to the fabric, plus a detailed statement of the furniture and equipment required. The basis of the latter can be a room schedule; an example of this document is given by Metcalf[4]. The use of this document is not recommended in the programme given here: it is certainly possible for room schedules to be provided by the librarian at the request of the architect as part of the secondary brief but they should not be used as primary documents.

Network analysis
In very large projects the architect will be responsible for an enormously complicated operation and he may make use of the techniques of network analysis to control activities of great complexity whose interdependence in both time and action is such that a sequence of steps must be meticulously followed in order to avoid disastrously expensive delays.

On pp 22–3 and 174 two examples are given of networks applicable to building operations in which a librarian may become concerned. The university example (reproduced by kind permission of the RIBA) shows the great complexity in university building work. It is not particularly designed to apply to university *libraries* but shows clearly the large number of officers, committees and other powers who will inevitably be involved in the project.

The example on pp 22–3 shows in more detail a programme network for a public library building; note that the architect concerned is the authority's own architect and planning officer, and is therefore more closely involved in the committee procedure than would be the case if a consultant architect had been employed. Also more events concern officers within the authority than is the case in the university example; this is because, in this particular instance, the authority was itself a planning authority, and therefore some consents (see page 42) were obtainable through officers of the authority (eg planning officer, medical officer of health). The analysis is in two stages: the first concerns the actions leading up to the acceptance of the feasibility report, and the second that applying to the production of the sketch plan and working drawings. In practice the architect will use a third network to control activities at the stage of tender and construction on the site, but these will be of little real concern to the librarian.

Despite their apparent complexity these networks are basically simple, showing the progress of activities (indicated by arrows) in an exact sequence as they lead up to certain events (indicated by circles). These events are key points beyond which no progress is possible without some form of authorisation; where such events involve a number of officers or committees simultaneously the circles become ovals to show who is involved. Many of these events will have predetermined dates (eg meetings of the authority council).

Architects are familiar with network methods which are part of the technique of critical path analysis; if a librarian is to understand how the project is progressing he should at least know something of the methods used; titles of simple introductions to critical path analysis and networks are given at the end of this chapter[5-7] but an increasing number of senior librarians are becoming familiar with these and other such techniques as part of their general library management duties.

A network such as this need not be created anew for a library project because the responsible officers of the authority may have already prepared and used a similar scheme for other building projects. All that will be necessary will be for minor amendments to be made where procedures are deemed unnecessary and for the "client" to be the relevant officer or responsible committee.

Such a network will have time implications, and progress will obviously depend on the degree of completion of one activity before the next can take place. From this basis will be produced the timetable of operations that will form part of a periodic report from the architect to the authority.

STANDARDS

One of the librarian's most obvious tasks is to tell the architect, by means of the brief, how big the library should be. He should do this, not in square or cubic metres or feet, a judgment alien to his training and experience, but in numbers of readers to be expected (and at what times), numbers of books to be housed, equipment to be installed and reader services to be provided. He will also say how long he expects the building to last and how much room for expansion and allowance for change is required.

The information falls into two categories—persons (both readers and staff) to be accommodated, and material to be housed; these matters are for the librarian's decision alone, given the concurrence of his authority. Where his task is to transfer unchanging operations from an old library to a new one he will already have the practical local experience to visualise the new service in quantitative terms. Similarly it is easy enough for a public librarian who has to create a new branch library basically similar to those he already runs, to find what numbers of readers and books have to be accommodated. It is simple for a school librarian to know how many scholars he has to seat but not so simple to discover what book stock provision should be made. It may be very difficult indeed for a librarian who has to create a completely new library of any kind, and perhaps most difficult of all for a college or university librarian when the library is to form part of a new venture, whose boundaries, both physical and intellectual, have yet to be clearly defined. In such cases, very clear thinking is needed.

The librarian will get his greatest help from a study of similar projects carried out by others. Reading, visits, correspondence with colleagues, all these will help him to produce an estimate of the quantities concerned—books, readers and services. Unfortunately, the figures he obtains in this way are not likely to impress his authority when he seeks its concurrence. He would find it helpful to be able to quote official standards relevant to his own case; published guide-lines describing the official or co-operatively agreed levels of size, staffing, equipment and, above all, finance, which have been found appropriate for producing an acceptable standard.

Such guide-lines seldom exist; certainly the most helpful figures are derived from the experience of other librarians. "Official" statements normally turn out to relate to financial limits, the main yardstick with which officialdom is concerned. As Havard-Williams has said[8], "Whether you have one seat for every three students or every ten will depend on whether the financial authorities are convinced that it is an essential service to provide seating on the scale 1:3 or 1:10." The figures which can be obtained from fairly official bodies are consistent neither in level nor in approach. In a college library the authorisation may be in terms of percentage of seats and number of books per student; in a public library it may be volumes per head of population; in a hospital library, expenditure per patient. It is not that there are no published standards, but that they are diffuse, inconsistent and irrational. Those which exist have emanated from many countries and have not been codified into a single document.

At international level the work of the Standards Committee of the International Federation of Library Associations has produced, and continues to produce, valuable work but because of the immense variation in the development, attitudes and authorities in different countries, standards must inevitably be less than precise in their application to particular libraries. Standards quoted from foreign countries can be helpful but they suffer from the disadvantage that even theoretically universal institutions such as public and university libraries differ widely between countries. It is also unfortunate (if inevitable) that controlling authorities are less likely to be impressed by standards quoted from foreign countries: they always prefer "official" statements, preferably emanating from their own government.

The major British official recommendations for libraries of all kinds, and implications to be drawn from other governmental statements, are given in appendix I, with extensive quotations from *Standards for library service*, by F. N. Withers[9]. This book, a most valuable research project, was written under the auspices of the International Federation of Library Associations for UNESCO and covers public, school, university, college, special and national libraries: its value is limited only by the great difficulty of making comparisons among such diversity.

The standards quoted may serve as a rough guide and as a useful source to help to persuade the authority, but they are not given in detail because they need to be read in context. Librarians will (should) already be familiar with them; architects may find them of value because they can help in the task of relating requirements expressed in numbers of persons and books to appropriate allocations of space.

REFERENCES

[1] RIBA *Handbook* op. cit. Appendix B part 3.564 (O5)

[2] Ibid Appendix A to part 3.525

[3] Design guide for libraries. *In Architects' Journal*, 21 February 1968, pp 443–453

[4] METCALF, KEYES D. Planning academic and research library buildings. McGraw-Hill, New York, 1965, p 369

[5] LOCKYER, K. G. An introduction to critical path analysis. Pitman, London, 1964

[6] BATTERSBY, A. Network analysis for planning and scheduling. Macmillan, London, 1964

[7] FAIRHURST, H. H. Planning and control of engineering and building construction by use of the critical path network. T.R. Report 1030 Min. of P.B. & W. 1963

[8] HAVARD-WILLIAMS, PETER In *Libri* v 21, 1971, pp 374–385

[9] WITHERS, F. N. Standards for library service. Unesco, Paris, 1970

3 Primary brief

It is now the librarian's task to start the programme by telling the architect what the client, ie the authority, wishes to create. He does this by means of the brief, which is basically a statement of user requirements in terms of accommodation, function and standards. The brief should provide the basic information required by the architect for his design, but he will himself take part in the planning process in order to equip himself to create the design.

Although it is possible to have a verbal brief, common sense dictates that it should be written in order to serve as a source of reference. It is no exaggeration to say that this is the most important part of the whole scheme; however magnificent an architect's creation may appear to be, it must fail utterly unless it meets the need for which it was designed; however skilful the architect may be in solving a problem, the solution is useless if he has not grasped the problem's true nature and extent.

While the brief is primarily a statement to the architect of a problem, with all its implications in the fields of space and organisation, it has a secondary value in that it forces the librarian to organise his own thinking and to examine the organisation and methods of his proposed library. The first requirement then, is that the librarian should be quite sure in his own mind exactly how the new library is to operate, both generally and in detail. Vagueness at this point will inevitably result in an unsatisfactory end product.

This first brief should be prepared by the librarian and addressed to the architect but in fact, if teamwork is already in process, it will have been preceded by general discussions within the team which will ensure it a sympathetic reception. In the case of simple designs which might be repeated in the future (for example, a series of small branch libraries), the architect could produce some preliminary design ideas which might be used as a basis for team discussion leading to the production of a jointly prepared definitive brief. See *The design of small branch libraries*[1].

In most cases, however, the responsibility for producing the brief should lie with the librarian, and the result should be on paper because the architect is entitled to have a document which will be his authority to spend valuable time in working in a certain direction. At its most elaborate the brief can be divded into three elements:

statement of the purpose the library is to serve and the place it is to occupy within the social, educational or commercial framework: the library's relationship to the other institutions, departments or sections of its environment;
detailed record of the library's exact requirements as an operational unit, including quantities of books and other materials to be accommodated, the readers to be served, their needs and the times when they will be expressed, staff to be housed, and the physical relationship between these different elements;
record of the limitations imposed by the authority: the chosen site, any known height or access restrictions together with the financial and other controls which have been determined.

In a small and uncomplicated project these three elements may be combined in one simple statement. In any large scheme however, it is better for them to be elaborated systematically if only because team consultation can then take place on each section, as questions arise in the mind of the architect moving towards his solution. In this book the statement of general aims is included in the primary brief, although in the event it is often produced as a separate document.

What has so far been called "the brief" is in fact the first stage—the primary brief: the secondary brief is initiated by the architect, who asks the librarian for specific information after he has made a feasibility study and realises that he needs to know more.

Although the brief will be chiefly in words there will also be diagrams—for example of area relationships, access priorities, material and reader progress routes. It is most important that the librarian should express these essentially spatial factors in a merely notional manner and not restrict the architect by prejudging the way in which he will solve the problems. Areas should be shown very roughly and without any attempt to formulate their shape, otherwise the architect would be justified in considering the diagrams as an exact indication of required area shapes and sizes. Where a particular requirement concerns matters affecting the whole building, for example communication networks, they are better tabulated, so that the whole question can be studied separately.

When the librarian has sent the completed primary brief to the architect he should, as far as is humanly possible, stick to it. Inevitably changes will be made, but they should arise from changed circumstances, not from changed ideas. The time for the librarian to think hard is before writing the brief, not afterwards. Any necessary changes must be notified, in writing, to the architect as soon as possible: all changes cost time and money, but the later in the scheme they occur, the more expensive they become. At a certain point, usually before detail design begins, the architect is entitled to impose a freeze date; a point beyond which no changes in the brief should be made; changes after that date may be inevitable but they will be very expensive indeed.

In the brief it will be necessary to call for flexibility—a factor that often bedevils the solution proposed in response to the statement of the problem. Few libraries are now created except as part of larger organisations, and on the change and development of those organisations library design is utterly dependent. But flexibility is an expensive luxury and it should never be used as a substitute for forethought.

STATEMENT OF AIMS

Perhaps the most difficult part of the brief to write, this statement has to express clearly and concisely the part the library is intended to play in the life of the community or of the parent organisation. The terms of the statement need to be quite different from those the librarian used when he presented to his authority a case for creating a new library; no polemics are called for, no generalisations on cultural, social or economic advantages to the community, but a definition of objectives, both immediate and long-term. In order to do this it may be necessary to explain the programme and objectives of the parent institution itself.

This is particularly important in the case of a school, where the library's contribution depends directly upon the educational methods to be used. In the traditional pattern the school library was a place where books were kept and where children went to read them at certain hours; today in increasing numbers of schools the library is a dynamic centre which exploits media of many different kinds and which is continually in action, with contacts in both directions from each element of teaching and learning. Unless the architect knows this he can hardly design a framework appropriate for the proposed activity.

It is equally important for the statement to show what the library has *not* to do. A library in a hospital may be planned to serve the recreational needs of the patients, or of a certain section of the patients, the medical staff, the technical staff, the professional and recreational needs of the nurses. The combinations of these variables are infinite and the architect must know exactly which applies in a particular case.

From the statement the architect will see a picture of the library as an operational unit and from this he can visualise the environmental conditions which he must create to meet the aims. The library's programme in detail—activities, users, contents and methods—will be discussed later: there is no reason for this first section to record a planned programme of library actions; only the end which it is hoped the new service will attain.

CONTENTS TO BE ACCOMMODATED

Because shelving space is so valuable, and because library stocks are expanding at a tremendous rate in line with the information explosion, it is every librarian's duty to consider possible economies in the storage of books. To each of the alternatives there will be objections because they involve much planning and extra work.

Weeding the stock
This very unpopular recommendation will raise the hackles of most librarians; nevertheless, it is every librarian's duty to ensure that each book in his stock justifies the high cost to his institution of storing it.

Separate storage of less-used books
All libraries place the most-used books in priority positions: this principle can be extended, after a survey of stock use, to creation of shelving sequences based on frequency of use, the least-used books being housed most economically, the most-used closest to the service point. Surveys of the use of materials in large libraries (Fussler and Simon[2], Colley[3], Bush et al[4]) seem to lead in a general way to the conclusion that books which have not been used for several years are not particularly likely to be used for several more years. It should be possible to make a systematic survey of the library's stock, identify books which seem to fall within this category, and remove them to a place where storage is cheaper. Access to this separate storage will be slower and more expensive, and there is always the book or section of books which suddenly comes into active demand because of a shift in public interest or in the curriculum; nevertheless considerable saving could result.

Books which have been established as likely to be the least used can be stored in various ways to save library space[5]:

Off-centre storage Housing books in warehouses away from expensive sites saves a great deal of space, but at a high cost in delay in retrieval and consequent reader frustration.

Co-operative storage Schemes whereby libraries associate for the common storage of books in little demand are already in operation, with some success.

Storage in basements and stack towers Numerous examples of this solution have appeared and the architect will know the relative advantages and disadvantages, in both design and overall cost. Perhaps the only new idea is one proposed in some overcrowded American universities on restricted sites whereby underground areas between existing buildings are excavated for use as overflow storage. This action is being taken beside the new Guildhall Library in London.

Sizing
Because the height of the shelf must be determined by the height of the tallest book on that shelf, the more single-size sequences there are, the more economically the stock can be shelved. The necessary disadvantage of single-size sequences is that the reader has to look in several sequences to find the book he needs; even if the different locations are recorded on the catalogue entry, confusion will still be caused. This disadvantage naturally applies less to little-used books in closed stacks, so the possible space savings in closed stacks by storing according to size must be considered.

J. Grady Cox[6] considers this problem from a mathematician's angle. He quotes earlier claims of space gains in storage by size, ranging from 25 per cent (Rider) to 250 per cent (Midwest Inter-Library Centre), but his own conclusions are less easy to summarise without extensive quotation. He sees two possible methods of using sizing: "within shelf" has several given shelf heights running throughout the stacks, each in its own shelf location sequence;

in order to locate a book in this arrangement it is necessary to know first the size sequence and second the location symbol. "Within stack" on the other hand, uses only one shelf height in one group of stack units; in this case it is necessary to find the group of stacks holding the size of books and then trace the location symbol within those stacks. Cox shows that the "within stack" system gives slightly better space saving. He also shows that between three and five is the best number of size sequences in most situations.

Further space savings can be made when the top shelf of a shelving unit is open, so that there is no limit (other than the ceiling) to the height of books on it. However this gain is achieved only when tall books are stored on the top shelf—not a practice which many librarians will relish.

Against all these space gains—and they can be considerable— must be offset the cost of selection, transfer, alteration to records and other initial costs; these will be very small indeed in the long run compared with space savings over many years, but the cost in staff time of continual access to these books may be very high. The librarian must be quite sure that the possibility of frequent retrieval has been well assessed and can be discounted.

In addition to listing the quantities of material, the librarian must also show:
access conditions under which material is to be housed;
size sequences in which books are to be shelved and the quantities in each sequence;
allowance to be made for future expansion
the librarian's preferences as to shelving.
Each of these factors is of great importance and must be considered carefully before being committed to paper; but it should be remembered that the architect is at this stage concerned only with general space allowances; there will be no need to go into such minor matters as the number of reference books in the children's library.

Access conditions
The variations are:
books which are to be freely available to readers in fairly spacious browsing conditions (open access);
books to be housed more economically in formal rows of shelving but still available directly to readers (open stack);
books to be housed as closely (and therefore economically) as possible because only staff will have access to them (closed stack). Ways of computing space allocation for each of these categories (including compact storage methods) are suggested in chapters 8 and 9. In general, public, hospital, school and some college libraries will use open access with a small proportion of closed stack; large public libraries will use open access but with a larger proportion of closed stack. Most university and some college libraries will be very largely open stack with a small proportion of open access, and with a varying, but usually very small, proportion of closed stack.

Size sequences
A single size sequence of books is seldom possible but in most libraries more than 90 per cent are less than 280 mm (11 in) tall (see chapter 8). In popular libraries most books are less than 250 mm (10 in) tall and such libraries can house the bulk of their open-shelf stock on bookcases with shelves at 280 mm (11 in) centres (with encyclopaedias and quick reference books at 330 mm (13 in) centres) and most other books in a single over-size sequence at 500 mm (20 in). Books larger than this in general open-access libraries will be very few and will usually be shelved flat. At this stage it will be enough to compile a round estimate of books for each operational section, subdivided into those under and over 250 mm (10 in) tall, and those which need to be laid flat: a sampling of the stock will give such a figure. Depth of books need not be considered—in general, tall books are also deeper—but thickness is important. The thickness of the average book in each of the operational sections should be given, because without this

information numbers bear little relation to space requirements. Some music scores are thin, most directories are thick; so much is obvious, but further variations in any particular situation will be unknown to the architect.

Expansion allowance

There is no need to re-emphasise the fact that libraries of all kinds are expanding at an enormous rate, and that there is no sign of a halt. Growth of demand, official policy and a steady increase in the number of books published each year make this an inevitable process and the call will certainly continue to be for more space for books and for readers. Planning a new library takes several years; the stock to be accommodated on the opening day therefore, will be larger than was estimated when planning started. To spend a great deal of money on a library that will be inadequate in a few years is so patently absurd that it is is absolutely essential for the librarian to estimate the size of the library at a given future date, and to relate all his space requirement to that date. Havard-Williams[7] points out that a university library growing at the rate of 5 per cent a year, and starting with a stock of 600 000 volumes, will have to house 2 032 000 after twenty-five years. This indicates the seriousness of the problem. Public and other more popular libraries will grow less dramatically because they discard more books, but every librarian must think hard, choose a date at the very least ten years ahead, and plan to have sufficient space to house books and serve readers at that date.

This figure alone is not enough to enable the architect to make effective plans: even if enormous expansion is expected after a few years, no one would wish to open a new library that is three-quarters empty. The architect will plan for expansion, both in general and in detail, at the same time producing a library of acceptable form on the day of opening. It is therefore necessary for two sets of figures to be provided when expansion is expected: those applicable on the day the library opens, and those which will

Materials to be housed—books

	Under 250 mm (10 in) tall		Over 250 mm (10 in) tall		Laid flat	
	At opening	In x years	At opening	In x years	At opening	In x years
Open access areas						
1 Bibliographical						
2 General reference						
3 Special reference (commercial, technical, etc)						
4 Adult lending						
5 Children's lending						
6 Local history						
7 Music						
8 Arts						
9 Others						
Closed access areas						
10 Local stacks for 3 to 9 above						
11 General stack						
12 Compact shelving stack						
13 Special collections						
14 Extension services stack						

Number of books per metre or foot run of shelf in each of sections 1 to 14 above . . . .
Top and bottom heights of shelving preferred in sections 1 to 14 above . . . .
Distance between stack centres preferred in sections 10 to 14 above . . . .

*Materials to be housed—other than books**

	Location†	Open access		Closed access		Method of storage‡
		At opening	In x years	At opening	In x years	
Periodicals:						
Current only						
Current plus x back issues						
Back issues						
Newspapers:						
Current only						
Current plus x back issues						
Back issues						
Sheet maps						
Photographs						
Prints						
Broadsides						
Cuttings (no of boxes)						
Slides						
Pamphlets						
Sheet music						
Gramophone discs						
Audio tapes						
Video tapes						
Microfilms reels						
Microfiche						
Microcards						
Film reels						
Film strips						
Pictures						
Other materials						
Catalogue cards						

* Any non-book form that has been bound up to form a volume, or is to be kept in boxes and stored on book shelving, will be recorded under books.
† Show in which of the sections 1 to 14 in table 1 material is to be housed.
‡ Gramophone discs may be laid flat, stored on edge in pigeon holes or in open trays; microfilm may be in boxes on shelves, in vertical files and so on. See Chapter 9 for alternative methods.

apply at a chosen date some years ahead. It is difficult indeed to provide such figures, but they must be provided and only the librarian can do this.

Shelving

The space allowances which the architect will make to house the materials listed will depend on the height to which he shelves books, the distance apart of the stacks and many other factors. On these matters the librarian should indicate his *preferences*; he cannot be more specific because structural and design considerations may prevent the architect from accepting these preferences as positive instructions.

The great bulk of the material to be housed will be in the form of hardbacked books; separate record must be made of all other forms—and in many libraries there will be a surprisingly large number of these. Methods of, and space requirements for, housing various forms of library material are discussed in Chapters 8 and 9. The operational divisions in the following tables are those of a large public library building with conventional reference and lending divisons, but the principle can easily be applied to any type of library. Something along these lines will serve as a useful guide if completed and handed to the architect.

ACTIVITIES AND USERS

The architect will have a general idea, both from the statement of aims and from his own experience, of the likely activities within the building, but this is not good enough; he needs to know in some detail how the librarian (representing the authority) visualises them in operation. It is important that this information be given in a systematic pattern; if a particular activity is omitted the architect is entitled to assume that it is not to be included.

The total activities in the library can be separated into two sections: user services, divided into: user activities, their quantity, frequency and timing; and staff activities in serving users; technical services —staff activities in providing the framework and materials for user service.

The information should be given to the architect in two ways: the first will list all major activities in the library, with an estimate of the numbers of persons (both staff and readers) involved, and the hours when these activities will take place. The second, in the form of a series of diagrams, will show the practical relationships between these activities and the priorities in terms of nearness and separation, which the librarian would wish to give to them.

These priorities will apply to both the relative proximity of activity areas, and the access routes between the areas.

List of activities and users

The list should show both *what* is to happen and *when*. Hours of opening must be given, also an estimate of the varying amount of reader use of each section of the library during those hours. Many points will be difficult to predict but the librarian must make an attempt. However inaccurate his estimates turn out to be, they will at least be more realistic than those which anyone else can make. Some terms may need explanation: "reference library" may seem self-explanatory, but what will the readers be doing there? Browsing, consulting books or studying for long periods? If the answer is all of these, it would be useful to estimate the proportions of users engaged in each activity, and at what times the proportion can be expected to change.

User services
Hours of opening
Peak hours of the day
Peak days of the week (also of the year, particularly in educational institutions)
Number of readers (where applicable these figures should be provided separately for each major section of the library):
      at peak hours on a peak day
      at normal times

Length of time readers will stay (where applicable these figures should be provided separately for each major section of the library):
      at peak hours on a peak day
      at normal times
Number of reader seats to be provided (at date of opening and at a given future date) in the areas listed below: where applicable give separate figures for open seating areas and carrels: note where microform reading machines will be required:
      bibliographical
      general reference
      adult lending
      children's library (give age range)
      young adults' library
      periodicals
      newspapers
      music
      special reference (commercial, technical, etc)
      local history
      arts
      other departments
      typing rooms
      other areas (exhibitions, etc)
      outside the building or in courtyards

Associated activities—number of seats in:
      story hour rooms
      creative activity rooms for children
      language learning areas
      meeting rooms (give hours of opening)
      lecture and film shows (give hours of opening)   Indicate general nature of equipment to be provided
      music recitals (give hours of opening)
      exhibitions (give size and basic purpose)

Facilities for readers (showing location):
      document copying (staff or reader operated?)
      television
      video-tape reproduction
      audio reproduction
      microform viewing
      sales points
      automatic phone answering service
      external book return slots
      leaflet or pamphlet racks
      poster display

Public refreshment services:
      hours of opening
      number of seats
      type of service and staffing
      type of refreshment
      water dispensers

Storage of readers' belongings (with location):
      number of coat hooks
      number of lockers
      briefcase or handbag accommodation at tables
      attendant operated bag deposit stations

Public lavatories:
      numbers to be catered for—men and women
      type of towel system
      incinerators

Public telephone(s) (with location)
First-aid room for public use
Other provisions—book shop, vending machines, etc

Staff activities in serving users
Direct reader service: number of staff on duty at the following points at normal and peak times in each of the sections listed under "Number of reader seats" above:
>   security points
>   book issue and return counters
>   readers' inquiry desks
>   other

External activities for which the library is to be the headquarters; number of persons to be catered for in:
>   branch library supply and service area
>   school library supply and service area
>   welfare libraries supply and service area, (handicapped readers, prisons, housebound readers, etc)
>   privileged readers (for example, a room for teachers to select books from a display range. These areas will be fairly small in many libraries but large and important in others, particularly in county library headquarters.)

Mobile libraries: number and size of vehicles to be housed and their servicing requirements (petrol, oil, air, etc)

Technical services
Staff working accommodation, each with numbers of staff to be allowed for at peak times, with types of staff involved (clerical, porters, attendants, etc):
>   administrative offices, clerical, typing, machine operating
>   executive offices (indicate each post)
>   secretarial offices
>   accessioning area
>   cataloguing area, both cataloguers and typists. (In some special libraries such intensive activities as scanning and abstracting are, for convenience, included here.)
>   processing areas
>   receipt and dispatch area
>   post room
>   Telex centre
>   Xerox room

>   photographic laboratory
>   bindery or repair room
>   printing department

(The complexities of these three departments necessitate separate statements of their equipment and operation before the architect can estimate the space he needs.)

>   poster artist's studio
>   workrooms (indicate location)

Staff rest accommodation, with numbers (if there is to be a physical division then there must be separate numbers given for men and women or for staff and porters):
>   lounge
>   tea room } with general indication of range of equip-
>   kitchen } ment needed
>   staff lavatories, with numbers, men and women, for all locations
>   lockers, number and location. In rest rooms or lavatories? (Will staff go direct to rest areas to remove outdoor clothing or should a locker area be provided near the staff entrance?)
>   staff first-aid room

Other areas (in square metres or feet) with location if more than one:
>   strongrooms
>   stationery store
>   furniture store
>   cleaning materials store
>   other stores (stacking chairs, display screens, etc)

Other facilities
>   parking: number of cars
>   number of motor cyles
>   number of bicycles

At peak times; controlled or uncontrolled; covered or uncovered; staff only or both public and staff

>   pram park: number, inside building or under canopy outside
>   points where dogs may be tethered outside building
>   access for disabled persons (other than the statutory provision)

Sizes of areas
An alternative, or perhaps additional way of showing the amount of space needed for the various sections of the library is to draw up a scale diagram. The example given opposite is the one the librarian of the University of York included in his brief: it is of particular interest in that it can be compared with the result—the plans of the four-storey building showing the architect's design solution. From these it is clear that the spaces shown within a perimeter had no exact positional significance although certain relationships were implied by their proximity in the diagram. It also shows the confidence which obviously existed between librarian and architect and which must have resulted from a number of amicable meetings. Without such understanding a diagram such as this would risk misinterpretation.

Relationships between areas
Up to this point the brief has been a specific and detailed statement of requirements. There follow sections of more general comment on matters relating to the operating and environmental conditions of the future service. These are for the librarian to decide; it is certainly possible, and not uncommon, for such matters to be left for the architect to raise when he finds that he needs the information but the principle followed here is that it is better for them to be dealt with in the brief. After having read the brief the architect will be in a position to ask more specific questions. Moreover, it is safer for all possible points to be covered in a systematic document that will make absolutely certain that they do come to the team for consideration.

One of the earliest decisions the architect will be called upon to make concerns the relationships in space between the various operational areas and the priority of access routes between them. The obvious answer is for the librarian to show by means of a diagram which sections should be closest together, which fairly close, and so on. A little experience will show that this can be an exceedingly difficult task; any such diagram must invariably carry inferences as to the positioning of the areas, and this is a matter which the architect must approach with a completely open mind in order to develop a design. Precommitment by the librarian, even if inadvertently, can have a surprisingly hampering effect on the architect: the information needed can be best given by means of the table on page 32.

This table shows the relative proximity between the main sections of a medium sized central public library, in which one loan control is to be centrally placed and so outside any single department. The architect will need to know which sections are to be more, or less, close together but he also needs to know when they should specifically be placed far apart—for example, noisy staff areas (bindery, typing rooms, etc) must be kept away from quiet public areas. He also needs to know where the relative placing of sections is immaterial to the librarian—this is all positive information.

A far more advanced example of such an analysis is to be found in the *Site selection study* of the Metropolitan Toronto Library Board[8]. This used an interaction matrix to chart the degree of interdependence of each component of a future central library with all other components. Ninety-nine basic components were identified, giving 4901 separate interactions to be considered. This exercise concerned the planning of the central library services of a metropolitan area, not merely those of a single building, but it is nevertheless well worth studying.

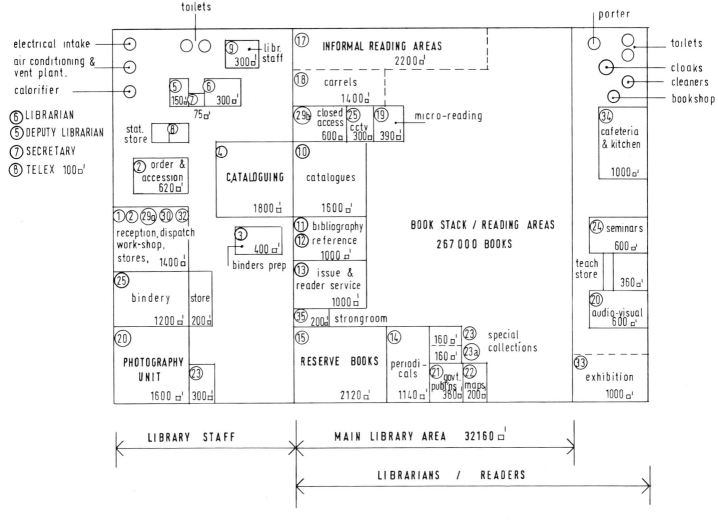

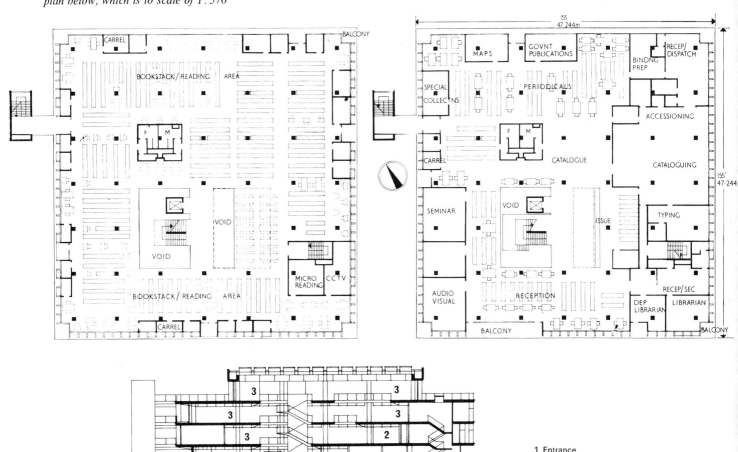

*University of York: relative areas of departments. Compare with
plan below, which is to scale of 1:576*

1 Entrance
2 Circulation desk and catalogue
3 Reader/stack area

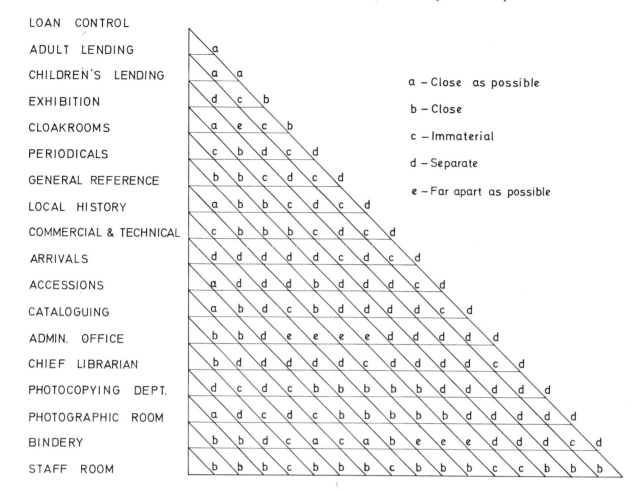

LOAN CONTROL
ADULT LENDING
CHILDREN'S LENDING
EXHIBITION
CLOAKROOMS
PERIODICALS
GENERAL REFERENCE
LOCAL HISTORY
COMMERCIAL & TECHNICAL
ARRIVALS
ACCESSIONS
CATALOGUING
ADMIN. OFFICE
CHIEF LIBRARIAN
PHOTOCOPYING DEPT.
PHOTOGRAPHIC ROOM
BINDERY
STAFF ROOM

a – Close as possible
b – Close
c – Immaterial
d – Separate
e – Far apart as possible

Relationship between sections in a multi-storey building

When the library is obviously going to consist of more than one floor the librarian must say not only which areas need to be close together, but also which need to be on the same level, listing them again in order of priority. Attention will first be directed to the main (usually ground) floor because it is obviously sensible that areas most used by readers should be nearest to the entrance. It should not be forgotten that readers (particularly serious students) are not at all reluctant to use upper, and therefore quieter, floors if lifts are adequate.

Among the factors to be considered in this example of a central public library are the following (under each heading the numbers indicate priority):

Same floor as main entrance:
1 Exhibition area
2 Loan control
3 Adult lending library
4 Children's library
5 Cloakrooms
6 Periodicals room
   etc

Same floor as goods entrance:
1 Unpacking area (must be same level)
2 Accessions area (same level, unless a goods hoist is to be provided)
3 Bindery (same level, unless a goods hoist is to be provided)

Same floor as adult lending library:
1 Department workroom
2 Department stack
3 Children's library
   etc

Same floor as general reference library:
1 Local history library
2 Technical library
3 Departmental workroom
4 Closed stack (if not on same level, a book hoist will be needed)
   etc

It will presumably be taken for granted that public access between departments not on the same level will be by both lift and stairs. Access for staff may be by stairs only where distances are small, staff movement is not very frequent and no loads will be carried.

Access routes

Area relationships are closely concerned with access routes: to operate efficiently the library must be planned so that there is minimum interference with main routes through the building of both readers and materials. These routes are best indicated by simple diagrams showing notional areas linked by arrows. Priorities can be shown by changes of colour or markings of the arrows. The areas shown should not be shaped, nor should they attempt to show relative size.

In small libraries the relationship and reader routes can be shown very simply:
In less simple examples it will be necessary to show where traffic will vary at different times of the day.

An example is given here of a diagram which concerns the technical processes to be carried out in a university library: it was produced by the librarian of the University of York and given to his architect as part of the brief. Although he has shown the main progress taking place and indicated where sections form separate natural divisions, the librarian has been careful not to scale or shape his diagram in a way that might limit the architect in his response. The design solution can be seen in the plans on page 31. At this stage the information given concerns only the placing of

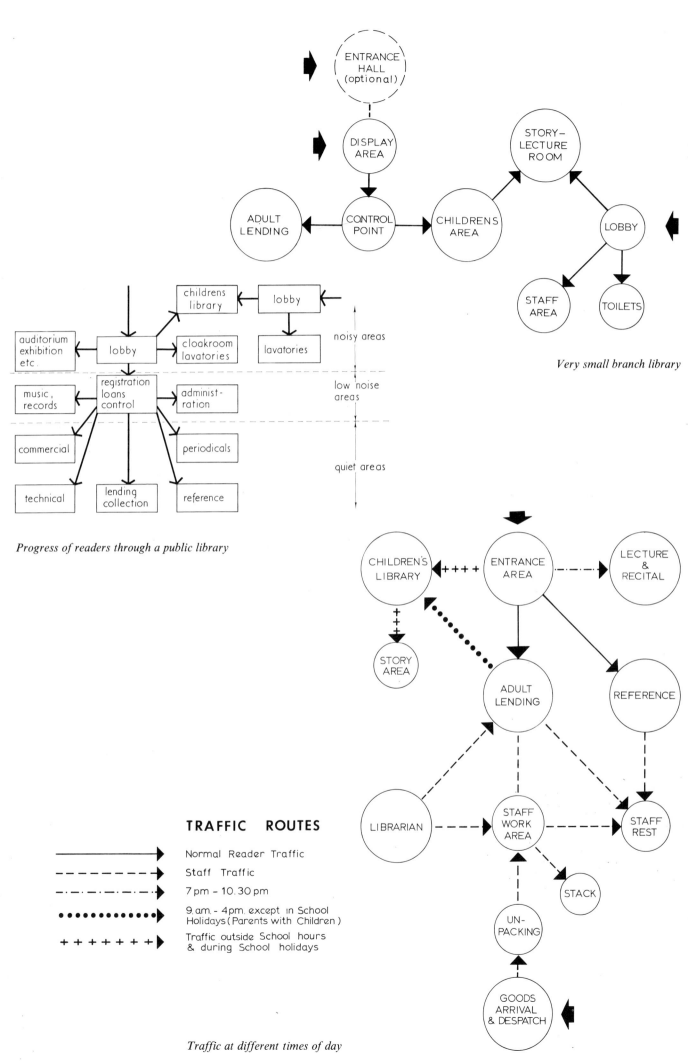

ENTRANCE
HALL
(optional)

DISPLAY
AREA

ADULT
LENDING

CONTROL
POINT

CHILDRENS
AREA

STORY-
LECTURE
ROOM

LOBBY

STAFF
AREA

TOILETS

Very small branch library

childrens
library

lobby

lobby

cloakroom
lavatories

auditorium
exhibition
etc.

lavatories

noisy areas

registration
loans
control

administ-
ration

low noise
areas

music,
records

commercial

periodicals

quiet areas

technical

lending
collection

reference

Progress of readers through a public library

CHILDREN'S
LIBRARY

ENTRANCE
AREA

LECTURE
&
RECITAL

STORY
AREA

ADULT
LENDING

REFERENCE

LIBRARIAN

STAFF
WORK
AREA

STAFF
REST

STACK

UN-
PACKING

GOODS
ARRIVAL
& DESPATCH

TRAFFIC ROUTES

Normal Reader Traffic

Staff Traffic

7 pm – 10.30 pm

9.am. – 4pm. except in School
Holidays (Parents with Children)

Traffic outside School hours
& during School holidays

Traffic at different times of day

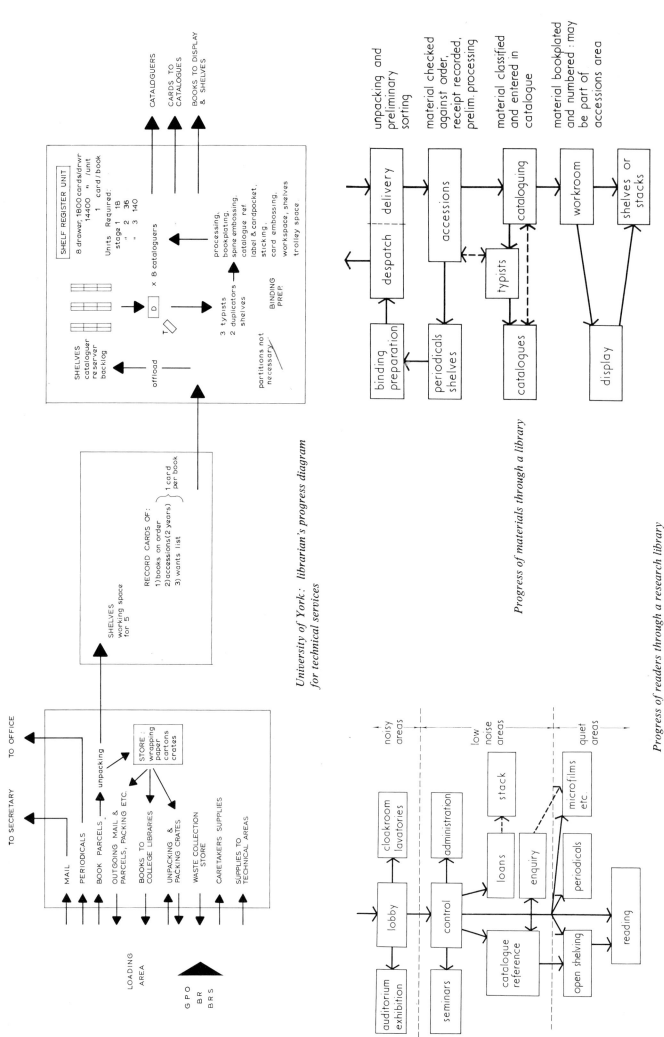

SHELF REGISTER UNIT

8 drawer, 1800 cards/drwr
14400 " /unit
1 card/book

Units Required:
stage 1   18
"   2   36
"   3   140

× 8 cataloguers

processing,
bookplating,
spine embossing,
catalogue ref
label & cardpocket,
sticking,
card embossing,
workspace, shelves
trolley space

3 typists
2 duplicators
shelves

BINDING
PREP.

CATALOGUERS

CARDS TO
CATALOGUES

BOOKS TO DISPLAY
& SHELVES

SHELVES
cataloguer
reserver
backlog

offload

partitions not
necessary

RECORD CARDS OF :
1) books on order
2) accessions(2 years)   1 card
3) wants list   per book

SHELVES
working space
for 5

TO OFFICE

TO SECRETARY

MAIL

PERIODICALS

BOOK PARCELS

OUTGOING MAIL &
PARCELS, PACKING ETC.

BOOKS TO
COLLEGE LIBRARIES

UNPACKING &
PACKING CRATES

WASTE COLLECTION
STORE

CARETAKERS SUPPLIES

SUPPLIES TO
TECHNICAL AREAS

unpacking

STORE :
wrapping paper
cartons
crates

LOADING
AREA

GPO
BR
BRS

*University of York: librarian's progress diagram
for technical services*

unpacking and
preliminary
sorting

material checked
against order,
receipt recorded,
prelim. processing

material classified
and entered in
catalogue

material bookplated
and numbered : may
be part of
accessions area

despatch   delivery

accessions

cataloguing

workroom

shelves or
stacks

binding
preparation

periodicals
shelves

typists

catalogues

display

Progress of materials through a library

noisy
areas

low
noise
areas

quiet
areas

cloakroom
lavatories

administration

stack

microfilms
etc.

lobby

control

loans

enquiry

periodicals

auditorium
exhibition

seminars

catalogue
reference

open shelving

reading

Progress of readers through a research library

34

operational sections and the access routes between them. Traffic patterns within each area, and the layout of furniture and equipment which will depend on these patterns, will arise at a later stage. Similarly the diagrams and lists will show only the progress of people and materials through the building. Telephone and similar methods of communication which have no direct bearing on the space allocation will be shown in a separate communications chart (chapter 4). The transport of small amounts of material (single books, photocopies, etc.) is a matter of document conveyance and is also dealt with in chapter 4.

Producing the "activities and users" part of the brief will inevitably require a great deal of time and thought but without this information the architect may well produce sketches that are quite unacceptable to the librarian and much expensive time will have been wasted.

LIFE OF BUILDING, EXPANSION AND FLEXIBILITY

When drawing up his requirements, in terms of both materials and use, the librarian will have in mind a date, which he has agreed with the architect, up to which these requirements will be valid. In all types of libraries evidence suggests that continuous expansion will be called for in the foreseeable future. Factors of great importance are the effect of the continuing growth in both publishing and in education, as both factors will inevitably mean an increase in reader demands.

During the last ten years the production of information material which any responsible library must make available has grown enormously. In 1955 19 962 books were published in Great Britain; in 1970 the figure was given as 33 489, an increase of 68 per cent. The growing awareness of, and demand for, books published abroad adds to this already impressive expansion.

In the field of formal education numerous official statements show that the recent enormous increase in numbers of students is to continue at an even faster rate. The total of students receiving higher education is to double in the next ten years and reach 825 000 by 1981[9]. The number of pupils in schools is to increase from the 1968 figure of $7\frac{1}{2}$ million to $9\frac{1}{2}$ million in 1980 and over 11 million by 1990[10]. The number of trained teachers is to rise from 318 000 in 1968 to 609 000 in 1986[11]. These figures certainly cannot be relied upon, but the changes announced almost daily are always increases. It must be remembered too that apart from library needs in education itself, increased demand will result from the higher proportion of the population which has been given the chance to read widely.

Metcalf[12] has said:

"Academic and research libraries, until they become what may be called mature institutions, tend to grow at the rate of 4 or 5 per cent a year, doubling in perhaps sixteen or seventeen years. This has been true (in America) for at least two centuries. In due course libraries may become mature and the growth rate will slacken. It may go down to 2 per cent a year, doubling in thirty-five to forty years, instead of half that time, but in general that does not occur until the library is so large that even 2 per cent is a serious matter."

Although these figures of expansion are familar to librarians and must be faced, it is of vital importance that they are not taken too literally. They are growth factors and must be assessed while bearing in mind other developments which might work in the opposite way. Even if we know that publication and reader demand will continue to increase for the next twenty years, this does not necessarily mean that a new wing must be added to a library to cater for the pressure on space. It may well be that factors of improved communications, co-operation, micro-storage and technological innovations as yet unknown will produce such a drastic reform in space use that no increase will be called for. It may be that the need in the future will be, not for more space, but for a greater opportunity for flexibility in the use of that space. Because a new library will have to last for a great number of years

it will, at the very least, be helpful if space can be allowed for expansion: the drastic alternative is planned obsolescence. If there is room on the site where a new wing may be built in the future, this must be a feature of the brief. If no such space exists but long-term expansion is nevertheless expected, the architect may be asked to plan to add floors to the building at a later date. He can deal with either contingency only if he knows about it from this very early moment, but even so he may not be free to plan for a stipulated future expansion on the site if other requirements in the brief tie his hands. For example, a librarian who insists on maximum daylight provision forces the architect to provide glass walls and any expansion must therefore take place upwards or by extensions at an angle to the initial building.

Expansion can take place either laterally or vertically. Possible future expansion upwards is a highly questionable idea; at the very least it calls for a heavier basic structure (which adds greatly to the cost) and special attention to the size and positioning of the core elements (stairways, lifts, book conveyors and mechanical services). These core elements matter enormously also in the case of lateral expansion; the example of the layout of the University of Essex library (pages 49, 52, 68) shows it can be achieved effectively, given careful thought at an early stage. For aesthetic (and often structural) reasons the architect may dislike the solution of siting the core elements outside the main structure but to the librarian this idea has great attractions. It frees him from the internal obstruction (visual, aural and physical) of these elements and can add considerably both to his freedom to use an open-plan layout and to the percentage of space available for library operations.

When expansion within a given period is a known requirement, then the architect can allow for this by using partitions for perimeter walls and removing them later to fit an extension onto the library. Recent examples of this are to be seen at the Hatfield Polytechnic where a wooden side wall has been built for later removal, and at Thurrock Central Library which had a demountable brick wall on part of one side; this was to be removed when the second stage of the project was reached, and the operational services were resited.

Because many of the famous buildings of the last century were notable for their functional rigidity, and because new methods of construction have given the architect more freedom, many librarians have jumped with relief to the idea that flexibility is the solution to all problems. This may well be so, but it is important to stress, what every architect knows well, that flexibility in itself is both a limiting and an extremely expensive requirement. It should be obvious from a comparison of library buildings of the pre- and post-second war periods that elimination of loadbearing walls and use of the open plan and demountable partitioning have added enormously to the team's freedom to plan for future internal changes.

For such open-plan layouts a price must be paid. If absolute flexibility on each floor is required, then the architect will be limited in his choice of design solutions. For example, it is not possible to feature sections of roof lighting or to emphasise control areas by top lighting, without either limiting flexibility or making expensive arrangements so that these features can be moved to other parts of the floor if required. Absolute flexibility means that lighting, heating and floor loading must be planned everywhere according to the highest special requirements of the most intense individual demand; it is possible but it is expensive. The opportunity for change is not needed only to meet growth in numbers of books and readers. Standards of physical comfort, both for staff and readers, have risen sharply in recent years and it is reasonable to assume that they will continue to rise. It may be that expansion will be necessary merely to house present numbers of readers and staff in conditions considered acceptable in the future.

The experience of professionals involved in library planning is necessarily based on experience of libraries of the past—at best of the recent past, because few institutions are changing and expanding faster. Even the period of gestation of a new library will see development in library needs and technology which can make the new building out of date at the opening ceremony. The library planning concepts of only a decade ago are now inapplicable and it is up to the librarian to predict, as far as his vision allows, the effect of changes of the present on the service he hopes to give in the future.

To take the most obvious examples, the librarian must allow for the growth of publication in microform, for developments in the storage and retrieval of information by computer, for closed-circuit television link-up of information sources, and for both reference to and loan of video-tapes. But these are only internal changes: more important are the coming changes in the whole ambience of library and information provision, the linking of libraries which are at present concentrating on their separate functions. A national network, the association of libraries within multi-cultural concepts, and— even more important—the impact of new ways of conveying information direct from central source to home-based reader—these must drastically affect library planning.

Another factor of change is to be seen in the complete transformation which may be forced upon an established institution. Colleges become polytechnics, secondary schools become comprehensive, county district libraries become central libraries for new towns and so on. The necessary alterations may seem impossible to achieve, particularly at short notice, but they have to be achieved somehow. Even small changes in function can drastically affect a library: the alteration of college library policy in favour of short-term loans will have repercussions on storage requirements close to the service counter. The expansion of the number of readers and books will obviously call for more space for both elements, but it also means that more space will be needed for staff operations. If full attention is paid to flexibility at the outset then the job becomes so much easier.

Although the librarian is aware of modern technological advances in his profession and has asked himself what effect these might have on the library, there is still a danger that he will have done so within a functional outline which he has automatically come to accept, but which, when the new building is halfway through its life, will be seen to be the practice of an earlier period. All librarians listen to experts on new mechanical methods; they attend conferences and discuss the enormous differences which technical breakthroughs *could* mean to libraries of the future; however cautious they may be in committing themselves they have to admit that communication by satellite, direct copying over vast distances, computer retrieval of huge masses of information resources at high speed will someday drastically alter the service they are called upon to give. "Someday": but by the very speed of advance in this field and, equally important, by the swift reduction in costs of techniques which, at the moment, seem impossibly expensive, it must be obvious that "someday" is likely to be within the life of the building which they are at this moment planning. It is not enough, therefore, to listen complacently to the experts predicting the great changes that will come by the year 2000. These changes may well have to be accommodated in the building which is to be put up in the 1970s.

The librarian directly concerned with a service which is part of formal education can see that his work will be affected by an educational climate in which education is learner-, rather than teacher-, based; where the student will be accustomed to using an audio-visual device which "answers" his questions, crystallises his vague requirements, brings before him the references he calls for (wherever they may be located) and gives him a personal copy at the push of a button. The whole place of the library in the educational machine needs reconsideration; it will be dominated no longer by the storage and location of books, but by the sophistication of the machinery at hand for providing not the book but the information required. The school or college librarian, therefore, must bear in mind that his library may have to provide for each reader, not a table space and access to books and the machinery that will bring them to him, but a carrel equipped with individual machines *which do not at the moment even exist*. It must be apparent that the most important factor in the whole building project is the librarian's ability to predict, and to do this he must familiarise himself with the most advanced thinking in this field.

No more exact guide can be given: throughout all the detailed exercises which the team must carry out in preparing the brief and applying quantifications, these nebulous considerations must be held in mind. Modular building methods may have given more freedom within the library itself; of greater importances are the changes which are fast breaking down barriers between the whole corpus of recorded knowledge and the reader who needs access to it.

REFERENCES

[1] The design of small branch libraries: a brief prepared for use in the county architect's department in collaboration with the county librarian. Nottinghamshire County Council, 1963.

[2] FUSSLER, HERMAN H. and JULIAN L. SIMON Patterns in the use of books in large research libraries. University of Chicago Press, Chicago, 1969

[3] COLLEY, DAVID I. The storage and retrieval of stack material. In *The Library Association Record*, v 67, February 1965, pp 37–42

[4] BUSH, G. C., H. P. GALLIHER and P. M. MORSE Attendance and use of the science library at MIT. In *American Documentation* v VII no 2, 1956, pp 87–109

[5] CASSATA, MARY B. (editor) Book storage. In *Library Trends* v 19 no 3, January 1971 (Contributions in this issue deal with possible solutions to book storage problems)

[6] COX, J. GRADY Optimum storage of library material. Indiana Purdue University Libraries, Lafayette, 1964

[7] HAVARD-WILLIAMS, P. Op cit

[8] METROPOLITAN TORONTO LIBRARY BOARD Metropolitan Toronto Central Library programme and site selection study. The board, Toronto, 1971

[9] COMMITTEE OF VICE-CHANCELLORS University development in the 1970s. Committee of Vice-Chancellors, London 1970

[10] MINISTER OF STATE FOR EDUCATION AND SCIENCE In *Parliamentary Debates*, Commons, 5 November 1971

[11] *Statistics of education.* HMSO, London, 1968

[12] METCALF. Op cit p 12 (Gives details of the author's prognostica-cations on the growth of American research libraries)

4 Primary brief (continued)

SPECIFICATIONS AND SPECIAL PHYSICAL CONDITIONS

It is not the librarian's duty to attempt to instruct the architect in matters concerning the structure, materials or appearance of the future building, but it will be necessary to communicate to him any client requirements that will limit his freedom in this field. The building may have to form part of a campus, a cultural centre, or a shopping precinct where conformity with certain design principles is considered essential.

Similarly the architect can be relied upon to produce atmospheric conditions for the interior of the building which conform to best modern practice but it will be necessary for him to be informed of any special conditions which may apply in a particular case. If rare and fragile material is to be housed the architect will make special arrangements for light, heat and humidity control for the building, or for the appropriate sections of the building. If fumigation is used in conservation of old material, then special ventilation arrangements will be needed.

The question of whether to ask for full air-conditioning is a difficult one. Although air-conditioning is undoubtedly the best method at present available for providing clean air of the correct temperature and humidity it has two drawbacks: the minor one is that it tends to use space and limit flexibility by its requirements in machinery and trunking; the major one is its cost, which for a good installation can be very high indeed. The Parry report[1] stated that full air-conditioning was "essential" for British university libraries, but the University Grants Committee has not yet given unqualified approval to this recommendation in financial terms. Even if the library cannot afford full air-conditioning initially, the architect can be asked to allow ducting and space so that plant can be provided when funds become available.

If old or fragile materials are to be displayed, or if paintings, prints or photographs are to be featured in an exhibition or art gallery area, the architect will need to plan suitable housing conditions. It would not be appropriate for the librarian to go too far into the practical details—to stipulate, for example, lighting levels—because the architect will be familar with the recommendations of the Illuminating Engineering Society, but he must be told what the materials are likely to be and for what periods they are to remain on display.

The architect will be aware of the Chronically Sick and Disabled Persons Act 1970 and will take into account its requirements in terms of access to the library by disabled people. He will see that ramps or lifts are provided so that handicapped people are not debarred by stairs, but he needs to know what special allowance should be made so that disabled persons, particularly those in wheelchairs, can have access to catalogue cabinets, book shelving and other facilities. To what extent the special design of these elements is to affect the general provision for the average reader is a matter for the librarian to assess. Hospital and welfare librarians will find this a matter of crucial importance.

Under "Activities and users" (Chapter 3) information will already have been given about rest and eating facilities but if, for example, smoking is to be allowed in all, or any part, of the library the fact must be stated in this part of the brief. Although it may seem obvious, it would be as well to tell the architect which areas are to be particularly designed to allow quiet, undisturbed study and which areas can have an atmosphere of businesslike bustle. When in doubt it is better to include information which might appear obvious rather than risk a misunderstanding.

THE SITE

Libraries which form part of a larger organisation in a building complex will seldom have much say in the choice of site. In a university the master plan will probably have fixed the library site. In a school or hospital the library site will usually be a section of a building rather than a piece of land on which to build. The public library, on the other hand, must take the question of site selection very seriously because so much of its success in attracting readers will depend upon its position. There may be little choice: the site may have been earmarked for years even though the money or permission to build, could not be obtained.

Even when the question is only where to place the library within a building (school, hospital, commercial office block and so on), a conflict of interests will arise. The library will need to be central, easily accessible for all major activities of the institution, close to a main entrance but never usable as a thoroughfare: these will also be the requirements of most other special interests within the organisation, and the library is unlikely to get absolute priority. If the ideal, centrally-situated position is denied to the library, there is consolation in the fact that such a position would almost certainly have prevented lateral expansion.

When the problem concerns a site for a separate building and the librarian has a choice, he will discover that he has to deal with many agencies before he is able to persuade the authority to accept what he has chosen. A planning officer may be responsible for a local development plan; the surveyor to a university may have strong views on library siting; other competing interests may be met when a suitable site is found. In most cases there will be officers to be consulted, committees to be persuaded and some opposition to be overcome before a suitable site can be secured, but first the librarian must be clear in his own mind what features of a particular site are important to him.

In the case of a public library that is not to be a part of any cultural or educational complex, he will want a site which is central and easily accessible from main traffic routes by those it is designed to serve. Some interesting studies[2] have been made of the criteria needed when choosing sites for public libraries in new towns. The conditions here are ideal for a clear study of principles because the areas are unencumbered by existing buildings. The studies have been particularly directed to the importance of the siting relationship between the public library and other crucial elements of community life—houses, shops, industry, civic centres and so on. The methods used in assessing the various social factors will be new to most librarians, particularly the use of mathematical models and cluster analysis.

A very fine example of site selection by highly systematic procedures is to be found in the *Site selection study* of the Metropolitan Toronto Library Board[3]. Here the team considered ten sites as potential locations for a new central library and after questioning all the experts available, both planners and librarians, distilled the requirements into fifty-eight evaluative criteria (excluding site cost). Each criterion was given a number relative to its assessed importance, tabulated and totalled, in order to "prove" which site was the most suitable. At the head of the table of "first level criteria" were "metro-wide access", "development potential of the site" and "availability"; in the second-level criteria, and awarded a higher relative score, were such factors as "positive contact with major pedestrian ways", "positive contact with public open spaces" and so on. Few situations will ever call for such an elaborate approach (and it has been suggested by critics that the wrong questions were asked) but the methods used are worthy of study. Working without the benefit of such expert help but with his own experience as guide, the public librarian will usually recommend a position where a great many people come for other essential routine needs—shopping, public transport, other cultural and recreational centres and so on. The most suitable association has always been found to be with shopping, but local authority representatives usually tend to favour a site near the town hall on the grounds of civic dignity. All public librarians will oppose the suggestion, always made by town planners, that the library should be placed in a quiet backwater and so ease the pressure of demand for "main street" sites. A key position in a busy street may be expensive but, like any other businessman, the librarian knows that out of public sight is out of public mind, and an underused public service is potentially a waste of money. A good comparison is between the central libraries of Manchester and Sheffield, the only two large central libraries built in England during the early 1930s: Manchester has a central library on a magnificent site and, partly because of its grandiose architecture, is known to every citizen and serves as a symbol of the city; Sheffield's functionally better planned library is in a central backwater and attracts fewer new readers. A strong argument for the quiet area in the past was the problem of noise, but this is much less important today because it can largely be controlled by the architect. All this may be another way of saying that the site should be "next to Woolworth's" but it is of the greatest importance.

Because the public library will serve its community far into the future it is important to take into account the position, so far as it can be estimated, in thirty or forty years' time. Despite the steadily increasing use of city centre libraries in Great Britain, account must be taken of the tendency for urban centres to become depopulated. If the centre of a large city is likely to be cleared of residents in the future it may be that its library should be planned to serve the day-time business community only; library services for residents would then be based in residential community areas, or even in large shopping complexes outside the city. On the other hand there is some evidence that in America residents are showing a tendency to return to the 'deserted' down-town areas. Perhaps the siting priorities of the future should be concerned with vehicle rather than pedestrian access; this might mean that the ideal site will be one close to main motor roads and with large parking provision. Far-fetched as this may seem at this moment, it is probably more realistic than to use very expensive space within a city for car parking space for library users. The high proportion of the "library" space in the new Central Public Library in Washington DC, which is devoted entirely to car parking throws into relief a problem that will grow larger every year. A parallel problem concerns the administrative headquarters of a large public library system. Traditionally housed in a central library in the heart of a city, it is becoming ever more expensive to maintain and less convenient for delivery and dispatch of books. A separate headquarters outside the central area with better vehicular access and a much lower rent might offset the disadvantages of separation of the public service from its administration. The explosion of the traditional central library into a series of smaller buildings, each housed among the people it is intended to serve, may be the way of the future. Business libraries and day-time lending libraries in city centres, arts and music libraries near cultural and educational precincts, technical libraries close to industrial complexes—these suggestions, anathema to the librarian who regards each member of the community as a potential user of all sections of the service, may have to come unless in future funds will be provided on a more generous scale than at present. Where any choice is open to him the librarian should strongly resist the suggestion that the library should share premises with any other activity. A combination of social services within a single building has immense appeal to planners with no practical experience of the problems which it causes. Shortly after the second world war a variety of such schemes arose in the British

public library sector—association with community centres, health centres, local government offices and so on, but experience proved most of them to be social failures. The new fashion is for "educational centres"; one must wait and see.

Whatever the social reactions, problems are inevitable on the structural side; different activities have their own spatial and operational needs which can seldom be catered for efficiently in the same building. A library works best when it is planned as a library, not as a section of a multi-purpose building: if a new library can by financed only by becoming part of a commercial block, or with shops below or offices above, then the librarian will have little choice, but even if he is given the priority ground floor position, he will find that the structural module has to be chosen to suit an alien purpose and that large pillars and ducts will be needed to carry services to other floors.

It is obviously of the greatest importance that, if choice of site is possible, the architect should be closely involved in the decision. If the choice has already been made, the librarian can do no more than show in the brief where it is to be, giving all the conditions and restrictions known to him. The architect will soon find that there are more.

SECURITY

This is more of a problem for the librarian than for the architect. It is not the layout or the design of machinery which are difficult, but the policy decision as to the extent to which security of the book stock is to be maintained at the expense of freedom of access by readers.

Ideally, in an educated society, there should be little need for barriers and checks; in practice, unhappily, this is not so. The reasons which lead to loss of and damage to books and other materials should be discussed by the design team in order that they can be fully aware of the difficulties and of the acceptable risks. The problem is a very real one in universities, colleges and large public libraries, all of which will hold stocks of rare books; "rare" in this context can refer to those which are in excessive demand and scarce as well as to those of a high monetary value. Where most of the stock consists of books in fairly even demand and the titles are easily replaceable, as in most public lending and school libraries, it may be easier to "trust the people"; the resulting losses, though costing money to replace, will not be as damaging to the library as when intrinsically valuable items, or books in great demand, are lost. Whether the authority is prepared like a supermarket management, to accept a certain level of losses as an operating cost is another matter; the authority may feel that its duty to the public calls for a high level of security, even though the cost be higher than that of possible losses. There follows the question of what the authority is prepared to do when theft or attempted theft is detected; educational and other "closed" institutions may be able to use their own sanctions, but a public library has little alternative but to prosecute at a cost that will almost always be uneconomic in the particular case but which, by the resultant publicity, may deter other potential thieves.

Theft of books
Book thieves are motivated by:
Cash value This reason is much rarer than might be expected. Because most library books are "mutilated" (in the sense that they are marked with ownership stamps and labels) they are not really saleable. The great exception is the rare and valuable book, but such books will usually be kept in strongrooms and issued under strict conditions to readers who can produce proof of identity.

Ad hoc need Students are the main culprits. They "must" have the book for their studies; the conditions of study in the library do not appeal to them or they want to continue studying in their own rooms. The book they need may be unobtainable for this purpose so they steal it. This is very reprehensible but one can see the driving force; much less reasonable is the student who steals to save his book grant for other purposes. A lesser, but still large group consists of "shy" readers, who will steal books on sex rather than borrow them openly.

Absent-mindedness Many books are taken by honest people who find them in their possession when they get home and are too lazy or too embarrassed to return them.

Mutilation of books
This is another form of theft. It is caused by:

The collector He is one of the great menaces to libraries of all kinds. Fundamentally decent people often become unbalanced when under the spell of a devouring hobby; every reference librarian knows how much care has to be exercised when issuing volumes of illustrations of old trams, trains, ships and so on, even in well-supervised reading rooms. Hobby fanatics will even use razors held in their palms to cut out desired sections, and their ingenuity is considerable.

The engravings thief—a more recent development. The vogue for framed engravings and maps has produced a type of thief who cuts engravings out of illustrated books, especially of topography or costume, in order to sell to unscrupulous print dealers.

All this may seem a sweeping condemnation of the community; but as every librarian knows, book thieves and mutilators form a very tiny proportion of the great mass of readers. The problem is to deal with them in the interests of the majority without disturbing general freedom to use the library. Various alternative methods of obtaining the required degree of security are discussed in chapter 16.

Controls
The architect will need answers to the following questions:
Is a physical barrier or control to be placed at the exit from the building, or from any room, and is it to be manned? Is a detection device to be installed, and if so has the librarian decided on a particular product?
Is a bag and coat deposit station to be installed? If so an estimate of the highest number of coats and bags to be housed will be needed. (The latter point must be taken very seriously: a busy library which proposes to use such a method for the first time will find that an alarming amount of space will be needed for storage.) Is the station to be manned or is there to be locking self-service equipment?
Is visual supervision of a particular reading area to be given priority? Is the supervision to be obvious (even blatant) or hidden? In what position are strongroom and safe facilities to be installed and to what degree of security? There is a vast difference in cost between a strongroom, a safe (which is fire- and water-resisting and secure against amateur thieves) and a burglar-proof safe.
In what positions are built-in cash safes to be provided?

COMMUNICATIONS

It seems simple enough to tell the architect what communications are needed between the different sections of the library; as the structural implications are very small indeed, he will be able to allow for the necessary equipment without difficulty. It seems to involve deciding what communication is wanted, then finding equipment to provide it, but this is not quite the case. One is aware of the possibilities of communication only when there is a reasonable chance that it can be given practical form; before closed-circuit television was available, no one asked for a direct visual link between widely separated departments: the availability of the system came first. It is therefore important that the librarian should be aware of the various possible devices.
The normal way for the librarian to tell the architect about his

requirements in all these communications methods is for a schedule to be prepared showing, room by room, what equipment will be required. A neater solution to this problem is a communications diagram (see pages 32 and 60).

Telephone—external
Where the library is to form part of a larger establishment which has its own central telephone exchange (switchboard), it is obviously more efficient from the reader's point of view if incoming calls can be routed directly from that exchange to the required section of the library. The librarian will see that the exchange operators are adequately briefed on the range of activities of each section. If, however, the library is independent of such a group exchange, then the question to be decided is whether it is more efficient and economical to have a private exchange (which means that the reader's call will be handled twice) or whether each major department should have a separate number. The disadvantages of the latter are the cost of extra lines (to be offset against the savings in not having a private exchange and operator), and the frustration caused to the reader who calls what he thinks is the correct department, only to be told that he must ring another number. Direct transfer systems can meet this objection: discussions with the telephone engineer for the district will show what equipment will be most efficient and economical.
If the library is large enough to have its own exchange, this should be placed out of sight and hearing of the public services. Except in the largest libraries, where more than one operator may be needed, the exchange should be near enough to a staff workroom for relief to be available at short notice. In small libraries where an exchange cannot be justified, the placing of the main incoming lines presents problems; too often it is found on the service counter where calls interfere seriously with public service. An estimate should be made of the frequency of calls to the various sections (book inquiries, information inquiries, book renewals and so on) and the telephone placed where the greatest number of calls can be quickly handled with the minimum interference with other services. In a branch public library the best place is often the inquiries desk; even though this may mean that a professional member of the staff must take all calls it may be better than interrupting the relatively busier "books-in" counter. At busy times the flow of book-renewal calls can be a great problem: is such provision necessary? Would it not be better to have a longer period of loan and to ban phone renewals, which are largely motivated by the wish to avoid paying fines?
The whole question of telephone inquiries needs careful thought before any decisions are committed to paper. In most libraries a high proportion of such inquiries can be answered from a comparatively small collection of quick-reference books and there is something to be said for the system developed most efficiently at the Enoch Pratt Free Library at Baltimore, Maryland, where all information inquiries go directly to one of a group of telephones situated beside a revolving bookcase which holds about a thousand quick-reference books; these telephones are permanently manned by staff devoted entirely to this purpose, the number of telephones in use varying with known peak periods of demand. The expense of such special staffing arrangements, and the necessary duplication of many of the books, must be balanced against the inefficiency and frustration caused by staff attempting to serve readers in person while being constantly interrupted by telephone inquiries.

Telephone—internal
Recent advances in telephone systems enable a wide range of internal calls to be made on the telephones used for external calls. Would this arrangement be better than a parallel internal communications link, or are the external lines likely to be too busy? If a combined internal/external system is to be chosen, should all phones accept outside calls or only certain selected ones? Telephonic communication is not cheap; the demand for more telephones within the building (and demand always grows) can add considerably to the running costs of the library: on the other hand

it is much better to have an adequate network planned beforehand than to add lines later.

In some organisations it may be necessary to trace certain members of the staff who may have several working bases, and in extreme examples a pocket point-to-point radio might be justified. If so, this should be included in the brief because it is obviously more efficient to install an aerial loop in a new structure than in a completed building. Perhaps a pocket paging device might be acceptable as a much cheaper alternative.

Visual communications

The coming of closed-circuit television has given libraries the opportunity to bring a reader in a remote part of the library (or campus) a page of information, instantly, without the reader leaving his work. This is potentially a great step forward but at present it has several serious drawbacks, the most important being that it is wasteful of staff time (if economical of the reader's). Someone has to locate the required information: one day a computer may do this; until then it must be staff. At present if the information is on more than one page, someone has to stay with the machine and turn the page, at the same time keeping in telephone contact with the reader. It is not difficult to believe that mechanical answers to those problems are just around the corner, but at this moment it is an expensive luxury, justifiable perhaps when a whole group can make use of the machine in class but seldom for an individual reader. Technical improvements may alter the cost balance and other uses can certainly be found for the equipment. If story hours are held in a number of branch libraries at similar times, it might be possible to have a broadcast from a central children's library: this kind of service may become more feasible in public libraries as the systems become larger and more integrated. If consideration is being given to the installation of a closed-circuit television system, its other uses, for example as a security aid in preventing book pilfering, should be discussed at the same time. Any machine which reduces staff involvement in the transfer of information from a central source direct to the reader must be studied seriously. Facsimile transmission systems (chapter 14) cannot at the moment deal economically with the problem of automatically transferring information from books direct to a distant source, but this development may come. It is certainly possible, with ordinary equipment now available, to produce an offprint of information stored on microform by using a reader-printer and then to feed the sheet into a facsimile transmission machine which will almost instantly reproduce the information at a distant terminal. Elaborate perhaps, but in some circumstances this could be justified and even economical.

The transmission of book identifying information between inquiry desk, bookstack, cataloguing department and so on is traditionally made by telephone or by pneumatic tube. Thought should be given to the possibility of using modern facsimile transmission equipment or closed-circuit television apparatus for this purpose (and this is discussed in chapter 14.) Before any such decision is made there should be a study of the comparative efficiency and operational costs of each alternative in the situation visualised.

Book transport

Deciding on the methods needed to move books within the building may, in a small library, be merely a matter of comparing the efficiency of the book trolley against carrying by hand, but in a large library a mechanical system will usually be called for. Horizontal transport can be by conveyor belt (enclosed in public areas but probably open in stacks). For vertical transport the choice is between book hoists of the positive stop variety, or paternosters. A combination of horizontal and vertical calls for special equipment; systems are available which allow for careful handling of books.

The finding, delivery and return of books from the stacks of a large library involves a series of operations requiring enormous expense in staff time over the life of the building. The librarian will therefore consider with great care whether the considerable cost of installing an automated system of retrieving books would not be an economy in the long run. When such a system can also offer the advantage of needing less space for compact storage (essentially the elimination of access aisles and the opportunity to have higher stack tiers), then the long term saving may be much greater. Equipment for all these purposes is considered in chapter 14.

COST IN USE

This term denotes the complicated exercise by which the architect will establish the factors in shape, structure, materials and so on that will produce the most economic new building. The complication arises from the need to arrive at a balance of initial and running costs, and this involves attempting to correlate two sets of cost figures which have entirely different bases. Initial costs are predictable; running costs depend on many uncontrollable and unpredictable factors. Obviously the total initial cost of the building will be small compared with the running costs throughout its life; it is therefore important that the librarian should understand the principles underlying the architect's decisions and that he should bear cost-in-use considerations in mind when drawing up the brief. An interesting series of articles in *The Architects' Journal*[21] on cost-in-use studies for the design of new schools is a helpful introduction to the subject.

Although every feature of the design affects this issue, there are three fields in particular which should be considered by the librarian at this point, and on which his comments and recommendations may help the architect in producing his first sketches. They are the requirements for the mechanical services (heating, lighting, ventilation etc), the employment of maintenance staff and the the employment of library staff.

Mechanical services

Because of the technicalities involved this must be a matter for the decision (or at least the recommendation) of the architect on the advice of the specialist consultants. If however the librarian asks for too critical a range of temperatures and humidity levels, highly sophisticated equipment will be necessary; this will not only cost more initially but its running costs may include labour charges for maintenance engineers. If such costs would be unacceptable then the architect is wasting his time in designing for such conditions. This may seem very obvious but it is worth taking seriously: a librarian who asks for perfection in all fields when he is well aware that the future running budget will be limited, is simply creating a situation in which economies will eventually be made in the only truly flexible item in his budget—the book fund.

Maintenance

When the architect has completed the building and left the scene, maintaining the building will be the librarian's responsibility. For this reason he will be well advised to state clearly to what extent the architect is to be restricted in his choice of materials and methods in order to plan for economy in maintenance. Because need for constant maintenance in certain parts of the building can cause chaos in the service and add enormously to costs, the librarian is within his rights in doing this, but he must remember that any stipulation of maintenance-free materials and equipment is likely to add heavily to the initial cost. He must sum up the factors applicable in his own case. For example, doubling the number of fluorescent tubes in each fitting and having alternating switches is an economy in the long run but is expensive initially; alternatives such as this can be found in almost every part of the building and its fittings.

If maintenance staff will be available for a strictly limited number of hours a week, the architect should be informed. If cleaning can take place only in the late evening or early morning (common in schools and busy public lending libraries), or all major maintenance tasks can be carried out only in college vacation time, then these limitations must be made clear as they may affect the choice of materials—particularly flooring. Electrical fitments which require skilled attention may be inappropriate in a small branch library with only one general-duties janitor. For instance the fashionable cluster of lamps hung high over an entrance hall requires at least two men with long ladders whenever a single bulb fails—a major drawback when the branch library is several miles from central sources. Similarly, a floor which requires sanding and resealing at regular intervals can be a permanent embarrassment.

Staffing

A major factor in the cost of running a library service is the number of points which must be manned at all times. Allowing for shift working, sickness and holidays, at least two staff will have to be employed for each point. To provide more points than the librarian really needs for his service requirements is therefore a major financial hazard, so a good understanding between librarian and architect on this matter is vital.

Economy of staffing is a particularly important question in small libraries where the number on public duty at off-peak times must be minimal. Placing a children's library where it can be visually supervised from the lending counter at quiet periods, rather than putting it on a different level or in a separate room, can make a great difference to staffing needs. The design and layout of control counters is critical; if only one person is available at off-peak times, then an island counter is essential (see chapter 10). Similarly, separate entrances to a building or to a single section will present control problems and if the librarian asks for such an arrangement he must realise that it will imply either extra staff or some loss of control.

One cause of conflict can be the librarian's insistence on visual supervision of every part of the library where readers are allowed. This will probably clash with the architect's design ideas; in the past bookcases were sited so that they radiated from a single control desk, allowing a view of every part of the library, but other alternatives are now possible provided that the problem is clearly stated at an early stage.

END OF BRIEF

The brief may seem to have developed into a formidable document, particularly in a large undertaking. The architect will supplement it by asking questions and by himself exploring factors which will affect his decisions. He may survey the community to be served, the characteristics of the locale and the potential readership to satisfy himself as to the true, if unwritten, aims of the library. Architects are trained to make this kind of preassessment and in many projects it is an essential exercise. Such an assessment should first have been made by the librarian (or library consultant), who will have specialised knowledge of both the service and the community, but this does not mean that the architect will not wish to make his own survey. He should however be provided with a full record of the librarian's views and these views should be given careful consideration.

From this point onwards the architect, as leader of the team, will ask, examine and propose. The librarian's task will be to study the architects' proposals, be quite sure that he understands all their implications, and comment on them. Having written the brief the librarian must stand by it; all changes cost money and the later they are made, the more expensive they become. It is inevitable that he will want some change but if he has given full thought to every point in the brief these changes can be kept to a minimum. Where the project is the conversion of use of some rooms in a larger institution, such as a hospital, the administrators will be familiar with the process and may have a standard series of forms which have to be used. There may be a form for each room to show the contents and function, followed by a workflow analysis or diagram and a description of the furniture and equipment required. Alternatively there can be a data sheet to record in a standard form the contents and function of each room, and an activity unit data sheet to record the furniture and equipment and its purpose. This procedure is not recommended here: even if the full procedure of writing the brief does not seem to be justified, the architect will need to be given information covering the same range and if this is given under the heads of the brief, as they have been suggested here, the discipline has many virtues, not least in ensuring that nothing of importance has been omitted.

COST LIMITS AND CONTROLS

The authority may have stipulated a cost limit for the project. This is a perfectly reasonable stipulation and one which the architect will take into account in his feasibility study. The cost control can be based on so many pounds per book, per reader, per square metre or foot, per cubic metre or foot, or as a proportion of the total cost of a larger project (eg a new college) but in practice it will also be a global sum; even where higher authority (eg government) permission is given on a cost per square metre or square foot basis there will also be a limit to the total cost.

Before a cost limit is stipulated it should be clearly understood that, if the quantity requirements of the brief are firm, the architect may have to use lower standards of quality (in materials, finishes, etc) in order to meet it; this will be clearly shown in his feasibility report where responsibility for acceptance is firmly placed upon the authority. If possible the accepted target figure should be one that arises out of the feasibility study, or an amendment to that figure, not one that was arbitrarily chosen before studies were even begun.

In setting an initial cost limit the authority should consider very carefully what its impact will be on the cost-effectiveness of the space provided. The more effective the use of space, the greater the purely financial cost, because of the additional seating, shelving and furniture which can be accommodated. In general the larger the library, the smaller the proportion of non-assignable areas (ie architectural features such as walls, columns, vestibules, stairways, etc) required, so that an increase in size may produce functional economies. A fairer cost criterion might be the cost per reader, or per book housed, but it is difficult to see how such a true cost effectiveness can be computed for a library. Designing down to a price can mean that extra library staff will be needed for service and security and this will have to be paid for in the long run. This underlines the importance of including in the brief all possible information about operating conditions.

In order for the cost limit to have any real meaning, it must relate to a particular moment in time. In periods of inflation the architect cannot be responsible for increases beyond, for example, the time of tendering, unless a given allowance for inflationary price rises is to be included. If all tenders exceed the limit and reductions are necessary, the librarian will have to decide what to give up: if this is not done, cuts will have to be made in the standard of controllable items—floor covering and finishes—and this can mean a poorer appearance, reduced comfort and possibly higher costs of maintenance and renewal.

A cost ceiling based on the cost of a similar library elsewhere should not be hastily applied without bearing in mind hidden differences. Construction may be more expensive on one site than on another, for example in a crowded situation, in the centre of a metropolitan area, or where a token service has to be operated from part of the site while construction is in progress.

When the architect knows the cost limit he will begin, with the quantity surveyor, to assess the proportions to be allocated to the various building elements. Throughout the progress of the project he will maintain, and where necessary amend, his apportionment so that no one element is allowed to cost disproportionately more at the expense of others. When, at a later stage, he receives the specialist consultants' recommendations he will compare the cost implications of each recommendation with his original theoretical allowance and so retain continuous cost control of the operation.

Consents

The consents from outside powers which have to be obtained at various stages of the programme are many and varied, and it is right that it should be so. The community has to be protected against the results of irresponsible building, but the restraints used to provide this protection mean work and, therefore, time and money, in any architectural scheme. Some of the limitations apply to all buildings, (eg the local authority's planning approval), while others apply only to certain kinds of building (eg building and fire regulations for public buildings).

Some of the chief controls and their authority are:

planning (both outline and detail) and utilisation (purpose of building), appearance, height, etc—local authority and central government;

traffic matters—local authority and police;

conformity with local building by-laws—local authority;

drainage, sanitation and matters concerning the handling of food —health department of the local authority;

fire safety—local fire prevention officer;

working conditions—factory inspectorate (for both offices and "factories", eg library binderies).

For a fuller list see the RIBA *Handbook*[5].

Most of these controls are in the hands of the local authority but they are specialist matters and are dealt with by different departments. Powers differ in various parts of the country—for instance the district surveyors in inner London have far greater discretionary powers than their nearest equivalent, the building inspectors elsewhere; the position in most matters differs very considerably in Scotland and Northern Ireland.

Undoubtedly, the most important of the powers belong to the local authority in its capacity as local planning authority. This body will have to be consulted from the earliest moment in order to obtain outline planning approval and the final scheme, in every detail, will have to be submitted to the same body (and in some degree to the central government) for final approval. What the librarian seldom appreciates is that this is not just a matter of submitting drawings and receiving them back stamped "approved" or "disapproved". While the architect is conceiving possible solutions to the problems raised by the brief, he will have to turn, time and again, to the planning officers to see whether what he has in mind would be acceptable to them. Planning powers cannot be neatly defined in published regulations; they are developed locally by the council on the recommendations of its officers. New proposals are tested against agreed planning ideas which are continually being developed. The reply to a request for approval is not necessarily a simple yes or no; the planning officers are working towards a concept of a satisfactorily planned area as their council has decreed; they may make concessions towards an architect's ideas in one direction if he will meet their wishes in another (usually a more important one). The result is an almost continuous dialogue in which the personal qualities of the architect are of real importance. If he is preremptory and unyielding in his approach, he is less likely to be met with a reasonable answer than if he is flexible and willing to compromise. A final point for the librarian to note is that consent must be obtained from some authority for almost every major change he causes the architect to make. This means more time, more delay, more expense.

In addition to compliance with statutory powers, the architect is responsible for seeing that his proposals do not affect the rights of others. He will need to use legal expertise in his search for any possible restrictions upon the use of the land which may form part of the site, as well as for any effect which the proposed building may have upon the access routes, rights of way or natural light rights of adjoining properties.

The librarian will state in the brief whether any consents have already been obtained, for example outline planning approval for the use of a site for library purposes. The architect will certainly double-check, but a record of previous discussions with the planning authority is very important.

OTHER MATTERS

Timetable

When the initial proposals for a new library were approved in principle, the authority had in mind a general idea of a date of completion, and this date may have been communicated to the architect. It may be that after preliminary studies he will find this date unrealistic and he will say so in his feasibility report. If the authority accepts the report it will also accept the timetable which the architect then proposes. This will show approximate dates for submission of the various reports and drawings which mark the salient points in the operation; it will be kept up to date (and inevitably amended) by such devices as bar charts, but it should be distinguished from the programme which the architect will keep in a far more elaborate form to assist him in controlling the work. Such a programme schedules in some detail large numbers of related and interdependent activities for which a logical and pre-planned order is of the first importance.

Liaison

The question of appointment of architect, quantity surveyor and consultants has already been considered, as has the setting up of the design team. It remains only to emphasise the importance of stating clearly where the responsibility is to lie for decisions, particularly those which alter earlier understandings. If the librarian is to represent the client in all day-to-day matters then it is up to him to ensure that he has his authority's backing for his decisions. Consultants will report to the architect who (except when formal technical reports are called for) will usually communicate with the client authority only through the librarian. Alternative methods are referred to on page 20. Whichever method is used, it is vital that all concerned are quite clear about the procedure to be followed. The architect will have to liaise with other powers who have to give consents and some of these may be officers of the authority (particularly when it is also the local planning authority); in these negotiations the librarian will have no part to play.

Study of brief

The architect will by now have received a great deal of information, but before he can make use of it he will have to use a number of conversion factors. To take the easiest example, he will have been asked to provide seating accommodation for a certain maximum number of readers. Before he can work out space allocations he must know not only how much space an average reader takes up when seated at a table but also the space allowance within the building to be allowed for each reader—a very different matter because of the need for movement of readers, access to tables and immediate circulation space. To this he will add the space for general access routes, for readers to consult books on shelves and many other factors.

No architect is likely to approach the subject from scratch and start to measure books and readers to see what space they occupy: he will expect to use established standards for each element. Unfortunately the experts disagree on almost every aspect of library estimation, not out of cussedness but because conditions and materials in libraries vary so enormously. When a basis for estimation is quoted in this book the rationale of the measurement is indicated, so that the architect can decide whether or not it applies to his particular situation. If ready-made guides are accepted without question, the variations in space which could be assumed are simply enormous.

At this very early stage the architect will make a very rough assessment of the space requirements of the various areas; he cannot afford to go into detail as yet but he would like to have a general idea of the square and cubic metres or feet involved. This is where the library consultant would show his real value, but in his absence the architect will be glad of the roughest general guide to the space requirements of a given number of books and readers.

He may do this by resorting to various formulae, such as the Cubook (pages 86–90) or the vsc formula (see page 165). Unfortunately, these have been used out of context in the past and without consideration for the great variation between libraries of different types.

To supply height, depth and space conversion factors which can be applied to libraries of all kinds is an impossible task. The table below, based on findings recorded throughout this book, is given, reluctantly, and without quoting any authority. These findings can be dangerously wrong and should be used only if there is no opportunity to study the circumstances of an individual case.

Popular open-access rooms

Books per single-sided 900 mm (3 ft) tier (3/4 full, 5 shelves high)	120 to 130
Current periodicals on open display, each	90 mm² (1 ft²)
Depth of single-sided tier	200 mm (8 in)
Height of wall shelving—adults' library	2 m (6 ft 6 in)
—children's library	1500 mm (5 ft)
Height of island bookcases	
—adults' library	1350 mm (4 ft 6 in)
—chilren's library	1350 mm (4 ft 6 in)
Height from floor of bottom shelf (for very small children this can be as low as	380 mm (15 in) 75 mm (3 in)
Distance between freestanding bookcases	2 m to 3 m (6 ft to 9 ft)
Overall capacity*	65 vols/m² (6 vols/ft²) 17 to 65 books/m³ (0·5 to 2 books/ft³)
Space per reader (other than at tables)	460 mm² (5 ft²)

Study and reference areas:

Absolute minimum space taken up by one reader	0·93 to 1·2m² (10 to 13 ft²)
Space allowance for one student or reader	2·3 m² (25 ft²)
Space allowance for one carrel user	3·7 m² (40 ft²)
Space allowance for one research worker	3·25 m² (35 ft²)

Public reference libraries—allow 1 seat per 500 population served. 7 m² (75 ft²) per 1000 population served.

Open stack 2·3 m (7 ft 6 in) high, shelved close to ceiling (3/4 full)	130 books/m² (12 books/ft²) 50 books/m³ (1·5 books/ft³)
Books under 300 mm (11½ in) tall in these conditions	130 to 180 books/m² (12 to 16 books/ft²)

*Compare these figures with the annual survey of newly built public libraries in the US carried out annually for the *Library Journal*, which produced the following summary: Books per square foot: 1969 4·7; 1970 4·5; 1971 3·8.

Books per single-sided 900 mm (3 ft) tier (3/4 full, 6 shelves high)	140 to 150
Bound volumes of periodicals per single-sided 900 mm (3 ft) tier (3/4 full, 5 shelves high)	75
Reports in laterial filing cabinet single-sided 900 mm (3 ft) wide, 1800 mm (6 ft) high	750 to 1450
Closed stack 2·3 m (7 ft 6 in) high, shelved close to ceiling (3/4 full)	120 to 130 books/m² (11 to 12 books/ft²) 50 books/m³ (1·5 books/ft³)
Books under 300 mm (11½ in) tall in these conditions	180 to 220 books/m² (16 to 20 books/ft²) 70 to 80 books/m³ (2 to 2¼ books/ft³)
Compact book storage	330 to 440 books/m² (30 to 40/ft²) 120 to 170 books/m³ (3½ to 5/ft³)

To allow storage space for expansion: estimate additions (less withdrawals) for each year.

Books—(additions ÷ 120) $\times \frac{9}{10}$ = m² required
(additions ÷ 120) × 3 = ft² required

Periodicals (bound)—(additions ÷ 75) $\times \frac{9}{10}$ = m² required
—(additions ÷ 75) × 3 = ft² required

Work space per head of staff	11 m² (120 ft²)
Cataloguing staff	13·5 m² (150 ft²)
Capacity of catalogue drawer	1000 cards (300 titles)
Weight of a shelf of books (900 m (3 ft) long ¾ full)	12 to 14 kg (25–30 lb)
Weight of a shelf of directories or bound periodicals	22 to 25 kg (50–55 lb)
Percentage of students who will require seats in an academic library—30 per cent	

For a more detailed set of formulae, see Metcalf[6].

Note—Order of following chapters

Because so many elements of a library are common to all buildings, and others are common to all public buildings, the architect will be dealing with matters which are thoroughly familiar to him and quite outside the librarian's province. For the rest of the programme, as followed in this book, matters which concern the architect only—structure, mechanical services, layouts of entrance halls and corridors, exterior cladding and so on—will be discussed solely as they impinge upon the librarian's direct concerns.

Other features still within the architect's jurisdiction, such as lighting, floor covering, shelving, furniture and so on, will be considered in more detail because the librarian will have something to contribute from his professional training and experience. He will know, and need to know, less about them than an architect, but familiarity with the various alternatives and their peculiar strengths and weaknesses will enable him to see the functional problems against a range of possible solutions. For example, it is not his concern to stipulate the flooring material, but he should record the required physical conditions needed to which flooring will contribute. When he sees what flooring materials are proposed, he will comment upon them from his own experience and from his study of other libraries. The architect need not take these as more than comments but it is important that he should have them.

REFERENCES

1. Parry report. Op cit p 92
2. OSBORN, E. The location of public libraries in urban areas. *In Journal of Librarianship* v 3 no 4, October 1971, pp 237–244
3. Metropolitan Toronto Library Board. Op cit
4. *The Architects' Journal*, 7 January 1970, with subsequent discussions in the issues of 28 January, 11 and 28 February and 4 March 1970
5. RIBA Handbook. Op cit, part 3.270
6. Metcalf. Op cit, appendix B, pp 387–398

5 Feasibility study

Now that he has received in the brief the basic information, the architect can begin the process of design. It is difficult to dissect this process and to fit it into a programme of activities because it is composed of both rational and intuitive elements. The whole question of the design process is being studied; not only the mental processes by which creative ideas evolve but also methods by which these can be stimulated and systematised. These studies are important, both in producing more effective creativity in a designer and in encouraging group decisions and participation in an area where the initial impulse arises from an irrational, and therefore highly subjective, element.

In the *Handbook of architectural practice and management*[1] an attempt is made to outline the process of design by breaking it into a series of phases: 1 Assimilation; 2 General study: part I Investigation of the nature of the problem, part II Investigation of possible solutions or means of solution; 3 Development; 4 Communication.

It is made clear in the *Handbook* that "in practice the mental activity [of the designer] tends to make short flashes from one phase to another according to results achieved and the ideas that are stimulated by the work". It is obvious that, while there will always be feedback of ideas from later to earlier phases, the more effectively the earlier stages have been thought out, the less delay will arise from later rethinking.

These matters are fundamental to the professional architect's world and they are mentioned here only to show how complex and personal must be this stage of the operations. To the librarian the position is that the architect, having received a full statement of the client's requirements and knowing the site, has to consider how to accommodate requirements in an acceptable way while bearing in mind various constraints.

At its simplest then the architect, knowing the required functions, contents and physical conditions, has to associate them on a known site, place them in a spatial relationship which will enable the known functions to be performed and choose a suitable envelope in which to enclose them. In practice this is a question of trial and error: during the design process the architect will have visualised many different solutions and sketched many "envelopes", testing each against the known needs and restraints. The relationship of operational sections, movements—human and material, provision of mains services, consideration of external elements, natural light, outside noise, access routes—all these factors will be used in shaping and refining his early vision.

Some of the factors affecting his aesthetic conception are given below: there can be no rigid order in which these matters are considered and he will continually hold them in his mind and balance them against aesthetic factors which must be largely subjective. At this stage he is concerned to see whether the project is feasible; later, in his outline planning, and then again in the scheme design, he will be concerned with the same subjects but for different reasons and in different degrees of detail. It is never possible to say dogmatically that heating problems are considered at this stage, reader circulation matters at that. The architect will work with his technical experts in collecting information, trying out ideas, finding ways to avoid constraints, measuring, costing and comparing alternative ways of providing a feasible solution.

SITE FEASIBILITY

Selection of the site has already been considered. In too many cases this question will have been settled long before the architect came upon the scene but in some cases he may already have been involved, particularly where the library is within a university campus. It might happen that the architect is forced to report, after investigation, that the chosen site is not feasible for the successful accommodation of the proposed materials and functions. He may make alternative suggestions, either a change of site or (more frequently, in view of a possible firm precommitment to the site) variation in the proposals in the brief. Where a separate building is to be erected the points which follow below must be given close attention: where the site is within an existing complex or part of a building designed basically for other purposes, many of the points are inapplicable.

From the requirements of the brief and his knowledge of the site, the architect will already have general ideas as to the height and shape of the building. He must now consider:

the relationship with existing buildings in the immediate neighbourhood, with regard to both the general environment and possible limitations on his freedom to plan;

adequacy of the site for future extensions to the building, and the relationship of the library to other buildings which may later share the site: in particular external circulation routes will need careful study and discussion with those who will be responsible for other buildings;

noise factor—if noise from the immediate surrounding area is inevitable (traffic, student movement and so on), physical provision for protection must be made in the structure, layout and surfaces;

immediate surroundings—whether space is available for gardens or other areas to insulate the library from its neighbourhood or to improve its appearance;

car parking—a fast growing and space-consuming requirement, will have been indicated in the brief but co-ordination with other arrangements in the complex may be possible or it may be provided underneath the building: the planning authority or the police may have relevant regulations;

access routes—the possible need for weather protection for readers approaching the building: access for servicing may be a major problem and may have to be kept quite separate from the public approach.

Other equally important considerations in the viability of the site require the expert advice of the specialist consultants (especially engineers) who form part of the design team and who must now be approached. Points include:

geological basis of the site: a soil engineer may be needed to advise as to its suitability for bearing a multi-storey structure; a layer of rock immediately below the surface may mean that the excavation of basements would be too expensive, water hazards may be similarly restricting, or there may be mining subsidence problems;

availability and adequacy of mains services—water, gas and electricity supply, drainage and sewer access: plumbing and drainage experts may be involved and almost certainly consultants on the heating, cooling, ventilating or air-conditioning system envisaged (at this stage only general principles and major drawbacks need to be considered);

suitability of the preliminary design for incorporating the ducting, trunking and machinery for mains services: this will include study of the access routes, both those needed for maintenance and renewal of the services themselves and those for vehicles used by the service engineers.

Edinburgh University Library

When these, and many other factors have been assessed, the architect is in a position to study the question of orientating the building to make the best use of both site and possible design. He will visualise the impact which the completed library will have upon the passer-by, the effect of natural light at different times of day and at different seasons. He will also be able to plan the main approach route and the approaches to any other entrances to the building, again working in close consultation with the local planning authority.

Expansion allowance on site

If the brief required provision for expansion to be made horizontally, then preliminary designing will be complicated by the need to place access routes and physical services where they can be used in the expanded building of the final concept. The examples below, of four recent British university libraries, show site factors and expansion plans made for very different site conditions. (It would be difficult to make a direct comparison using other types of library; few have so many elements in common as do university libraries. A public library for example, because it has to serve so many different age groups and levels of reading will exhibit local variations which could make such a comparison meaningless.)

Comparative size of library projects

University	Functional area			Comparison with Edinburgh (per cent)
		(m²)	(ft)	
Edinburgh		23700	249600	100
Essex*		4750	51300	20
Lancaster	phase 1	2190	23600	9
	phase 2	3640	39200	16
	phase 3	6350	68600	27
Warwick	phase 1	5700	61400	25
	phase 2	10700	116400	47

* Number of reader places has been reduced from 887 to 710 with the provision that reader places will be provided in residential accommodation.
Note Functional area has been chosen as the basis for comparative size because this indicates the effective size. Figures are given to the nearest hundred, and compared with Edinburgh which is the largest project.

Edinburgh Town planning authorities enforced height restrictions. The university's comprehensive plan for the George Square area required the building to sit on a pedestrian podium at ground level with traffic circulating at lower ground level. Site slopes from north to south. Plan arranged to allow for future extension to the south-east.

Essex University Library

Essex The architect has to take up as little of the available site as possible to allow for future expansion of the university, and to keep the concentrated atmosphere of the development plan which is essentially urban in character. The building is sited in a quayside "piazza" bounded by the lake on the east. These factors necessitated planning vertically to six storeys. Building designed to allow addition of a further wing (stage 2) which will double the initial size with further expansion in stages 3 and 4.

45

Warwick University Library

Lancaster University Library

Lancaster The building is central in the university complex and is to provide other amenities, including bookshop, exhibition hall, coffee and snack bar and a recreational "public" library. Planned for construction in three phases to form a completed building round a central courtyard, each successive phase is to provide a workable unit with minimum disturbance in changeover. The possibility of further expansion on an adjoining site after the original three phases are completed was to be considered.

Warwick Building is to be centrally placed with a view to easy access from faculty buildings and to include a coffee bar. The library is to provide a room suitable for meetings of university societies, picture exhibitions, etc, and to act as a centre of university life. The site is in open country on the outskirts of Coventry. The top two floors are to be allocated to the humanities department until required for library expansion to phase 2. Site allowance to be made for further expansion up to treble the size of building illustrated.

SPATIAL RELATIONSHIPS

From the brief the architect will see the priority which the librarian wishes to give to certain functional areas; applying this priority rating to the spatial allocation which is already crystallising in his mind he will arrive at a solution of the interdependence of operational areas which is, in many ways, the most important spatial factor in the whole concept. In doing so he will try to disregard

the many matters of detail that will constantly arise.

In large projects, which will inevitably be multi-storey, the architect has to conceive a relationship between large masses of books and large numbers of readers which will give the required degree of freedom of access. In the case of a very large closed-stack system he will wish to keep the mass of books housed closely together for space economy and he will study the various classical alternatives of relationships with reader spaces. Thompson[2] illustrates five such plans:

reading room above and bookstacks below,
central reading room surrounded by bookstacks,
reading room in front and bookstacks behind,
bookstack in the form of a tower,
central bookstack with surrounding reading rooms.

Imagination could suggest other alternatives but there are many working examples of these five which may be studied to determine their strengths and weaknesses.

In an open-access or open-stack library the decision will be less dramatic in that most reading areas will also house books; the problem will be more closely bound with degrees of access and priority placings of particular services. Examples of the four university libraries previously quoted show the different stack requirements and solutions.

Stack requirements
Edinburgh Open access generally to encourage undergraduates to explore stacks. Some closed stacks for rare books. Floor structural loading to permit complete interchange of book storage and reader space if required. Bulk of each floor to fit exactly and without horizontal voids over the floor below. Columns kept to the same size 914 mm × 457 mm (3 ft × 1 ft 6 in) as stacking units, and laid out on a module of 8·23 m square (27 ft square).

Essex Open access stack to be the core of the building with reading areas surrounding it at all levels. Main library services to be integrated as closely as possible on one floor and adjacent to main staff workrooms.

Lancaster A diffused "modular" library was requested, but after discussion modified to provide a bookstack core with perimeter reading bays. Open access generally with some closed stack for rare books. A module of 5·486 m square (18 ft square) was adopted for convenience and economy. Full bookstack loading has been allowed for throughout, to promote flexibility for future planning.

Warwick Open access generally, with reader services and closed stack for less used books at basement level. Structural obstruction kept to a minimum and grouped to give the greatest possible freedom for rearrangement. Planning is based on a 1·524 m (5 ft)

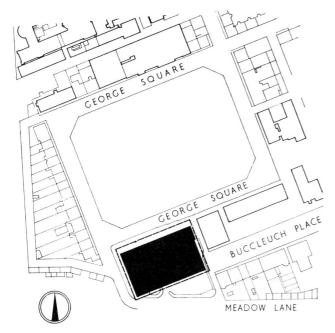

Site plan, Edinburgh (1:3750)

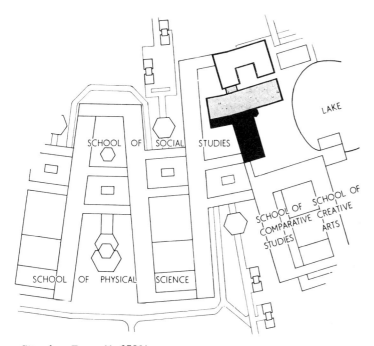

Site plan, Essex (1:3750)

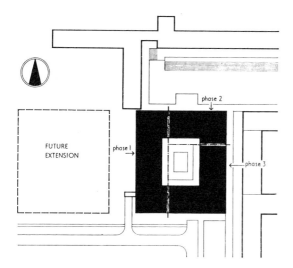

Site plan, Lancaster (1:2000)

Spatial analysis, Edinburgh

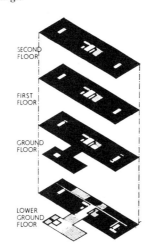

Spatial analysis, Warwick

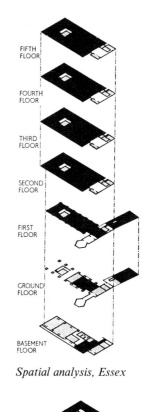

Spatial analysis, Essex

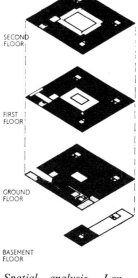

Spatial analysis, Lancaster

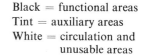

Black = functional areas
Tint = auxiliary areas
White = circulation and
unusable areas

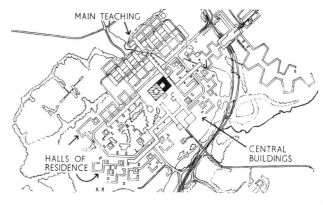

Site plan, Warwick (1:13200)

47

Space allocations compared

University		Total volume as percentage of equivalent volume	Total contained volume as percentage of equivalent volume	Contained volumes as percentages of equivalent volumes			Contained volume as percentage of total volume
				Functional	Auxiliary	Circulation	
Edinburgh		118	106	107	109	112	93
Essex		134	120	111	108	104	82
Lancaster	phase 1	112	98	98	95	102	88
	phase 2	105	92	95	70	99	88
	phase 3	98	93	97	63	99	89
Warwick	phase 1	175	90	90	89	90	74
	phase 2	121	90	90	90	90	74

module relating to a single-sided table spacing 610 mm table with 914 mm space (2 ft table with 3 ft chair space). Book stacks are freestanding and movable.

SPATIAL ANALYSIS

Analysing the proportions of the building which are to be allotted for the various purposes is a complicated exercise. In the first place a basic volumetric analysis will distinguish between:
the total volume: that contained by the external perimeter and the height from lowest floor surface to outer surface of the roof;
the total contained volume which is in effect the volume of air contained within the visible parts of the exterior.
the equivalent volume, which is calculated by assuming a standard floor-to-floor height of 3 m (10 ft).
The analysis on page 47 of the same four university libraries shows how the differences in basic design have already caused great variations in the proportions of the different spatial measurements given above. Reference to the plans and spatial analyses of these libraries (pp 66–9) will illustrate how the differences have affected space allocations.
The librarian will be less interested in this than in seeing that the library's operational areas occupy as high a proportion of the total space as possible. American books tend to use the terms "non-assignable space" or "architectural space" for the difference between the gross area and that usable for the library's purpose (including the machinery necessary to create acceptable atmospheric conditions). Non-assignable space therefore includes walls, columns, entrances, vestibules, corridors, stair wells, and other spaces used for transport and communications, unusable space under sloping roofs and so on. A distinction of more immediate use to the librarian is one between "functional", "auxiliary" and "circulation" space: the term auxiliary refers to areas which house activities concerning the building but not its operation as a library—such as heating, lighting, ventilation as well as open spaces. A comparison is given now of the relationships between these areas in the same four university libraries. No immediate conclusion will occur to the librarian on studying these figures and the appropriate plans, but they will help him to grasp some of the factors involved if he is to reach his aim—as high a proportion as possible of functional space.
An interesting exercise in architectural design potential is shown in the *Site selection study* of the Metropolitan Toronto Library

Board[3]. This applies relevant criteria about spatial relationships and critical placing to both plan and isometric drawing, working without any design preconceptions. The conclusions drawn, especially those relating to the positioning of the stack in a large central library, are most illuminating.

THE BUILDING

The most immediately obvious result of the design concept will be the external shape of the building. The architect will wish to create a shape which not only encloses the functions satisfactorily but also makes a certain impact upon the user and the passer-by, interacting with its surroundings in an agreeable way. He will also have the not unnatural wish to achieve some degree of originality. In this lies temptation: he will do well to visit some "striking and original" library buildings and note the price which users and librarians have had to pay for this originality, in terms of inconvenience, extra staffing and large heating, ventilating and maintenance bills. A few architects, mainly eminent practitioners with a "style of their own" have been responsible for some functionally appalling buildings which are notorious in the library profession.
On the other hand, librarians have been flogging a dead horse for decades now in their dislike of architectural "monumentalism". Contemporary architects have reacted against this style far more than have librarians and no such danger is likely today. Fashions do exist among architects however, and it may be that the present-day equivalent of monumentalism is the love of artistic gimmickry, such as fountain courts and gardens, open stairways to mezzanine floors, and glass walls.
In the relationship lists and diagrams the librarian will have asked for a pattern of association between activity areas which will be virtually impossible except in a spherical building; this the architect is unlikely to provide (although the Humanities library of the University of California at San Diego is a step in this direction) but he might be tempted towards a circular one. There are precedents—not only the well known ones of the British Museum Reading Room, Library of Congress, Manchester Public Library and the Brotherton Library of the University of Leeds, but also recent lending libraries at Fulwell Cross (London Borough of Redbridge), Bourne Hall (Epsom and Ewell, Surrey) and Jesmond District Library, Newcastle upon Tyne. At least one

University	Functional area		Areas as a percentage of total area		
	(m²)	(ft²)	Functional	Auxiliary	Circulation*
Edinburgh	23 700	249 600	87	7	6
Essex	4750	51 300	73	12	15
Lancaster	6350	68 600	85	8	7
Warwick	10 700	116 400	80	8	12

*Circulation area here is taken as including general (other than functional circulation), also all unusable space.

Jesmond District Library, Newcastle upon Tyne CB

Bourne Hall Library, Borough of Epsom and Ewell

West Norwood Library, London Borough of Lambeth

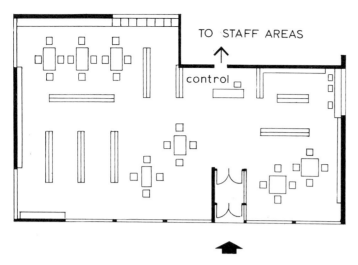

Library of 180m² to 270m²

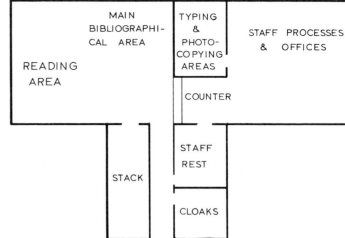

Small special library

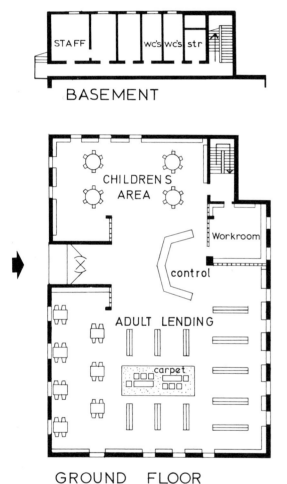

Library of 460m² to 930m²

In very small libraries there will be little real choice as to shape. If it is to be an independent building and open plan, then maximum use will be made of natural lighting and this almost always means window walls. There must be adequate space for circulation, a central main entrance and control counter for economy in staffing, and nominally separate areas for children, adult lending and study. A typical library of 180 m² to 270 m² (2000 ft² to 3000 ft²) holding 5000 to 10 000 books is shown above, with one of 460 m² to 930 m² (5000 ft² to 10 000 ft²) holding 15 000 to 20 000 books. Apart from the positioning of some staff areas in a small basement in the larger, there is little difference between these plans; the only real variations found in libraries of this size will be in arrangement of the shelving and furniture.

Above this size complications arise chiefly because the demarcation between service areas, even in an open plan library, must become more marked. Nevertheless the movement towards full flexibility in libraries of this kind can be seen clearly in a comparison of the plans of two large branch libraries, Yardley Wood, Birmingham, 1936 and Seacroft, Leeds, 1964 opposite.

Small libraries which must occupy a part of a building which is used by the institution which it serves, particularly school and special libraries, seldom have this freedom to choose the perfect shape. The area will often be the wing of a building and because the heart of both these libraries will be a service and the two main elements a reading area and a staff area, L and T shapes are commonly used, the entrance and the reader service point being at the junction of the laterals. An obvious layout is shown.

Height and number of floors

Because movement of all reader and staff operations in a library is more efficiently carried out in a horizontal than a vertical plane, and because second and subsequent floors, with their need for complicated mechanical services, lifts and staircases waste space and money, a single-storey library is usually the most economical. Not invariably however: in a very large building on one level the horizontal distances involved must pose serious problems. In theory one needs a second floor when horizontal movement on a large ground floor becomes less efficient than vertical movement to an upper one; in practice it is when the ground floor site gives too little space for all the activities required.

The architect's decision on building height may arise out of area planning considerations within the constraints of the site. It will certainly be limited by planning height restrictions and by cost, but he has some choice in the number of floors to be obtained in a given overall height if he varies the thicknesses of intermediate

of these should be visited and its problems studied before such a risk is taken. Similar parallels of great value can be found with other "original" shapes—there is little which is really new.

The square shape has many advantages, particularly minimum distance between extremities, maximum opportunity for re-arrangement and an optimum external wall to floor area ratio which produces economies both in building costs and in the lower heat gains and losses through external walls. For a most convincing assessment of the cost increases caused by the choice of "irregular" shapes, see Metcalf[4]. In many cases however the architect may declare that a square building would be ineffective, dull, wasteful of site and incompatible with the environment—and he is the man who is making the decision.

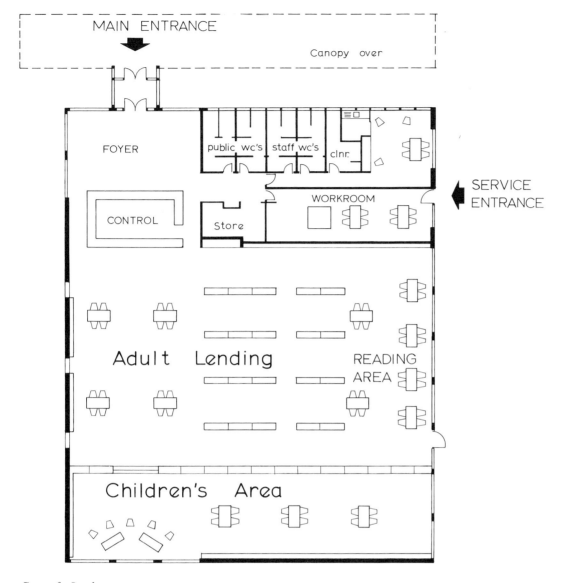

Seacroft, Leeds

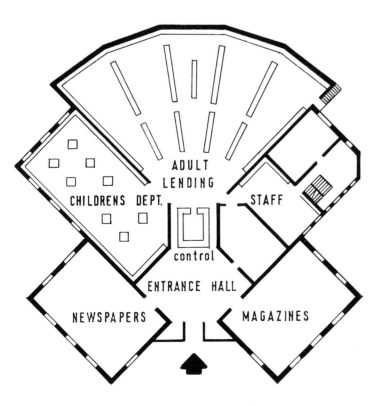

Yardley Wood, Birmingham

floors (see Chapter 7). He will also bear in mind the requirement of possible or agreed expansion and may consider making the foundations sufficiently heavy to allow for a further floor or floors to be added later. This in theory: in practice there are serious objections to later expansion upward. Building operations are violent, noisy and dirty, and when carried out on top of an already operating library they are very costly indeed. It is better to build at the outset more floors than are required at first; they can be used for other purposes until the library needs to expand. Usually such a decision will have been made by the authority at an early stage but fundamental thinking by the architect can produce such a possible solution in the feasibility study.

Because he is an expert on the optimum use of space the architect may suggest radical solutions which had not been envisaged in the first concepts: many a scheme has been rethought and a new brief prepared because the architect made proposals involving ideas which were new to the client. The site itself may offer interesting opportunities: a sloping site can make possible both a variation in floor levels and an alternative to having a ground floor entrance. An entrance at the middle level on such a site can be a most useful expedient. In ways such as these the architect can make a virtue of an unusual site and at the same time create an original design at a lower cost. When floors are planned on different planes or in differing sizes the effect throughout the building can be most striking (Humanities Library, University of California at San Diego and, in a lesser degree, Essex University), but there is always a space loss compared with the simple cube. It is up to the architect to reconcile the balance of advantages and disadvantages before making his proposals.

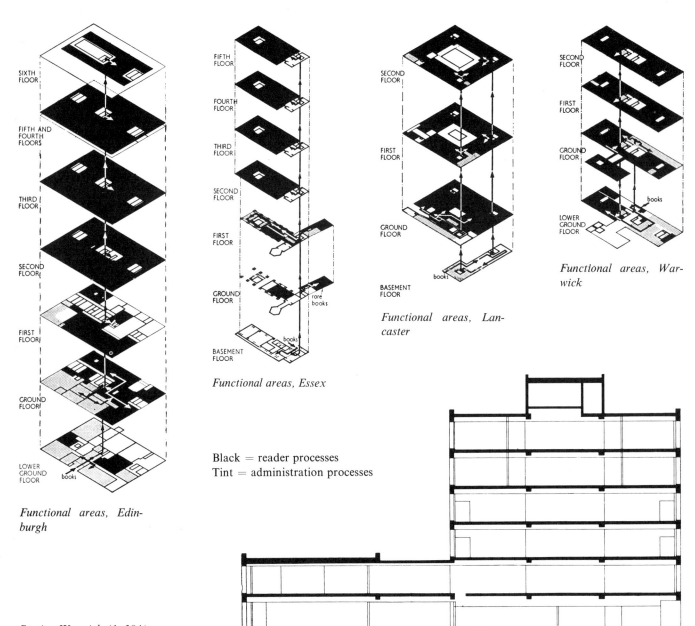

SIXTH FLOOR
FIFTH AND FOURTH FLOORS
THIRD FLOOR
SECOND FLOOR
FIRST FLOOR
GROUND FLOOR
LOWER GROUND FLOOR — books

Functional areas, Edinburgh

FIFTH FLOOR
FOURTH FLOOR
THIRD FLOOR
SECOND FLOOR
FIRST FLOOR
GROUND FLOOR — rare books
BASEMENT FLOOR — books

Functional areas, Essex

Black = reader processes
Tint = administration processes

SECOND FLOOR
FIRST FLOOR
GROUND FLOOR
BASEMENT FLOOR — books

Functional areas, Lancaster

SECOND FLOOR
FIRST FLOOR
GROUND FLOOR
LOWER GROUND FLOOR — books

Functional areas, Warwick

Section Warwick (1:384)

Housing the function

As the architect assesses the various factors involved and a picture begins to form in his mind of a possible spatial approach, he will look again at his early ideas and will notionally divide the areas which he intends to devote to library functions between the two elements of reader processes and administrative processes. The tables and diagrams below illustrate the solutions of the architects of the four university libraries:

Provision for reader activities

Edinburgh	Open access stacks and reading areas. Reading-rooms. Periodicals room. Palaeography room. Seminar rooms. Study rooms. Carrels. Typing carrels. Listening rooms. Microfilm areas. Map room. Lounge (canteen facilities).
Essex	Open access stacks and reading areas. Research rooms. Periodicals room. Microfilm unit. Blind readers' carrels. Readers' typing carrels. Exhibition space. Xerox unit.
Lancaster	Open access stacks and reading areas. Periodicals room. Carrels. Typing carrels. Seminar rooms. Microfilm units. Audio-visual aid units. Photographic unit. Bookshop. Exhibition hall. Recreational library. Coffee bar.
Warwick	Open access stacks and reading areas. Carrels. Research rooms. Periodicals rooms. Photographic and microfilm units. Xerox unit. Seminar rooms. Coffee bar. Listening rooms. Readers' typing carrels.

Analysis of functional areas

University		Administrative processes (per cent)	Reader processes (per cent*)
Edinburgh		12	88
Essex		10	90
Lancaster	phase 1	26*	74
	phase 2	16	84
	phase 3	9	91
Warwick	phase 1	17	83
	phase 2	12·5	87 5

* Estimated

The architect will also need to make a survey of the reader circulation routes that will follow from these space allocations, with particular relation to the main entrance and exit. For reasons of security it is assumed that wherever possible there will be only one main entrance and one main exit, and that they will be located together. The obvious answer is for this to be placed in the centre of the ground floor of the building but there is a body of opinion which holds that this placing has many design disadvantages. The diagrams opposite and following show the thinking of the different architects to the basically similar problems of the four university libraries.

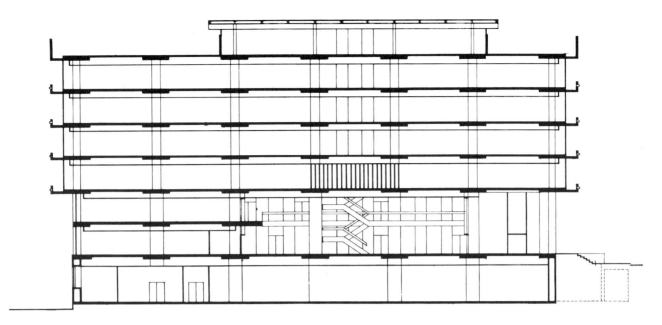

Section, Edinburgh (1:384)

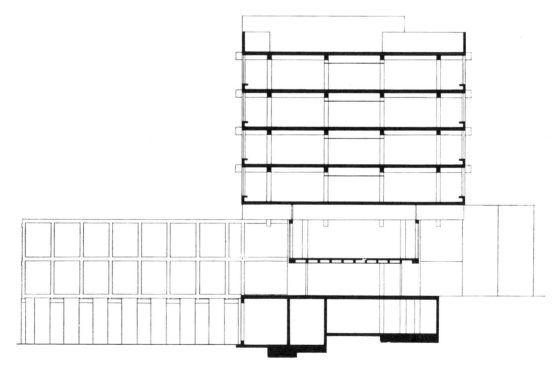

Section, Essex (1:384)

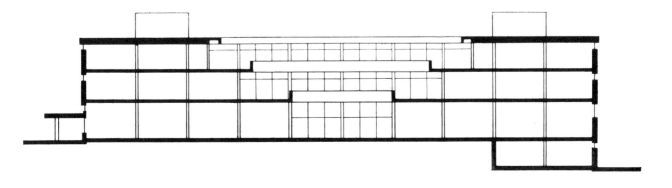

Section, Lancaster (1:384)

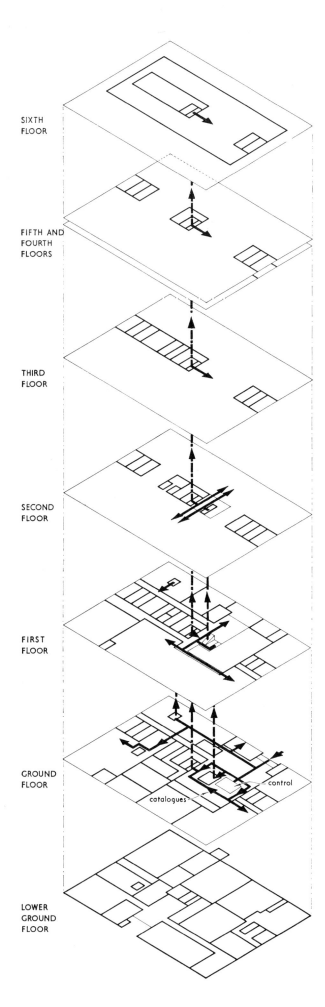

SIXTH FLOOR

FIFTH AND FOURTH FLOORS

THIRD FLOOR

SECOND FLOOR

FIRST FLOOR

GROUND FLOOR

catalogues

control

LOWER GROUND FLOOR

Reader circulation, Edinburgh

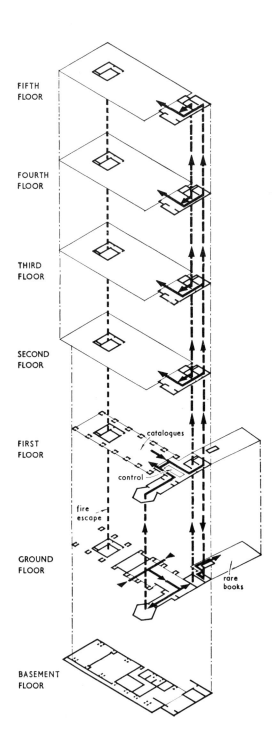

FIFTH FLOOR

FOURTH FLOOR

THIRD FLOOR

SECOND FLOOR

FIRST FLOOR

catalogues

control

fire escape

GROUND FLOOR

rare books

BASEMENT FLOOR

Reader circulation, Essex

Atmospheric conditions

The services aim to provide thermal comfort and atmospheric conditions acceptable to both staff and readers and conditions in which books and other materials can be satisfactorily preserved; see chapter 17 for details. The methods used in providing them affect the plan by their space needs and their costs, both initial and running. The architect must balance space and cost factors: the heating engineer will be able to supply cost estimates for various alternatives.

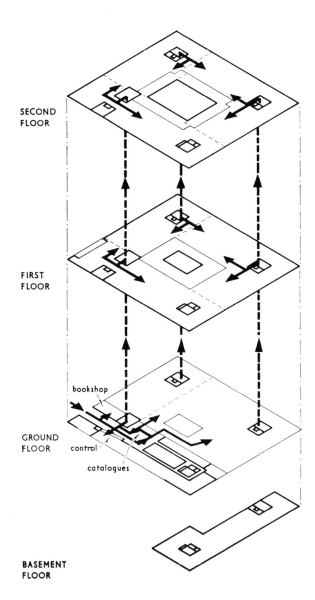

SECOND FLOOR

FIRST FLOOR

GROUND FLOOR control
catalogues

bookshop

BASEMENT FLOOR

Reader circulation, Lancaster

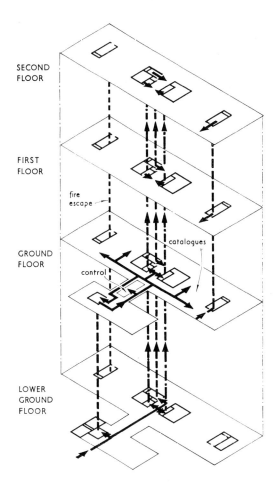

SECOND FLOOR

FIRST FLOOR

fire escape

GROUND FLOOR

control

catalogues

LOWER GROUND FLOOR

Reader circulation, Warwick

As a rough guide, heating, lighting, and ventilating provision will represent 20 to 30 per cent of the structure costs. Separate estimates will be produced for each but the running costs of the three elements are interlinked in many ways; for example, heat produced by high level lighting installation can sometimes be utilised in the heating system. The costs are also affected by design factors: the lighter the structure, the greater will be the need for cooling; in a large building, internal areas will at times need cooling more than perimeter ones.

The equipment used to produce heating and cooling have normally to be housed within the building. In a few cases this may not be necessary: district heating and small loads of electricity are obtainable without special plant: a library using a great deal of electricity—the figure has been placed as low as 100 kW—will need its own transformer and a special chamber to house it. (In order to relate this figure to a librarian's experience, one large electric fire uses 3 kW.)

Fenestration

Because the appearance of a building and the internal atmospheric conditions will be so greatly affected by the size and position of windows the architect will treat fenestration as a fundamental matter of design, not merely as a way to provide natural lighting. While wrestling with various design concepts, therefore, he will be free to exercise his imagination only when he has digested the arguments for and against the use of large areas of glass in library walls. These arguments are by no means clear cut even with regard

to human needs for natural lighting. Metcalf's[5] experience is that even large reading areas completely without windows are acceptable, both physically and psychologically, to readers. Thompson[6] on the other hand believes that daylight is essential. We in Great Britain have had little experience of libraries completely without windows but there is certainly no physical need for natural light: whether there is a psychological need is another matter, some experts hold that the eye needs a distant view as a relief from short distance concentration. Even if a window light is no longer thought absolutely necessary, it may be that windows offer psychological advantages in giving a change of view: a recent example shows how this advantage may be gained without too great a light from above. In this connection it is interesting to see that a recent American university library shows "seats facing inwards from windows to avoid the distracting view"[7]. Certainly to provide light for reading purposes there is no need for the vast amount of fenestration which has become common in recent years but the architect may choose to have large windows for aesthetic reasons.

In addition to the day-time appearance of the building there is the great attraction which a well lit "shop-window" exercises on passers-by, particularly in suburban branch libraries. But when the architect considers these advantages, he must also be thoroughly aware of the accompanying disadvantages—limitation of shelving space, the troubles and costs caused by heat gains and losses, humidity and glare.

Before artificial lighting became as efficient as it is today, natural light was essential in all reading areas. In a very large building this forced the architect to provide internal light wells so that all rooms could have windows. These light wells are still seen: indeed this principle is used for the new Birmingham Central Library despite the enormous loss of space which it entails. In small single-storey buildings the interior court is fashionable but it has little connection now with the need for natural light: it is simply a design feature. It can be most attractive: and there is an undeniable advantage in giving the reader a sense of space by having a court (and possibly a garden) within the library walls. In some cases however, the reasoning behind the provision seems to be mis-conceived: reading in courtyards open to the sky may be a boon in California but in this country their use is restricted by the weather. If the architect contemplates such a design, he should first discuss it with the librarian who will assess the possible use by readers against the very large loss of usable space. Design is certainly the architect's responsibility but it is his duty to consult the client on a matter that will so strongly affect his use of space.

Structure

Even in his preliminary sketching the architect will have had ideas about the basic structural elements and the methods of con-struction to be used. He will be very conscious that different methods of construction can cause perhaps the greatest of all variations in the overall cost of the building, and if for only this reason he will give them very careful thought. If the building must be multi-storey and without internal loadbearing walls (in the interests of flexibility) then he will be very much concerned with the size of the structural grid and the columns. The latter, especially if they are intended not only to support a building several storeys high but also to carry air-conditioning ducts, may have to be several feet wide; the result could be a forest of columns almost as inhibitive of change as the internal walls they superseded.

The module is a unit of length used as a common denominator in planning a building. From it is developed the unit square and from this a grid square which can be the base for planning structural support. Very generally it can be said that if a ceiling can be supported by columns at corners of a grid square, internal walls can become merely convenient divisions between functional spaces. Elimination of the loadbearing wall is a great feature of modern buildings and it is particularly helpful in libraries.

The grid square is bounded by only four columns, the floor and the ceiling. Partitions can easily be erected between columns and as easily demounted; if the space so enclosed is of a size convenient for use as an office there will be little waste. In libraries with large book stocks it is even more important that the grid square should allow for the most economical layout of shelving.

The choice of a module is a complex matter requiring at an early stage a full appreciation of many different problems. These are not universal or easily definable. For example, in a multi-storey complex other factors may impinge: if offices over, or a car park under, the library are included in the scheme, reconciliation of a module appropriate to those functions with that appropriate to a library may pose difficult problems.

As far as the library itself is concerned, the architect needs to know the unit length and width of shelf he has to accommodate, and in the different functional areas (lending, reference, open and closed stacks, compact storage) the optimum dimensions *between* stacks and the optimum *lengths* of stacks. What may be acceptable in a little used closed stack will be quite inappropriate in a heavily used lending department. Different areas of the building may require quite different grids and this will be subject to many other structural, service and planning restrictions, so the librarian must state his parameters in the brief and leave the architect to work out the problem.

Standard shelving is traditionally made in 900 mm (3 ft) units and if mass produced shelving of this size is to be used the grid should be chosen so that shelving in a stack can run in either direction, with 5·4 m (18 ft) as the probable minimum acceptable length and 8·25 (27 ft) the maximum. Similarly we can take 1350 mm (4 ft 6 in) as a common size for the distance between stack centres; a square size divisible by both 900 mm (3 ft) and 1350 mm (4 ft 6 in) therefore will enable the direction of runs of stack to be altered by 90 degrees if required. In practice it is not quite so easy: for example the 900 mm (3 ft) of a standard stack bay is measured from centre to centre of the units, so six such units will not normally fit into an exact 5·4 m (18 ft) length. Similarly because the grid square, to the

architect, runs from centre to centre of the columns, the resultant space is not the same as that between column faces; the thickness of the columns will be a decisive factor. If a row of bookstacks is to run beyond (and to contain) columns, the size of the columns should for efficiency of shelving not use up more than one shelving unit; this implies a column thickness of 450 mm (18 in) or less. The between-column distance should also be suitable to accommo-date settings of tables and chairs, combinations of shelving and furniture and allow for standard-width aisles. 6900 mm × 6900 mm (22 ft 6 in × 22 ft 6 in) or 8400 mm × 8400 mm (27 ft × 27 ft) have been cited as the optimum sizes for grid squares in large libraries (for reasons given in chapter 8). Obviously the larger the clear space between columns the better for the library's purposes but there is a great deal more to the matter than this. The grid square can seldom be used continuously throughout any library building: some features, for example entrance halls and often lecture rooms, may need special arrangements whereby the columns bound larger areas. If column thicknesses are to vary on different floors, the grid square available to the librarian will also vary. A clearer concept is that of modules and zones within which the columns and internal partitions may be accommodated.

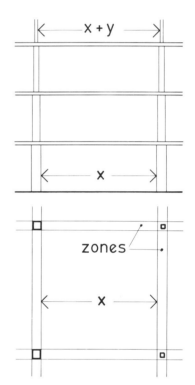

Zones for columns and partitions

Summary

These are but a few of the many questions inevitably affecting a judgment which is basically an aesthetic one tempered with practical considerations. Certainly the greatest influences on the architect's judgment will be his training, professional expertise, experience and, above all, the personal factors which make this an extremely difficult subject to rationalise. Completely different solutions will occur to him, be given tentative shape and be discarded for others, although it is often true that an architect is working towards a concept that was in his mind almost from the beginning. What is certain is that no other member of the team has any part in this operation; the power of the authority in this matter was largely delegated when it chose this particular architect to design its library.

COST FEASIBILITY

Before he spends too much time developing his first sketches, the architect will need to know whether what he has in mind is possible within the overall cost allotted for the project. Even if no firm limit has been given he must still have a rough estimate of probable costs; limits of cost per square metre or square foot may be laid down (or strongly "recommended") by outside authorities (in the UK the University Grants Committee or the Department of Education and Science). In any case he will have to present cost feasibility proposals to his client authority and so will need to see the overall financial position before he proceeds to more detailed planning.

The quantity surveyor will have been working throughout as part of the team, as will the engineering consultants, structural and service. Every proposal will have economic implications, every decision its cost consequences and these must be constantly kept under review if the budget is to be met. Even minor matters need to be assessed for their cost effect: the architect's wishes in the matter of finishes (floor and wall coverings, door furniture and so on) may not be detailed until a much later stage but the quantity surveyor will need to have a general picture of the quality standards of such items if he is to assess their probable contribution to the final costs.

It used to be normal for fixed price tenders to be invited at the appropriate stage but in periods of inflation contractors cannot be expected to gamble on prices remaining stable. In these circumstances they are likely to load their quotation to allow for price increases whether they occur or not. It may be wiser to agree to allow for payment of estimated increases in cost above the prices obtaining at the moment when tenders will be expected. The quantity surveyor will be equipped to verify these increases, which occur on wages and materials, so that the client can allow for these actual cost rises without having to face the price of a contractor's gamble. (See chapter 19.)

Despite the care with which the consultants and the quantity surveyor have prepared detailed cost figures, the architect will not accept them and submit them in a cost report without further consideration. He will go over them most carefully to decide whether any section is incurring costs disproportionate to its importance in the whole concept. Carelessness now may mean future cuts to meet a budget and if made later these cuts can usually be effected only by diluting reader services or using cheaper finishes. Such adjustments involve not only loss of amenities; the consequent delay and extra work can, by producing extra costs, increase the inefficiency of the operation.

FEASIBILITY REPORT

The report now submitted by the architect to the authority is his own responsibility, although it will embody the technical expertise and advice of various specialists. With the appropriate sketches and a summary of costs, it will be considered by the authority who may accept or reject it, or accept it with certain stipulated modifications. If the architect is willing to accept these modifications he will proceed to the next planning stage, or he will be reappointed for that purpose. In the latter case the other specialists will also have to be reappointed. At the same time the authority's general contract policy should be declared: whether the architect is now appointed to complete the operation, whether the building work is to be carried out by competitive tendering or by a modified form of tendering, or whether the authority intends to have any of the work carried out by its own Works Department.

Timetable

Included in the feasibility report was the architect's assessment of the time to be taken by each element of the project, and an overall time for its completion. He will make it clear that this is only an estimate, not a promise, because so many factors will be beyond his control. It might prevent possible confusion if a distinction is here made between a programme and a timetable: a programme consists of a record of related activities, and its essential is that these activities shall be carried out in a logical order. A timetable

on the other hand is simply a list of events set out against a list of dates; it may be shown in the form of a bar chart, or series of such charts, but it relates only to time, whereas a programme has also to show the activities and resources needed to conform to the dates in the timetable.

This timetable will be accepted by the authority, or the architect may be asked whether it can be amended in any way. Sometimes it is possible to shorten the period (the only amendment an authority is interested in) but this will be at a price. The extra cost will be caused by the allocation of extra staff and overtime working by the eventual building contractor. Probably the most important way to control cost is for the authority to give the architect enough time and information to complete his contract drawings and bills of quantity in great detail, but thereafter to resist all change, for change is always very expensive.

The position today on building delays has become critical. While there is always pressure by the client to complete the building in the shortest possible time, this often results in the preparation of information being rushed and inadequate. This is always bad policy because a contractor, working as he does in the competitive climate imposed by the need for tendering, will pick on any inadequacies in the information provided and may claim, with justification, that he was delayed by not knowing clearly what he was expected to build. Under the terms of the building contract he may claim extensions of time for uncertainties which cause delay and in such a case is entitled to be compensated for any resulting loss.

Another result of over-hasty preparation of contract information is that the architect will tend to leave certain matters to be sorted out later by including estimated provisional items and prime cost sums in the bills of quantity. There is a perfectly legitimate reason for doing this where work has to be undertaken by specialist or nominated subcontractors who will have special skills in technical fields. The architect may not wish such specialists to be appointed before the general contractor has been chosen, since the contractor may have worked with particular firms which he would like to use again, or may have objections to other firms proposed. The danger of leaving too many specialist jobs to be allocated later is that it creates problems of organisation, programming and control which may give the contractor legitimate cause for claiming extensions of contract if any of the specialists default. Such claims can be substantial and make complete nonsense of budget control.

Thus thorough preparation by the architect of all information before tender stage will make for a smoother run and, in the end, a cheaper contract. If he has enough time, items which in a rushed job would be the subject of later decisions, can be detailed and the responsibility for them placed squarely on the general contractor. The contractor can be far more effective when dealing with firms working directly for him than with firms nominated by, and accountable to, the architect. The elimination of all nominated subcontracts, with the whole burden of organising the contract falling direct on the general contractor, is the ideal but it is seldom achieved.

The timetable then is associated with the cost estimate and the architect will be prepared to give an alternative estimate for a different period, if necessary.

REFERENCES

[1] RIBA Handbook. Op cit. part 3.210 The process of design
[2] THOMPSON, ANTHONY Library buildings of Britain and Europe. Butterworth, London, 1963, pp 13–15
[3] Metropolitan Toronto Library Board. Op cit, pp 32–33
[4] Metcalf. Op cit, pp 42–43
[5] Ibid, pp 176–177
[6] Thompson. Op cit, p 38
[7] In Library Journal. 1 May 1971, p 1582

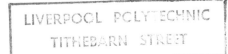

6 Secondary brief

When the feasibility report has been accepted and the draft timetable agreed, the architect will need more detailed information before he can proceed to the next planning stage. If team consultation has been continuous throughout there should be no doubtful points in the brief to be elucidated but there will certainly be need for amplification of detail. In addition, because the spatial relationship between the various sections has now been tentatively established, the architect is ready to consider in more detail the layout of each operational section, including the identification in general terms of the furniture and equipment.

To enable him to obtain this information he may draw up a questionnaire for the librarian to complete. This both pinpoints the matters on which he needs to know more and provides a document for the team to discuss. Metcalf[1] gives examples. A questionnaire alone is not enough. Because the librarian by now has studied first sketches (produced as part of the feasibility report), he has been able to visualise the new library and so to amplify and possibly amend the requirements in the brief.

The architect already knows the contribution each operational section is to make and the degree of priority in proximity between them. He now needs to know:

the pattern of operations to take place within each section,

the communications to be established between them,

further requirements which were not detailed in the primary brief,

the librarian's preferences, in general terms, in regard to materials and equipment.

To produce this information the librarian will prepare a secondary brief.

Many successful libraries have been created without the librarian being involved in such matters: many architects believe that they themselves, by observations and by experience, are the best judges, but it is the theme of this book that the best results are obtained by pooling the experience and expertise of all the professionals involved, and by free discussion within the team. The architect will certainly disagree with some of the librarian's suggestions, but it is most important that he should have them before him.

PATTERN OF OPERATIONS

An internal traffic diagram for each of the sections which formed the space relationship table (page 32) will be needed. There will be two different aspects, book services and reader services.

Book services

An example of the progress of a book from its arrival in the library, through the various essential processes to its destination on a shelf, is shown in a flow diagram, with an indication of the concomitant operations which it generates. Each of the sections involved is a workshop which the architect will have to plan, and to do so he must know, in some detail, what operations take place, in what order, and what special conditions are involved. Once again the librarian should not attempt to place these operations in any particular position, but show their relationships and priorities in proximity so that the architect can plan an economical and acceptable layout. The second diagram on p. 59 shows an example for a library bindery.

It will not be necessary to tell the architect that typists require decent working conditions or that the layout of a bindery must conform with Factory Act regulations; this is his business. The librarian's concern is to show how he wishes each section to operate. This will enable the architect to check his space allocation for each section and to design a layout. It will also guide him as to the exact needs for such elements as lighting, heating, windows and position of doors.

Book services are easy to plan because they involve quantities of materials which can be estimated and operating conditions which can be controlled.

Reader services

Reader services vary according to the infinite and unknowable trends of individual readers' demands, as well as the gradually changing pattern of library use. Some patterns are predictable; for example in the case of a new public branch library it may be possible to foresee the general character of use, in numbers of readers at times of the day and their traffic routes. In a small research or school library use may be predictable with even more certainty. Even in a new and complex library however, certain assumptions can be made: although there is no "average reader", the actions of certain large groups are predictable. The casual reader, the undergraduate, the research worker, have elements in common in their use patterns, although one person may himself at times form part of another group. It is most valuable now for the librarian to observe closely, and even to put himself in the position of a member of, each of these groups in turn and to try to visualise what he will do when he enters the library. The picture of the service which emerges may be very different from the librarian's usual view.

Not all readers find libraries inviting places; many combine inability to understand a catalogue with a built-in reluctance to ask the staff for help; how can such a reader be induced to help himself or to allow the staff to help him? The positioning of catalogues and readers advisers' desks alone is not the complete answer but careful consideration of the layout can be a first step towards solving the problem.

By drawing upon his experience the librarian can plan a compromise based upon reader needs, economy of staffing and estimated traffic patterns. The result, a notional placing of the operational activities and readers' movements within each section, can take the form of a traffic diagram. It will be the architect's task to translate this into spatial terms and to prepare a layout which includes the positioning of furniture and equipment.

In lending libraries the traffic pattern will be simplified in that most readers will go first to the book-return counter and then split up into various routes, going to the book-issue counter before leaving. Sections which use basically different materials within the same area (as in the diagram for a music and gramophone record library, facing) will present more complicated patterns, but any analysis of them by the librarian will enable the architect to make the fullest use of his colleague's professional experience.

In addition to providing such a diagram for each operational section the librarian may be able to clarify his original estimate of reader use. Now that he can see each section in its position, and as it relates to other sections and to access routes, he may be able to say that at a given peak hour, 200 readers will enter the section, that 100 will go direct to the study area and remain there for at least one hour, that fifty will go direct to the quick-reference area and then leave, that thirty will go direct to the quick-reference area and then to the study area, that twenty will go direct to the catalogue and so on. Such prognostications are very difficult to produce and may turn out to be wildly inaccurate in practice, but the librarian's experience is the only possible source for such an assessment and without it the architect will be less well equipped to proceed with his work.

COMMUNICATIONS

The ways in which readers and materials will move through the building were shown in the space relationship diagram, the materials flow chart and the traffic diagrams. From these the

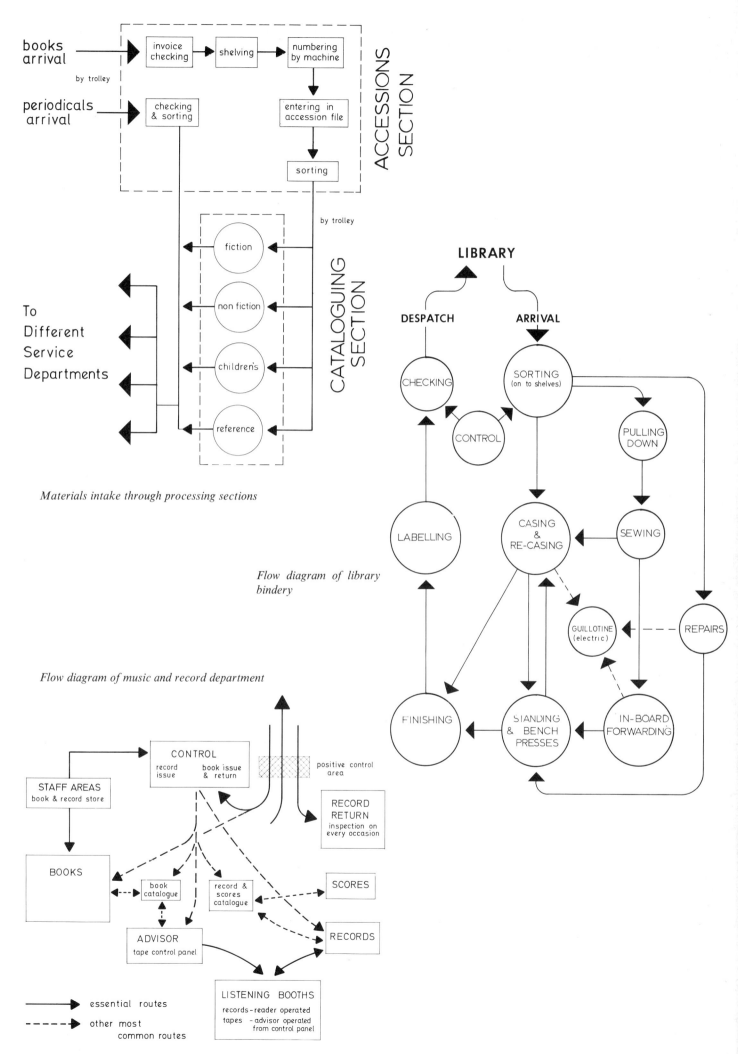

books arrival *by trolley*

periodicals arrival

invoice checking → shelving → numbering by machine → entering in accession file → sorting

checking & sorting

ACCESSIONS SECTION

by trolley

fiction

non fiction

children's

reference

CATALOGUING SECTION

To Different Service Departments

Materials intake through processing sections

LIBRARY

DESPATCH   **ARRIVAL**

CHECKING

SORTING (on to shelves)

CONTROL

PULLING DOWN

LABELLING

CASING & RE-CASING

SEWING

Flow diagram of library bindery

GUILLOTINE (electric)

REPAIRS

FINISHING

STANDING & BENCH PRESSES

IN-BOARD FORWARDING

Flow diagram of music and record department

CONTROL
record issue   book issue & return

positive control area

STAFF AREAS
book & record store

RECORD RETURN
inspection on every occasion

BOOKS

book catalogue

record & scores catalogue

SCORES

ADVISOR
tape control panel

RECORDS

LISTENING BOOTHS
records-reader operated
tapes - advisor operated from control panel

→ essential routes

⇢ other most common routes

59

architect will devise the necessary channels and machinery. It is now necessary for the librarian to show what telephonic and other methods of communication will be needed between staff operational sections.

Communications list for a large college library complex

Key: **A** Outside (GPO) line
    B Internal telephone
    C Closed circuit TV link
    D Telex link
    E Document facsimile transmission link

	A	B	C	D	E
Book return counter	1	1	–	–	–
Readers' adviser's desk	1	1	–	1	1
Periodical control desk	–	1	–	1	1
Map room	–	1	–	–	–
Special collections room	–	1	–	–	–
Stack control centre	–	1	1	1	1
Photographic section	–	1	–	1	1
Xerox section	–	1	–	1	1
Telex centre	–	1	–	1	1
Bindery	1	1	–	–	1
Closed-circuit television	1	1	–	1	–
Audio-visual room	1	1	–	1	–
Seminar room	1	1	–	1	–
Chief librarian's office	1	1	–	–	–
Deputy librarian's office	1	1	–	–	–
Administration office	1	2	–	–	–
Secretary's office	1	1	–	–	–
Cataloguing department	1	3	–	–	–
Accessions department	1	1	–	–	–
Delivery and dispatch office	1	1	–	–	–
Unpacking room	–	1	–	1	–
Staff restroom	–	1	–	–	–
Building supervisor	1	1	–	–	–

The list above is for a large college library. Few libraries will need such an elaborate network, but if the great increase in use and complexity of libraries continues this could be the pattern for many libraries in the near future. It is possible to give this information in the form of a diagram, but the list is entirely adequate and less liable to cause confusion.

LIBRARIAN'S PREFERENCES

The librarian should record his preferences for some of the materials and fittings. On many points he can have no views because they are not within his professional competence but in others his recorded preferences can be of value to the architect because either they arise from experience of use in libraries, or they will draw the architect's attention to possible problems.

Furniture and fittings
The critical sizes and layout of these items are dealt with in chapter 8, the materials and choice available in chapter 12. To the question, "Who is to choose the furniture?" the answer is that in planning the new library's environment the architect visualises the design, material and colour of the furniture, so to treat these as though they are an entirely independent matter is to destroy the unit of design. On the other hand, the librarian will be dependent upon the functional efficiency of the furniture and fittings for the successful operation of the library and he must agree every item proposed. In some contracts the freestanding furniture and equipment will be designated as "prime cost" items. This means that the architect is required to provide an estimated sum for them but not to provide them unless specifically instructed. In these circumstances, discussion and co-operation can still take place but its chief value lies in cases where all such items can be supplied under a particularly advantageous contract by a client nominee.
The level of comfort and convenience in library accommodation

has been rising steadily, and present-day readers expect much higher standards than were provided in the quite recent past. The architect knows this; there is no need to spell it out in the brief. Similarly, because the architect is responsible for the allocation of costs within the agreed total sum, he must decide what standard of fittings his proposals can support. He may wish, for example, to make savings by using a single manufacturer's range of supplies because of contract cost advantages. In all such cases it is essential that the librarian examine the specification for, and actual examples of, every piece of furniture or fitting it is proposed to purchase, so that he can check its suitability for its future function.

Lighting
Published lighting standards (see chapter 15) will be studied by the architect (who may also have the advice of a lighting consultant), but satisfactory lighting conditions are very largely a matter of personal preference. As it is impossible to ascertain the preferences of the future users, the views of an experienced librarian can be of great value. Intensity is not the only factor: colour, absence of glare, balance of natural and artificial light, types of artificial lighting and their fittings will all be involved.

Heating and humidity levels
These are the subject of recommended standards but are still matters on which the librarian should record his views. The methods of obtaining suitable conditions are not his world, but the effects of the various methods upon library efficiency certainly are. (See chapter 17.)

Materials and finishes
When considering these for floors, walls and ceilings the librarian will have in mind not necessarily the materials themselves, but the effect of library operations upon them: heavy trolleys may push up carpets, heavy traffic wear away flooring, children's hands can mark emulsion painted walls, footsteps can echo in quiet rooms— these are matters within his personal experience and in his comments he will pinpoint problems for the architect to solve. (See chapter 18.)

Shelving
What material does the librarian prefer, and why? It is worth asking this question, and in particular the second half of it, so that the priorities can be identified. What degree of adjustability is required? Is it the same in all areas? What is to be the height, depth, number of shelves, distance from the floor of the shelving? How many size sequences are there to be in each area? Does the librarian prefer canopied or topless shelving, and why?
In other matters the librarian will have little part to play. Enclosing elements of the building for example, are fundamental to the architect's conception of the whole: he will take into account their effect upon the appearance, cost and physical conditions. Such advice as he needs will come from the specialist consultants.

CLIENT NOMINEES

The architect is well acquainted with the materials and services offered by the supplier in many fields and any comment by the librarian will usually be superfluous. There are exceptions, however, when the librarian (with his authority's approval) feels so strongly that some firm's special equipment or materials are so exceptionally suitable for the project, that he will require its use in the library as a "client's nominee". The reason for this stipulation may be the wish to achieve uniformity within an institution or to take advantage of a highly economic supply contract which exists within the organisation.

The most extreme form of this nomination happens when a "systems building" technique is to be used. When materials and labour were scarce, immediately after the Second World War, co-operative ventures were developed by local education authori-

Complete package Library by Terrapin Reska Ltd

ties who began to plan primary schools with "kit" components. From these beginnings emerged CLASP (Consortium of Local Authorities, Special Programme) and, after its initial great success, other similar bodies. At first they concentrated on freestanding primary schools for which the components were virtually prefabricated, producing very considerable savings in both design work and construction on the site. There are now seven such consortia working in wider fields of education and in local government generally, especially in housing. No longer confined to producing simple buildings but obtaining advantages by the standardisation and coding of products, such schemes may attract authorities which are already using them in their education or housing interests. If a large local authority plans to build a dozen libraries to serve village communities there are obvious advantages in such standardisation of parts and the architect may be told to incorporate such materials and units in his work.

There is some resemblance between these schemes and the "complete library service" offered by certain library supply firms. These are based on a series of structural units, similar to those used to produce classrooms or offices, which can be assembled to produce a surprisingly wide variety of enclosures.

One such system available in Britain (Terrapin-Reska) is based on a module of 1·200 m (3 ft $11\frac{1}{4}$ in); a section, supported on timber columns, is of 20 m² (210 ft²). Another uses a plan module of 1·800 m (5 ft $10\frac{7}{8}$ in) with a vertical module of 400 mm (1 ft $3\frac{3}{4}$ in) from finished floor level. Spans in multiples of the module can give areas of almost any length without internal columns, provided that they are planned in a given series of patterns. If unusual shapes are required, internal columns will be necessary for support. The plan must of course be based upon squares or oblongs and this does limit the architect in his design.

The buildings are specifically planned for the economical layout of the firm's standard shelf ranges; the walls and panels are either of timber, plywood or chipboard, and a wide range of joinery is available for doors and windows. They are designed to be erected upon foundations or on a cement raft; underground services prepared within the site can be linked up. These buildings comply of course with British Building Regulations and are in every way viable as library structures. The suppliers have vast experience of this work and offer a wide range of furniture and fittings appropriate to the building design.

The great advantages of such a system are not only its cheapness and speed of erection but the economy offered in the design process, so often a bottleneck in architects' offices. It can be a most useful expedient where a service has to be provided on a certain site but where financial support for a full-sized permanent building is not forthcoming. If such a scheme is chosen it might be argued that there is no need for a separate architect. This would be highly dangerous; an architect is a professional whose services are entirely at his client's disposal to safeguard his interests. No commercial undertaking can do this impartially: by definition

they are partial because they have something to sell. It is also a complete misconception to imagine that a client is saving architect's fees in such a case; the fees are hidden in the total costs. Similarly a repeated design will always be cheaper, if sometimes less effective, than one conceived for a special purpose.

Services less comprehensive than these are offered by library supply firms who make furniture and shelving based on unit factory-made components. These can incorporate a very wide range of designs, although the basic materials and size standards will be the same. The advantage of price in such conditions is undeniable. Some of the firms also offer advice both in layout and design of furniture and shelving, as part of a package deal—"free" if the equipment is purchased; because of their wide experience over many years and in many countries this advice can be highly advantageous.

This is a difficult matter: the architect, when conceiving a design, will include the furnishings in it. To force him to use alien materials may upset his whole conception. On the other hand, the financial advantages of mass-production of this kind are undeniable and if the architect knows from the brief that such equipment is a client nomination, then he can plan accordingly from his earliest designs. The expertise available in such specialist firms also helps to avoid the pitfalls inherent in using firms without this experience. Even if no client nominees as such have been stipulated, the architect will allow in his estimates certain prime cost sums for specialist materials and services which he does not consider to be within the competence of the contractor himself to provide. These are chiefly proprietary products such as metal windows, lifts and hoists. With all specialist work, for example, hardwood flooring, it is as well for the contractor to be asked whether he wishes to tender for it; this he can do through a specialist firm whom he himself will appoint. As a general principle the more control the contractor has over specialists the better; subcontractors imposed by the architect are always a potential cause of friction, whereas if the builder himself appoints a specialist, he has more direct control over performance and can apply pressure without reference to the architect.

FURTHER INFORMATION

The architect himself may ask for the following facts in a questionnaire but it will save time if the librarian takes steps to supply the information as part of the secondary brief!

What sort of vehicles make deliveries, how often and at what times? Should unloading take place under cover, or are the loads so small that this requirement is unimportant? What tables, benches, racks and so on will be required for packing and unpacking? How much packing material will need to be stored nearby?

What machines are to be used in each staff work area? How many typewriters, duplicators, photocopiers and other machines, particularly those which call for power supply points?

What are the details of the equipment mentioned in the primary brief as reader service aids, such as microform readers, and photocopiers? Will there be ancillary items, eg if the photocopiers are coin-operated, is a coinchanging machine needed? Space requirements and power supply are particularly important.

Will cleaning be by contract or will the library have its own cleaners? Are there strict limits upon times when cleaning may be done? What are the preferences for materials and methods (such as vacuum dusting of shelves)? Are any unusual provisions needed for storage of cleaning materials? In which areas will cleaners' sinks be wanted?

How much waste accumulates weekly and how is disposal to take place? Does the local authority supply special bags for its disposal? (The architect can certainly find this out for himself, but it is the librarian's business.)

Where is postal delivery to be made? Entirely through a postal slot or by bag delivery? If there is to be a book-return slot for use by the public, are the books to remain in a box behind the slot, and if so, how many is it to hold?

Has the librarian a preference for lobby, porch, canopy or "dripping area"? Should absorbent mats be provided or will "barrier mats" be supplied on a contract basis? Where are cigarettes to be extinguished and discarded, and umbrellas left?

What sort of cycle stands will be needed? Dog rails? For how many dogs? What security must there be for a pram park?

What of signposting? Will a crest be used? Is the main sign to be large or small, lit or unlit, eye-catching or discreet? In how many places will there be notices to give times of opening of the various services?

Are there to be internal and external displays? How big will they be, and how much security will they call for? Lockable glass cases or just notice boards? Baize, peg-board, or pin-board?

Will there be shelf, tier or case guiding, or all three? What is the preferred method and material? How often are guides likely to be altered or moved? Must the guiding be protected against vandalism?

Will book supports be needed everywhere, or in some areas? What style is preferred?

Where are trolleys to be parked in off-peak times? Are they to be used as relief shelving; has the "hod" method been considered? (See chapter 14.)

Are floral displays, changed regularly under contract, desirable or acceptable financially?

Such a list can never be considered complete but to attempt one is to stimulate the mind into turning out problems which can be studied before the plans have crystallised, and for which the best solutions may be too expensive if left until later stages. It may seem that some of these matters are mere details which could be left until the programme is further on but it is only by completing the picture in his mind that the architect is able to try out solutions and to compare them with others which he has seen or studied. Above all he will be concerned with space allocations and critical dimensions and he can appreciate these only if he can assess all the many elements which can influence his decision. A strong recommendation from the librarian for carpeting throughout the library will influence the architect's approach to acoustic treatment as well as the overall balance of costs. The need for cleaners' sinks in certain rooms will affect his ideas for placing water supply, and therefore, perhaps his ideas on service scores generally. This is the time when the architect tries out different solutions, but without full information he cannot hope to make a satisfactory choice.

VISITS AND READING

With the foregoing information from the librarian, the architect will use visits, reading, observation, user survey studies and any other relevant methods to amplify what he already knows and to throw more light on the problem. Meanwhile the specialist consultants will be carrying out studies relevant to this stage of their own work. For example the mechanical engineers will consider possible types of installations and prepare estimated capital and running costs for each likely alternative, while the structural engineer will make similar studies into alternative structural systems, and so on throughout the whole group. Each member will advise the architect on the design implications of his various alternatives and keep the quantity surveyor informed of all financial implications.

The architect will of course bring to all meetings his own appreciation of modern development in design and materials. It is at this stage in the planning that the team will toss around and discard ideas in profusion. It is far, far better to "waste" a little time at this stage than to complete a library only to find that a new method or a new material would have drastically improved the result.

Visits

Visits to new libraries may seem to many to be light relief. In fact they are an exhausting and necessary duty: wherever possible they should be carried out by the architect and the librarian together. This principle, which lies behind all the activities of the Architect–Librarian Working Party of the Library Association, has proved conclusively that the contrast provided by the separate angle of approach of the two professionals gives an entirely new dimension to the vision of each. For tactical reasons it may be advantageous to take on the visit the leader of the authority's governing body; perhaps this particular occasion should be a return visit to the building which appeared to offer the most acceptable parallels.

Perhaps the most valuable exercise of all is to ask the librarian of a newly completed library what he would have done had he been starting again with hindsight; the result can be most illuminating. It is a mistake to visit only renowned or "successful" libraries: the reasons for the comparative failure of others will prove of great value. In others it may be found that popular votes of success or failure may have been too hastily expressed.

Even when time is short there can be no better investment than a painstaking visit to a recently completed library. Nor need visits be confined to libraries of a character similar to the one being planned. Views on the suitability of materials, costs of maintenance, new technical developments, ideas for traffic flow or staff economy can be acquired from libraries of all kinds.

Reading

There is a great deal of published information on newly completed libraries and the following list is far from comprehensive:

Library buildings A publication of the Library Association: for the years 1961–64 it was published annually in the *Library Association Record* but from 1965 it has been a separate publication. From 1961 to 1969 it was devoted to a survey of selected public library buildings erected in the previous year: from 1971 however, it has been covering a selection of new library buildings of all types. It gives information systematically, with tables, plans and photographs. However, it is selective, showing only libraries which the editors feel to be significant.

The Library Journal The December issue is largely devoted to new American library buildings of the year.

Articles in the library professional press These can be found in the publications of many countries but they all suffer from the disadvantage of brevity, and because they are usually submitted by the librarians of the buildings concerned they are uncritical.

Articles in the architectural press—in this country chiefly *The Architects' Journal* and *The Architectural Review*. Because these are written from the architect's point of view they complement those written from the librarian's angle. Articles of this kind concerning British libraries are listed in the bibliography.

The Library Association's files of plans, photographs, slides and facts concerning recently completed libraries may help to show which libraries are worth a visit.

Reference
[1] Metcalf. Op. cit appendix A

7 Outline planning

The architect's original planning conceptions may now need reconsidering in the light of new or altered requirements from the secondary brief and from the information gained in studies and visits. This is also the point where he has another long hard look at his sketches to see whether he has really made allowance for all the important factors. Is the shape truly functional? Are there as few changes of level as possible? Have the elements restricting flexibility of function been reduced to a minimum?

He will also incorporate the results of his dialogue with the various specialist consultants. Has full account been taken of the need to suppress noise? Are all those windows necessary for lighting, or, if they are purely for aesthetic effect, is not the price to be paid for them too high? Is it not worthwhile to install full air-conditioning and if so, where could the heavy plant be located? Should maintenance staff be residential to ensure supervision of the highly sophisticated machinery recommended, even at the extra cost and space loss caused by including a caretaker's flat?

These are but a few of many matters: in particular the architect will want to be sure that he is using the space to the best advantage and that the proportion of the space which may be used for the library's operation is as high as possible.

AUXILIARY AREAS

Reference was made earlier to a division between functional and auxiliary areas, and the various subsections of the functional areas were examined. The architect will now need to subdivide the auxiliary areas in order to check the suitability of his proposed allocation. The auxiliary areas can be divided into service areas and environmental areas.

Service areas

Main services: heating chambers, ventilating and air-conditioning plant, electricity substations, distribution and meter rooms, water tank areas, service equipment stores, cleaners' rooms and distribution ducts.

Sanitary.

Welfare: cloakrooms, restrooms, canteens, staffrooms, bicycle stores, garages.

The size and placing of these elements needs study; the diagrams opposite show allocations in the four university libraries.

Environmental areas

These are less easily defined because they arise from the architect's vision of the library as an attractive contribution to community life. They may include open spaces where sculpture can be displayed, areas with walls for paintings and displays generally, permanent art features (sculpture, murals, etc), gardens, internal courts for fountains or other pleasant features; to these must be added open spaces needed for purely architectural reasons.

The librarian will obviously be interested in seeing that as high a proportion of the building as possible is available for his operational use and would be happy to be able to consult "standard" figures to check that the architect is achieving this. There is however a limit to the value of systematising and comparing space ratios between libraries of a similar type, and here the limit has been reached. The architect decides on the environmental factors inherent in his design; he needs to bear in mind the proportions which have been notionally allocated by his plans, but beyond that point he will use his own judgment.

The ratio of both auxiliary and circulation areas to the whole will tend to fall as the size of the library increases, therefore, a large library must be more functionally efficient than a small one.

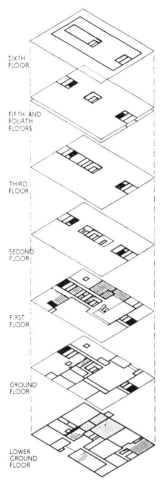

Auxiliary areas, Edinburgh

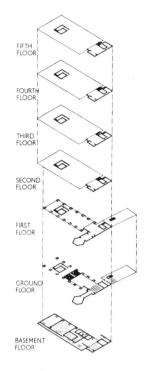

Auxiliary areas, Essex

Black = sanitary areas
Tint = services
Hatching = welfare areas

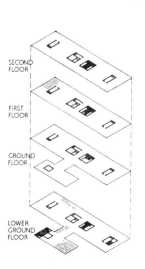

Auxiliary areas, Lancaster

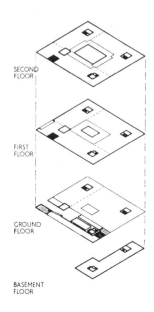

Auxiliary areas, Warwick

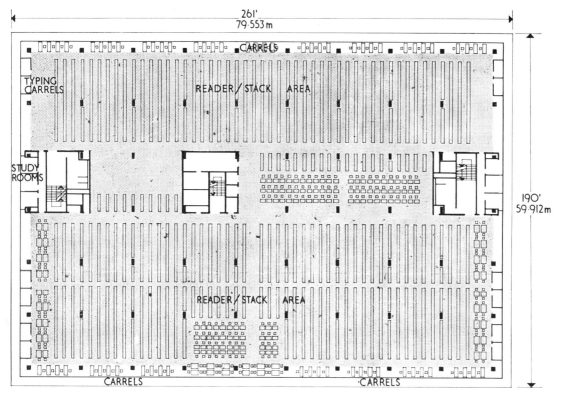

Edinburgh: potentially interchangeable area (shaded) on a typical stack floor. (1:576)

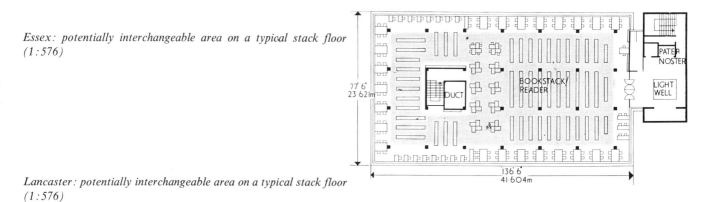

Essex: potentially interchangeable area on a typical stack floor (1:576)

Lancaster: potentially interchangeable area on a typical stack floor (1:576)

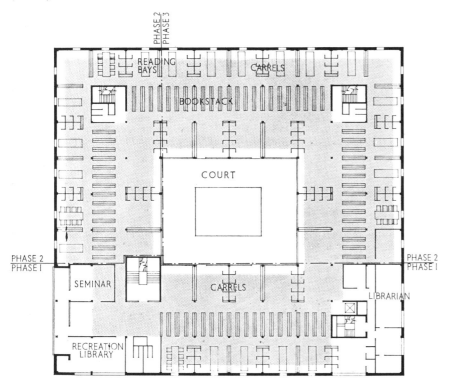

FLEXIBILITY AND ADAPTABILITY

The architect is likely to find the librarian's requirements in this field particularly irksome and perhaps entirely impracticable within fixed cost limits. Flexibility will be much easier to provide in a single-storey than in a multi-storey building because mechanical and sanitary services can usually be grouped together in a corner and, if a single roof span is possible, there need be no fixed structural elements to prevent a complete open-plan layout. With an even lighting plan, the same flooring materials everywhere and the use of demountable partitions there need be little difficulty in providing a thoroughly flexible layout. The open-floor single-room plan, divided only by bookshelves, has been widely used in lending libraries of all kinds.

In university libraries where the number of books required to be easily accessible is generally higher and the intensity of use per volume may be lower, the problem has a different emphasis.

Open-plan designs, besides offering infinite flexibility, give unity to the library and lead readers to books on all subjects. They produce a feeling of space and of colour (because books in publishers' jackets are themselves particularly colourful). Browsing areas can be notionally limited by bookcases lower than eye-height and by changes of furniture design; more definite breaks can be marked by tall bookstacks (which must of course be solid backed). Bookstacks like this but single-sided with panels on the reverse have been used effectively to produce a division between a reading area and a main library corridor. The chief difficulty in the open plan arises when attempts are made to accommodate both quiet (reference and study) and noisy (popular lending and children's sections) within the same open-plan area. Although this will be almost inevitable in smaller self-contained libraries, great difficulty will be found in preventing aural and visual distraction. There are no real solutions but noise problems may be partly alleviated by the generous use of noise-deadening material and even by installing low level hum to absorb peak sound frequencies. To prevent visual distraction it is sometimes possible to arrange to have higher bookcases as divisions and face all serious study seats away from reader movement. Use of semi-carrel fitments, or placing seats to face windows or book-lined walls is no disadvantage if sufficient space can be left around each reader to prevent the feeling of being penned in.

In multi-storey buildings, however, the position is very different; the structural requirements and the need for stairs and lifts will inevitably entail certain fixed elements and it is therefore much difficult to allow for full flexibility.

Large central libraries will have areas, and possibly whole floors, devoted to open access conditions but also areas or floors for closed stacks. University libraries will have large areas of open stack and various smaller areas of open access. By placing closed stacks at typical open stack distances (1400 m, 4 ft 6 in) they can later be opened to the public without alteration. Open stacks can be closed merely by fitting barriers or hinged gates. The only cost caused by this interchangeability is that the closed stacks cannot be arranged as economically as they would be with narrower aisles. To interchange either of these stacking methods with open access, however, means that the floor loading must be based on the highest single requirement and this may cause extra structural costs. If this is accepted and the grid and column sizes are carefully planned at the outset, it will be possible for stacks and bookcases to be resited when required without waste of space. The effects of this flexibility on lighting and floor finishes will be considered in later chapters.

Examples from the plans of the four university libraries show the potentially interchangeable areas on a typical floor in each case. The tables show the indices of adaptability and the limitations on flexibility created by the permanent structure.

Adaptability: permanent structural limitation

Structural data	Edinburgh	Essex	Lancaster	Warwick
Uniformly distributed load (lb/sq ft)	224	120	150	150
Grid dimensions	8·2 × 8·2 m (27 ft × 27 ft)	6 m × 6 m (19 ft 8 in × 19 ft 8 in) cantilever	5·5 × 5·5 m (18 ft × 18 ft)	7·6 × 7·6 m (25 ft × 25 ft)
Comment	Complete freedom of bookstack layout in either direction. Bookstacks could be laid at the following centres: 1170 mm (3 ft 10 in) 1375 mm (4 ft 6 in) 1650 mm (5 ft 5 in) 2060 mm (6 ft 9 in) Floor loading allows for Compactus shelving throughout; also for bookstacks at normal centres	Complete freedom of bookstack layout in either direction. Bookstacks could be laid at the following centres: 1195 mm (3 ft 11 in) 1500 mm (4 ft 11 in) 1985 mm (6 ft 6½ in)	Complete freedom of bookstack layout in either direction. Bookstacks could be laid at the following centres: 1100 mm (3 ft 7½ in) 1375 mm (4 ft 6 in) 1830 mm (6 ft) Floor loading allows for all normal bookstack bookstack centres	Complete freedom of bookstack layout in either direction. Bookstacks could be laid at the following centres: 1270 mm (4 ft 2 in) 1525 mm (5 ft) 1905 mm (6 ft 3 in) Floor loading allows for normal stack centres
Indices of adaptability	75	60	69	66

Note These indices are derived as the percentage of total floor area upon which either readers or bookstacks could be accommodated efficiently without major alterations.

Warwick: potentially interchangeable area on a typical stack floor (1:576)

In the new Birmingham Central Library the reference floors have a large central void, the closed stack forming one L shape, the other L holding the combined open access and reading area (see plan page 75). This offers unique advantages: the closed stack contents can relate to each subject area located conveniently at hand and there is good flexibility, although a partition wall would have to be removed to change the closed stack area to public use. The method depends on having a high level of loading throughout and is assisted by the use of a large 11 m (36 ft) grid square and a consequent absence of the usual forest of columns.

POSITION OF OPERATIONAL AREAS

The positioning of areas for the various reader services and the layout within each area are matters on which the architect will spend many hours and it is only to be expected that several drafts will be considered before a detailed proposal is put forward. Even after his insistence on the ubiquitous "flexibility" the librarian will have very strong feelings on this vitally important point. The examples below are again based on the four university libraries and show how very different have been the solutions which the librarian and architect together have achieved for this most complicated question.

Edinburgh

Type of university: ancient, established, urban
Type of library: to house the arts, science and social science collections
Location: urban site, city square
Date of occupancy: summer 1967
Architect: Sir Basil Spence, Glover & Ferguson
The building is on seven floors (lower ground to fifth) with entrance on ground floor. This floor contains control catalogue, current periodicals and technical services. First floor contains library administration and undergraduate reading-room; second floor another undergraduate reading-room, third to sixth are similar and contain stack and reader areas.
The library has full height glazing on all sides and each floor projects beyond the face of the window to form a continuous balcony. The structure is faced with precast units with a Portland stone finish.

Essex

Type of university: new (first students enrolled 1964)
Type of library: central collection
Location: rural site; the library is at the apex of the academic area
Date of occupation: summer 1967
Architect: Architects Co-Partnership
Stage 1 is in two wings: at the junction is the vertical circulation core. The main wing has a basement and six floors. The pedestrian entrance of the building is on the ground floor with cloakroom and bookshop. Library control, circulation desk, catalogue and technical services are on the first floor. The four upper floors, all similar, contain bookstack and reader accommodation. The other wing on three floors houses library staff and administrative accommodation.
Exposed precast concrete structure with sill to ceiling glazing.

Lancaster

Type of university: new (first student enrolled 1964)
Type of library: central collection
Location: rural site, on central spine of academic area
Date of occupation: phase 1 autumn 1966; phase 2 for summer 1968; phase 3 was scheduled for summer 1970.
Architect: Tom Mellor & Partners
On completion of phase 3 the building will be square on plan with a central courtyard. There are three floors and part basement. The entrance is on the ground floor which contains control, circulation desk, technical services and some reader space. First and second floors are devoted mainly to reader and bookstack areas.
The building is faced with brickwork.

Warwick

Type of university: new (first students enrolled 1965)
Type of library: central collection (with the exception of chemistry)
Location: rural site, centre of academic area
Date of occupancy: summer 1966
Architect: Yorke Rosenberg Mardall
This is a rectangular six-storey building. Reader entrance and control are on the first floor with a direct connection by bridge to buildings on the other side of the mall. The four floors above this are similar and contain stack and reader areas (fifth and sixth floors to be temporarily occupied by other users).
The ground floor comprises the library administration and readers' coffee bar.
The structure is faced with white glazed tiles and the infill panels are vitreous enamelled steel with large centre wing windows.

SPECIAL OPERATIONAL REQUIREMENTS

When making the initial allocation of areas for the different operational needs of a large library the architect will inevitably find that demands for groundfloor space will be far in excess of what is available. First there are those elements which *must* go on the ground floor—main entrance (except perhaps on a sloping site), goods loading, parking for mobile libraries: second, those which the librarian would *like* to have on the ground floor, such as issue and return counters and most-used departments. In the new Central Library at Newcastle upon Tyne the lending library is on the ground floor, but the central readers' advisory desk with all subject specialists in attendance, and the public catalogues (both reference and lending) are on the first floor. The city librarian has reported[1] that readers are reluctant to go up to the first floor for these services and then back to the lending books on the ground floor, so that it has become necessary to create another readers' advisory post on the ground floor. Both staff and readers have been asking for the lending library catalogue also to be brought down to this floor.

If a central bibliographical area, including public catalogues, is to be placed on the ground floor, then the housing of cataloguing staff can be come critical; as a backroom activity it might seem reasonable to place it on an upper floor where there is less demand for space, but this can necessitate either the creation of a staff catalogue separate from the public one, or alternatively (and usually in addition), frequent journeys by cataloguing staff to the public catalogues. Both expedients can be very expensive indeed and the librarian may insist that at least some provision be made on the ground floor for cataloguing and cognate staff processes. Similarly he may require that his own office, or that of a senior member of the staff, should be on the ground floor so that he can keep in close touch with the whole of the reader service. New books will go first to accessioning and other processing sections; again it may seem reasonable to house such backroom activities on an upper floor but this will inevitably cost time and energy in increased handling.

All these library service priorities have architectural implications which can be decided only by discussion. Sometimes the architect appears to take the external appearance of the building more seriously than he does the basic functional needs as when he leaves a ground floor as an open area (Hulme Branch, Manchester) or as a display area (Essex University), causing every user to make his way up by stairs or lifts to reach the library proper.

Subject departments

An alternative to the traditional division of public library buildings into lending and reference sections is the creation of subject

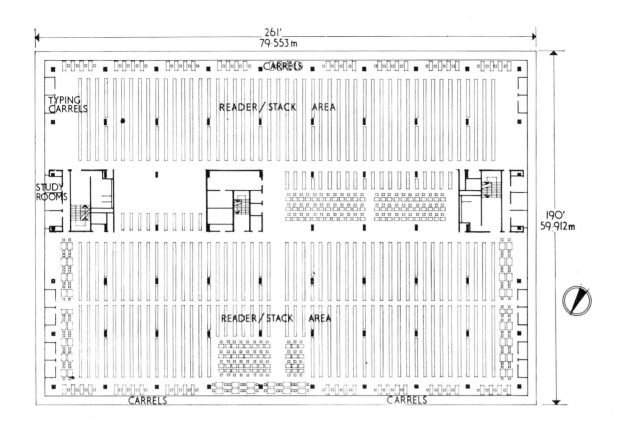

261'
79·553 m

190'
59·912 m

CARRELS

TYPING
CARRELS

READER/STACK AREA

STUDY
ROOMS

READER/STACK AREA

CARRELS

CARRELS

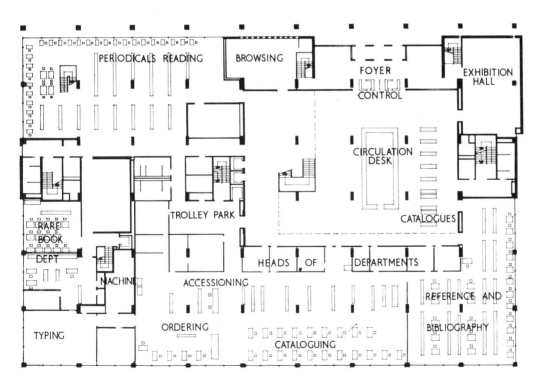

PERIODICALS READING

BROWSING

FOYER

EXHIBITION
HALL

CONTROL

CIRCULATION
DESK

TROLLEY PARK

CATALOGUES

RARE
BOOK
DEPT

HEADS OF DEPARTMENTS

MACHINE

ACCESSIONING

REFERENCE AND
BIBLIOGRAPHY

TYPING

ORDERING

CATALOGUING

Edinburgh: top, typical stack floor plan (1:576); centre, plan showing circulation desk, catalogue and administrative areas; bottom, section to same scale

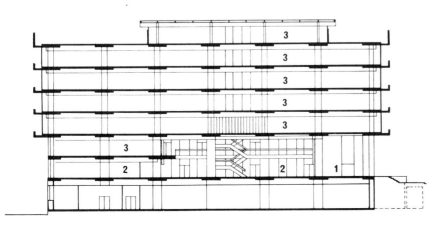

3
3
3
3
3
3
2
2
1

1 Entrance
2 Circulation desk, catalogue,
administration
3 Reader/stack area

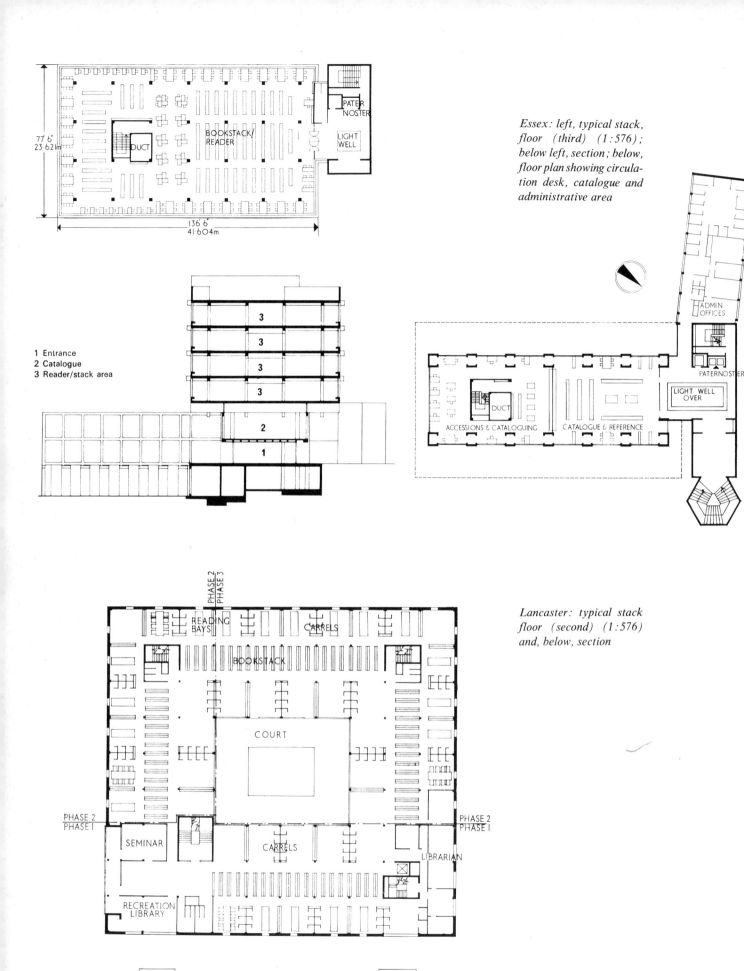

77'6"
23.621m

136'6"
41.604m

BOOKSTACK/READER

DUCT

PATER NOSTER

LIGHT WELL

Essex: left, typical stack, floor (third) (1:576); below left, section; below, floor plan showing circulation desk, catalogue and administrative area

1 Entrance
2 Catalogue
3 Reader/stack area

3
3
3
3
2
1

ADMIN OFFICES

PATERNOSTER

LIGHT WELL OVER

DUCT

ACCESSIONS & CATALOGUING

CATALOGUE & REFERENCE

PHASE 2
PHASE 3

READING BAYS

CARRELS

BOOKSTACK

COURT

PHASE 2
PHASE 1

PHASE 2
PHASE 1

SEMINAR

CARRELS

LIBRARIAN

RECREATION LIBRARY

Lancaster: typical stack floor (second) (1:576) and, below, section

3
3
1 2

3
3
2

1 Entrance
2 Circulation desk and catalogue
3 Reader/stack area

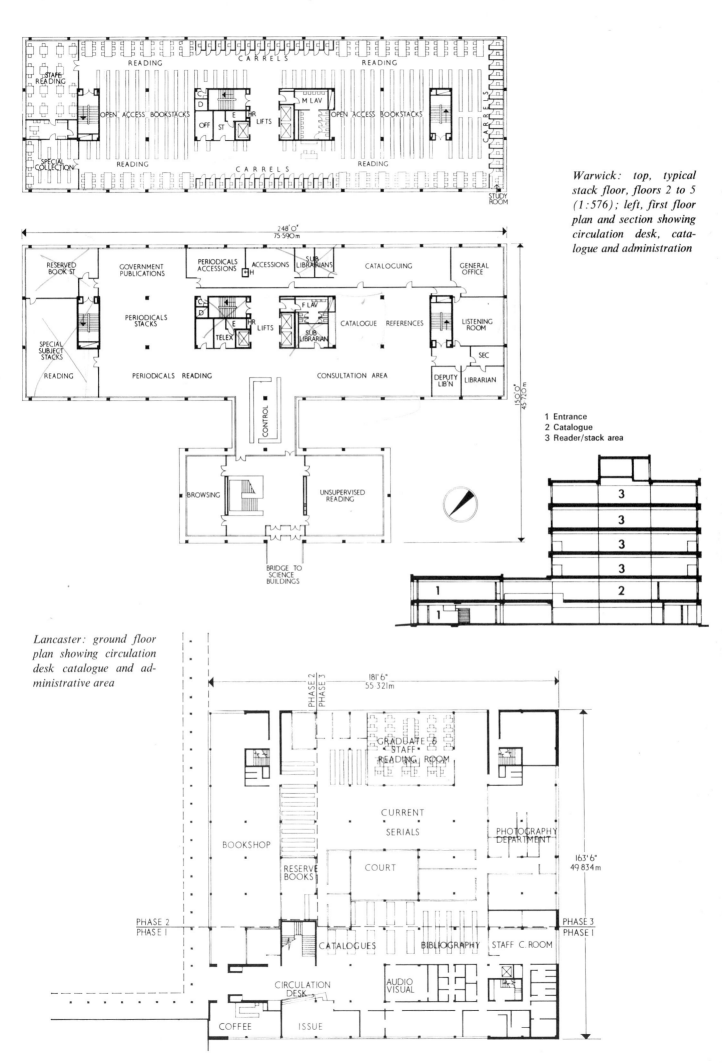

Warwick: top, typical stack floor, floors 2 to 5 (1:576); left, first floor plan and section showing circulation desk, catalogue and administration

Warwick — typical stack floor (top)

STAFF READING
READING · CARRELS · READING
SPECIAL COLLECTION
OPEN ACCESS BOOKSTACKS
READING · CARRELS · READING
M LAV
C D OFF E ST HR LIFTS
OPEN ACCESS BOOKSTACKS
CARRELS
STUDY ROOM

Warwick — first floor plan

248'0"
75.590 m

RESERVED BOOK ST
GOVERNMENT PUBLICATIONS
PERIODICALS ACCESSIONS
ACCESSIONS
SUB LIBRARIANS
CATALOGUING
GENERAL OFFICE

SPECIAL SUBJECT STACKS
PERIODICALS STACKS
C D TELEX
K E LE HR LIFTS
F LAV
SUB LIBRARIAN
CATALOGUE REFERENCES
LISTENING ROOM
SEC
DEPUTY LIB'N · LIBRARIAN

READING
PERIODICALS READING
CONSULTATION AREA

150'0"
45.720 m

CONTROL

BROWSING
UNSUPERVISED READING

BRIDGE TO SCIENCE BUILDINGS

1 Entrance
2 Catalogue
3 Reader/stack area

Section

3
3
3
3
1 · 2
1

Lancaster: ground floor plan showing circulation desk catalogue and administrative area

PHASE 2 · PHASE 3
181'6"
55.321 m

GRADUATE & STAFF READING ROOM

BOOKSHOP

CURRENT SERIALS

PHOTOGRAPHY DEPARTMENT

163'6"
49.834 m

RESERVE BOOKS

COURT

PHASE 2
PHASE 1

PHASE 3
PHASE 1

CATALOGUES
BIBLIOGRAPHY
STAFF C. ROOM

CIRCULATION DESK
AUDIO VISUAL

COFFEE
ISSUE

departments; these combine all reader-service functions for a single subject within what is almost a separate library. Each department may be self-contained in having its own issue and return counter, but it is normal for this function to be centralised for the whole building. In this case, for security reasons, the counter will control a single entrance and exit to the building. The subject department principle is, in effect, used in most university libraries, with a central bibliographical area provided separately but its application to public libraries is comparatively recent and is confined to those which can afford the extra space and extra staff which this system undoubtedly requires. In general, the trend to subject-departmentalised public libraries will call for larger buildings. Even when this principle is not fully adopted, most public libraries will create some subject departments, particularly where non-book materials form a significant part of the stock. Music, discs, tapes, films, prints, paintings and so on need separate treatment, if only for their peculiar handling and issue problems. This is very different from the subject departmental principle which involves a fundamental division of the entire service according to the readers' subject interest.

Medium sized public libraries, lacking the space or money to apply subject departmentalism overall, may use various diluted versions based on a so-called "service in depth" with conventional large, open shelving areas, but keeping together all material on subjects within certain interest groupings. Another step in this direction, but a much more perfunctory one, is division of the book stock and reader service into serious (information) and popular (recreation). An area will be given over to fiction and popular non-fiction, and another to serious non-fiction associated with reference books or having the reference area adjoining. This pattern is chiefly confined to small public libraries.

These service divisions are decided solely by the librarian but their implications will be felt by the architect not only in space allocation and furniture layout, but also in the interior environmental design which has to be appropriate to the mood of the service.

Dual-purpose rooms

Small public libraries, particularly those which treat seriously their position as a community centre, may need to provide lecture, film and music recital rooms; if these activities are to take place after the book service has ceased for the day, they may utilise certain library areas for the purpose by shifting the furniture and using flexible partitioning. This practice was common in Great Britain in the 1930s; it seems a very reasonable provision where a room will be needed only when another activity has entirely ceased, but it is to be deprecated except where there is the direst shortage of space and money. The library profession has found from bitter experience that dual-purpose rooms, and particularly dual-purpose furniture, are a menace. A possible exception is the adaptation of children's libraries for occasional use for story hours, but even here a specially designed alcove proves a great advantage with a very small loss of space. An alternative is to provide a story-hour room (without "kiddy-winky" atmosphere) which can be used for adult meetings in the evenings.

Single-room libraries

Most small libraries are on single floors, open access and open plan. They are in effect single rooms, the main layout factors being the position of windows, entrances and mains services. These libraries give a good opportunity to practise layouts, the possible variations being small. Wheeler and Githens[2] distinguish between the basic layout patterns and their main variants. In such simple cases the librarian's ideas as expressed in the brief and particularly in the traffic diagram can very swiftly be incorporated into sketch plans.

Most books on library planning contain layout plans of large buildings: because they are simple and interesting to study they can lead the librarian to believe that the placing of freestanding furniture is a really important part of the planning process, whereas in fact, it is a simple and pleasant exercise which can be

repeated until a satisfactory result is obtained. The real value of such plans is to students, enabling them to appreciate the dangers of inflexibility in structural elements and to visualise traffic and use patterns in different situations. The result of such study should be reflected in more efficient briefing, not in attempts by a librarian to translate these requirements into graphic terms.

No great harm will be done if a librarian does sketch out such a layout as an example, but only for a single-room situation. Once the position gets a little more complicated, and space relationships, circulation, and a thousand other factors outside his experience and training, have to be considered he must bow out. The more he has studied the question, however, the more valuable will be his comments upon the architect's layout proposals, after testing his functional requirements against the architect's own rationally designed layout.

PLANNING THE STRUCTURE

Some structural factors will have been largely predetermined by tentative decisions made at the feasibility stage: number of floors, positioning of heavy loads, choice of heating and ventilating machinery and so on. All implications of such decisions must be considered most carefully.

In the past most libraries were of the fixed-function type, consisting of a network of rooms, each designed to house some specific operation. This had many advantages: in a known situation it was economical of space in that each operation could be neatly framed, and it allowed each room to have a character and atmosphere suitable for its purpose. Dignity was obtained by impressive entrance halls and lofty reading rooms, and intimacy was created in other rooms by book shelves enclosing pockets of seating for readers. The great disadvantage of such libraries was that they were inflexible; in a world of fast-changing and fast-growing library needs they are entirely inappropriate. What is needed now, in its simplest form, is an interdependent network of open-plan areas with no internal loadbearing walls. This type, loosely called a modular building, means that, except in very small single-storey libraries, support for ceilings and upper floors will be provided by columns.

Structural grid

In planned modular libraries the architect will be guided in his choice of a grid size by considerations of loading, structural methods and cost. If use has been made of system planning based on mass production of some kind, his choice of grid and column distance may have been predetermined; if the building has to accommodate functions other than those of a library (an office block on upper floors for example), non-library considerations may be of dominating importance. In most circumstances, however, the grid chosen should be based on the needs of the clients; in this case, the librarian and the readers. The grid chosen will have a strong influence on the efficient use of the library space by its effect on the placing of shelving, readers' seating and furniture and, above all, in determining the amount of book stacking that can be installed. The relationship between the number of books which can be efficiently housed and the structural grid is dealt with in detail in Chapter 8 but it is not the only point of importance: if the grid allows for tables with seating between columns for six readers instead of eight and leaves unusable space in other areas, then the loss to the library as a working unit can be considerable. The grid should also allow for offices of reasonable sizes to be planned by fitting demountable partitions without column interference.

The Danish State Library Inspectorate's Committee has published a detailed survey of planning grids[3] and has made very definite recommendations. The committee first considered using functional modules based on various shelf lengths and found that no generally accepted shelf length would produce a structural module that would be acceptable for efficient shelving arrangements, both in linear run and in width of stack placing. They then took what they considered the optimum book-shelf centre-to-centre distance for a small public library (3 m), and argued that only this size of functional module can be efficiently used to obtain a suitable structural grid size; indeed they go further and suggest that "at every stage of the work of planning, the library's functional module should be used directly as the layout or planning module of P = 3 m".

The arguments are well worth considering but two points should be noted: First, the standards are meant to apply only to small public libraries (library premises in areas with populations between 5000 and 25 000) in Denmark. In larger buildings it is reasonable to take into account much larger structural grids which will offer greater flexibility.

Second, the possibility of using different shelf lengths within a single library is given full weight. Possibly this factor could be discounted in larger libraries because of other difficulties which may arise when shelf adjustments become necessary.

Columns

The choice of columns for a library of modular construction can be a crucial factor. In most aspects—material, strength, shape—the architect and his structural engineering consultants alone are concerned. With the positioning of the columns throughout the library and the size of the columns (and perhaps even more, the size of the column housings) the librarian is directly interested.

Column placing is a direct result of the structural grid chosen, although the columns are not necessarily placed at each corner of the grid. The positioning of columns at intervals inappropriate for the library's economic operation—shelving, reading, staff-housing—can be a disaster.

Column sizes will be affected by the structural system and whether or not the column housings have to carry service ducts. Air circulation ducts inside columns have the advantage that air can be directed out into semi-isolated areas such as carrels where normal heat flow might be impeded. In order to carry these ducts the column housings may be rectangular—one section providing the support and the other the duct space.

An interesting variation is to be found in the new Central Public Library at Birmingham (now in course of construction) where the large columns necessary to support an 11 m (36 ft) grid square and to house ducts have been made cruciform in plan, individual casual seating being possible against those columns where ducting has not been accommodated.

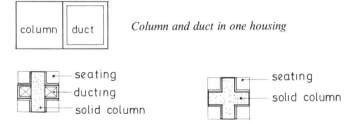

Column and duct in one housing

Birmingham: cruciform columns

The alternative, providing the ducts horizontally, might require thicker floors: the choice could be between these and very large columns which impede stacking and seating arrangements; if the librarian is to take any part in such a decision the architect must place the alternatives before him in terms which he can understand. The librarian will always prefer columns to be square in plan and as small as possible: 200 mm (8 in) square metal columns will suit him admirably. Columns as small in plan as this may be possible in single-storey buildings, but they will seldom be possible in multi-storey ones because fire regulations (in the UK) decree that all columns which support upper floors must have a certain number of hours' fire resistance and this means in effect that they must be enclosed, usually in concrete. If such small columns are used they should be painted in a bright

colour to make them noticeable to readers: neutral-coloured metal columns in a public service area (Redcar Branch Library, Teesside) saved a great deal of space but were a potential hazard in that readers tended to walk into them.

In areas used (or which might be used at some future date) for formal book-stacking, it is most important that each column should take up no more space than one half of a standard shelf length; two 450 mm (18 in) columns within a stack run will therefore cause the loss of only one 900 mm (3 ft) shelf and not upset the run of the other stacks. If the columns must be larger than 450 mm (18 in) in one direction it is better to have the longer side within the stack run, even accepting the loss of two shelf tiers, than to have it protrude into the between-stack space and thus force stacks further apart with a much greater loss of shelf space. It is possible to utilise the wasted space by making special shelves (at extra cost and loss of flexibility) or by putting in short consulation or reading shelves, but these are poor expedients.

Rectangular columns will, of course, limit flexibility in that a 90 degree change of direction of the stack runs will not be possible without loss of shelving efficiency. Serious consideration of the practical use of spaces left between columns, or outside columns, is always essential. If, for example, it is proposed to cantilever out beyond a line of columns to gain space on the periphery the extra space, however attractive, can be wasted unless it is at least 1800 mm (6 ft) wide and so usable for tables or shelving bays.

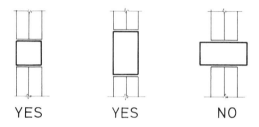

Columns should not project beyond stack runs

Park Branch, Borough of Swindon

Circular columns leave awkward, dirt attracting spaces on the floor around them; if they are absolutely essential (when converting an existing building, for example) it is possible, in reader service areas, to "lose" them by creating fitments such as catalogues around them.

Columns with a plastered surface need to be protected against the impact of book trolleys. The prevalent fashion for white painted columns in public areas may be visually attractive but should be accepted only after serious attention to the maintenance costs involved; readers inevitably handle columns as they pass them and many libraries are marred by grubby, finger-marked columns. "Washable" is a word librarians have learned to dread.

Although the grid will be basically square it is common in areas such as entrance halls, lecture rooms and so on for some columns to be omitted to give larger open spaces. It seems to a librarian therefore, that it would be structurally possible for similar larger columnless spaces to be provided elsewhere also—even in stack areas—but the architect may produce structural reasons why this is not feasible.

Columns should be uniform in section throughout their heights; the splaying of column feet will impede the use of book trolleys and can be a safety hazard. Tapering columns, which seem to attract some architects, can cause loss of shelving space: bookcases cannot be fitted close to them without looking awkward.

A space left between a column and a bookcase must be wide enough for a reader to pass comfortably. A narrow space, aesthetically desirable in order to allow the column to stand free, will leave the reader unsure as to whether he is to pass through it; inevitably some readers will squeeze through and the result again will be a grubby column.

The basic disagreement between librarian and architect on the subject of columns is that the latter may see them not only as essential supports but also as features of the interior design; the librarian will regard them only as hindrances and a cause of wasted space. Discussion on this subject at an early stage is vital: cost enters into it and may well be the determining factor.

Floor loading

To provide adequate foundations and a sound building with strength to withstand the required loads in all parts is a matter for the professional expertise of the architect and his consultants. All that need be discussed here is the peculiar nature of library loads. Books stacked closely together are heavy, heavier than an inexperienced person realises.

"Normal" books weigh 11·4 kg to 13·60 kg (25 lb to 30 lb) per 900 mm (3 ft) run of a single shelf, but certain categories (bound periodicals and directories for example) can weigh as much as 23 kg to 25 kg (50 lb to 55 lb) per 90 mm (3 ft) shelf run. If these are to be shelved several rows high, the result would be a very heavy floor load. If rolling stacks are installed, the load can be as high as ten times the normal book stack weight; firms who make the equipment will be able to supply exact figures.

Special consideration needs to be given to the equipment of a repair shop or bindery—guillotines and presses can be very heavy indeed. On the other hand people, in conditions where they have room to move about, are light and, strangely to a librarian, computer equipment appears to need only 2·4 kN/m² (50 lb/ft²).

In theory, to obtain full flexibility in a multi-storey building one has only to know the maximum weight per square metre or foot to be carried anywhere in the building and allow for this everywhere; in practice high loading levels have to be paid for in some way—larger columns, smaller grid squares, more expensive floors, deeper foundations. Economies may be obtained by sacrificing some flexibility in order to lower loading requirements, for example, by placing the heaviest loads—ventilating plant or rolling bookstacks—in a basement.

The floor loadings that may be regarded as permissible for libraries vary according to the structural characteristics of the floor concerned. The (British) University Grants Committee recognises

three characteristic floor structures[4] and provides standard equivalent uniformly distributed loads (udl) for them:

1 Structures capable of distributing a udl of 6·3 kN/m² (133 lb/ft²) in the direction at right angles to the line of the bookstacks, eg in-situ reinforced concrete. This loading is permissible if the floor to ceiling height does not exceed 2·75 m (9 ft).

2 When there are no spreaders for the loading, beams should be designated to carry a udl of 7 kN/m² (150 lb/ft²).

3 If floor to ceiling height is greater than 2·75 m (9 ft), udl load is reckoned as 700 N/m² (15 lb/ft²) for every extra foot height of potential bookstack.

In quoting to the structural engineer the maximum load likely to be required in the building the architect can use the experience of many other library planners. Faulkner Brown has said:[5]

"In order to support either bookstacks or reader spaces, the maximum superimposed floor loading takes on the nature of a constant. It is currently 7 kN/m² (150 lb/ft²). There is no evidence to show that the floor loading figure of 9·5 kN/m² (200 lb/ft²) quoted in *Bricks and mortarboards*[6] is necessary. Experiments that have taken place tend to show that 5·75 kN/m² (120 lb/ft²) live loads might be enough."

Stack positioning

The main purpose of the building will be to house books and readers in satisfactory conditions and relationships. Books in bulk are heavier than readers, and if a large part of the book stack is to be kept in closely packed conditions, then it is important at the planning stage to establish where they are to be placed. This problem was handled in the past by separating book storage areas from reader areas. Historical examples are given by Thompson[7] and Brawne[8]. To obtain a fair measure of flexibility in such conditions, the most usual arrangement today is for the book stack to form the core of the building, leaving the perimeter for reading areas, making the best use of window light.

Other alternatives are still used, particularly in closed access situations. The stack tower which has economic advantages (and it requires less aisle space) has had a vogue recently, but it is often expensive in retrieval and impracticable where reader access may be desirable at some future date.

Some libraries of an earlier period contained multi-storey stacks, that is bookstacks which supported other bookstacks, with access by integral stairways and catwalks, which were independent of the structure of the building. Such multi-tier stacks are still to be seen, though not as frequently as in the past. The uprights of the stack shelving system can be used to support a reinforced concrete floor, usually with the assistance of a capping plate. There are complications in such a proposal, conduits for example needing to be set into the concrete. These ideas, also the use of metal grid

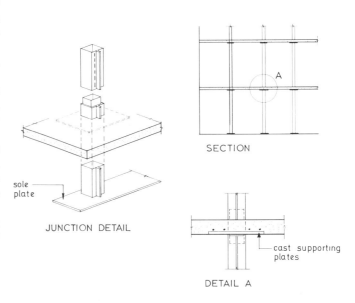

Uprights supporting a reinforced concrete floor

floors supported by stack uprights, produce savings on the basic
structure and may be acceptable in some countries. In Great
Britain it is very doubtful whether such a proposal would comply
with the Building Regulations, particularly the requirements of
Part D "Structure stability" or Part E1 "Requirements for periods
of fire resistance". If the proposed structure were of five or more
storeys, including basements, the requirements of Part D19 might
also be inhibiting. Instead of having a whole floor of reinforced
concrete supported in this way, gangways only may be supported,
the bookshelves being bracketed from the pillars which run
through the floors.

Service equipment

Heating and ventilating services in multi-storey buildings will
almost always require some heavy equipment. Even underfloor
electric heating may require a special transformer. The choice
and design will be matters entirely for the architect and the
mechanical consultants, but the librarian is interested in the
amount of space the equipment will take up and its position.
Briefly the alternatives for housing heavy service equipment are:
on the roof: not very usual except for lift housing, but it has been
done and has advantages for the intake of air for ventilation and
air-conditioning plant;
in an outbuilding: expensive both in site use and in heat losses in
transfer to the library;
in the basement: the obvious place for very heavy machinery with
possible savings in loading levels but occupying an area that
could be utilised for compact shelving, which is also very heavy;
on an intermediate floor of a tall building: unorthodox, but it is
said to offer savings in trunking costs because of its central
position. It is obviously unpopular with the librarian who "loses"
a floor; it may also be expensive in terms of sound insulation.
The first and second methods appeal to the librarian in that they
do not use any of the space he needs for library operations.
In the design of all service installations in libraries high priority
must be given to sound insulation of plant and equipment. Not
only do the main plant, boiler, fans, refrigeration plant and pumps
produce noise but ducts and pipes distributing air and water to
the building transfer it, often to areas most sensitive to noise.
Local equipment such as fan convectors must also be silenced.
Access for maintenance is another important matter: some
equipment requires regular maintenance and unless access points
are carefully placed considerable disturbance to readers can
result. Heating and ventilating machinery positions which are
not well thought out can prove very expensive in their effects on
library functions and space. Walls occupied by radiators or
grilles may be lost to the librarian as shelving space. A recent
British prize-winning library, which shall be nameless, has heating
fitments fixed at intervals on the floor of the open lending library
area. No librarian would award a prize to this arrangement.

Fenestration

In testing the draft allocation of areas within his general design
the architect will have to consider the implications of his proposals
for fenestration. If he has in mind the vast amount of glass in the
outer shell which is so common today, he must decide whether
it is reasonable to accept the many disadvantages, among which
are:

the need for machinery to control the considerable heat gain and
loss; in more than one modern glass-walled building dissipation
of heat costs more than heating and lighting the building;
the need to control the effect of direct sunlight on readers and
books: this can be by shades or light-breaks outside the building,
by special glass, or double-glazing with blinds, or by slanting the
heads of windows downwards: all have disadvantages in cost,
cleaning, operation and maintenance,
possible need for a higher level of artificial lighting in areas away
from window light in order to balance the brightness of direct
sunlight and to mitigate the sense of deprivation in readers who

Hull University Library

Jesmond District Library, Newcastle upon Tyne CB

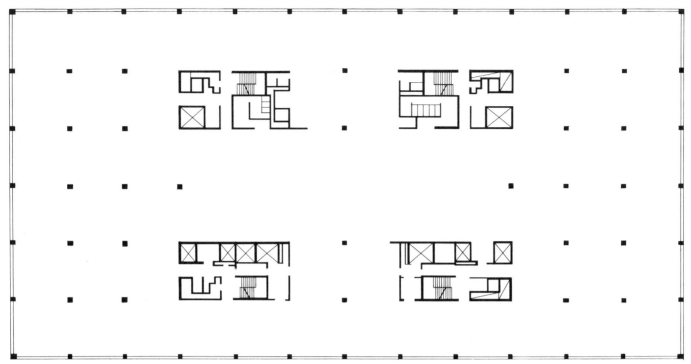

Public Library Washington DC, showing column-free central area (approx. 1 : 305)

can see a bright sky: darkened glass in windows can help to overcome this problem but it is not cheap;
loss of wall shelving space and of flexibility in both seating and shelving.

In all it can be said that glass walls are not usually suited to libraries. In open-access conditions clerestory windows (small windows running along the higher part of reading-room walls) may be an acceptable compromise; they can give the desired impression while allowing shelving to be installed on the lower part of the walls. However, with this type of window light is directly in the eyes of the reader as he chooses books and for this reason it is rejected by many librarians. Narrower but full height windows, zig-zag on plan, are another compromise but again there can be a serious problem of glare.

In single-storey buildings rooflights are still possible; very common fifty years ago, they fell into disrepute largely because of the difficulty of making flat roofs watertight. They have been revived more recently under the influence of Aalto, who, in his famous Vipuri libraries, used large round ceiling apertures and no side windows. This system has the disadvantages of interference with full flexibility and of an enormous variation in natural light levels at different times of day and year.

Artificial light will certainly be needed; the architect will know of the IES recommendations for lighting levels for different library functions and, with his lighting consultant, will have studied the contribution which both natural and artificial lighting make to the appearance of the library. They will also remember that the cost variation in different lighting plans and levels can be very considerable, both in installation and consumption of current and in the bills for cleaning and maintenance. The latter can be very heavy.

Position of stairways

In a multi-storey building the positioning of the core of stairs and lifts (and possibly of other services) will be one of the architect's major considerations. If placed centrally, they may need shielding to remove aural and visual interference with serious reading. If placed off-centre they will limit the flexibility of the building for changes in activities. In both cases it will be necessary for passageways to be left around the entrances to the stairs (if only for fire safety reasons) and this wastes space. An example of good thinking is in the plan below of the new Public Library of

Washington DC by Mies Van der Rohe. Despite the very large floor areas the centre portion has been left free of columns and the other areas are symmetrical for maximum flexibility.

A somewhat similar layout is used in the new Birmingham Central Library; here lavatories have been provided in the core areas but on alternate floors only. The plan (p. 75) shows clearly how the main floor areas have been left clear and security control established.

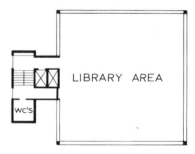

Building with outside stair leaving library area free

Stairs outside the building leave a good open-plan area for library use, but the single entrance to each floor may limit traffic routes and create bottlenecks. Fire regulations may also require a second stairway as an escape route.

Librarians have learned to be wary of architects who plan large open stairways as "features". Stairs like these, and symmetrical pairs of stairs rising from entrance halls, have proved to be sources of inefficiency, trouble and expense. They are the remaining traces of "monumentalism".

Core for reader service

Just as there are advantages in having a direct vertical relationship between the main services—lifts and staircases, water and sewage lines—so there can be a gain in having such a connection between reader service stations and other points, such as accessions departments and book stacks which will need access by hoist or conveyor machinery. To site all such service points close to lift shafts would impossibly restrict the planning of reader services but to insist that this vertically-operating machinery should be placed within open areas will restrict the architect in his freedom of design. Whatever solution the architect may produce he must discuss it with the librarian.

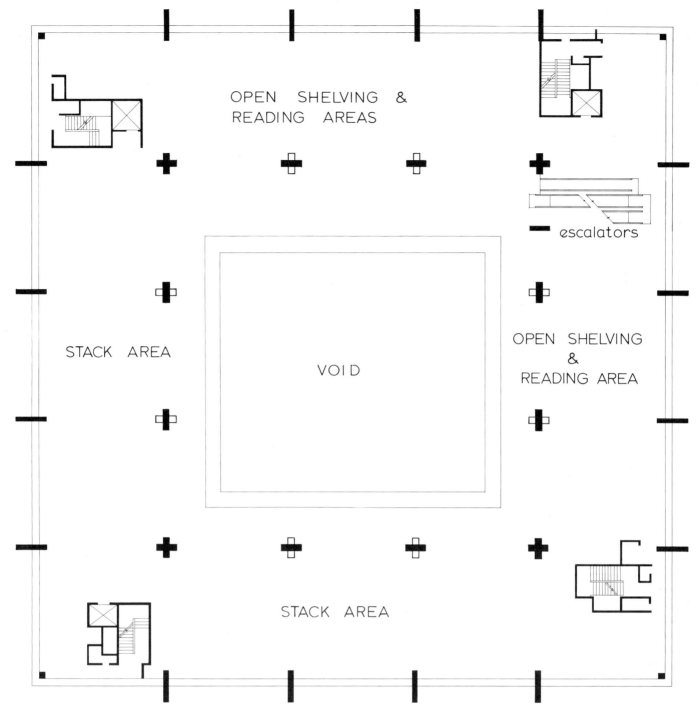

OPEN SHELVING & READING AREAS

escalators

STACK AREA

VOID

OPEN SHELVING & READING AREA

STACK AREA

Birmingham Central Library showing service areas with lavatories on alternate floors. (approx. 1:315)

Number of floors

The architect's own assessment of the contents to be housed, tempered perhaps by local planning requirements, will already have established the overall height of the building. By varying the structural design it is possible to get more or fewer floors into a building, depending largely on the acceptable floor-to-ceiling height of the rooms and the necessary thickness of the floors. Other factors, both structural and financial, will be involved; this is not a matter to be taken lightly, but if a library building can have either five floors, each with a floor-to-ceiling height of 2·75 m (9 ft) and floor thickness of 900 mm (3 ft), or six floors of floor-to-ceiling of 2·44 m (8 ft) and floor thickness of 600 mm (2 ft), then a difference of one-fifth of the total floor area of the library is involved—an extremely important matter. Of course it is not as easy as that; to build narrower inter-floors involves structural engineering decisions, and in particular different arrangements for the distribution of service ducts. Loading requirements for the entire building may have to be increased and heavier foundations thus necessitated; in addition the costs of a complete extra floor have to be met.

Conversely there may well be cost compensations: in some types of structure an extra floor can mean fewer brick or tile facings, and the air-conditioning may be more cost-effective. Lower ceiling heights and different service duct distribution can eliminate false ceilings. These matters are for the architect and his structural engineer; what very much concerns the librarian are the total area available for his operations and the floor-to-ceiling heights.

Floor-to-ceiling height

In a single-storey building there are obvious psychological advantages in having a reasonably high ceiling; the added costs are not excessive. Similarly on the ground floor (or more accurately, the entrance floor) of a multi-storey building the architect will wish to create an inviting prospect, possibly with a vista which takes the eye deep into the building. If there is insufficient space to provide a specific entrance area to give this required effect (and functionally the entrance hall is often largely wasted space), then the architect will probably wish to achieve his aim by building a high ceiling throughout the whole entrance floor level.

The librarian's priorities will be quite different: because the entrance floor is used by all readers, he will want every inch of it for library services. A fashionable compromise is for the area

Lending library with stairs to gallery reference library, Stockton District Library, Teeside CB

behind the entrance hall to be open but with a partial mezzanine floor around or in the rear of the room, an open staircase forming an attractive and eye-catching feature in the middle of the room. The librarian will consider such proposals with caution; to some extent a mezzanine is a "fixed-function" element and a bar to flexibility: unless it occupies a large part of the area (60 per cent has been suggested as a practicable figure), the space thus made available for book and reader accommodation may be poor compensation for loss of a possible whole extra floor. Moreover, readers will be inconvenienced by having to climb stairs to use key sections of the library and staff will have many extra journeys to fetch and carry books for them. The needs of disabled readers must also be taken into account: lifts to an open partial mezzanine are seldom practicable. The entrance floor itself may suffer by having in parts a low ceiling which makes readers feel cramped. For these and other reasons the librarian may insist that the efficiency in housing books and serving readers is at least as important as the psychological effects upon those first entering the building.

A series of voids has been used to create a mezzanine area with a fairly low ceiling. Central Library, City of Manchester

In formal study areas where on entrance the eye can travel right down the room, the ceiling needs to be of a height of at least 2500 mm (8 ft 3 in); where pressure on space is less acute, 2750 mm (9 ft) would be better, to avoid a claustrophobic effect. Metcalfe says,[9] "A room 7·6 m × 11 m (25 ft × 36 ft) which is enough for thirty-six readers is not unpleasant with a 2540 mm (8 ft 4 in) ceiling if ventilation is adequate." If the vista through the room is broken by high book-cases or partitions, for example in a university stack reading room where, in modern English practice the stack occupies the centre and tables the perimeter, a ceiling as low as 2340 mm (7 ft 8 in) can certainly be acceptable. For efficient shelving in such cases, a stack seven shelves high, giving an overall height of 2300 mm (7 ft 6 in) is necessary; a 2340 mm (7 ft 8 in) ceiling here may seem close but if the lighting arrangements are carefully considered it can be achieved. To have to reduce the height to six shelves because of lighting problems would, of course, be absurd. Readers in the perimeter areas, probably close to windows, will not be unhappy with such a ceiling height. Construction in reinforced concrete using "honeycomb" ceilings can give an even better illusion of height while, conversely, constructional requirement of deep beams (as in the University of Essex library) will waste a great deal of space. In the Manchester Central Library a mezzanine floor was fitted into a floor which had a total floor-to-ceiling height of only 4530 mm (14 ft 10½ in), the ceiling height of around 2135 mm (7 ft) being made tolerable by the use of a series of voids to break up the tunnel effect.

OUTLINE PROPOSALS AND SCHEME DESIGN

At the conclusion of the outline planning stage the architect will submit a report embodying all his conclusions and proposals up to this point. It will be his responsibility to co-ordinate and apply all the proposals made by the various specialists. Their recommendations will also have been notified to the quantity surveyor who will have been analysing the cost implications of every tentative decision reached by the team, and its relation to the cost limits. The report will include outline plans and elevations, possibly isometric drawings or an artist's impression, even a model. If some of these have been submitted in the feasibility report they may have to be amended and resubmitted to show the most up-to-date proposals. With the plans will be a new estimate of costs, broken down into various major headings but not usually detailed. The authority will be asked to approve this report before the team goes on to the next stage, that of developing the scheme design.

The architect may have to bring to the authority's attention certain matters requiring a specific decision; for example after full consideration of all alternatives, the team may have decided that certain of the brief's requirements are impossible within the limits laid down, either by the statutory authorities or by the client, particularly as regards cost limits. These matters will be for the authority to decide and the scheme cannot proceed until either the architect's proposals are accepted and the limits modified, or the brief amended so that the team can work out acceptable proposals.

Scheme design

With the outline proposals agreed, the team now sets out to prepare a full scheme for the project, going through the same procedure once again, each member carrying out further studies of his own special subject and its implications with regard to the plan as a whole. The proposals from each specialist will then be more specific, especially in space, access and loading, the effects of which will be most important to the entire plan. The specialists will also provide more details of prices so that the quantity surveyor can continue working towards a more realistic cost estimate.

The librarian will be concerned with many of the ideas, particularly those relating to layout, use of space and their functional implications. By this time the plans will be so far developed that every change will have an effect on space allocations already made and it is likely that the librarian's operational intentions will be affected. A very common example is that the heating engineer finds that in a certain area he will need a wider duct than had earlier appeared to be necessary; the architect will alter his drawings accordingly. The change may make a passage-way narrower than is acceptable and the obvious remedy would be for a nearby readers' service point to be moved a few feet. The librarian realises that this would result in a relationship with a book hoist that would increase the action needed to obtain every book from stack, and so add to the staff's work every working hour throughout the life of the building. He will report this to the architect, who after discussion, probably involving the heating engineer, will attempt to resolve the problem in a way acceptable to all concerned.

This example is not meant to show that the librarian's requirements are more important than those of any other officer, but that if he had not been kept informed, plans would have crystallised to a point when it would have been too late to make a change; the necessary alterations would have had expensive repercussions throughout the building. From this point in the programme therefore the librarian must be constantly involved and the developing plans must be sent to him for comment.

By the end of the scheme design stage the architect will have completed planning in general and made decisions on all matters except those of detail. Outline specifications will have been drawn up and necessary approvals obtained from the various powers. The result will be the presentation to authority of a completed scheme with a full explanation, references to the brief as it developed during the stages of consultation, a cost plan and a timetable. Only when authority accepts this scheme and all its implications is the architect able to move on to the next stage.

By the time the general outline of structure and layout have been established, there will have been identified a number of areas where decisions need to be made, at first in fairly general terms, and then, as the scheme progresses, in some detail, ending with a full and definitive statement of instructions to the contractor. In these subject areas the architect, or the specialist concerned, will

think out and test proposals, developing them at successive stages and bringing conclusions to the team to be tested for their effect on the spheres of responsibility of the other members. In these actions the librarian will be more and more concerned. From now, therefore, the succeeding chapters will deal mainly with aspects of the building in which the librarian will have a part to play by virtue of his experience and consequent opinions. The subjects are: furniture and equipment; layout and critical sizes as well as design and materials; floors; lighting; security and protection; heating and ventilation; enclosing elements; maintenance.

All these subjects are the province of an expert who knows more about them than does the librarian, but no expert knows as much as the librarian about the influence and the relative importance to library operations of the alternative solution to the problems which will arise in these sections. His voice must therefore be heard.

What if his voice is ignored? This may seem to be anticipating trouble but it is trouble which is too often met. In discussing with a librarian the weaknesses in operation of his new library, one hears, "I pointed out to the architect that this would make the library too hot/cold/noisy/cramped, but he assured me that this would not be so." What can the librarian do if he has reason to believe that one of the architect's proposals will turn out to be a failure in terms of the library's operations? If teamwork has been effective it will never happen, but the unpleasant possibility must be faced.

It must be accepted that the librarian is employed for his professional judgments just as much as is the architect. The librarian's judgment has no standing in technical matters of library building but it is pre-eminent where the library's future running is concerned. A serious disagreement therefore is a matter for the librarian's professional conscience; if he feels that his requirements are not being met then he must inform his masters of this fact, having given the architect notice that he will so so. A professional librarian, responsible to his authority for the effective operation of a library, cannot sit by and see erected a building which will, in his opinion, suffer from an avoidable operational inefficiency. In such a case the authority has no alternative but to consider this as a dispute between two professionals and it must either decide arbitrarily, or appoint another person, perhaps its own architect or another librarian, to give an opinion. If the architect's views are supported then the librarian can be content that he has done his duty; if he stands silent out of awe or friendship for the architect, he is betraying his professional trust. It must be said that such an event is very unlikely to occur, if the librarian has been accepted as a member of the team and not as a "client representative" who should stand on the side-lines.

REFERENCES

[1] WALLACE, A. *In Library World*, June 1971

[2] WHEELER, JOSEPH L. and ALFRED MORTON GITHENS The American public library building: its planning and design with special reference to its administration and service. American Library Association, Chicago, 1941, pp 219–287

[3] PLOVGAARD, SVEN, *Public library buildings:* originally issued by the Danish State Library Inspectorate's Committee for the compilation of standards for library buildings in 1967. Translated by Oliver Stallybrass. The Library Association, London, 1971, pp 51–64

[4] BROWN, HENRY FAULKNER University library buildings. *In The Architect's Journal.* 21 February 1968, pp 457–460

[5] Ibid

[6] EDUCATIONAL FACILITIES LABORATORY Bricks and mortarboards. The Laboratory, New York, undated, p 77

[7] THOMPSON. Op cit., pp 14–15

[8] BRAWNE, MICHAEL Libraries: architecture and equipment. Pall Mall Press, London, pp 14–25

[9] METCALF. Op cit., p 70

8 Layouts and critical sizes:
furniture and equipment

By this stage the architect has settled his ideas about the shape and layout of the building. He must now turn to each of the operational areas and consider in more detail the space allowances and layout of furniture and equipment. The size of each area will have been decided either by the amount of space which the authority feels that it can afford or by the application of a "standard" for that type of service.

In a single room of the library, or in a library which is in effect a single room, the librarian may be quite capable of arranging the furniture; librarians have had experience of the exercise of cutting pieces of paper to the shape and scale size of the items of furniture and equipment and arranging them on a plan to make a satisfactory layout. It will always be found that there are numerous ways of arranging the pieces and that some are more effective in their use of space than others.

A simple example concerns the placing of readers' tables and chairs: Reed[1] demonstrates that a number of single tables and chairs close to and facing, walls or windows use less space than a similar number placed against, but with tables at right angles to, walls or windows, while if the tables and chairs are placed in open space they need even more room. This is because, as Reed suggests, there is an unusable "halo" (he uses the figure of 450 mm (18 in)) around each working area and that the halo's shape will vary with its position within the room. It has never been suggested that the reader at a table will actually occupy the nominal 2·3 m^2 (25 ft^2) allocated; a more normal figure is 1 m^2 (10 ft^2), the rest being allowed to provide for a share of the aisles and necessary open spaces in the room. Similarly bookcases placed along walls occupy less space than those placed at right angles to walls, while the latter use much less space than island cases.

In the following sections critical sizes will be discussed for the various items of operational equipment, but in every case sizes and dimensions will vary according to the placing of the items relative to other items, to the walls and passages and to the peculiar requirements of the type of library.

BOOK SHELVING

The material to be housed for both staff and readers consists largely of bound hard-backed books. Furniture has certainly to be planned to hold microforms, sheet maps and computer products and sometimes for charter rolls, broadsides, rolled maps, prints and other inconveniently shaped material, but for the foreseeable future the bulk of holdings of libraries of all kinds will continue to be in book form. University and special libraries in particular, may have large numbers of periodicals, but, except for recent issues, they will take the form of bound books, or boxes which can be shelved as books.

The architect will know from the brief the quantity of material to be accommodated; his object will be to house the books in a way acceptable to those who have to handle them, in an aesthetically suitable form and as economically as possible, particularly as regards space. It is obvious that if he can house more in a given space he will save costs; in the case of large city, county, university and college libraries with stocks running into hundreds of thousands, or even millions, this can be a most important factor. If seven shelves can be installed per tier instead of six there will be a gain of one-sixth more storage space; if aisle widths can be reduced more ranges can be installed. For a full discussion of possible space saving methods by shelving design and layout; see Metcalf[2].

In other libraries the inconvenience caused by shelving books closely together may be out of all proportion to any gain. A popular library which can afford space for a large entrance hall and perhaps a car park cannot be well advised to pack books too closely together, when the space gain is comparatively small. To take the economical planning of shelving so seriously as to allow it to dominate such matters as ceiling height (and thus the number of floors which the building can hold) calls for a very careful study of the factors, and particularly the costs, which may be involved in structure, heating, lighting and so on.

Book sizes and shelf depths

There is little to be gained by the use of the traditional descriptions of books—folio, quarto, octavo and so on; they are both imprecise and difficult to determine. It has been well established that in most libraries at least 90 per cent of the books are less than 230 mm (9 in) deep: Metcalf says, "97 per cent of all books would go without difficulty on 230 mm (9 in) nominal shelves in a 508 mm (20 in) wide double-sided stack." In popular libraries of all kinds this is certainly so (except perhaps for junior school libraries with a high proportion of picture books, and for music libraries). Discounting then those libraries which have special problems because they hold large stocks of bound newspapers, music or art books, most libraries can save space if they standardise shelving at 230 mm (9 in) deep; indeed most popular libraries can afford to standardise at 200 mm (8 in) deep. The small difference between these figures may not be important in the majority of libraries but if double-sided cases can be limited to 400 mm (16 in) wide, more ranges may be fitted into the intensive shelving area of a large library, and this can be very important indeed.

A compromise which can allow the slight cost saving of having 200 mm (8 in) rather than 230 mm (9 in) deep shelves without loss of flexibility is to have a backless double-sided case 460 mm (18 in) wide, but to fit 200 mm (8 in) shelves, leaving a nominal 60 mm (2 in) gap in the middle of the stack: books up to 250 mm (10 in) deep can usually be shelved here by overlapping across the centre because the book opposite will usually be narrower. This will reduce the number of books requiring special oversize shelving. It should be noted that these sizes apply chiefly to wooden shelves where the specifications refer to actual widths, but not always to metal shelves whose width is often nominal, being rather less than half the width of a double sided case. It is also possible in closed stacks to house books deeper than 230 mm (9 in) in such conditions by allowing them to protrude over the fronts of the cases, although this is untidy and inconvenient.

Systems shelving units offer the opportunity to fit deeper shelves, particularly when held on brackets from wall strips; this has some advantage in flexibility. One large manufacturer (Terrapin Reska) produces shelves 200 mm ($7\frac{7}{8}$ in), 250 mm ($9\frac{7}{8}$ in), 300 mm ($11\frac{13}{16}$ in) and 350 mm ($13\frac{3}{4}$ in) deep, fitting any of them onto its uprights or wall strips. On the 200 mm shelf, a lip at the back of the shelf can be used when books are up to 200 mm deep; if deeper books are to be accommodated on the same shelf, the lip can be removed so that the books can protrude over the inner edge (in a double-sided case) into the gap between the shelves (see p. 79).

Books more than 230 mm (9 in) deep can be housed on special runs of shelving 300 mm (12 in) deep. As the majority of such books will also be too tall for normal shelving, oversize shelving bays must be provided to accommodate them. In stack conditions where the extra inches can be vital to shelving economy, it may be preferable to follow Poole, who says[3], "As a rule of thumb it may be assumed that a normal [American college] installation will require 80 per cent 200 mm (8 in) shelves, 15 per cent 250 mm

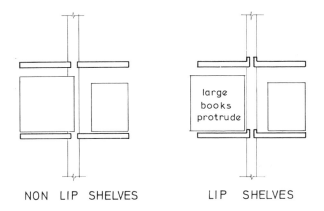

NON LIP SHELVES   LIP SHELVES

(10 in) shelves and 5 per cent 300 mm (12 in) shelves." It is debatable whether the space saving is worth the disadvantage of having three sequences instead of two. This is discussed under "Closed stack" later.

Shelf length

In the UK the standard shelf length has for many years been 914 mm (3 ft). It has been held, without any specific research to uphold the statement, that the reader's eye cannot encompass more than 3 ft in one glance. The late F. J. McCarthy produced the study below for the feasibility of scanning a 1219 mm (4 ft) shelf. Shelves longer than 914 mm (3 ft) are practicable now because u-section steel offers greater rigidity than either wood or the older type of metal shelving. Longer shelves can save some space (provided that their use is planned when the module is chosen) but the gain is slight and the shelf has usually to be rather thicker than the 20 mm ($\frac{3}{4}$ in) of the conventional wood shelving. Indeed, the 50 mm (2 in) thickness of some u-section shelving can result in one shelf less per tier—a serious loss. What is important is that the shelf length unit shall be consistent, or at least that there shall be as few sizes as possible. Any librarian who has had to move books and shelves in a library where some shelves are not *quite* the same length will echo this from his heart.

With the change to metric measurements in building the equivalent of the standard 3 ft shelf is 900 mm and this enables new shelves to be interchanged with old ones. To change to a measure of 1 metre simply because it is a tidy unit seems not to serve any useful library purpose, but in the long run the trade may be forced to concentrate on this unit of length for modular reasons in the building industry. At the moment several manufacturers of systems offer 750 mm, 1 m and 1·5 m; these can fit in with different modules but not with existing 3 ft bays.

Shelf height

The question of the distance apart at which shelves should be fixed is of course mainly of interest in that it affects the number of shelves fitted per tier; if equally convenient for the reader there is obviously a great gain in space if six rather than five shelves of books can be accommodated.

In libraries whose stock consists of books for general reading it is possible to house the vast majority at 280 mm (11 in) centres; this, with 20 mm ($\frac{3}{4}$ in) for shelf thickness, means 260 mm ($10\frac{1}{4}$ in) clear and, allowing 13 mm ($\frac{1}{2}$ in) for fingers to be inserted above the top of the book, will accommodate a 240 mm ($9\frac{1}{2}$ in) book comfortably and a 255 mm (10 in) one without too much trouble. Such an arrangement can have many advantages in housing the maximum number of books within convenient reach of the average reader. For books that will not fit onto those shelves an oversize sequence will be necessary. There will always be the temptation to make the distance 300 mm (12 in) rather than displace a book which is just too large for 280 mm (11 in) centres, but if this is done it may cause the loss of one shelf per tier. A conventional expedient has been to allow one deeper shelf per tier (usually the bottom one), but this can never accommodate the really large books and the inevitable result will be three sequences of books. The recommendation is two sequences only in popular libraries: one at 280 mm (11 in) centres and a special oversize sequence which can be clearly labelled and referred to by location symbols in the catalogue. This does not apply to the quick-reference collection; it is more economical of space to have a special tier at 330 mm (13 in) centres for encyclopaedias than to house them in a run with much smaller books.

A decision on this matter is vital when fixed shelving is to be used but in practice it is advisable with regard to adjustable shelving. The top and bottom lines of shelving units are important in the appearance of the room, and the height of these lines (and of course the distance between them) severely limits the use of even infinitely variable shelf fittings. A most attractive run of low

Book boxes for small children, Redcar Library, Teeside CB

Shelving boxes for small children. (Library Design and Engineering Ltd)

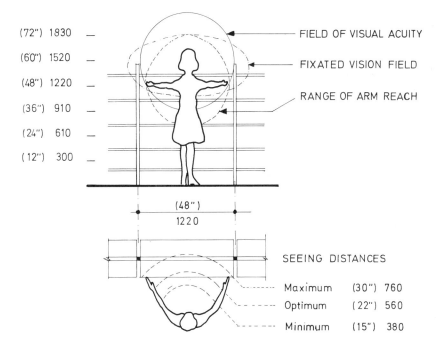

Scanning a 1219mm (48in) shelf

Shelving sizes

	300 mm (12 in)									400 mm (15 in)								
Bottom space																		
Fascia	50 mm (2 in)			75 mm (3 in)			100 mm (4 in)			50 mm (2 in)			75 mm (3 in)			100 mm (4 in)		
Shelving space ie no of shelves at 280 mm (11 in)	4	5	6	4	5	6	4	5	6	4	5	6	4	5	6	4	5	6
Overall height mm	1475	1750	2030	1500	1775	2050	1525	1800	2085	1550	1830	2110	1575	1850	2135	1600	1880	2160
inches	58	69	80	59	70	81	60	71	82	61	72	83	62	73	84	63	74	85

island cases was designed by an architect to allow a vista throughout the room; they would hold two shelves of books only, but the addition of 75 mm (3 in) to the overall height would have allowed a third shelf to be fitted.

The overall height of shelving in an open-access library is an important factor in the design. Wall shelving should never be higher than 2 m (7 ft) to the very top and 1·8 m (6 ft) is usually better. Height of an island case depends on its position: where a vista is called for 1·375 m (4 ft 6 in) is a good height and 1·5 m (5 ft) is the maximum, but for cases at right angles to wall shelving, the wall shelving height can be followed. No shelf for use by the general public should be less than 300 mm (12 in) from the floor, while for island cases a 400 mm (15 in) space at the bottom gives a surprisingly large increase in lightness of appearance. The depth of the fascia must be considered before a decision is made: if a generous space is needed for tier guiding then room for shelving will be reduced. In closed and open stack tier guides are less important than in open access and methods more economical of shelving space can be used. (See page 126.)

Rather than make an arbitrary decision as to overall shelving height it is better to make simple calculations from a list of alternatives (see table above).

When adjustable shelving (including wall-mounted bracket shelving) is to be used this may seem over-elaborate but it can be a useful exercise to produce a figure which can then be tested for other combinations of shelf spacing. The final choice will affect the appearance and the efficiency of the library for many years.

The sizes discussed above are for adult libraries, but as books for older children are similar in size the important factor is convenient access heights for children. Obviously, these will differ according to the age ranges of the children concerned: the diagrams below show the best shelving heights for fourteen-year-olds and six-year-olds respectively.

The Danish State Library Inspectorate[4] decree a height of 1600 mm (5 ft 4 in) in junior schools but this seems too high because these children will need a large number of picture books calling for

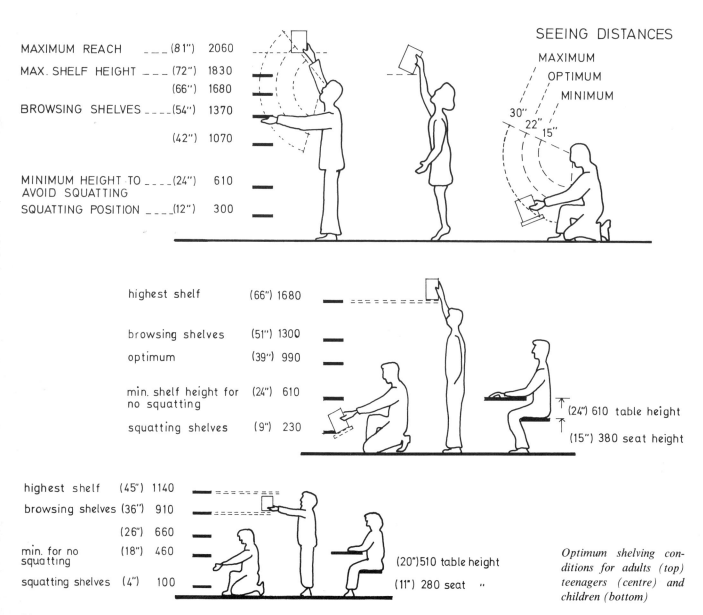

MAXIMUM REACH ___ (81") 2060
MAX. SHELF HEIGHT ___ (72") 1830
(66") 1680
BROWSING SHELVES ____ (54") 1370
(42") 1070
MINIMUM HEIGHT TO ____ (24") 610
AVOID SQUATTING
SQUATTING POSITION ____ (12") 300

SEEING DISTANCES
MAXIMUM
OPTIMUM
MINIMUM
30" 22" 15"

highest shelf (66") 1680
browsing shelves (51") 1300
optimum (39") 990
min. shelf height for (24") 610
no squatting
squatting shelves (9") 230
(24") 610 table height
(15") 380 seat height

highest shelf (45") 1140
browsing shelves (36") 910
(26") 660
min. for no (18") 460
squatting
squatting shelves (4") 100
(20") 510 table height
(11") 280 seat "

Optimum shelving conditions for adults (top) teenagers (centre) and children (bottom)

display shelves. Such fittings can be very conveniently provided by systems shelving units.

In junior schools and parts of children's libraries the bottom shelf can be as little as 75 mm (3 in) from the floor because small children like to sit on low stools or on carpeted floors. Common sense and familiarity with children's needs will dictate the answer. A practice to be deprecated is that of buying standard shelving units for a whole library and then leaving the top shelf empty, or blanked off as a display shelf, in the children's library. If a library is worth providing, it is worth planning according to the needs of its users. Recommendations relative to shelving for children's libraries are given in *School library resource centres*.[5]

In special libraries the layout of shelving and its association with reading needs will indeed be "special" and individual. The total book capacity will be small (compared with universities and central libraries) and the accent will be on speed of access to the material. There will seldom be any call for very long runs of books or need for large open seating areas and it is common for individual study tables to be placed close to, and often within, the shelving runs. Because there will be comparatively little browsing or casual use, books can be housed seven shelves high and runs of bound periodicals and reports, being in very great demand, are likely to be positioned close to the focal point. Current issues of periodicals and reports will usually have absolute priority; periodical shelves adaptable within proprietary shelving runs have much to commend them here (see pp 97–99).

The layout of such libraries will be complicated by the need to house banks of vertical files, photo-copying equipment and so on in a tight operational area convenient for instant use. The concentration upon speed and efficiency of operation in a library designed specifically to meet a known and limited need will dictate layout of shelving; because the needs of each special library are "special" it is impossible to generalise, but a sound survey of the problem has been produced by Anthony[6].

Shelf loading

Poole says[7]: "All standard book shelves [in US] are presently designed to withstand loads of 2 kN/m² (40 lb/ft²) with no permanent deflection and with no temporary deflection in excess of 20 mm ($\frac{3}{4}$ in)." In the UK this depends on the specifications of individual manufacturers as no standards exist (performance tests for various types of shelving would be an asset to the profession). Poole also notes that 300 mm (12 in) gramophone records produce a load factor of 2·39 kN/m² (49·5 lb/ft²) on a 300 mm (12 in) shelf. However the writer's experience has shown that there are runs of books (directories and bound volumes of periodicals for example) which weigh more than 2·4 kN/m² (50 lb/ft²). If an average book weighs between 0·5 kg and 1 kg (1 lb and 2 lb), than a 900 mm (3 ft) shelf of such books, three-quarters full, weight 11 kg to 22 kg (25 lb to 50 lb). To discuss the weight of a square foot of books is seldom helpful because when housed upright on shelves, a 300 mm (1 ft) run of average books will take up an area 300 mm (1 ft) × 200 mm (8 in): to render this in square measure serves no useful purpose. The relative bearing qualities of wood and metal shelving are considered in chapter 12.

Books per shelf

This subject has generated a surprising amount of heat among the experts, mainly because they seek a general solution to a problem with so many variables. In closed access conditions with a completely finite stock, or in other than subject sequences (for example, where large runs of defunct serials are housed) shelves may be completely filled, but in few other cases. Even in a normal closed stack, space must be left for additions within a classified subject sequence. In open stack where books are continually removed from the shelves, and even more in open access where there must be room for a great deal of casual handling, from a fifth to a quarter of the shelf should be left empty, if only to make life tolerable for staff inserting returned books. This space allowance applies right up to the end of the life expectancy of the building; the notion that a space is left on each shelf for expansion, and that when these spaces are all filled the building is ready for replacement, is based on some of the woolliest thinking in the profession.

The table below gives a generally accepted estimate for shelves *three-quarters full*; because books vary so much in thickness all "averages per foot" must be vague; Other inconvenient details are ignored: a 900 mm (3 ft) shelf is usually between 1 in and 2 in shorter than that dimension, 3 ft do not really equal 900 mm, and so on. For general estimating purposes this table is accurate enough.

Number of books per shelf

Type of book	Number per 300 mm (1 ft) run of shelf	Number per 900 mm (3 ft) run of shelf
Children's books	10 to 12	30 to 36
Loan and fiction stocks in public libraries	8	24 to 25
Literature, history, politics and economics	7	21
Science, technology	6	18
Medicine, public documents and bound periodicals	5	15
Law	4	12
Averages	7	21

Fixed and adjustable shelving

It seems reasonable to suppose that to obtain the best use of space within each tier, adjustable shelves should be used—either infinitely adjustable by Vernier type fittings or, more usually, by inch divisions. Such shelves are normally used, but mainly from habit rather than clear thinking. The size range to be housed is not large: at least 90 per cent of books are less than 230 mm (9 in) high and most of the other 10 per cent will need special oversize shelving because of the greater depth of these books. Shelves can thus be fixed at intervals of slightly more than 230 mm (9 in) to hold the bulk of the book stock; 280 mm (11 in) centres are the most convenient.

Fixed shelving has the advantage of giving a neater and more regular appearance and in many cases it is cheaper. If a lending library uses shelving at 280 mm (11 in) shelf centres (height), with reference shelves on 300 mm (12 in) and encyclopaedias, etc, at 330 mm (13 in) (or both the latter on 330 mm (13 in)), it is surprising how little adjustability will be missed.

Adjustable shelving will definitely be needed in the following circumstances:

where the need for a single sequence of books to contain a large proportion of the library's stock is greater than the need to make the best possible use of space: for example, in a closed-access special library where books are added to stock in the order of receipt;

where the stock contains separate long runs of large and small volumes (eg bound periodicals and annuals) without any certainty that their location can remain fixed;

for housing bound volumes of newspapers: these should be laid flat and, because of the variation of thickness in volumes over the years, much space will be wasted unless shelves are adjustable. (Paradoxically such newspaper storage cases are seldom offered with adjustable shelves.)

Adjustable shelving allows greater flexibility, and in particular the opportunity to fit an extra shelf into each bay of popular books (especially fiction) without having to commit that bay to holding fiction for ever. On the other hand many experienced librarians would be surprised if they discovered just how seldom the vaunted flexibility was in fact used in their libraries, and what it had cost. The position is altered when "systems" shelving is used. Because these products are assembled from standard components they offer the economic advantages of mass production and they can give flexibility at no extra cost. (See chapter 12.)

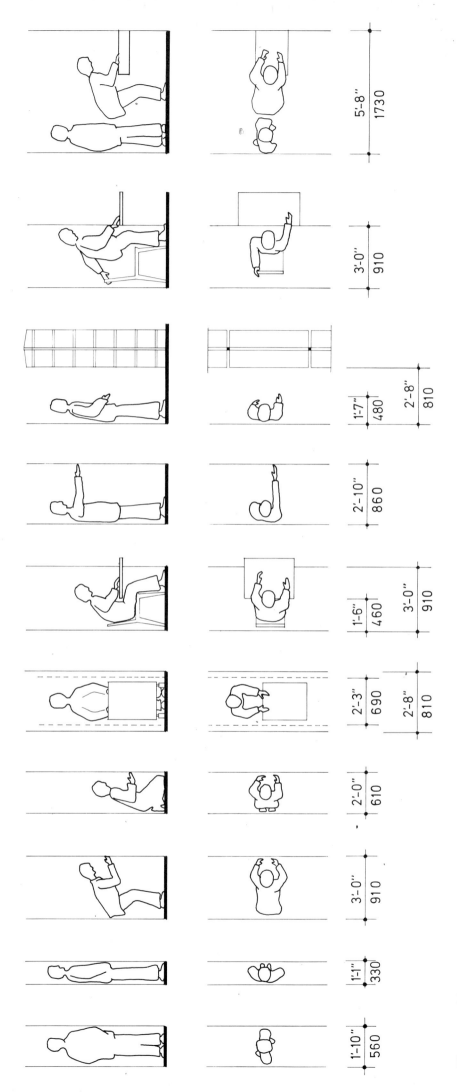

This page and facing page: Minimum clearances for various attitudes in shelving areas

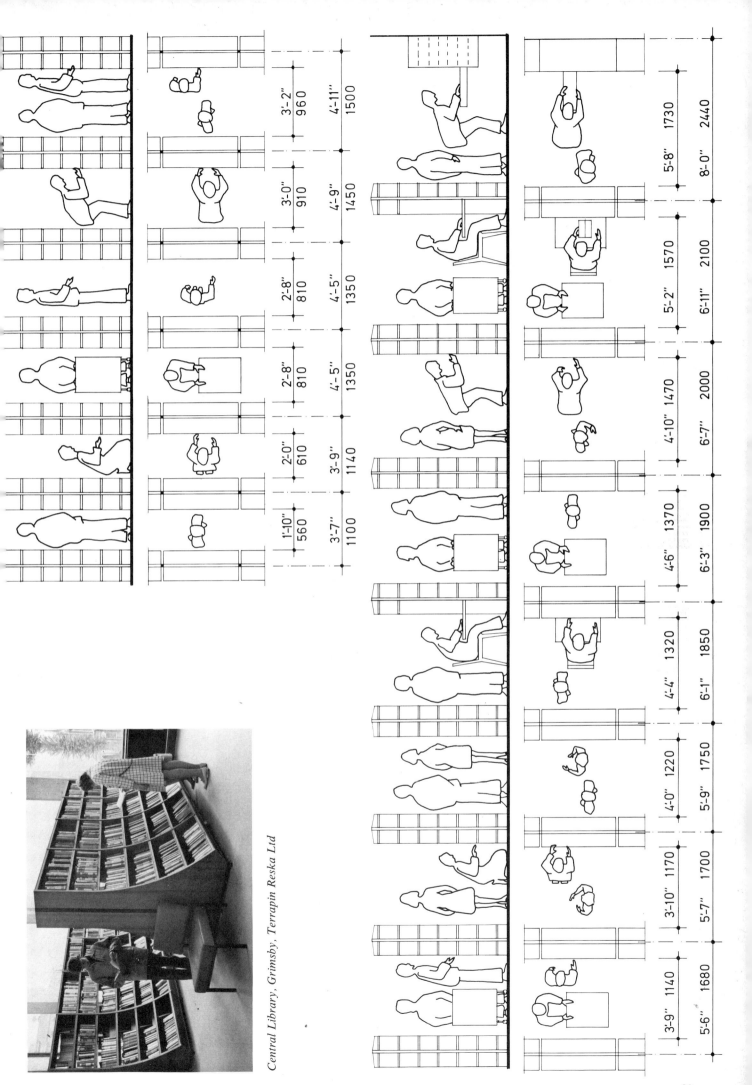

Central Library, Grimsby, Terrapin Reska Ltd

3'-2"	4'-11"
960	1500

3'-0"	4'-9"
910	1450

2'-8"	4'-5"
810	1350

2'-8"	4'-5"
810	1350

2'-0"	3'-9"
610	1140

1'-10"	3'-7"
560	1100

	3'-7"
	1100

5'-8"	8'-0"
1730	2440

5'-2"	6'-11"
1570	2100

4'-10"	6'-7"
1470	2000

4'-6"	6'-3"
1370	1900

4'-4"	6'-1"
1320	1850

4'-0"	5'-9"
1220	1750

3'-10"	5'-7"
1170	1700

3'-9"	5'-6"
1140	1680

Tilted shelves

Lower bookshelves can be tilted slightly upward so that the sloping book spines are easier to read. This is largely a matter of taste; there are proprietary bookcases of this kind on the market but, because they take up considerably more floor space, they are seldom used except in casual open-access conditions. The County Libraries Section of the Library Association states that "a rake of 150 mm (6 in) in the overall height of the shelves (ie the bottom shelf is set forward 150 mm (6 in), so that the whole bookcase slopes and all the shelves are slightly tilted) can be recommended as satisfactory and aesthetically pleasing; this does not cause books to slide back on painted shelves, but polished hardwood should be finished with a matt or eggshell finish." An extreme example of this is Grimsby Central Library where the lower shelves are quite heavily tilted, the shelf depths varying from 200 mm (8 in) on the top shelf to 690 mm (27 in) on the bottom (page 83).

Some may consider the effect grotesque and the upper shelves are certainly further away from the reader; the arrangement takes up space of course, but it is only fair to say that Grimsby reports favourable reader reaction to the experiment. A compromise is to have only the bottom shelf tilted, and this can be done, even in stack, at a smaller loss of space. Unless the lighting is particularly bad it is difficult to follow the reasoning of those who would do this in a formal stack at the price of reducing the aisle or placing stacks further apart.

Layout of shelving

Except in popular open-access rooms where the book shelving plays an important visual part in the internal environment, the aim is to house as many books as possible in conditions convenient to both staff and readers. It is very necessary, therefore, to take account of the human engineering elements; arbitrary recommendations are no substitute for a study of the measurements relating directly to those of the human body. The drawings on pp. 82–3 show better than any tables the distances, heights and depths which are convenient for readers.

These are the best conditions for reader use but the librarian may decide that some slight inconvenience may be acceptable to readers (for example, shelves starting lower and ending higher) in the interests of housing books more economically. The decision will depend on the expected clientele and upon the type of shelving; for this reason the housing requirements considered in detail later are dealt with under the separate headings of closed stack, open stack and open access.

It was suggested earlier that the architect should choose a structural grid related to the module most vital to his client's interest, and that this is the unit of shelving. Where large numbers of books have to be accommodated in stack conditions the positioning of the columns is perhaps the most important factor of all and this will have a very close relation to the structural grid. If a grid of 11 m (36 ft) can be chosen (an expensive and much-to-be-desired luxury), the columns will be so far apart that stack shelving distances will no longer be critical, but where such a large grid would produce an impossibly expensive structure then, if a standard 900 mm (3 ft) shelf is to be used and the stack centre-to-centre distance is to be 1375 mm (4 ft 6 in), the most suitable grid size is 7 m (22 ft 6 in) square. Because of the greater strength of tubular steel shelving, shelves of 1375 mm (4 ft 6 in) can now be used and these can be fitted into the same grid with a slight loss of efficiency; a larger grid, preferably 8·25 m (27 ft) square, would be an advantage. The architect and the structural engineer will have other factors to take into account, but in general the grid chosen should be a multiple of both 900 mm (3 ft) and 1375 mm (4 ft 6 in) (or of other shelf lengths which are to be used).

The Danish State Inspectorate recommends[9] a "lay-out module" of 3 m, using shelves 1 m long. This can be used with grids of 6 m, 9 m or 12 m; the idea is applied with ingenuity and the simple diagrams show spacings of shelving, furniture and equipment based on the 3 m square. Within this square the inspectorate distinguishes between three shelving conditions:

general open access: stack centres at 3 m, aisle width 2·56 m;
near-stack (open stack): stack centres at 2 m, aisle width 1·56 m;
near-stack (closed access): stack centres 1·56 m, aisle width 1·06 m.

These figures are designed for small, single-storey public libraries where there will seldom be columns to complicate the issue. Columns waste vital shelving space and the librarian will wish to see them as small in plan as possible; steel columns 200 mm (8 in) square have a great appeal to the librarian, but the architect will have to take structural strength and many other factors into consideration. In a 7 m (22 ft 6 in) grid square, columns should preferably be no wider than 450 mm (18 in) so that two columns cause the loss of no more than a single 900 mm (3 ft) tier in stack shelving. If the columns have to be as large as 760 mm (2 ft 6 in) square, then 7·3 m × 7·3 m (24 ft × 24 ft) is probably a better grid size. Square columns allow for a future change of direction of the stack run without loss of shelving space; if the columns have to be rectangular, the stacks should be arranged with the stacks as a whole running so that their ends are against the short sides of columns.

CLOSED STACK

This forms a major part of the book housing of national, large city and county libraries and may be required in a lesser degree by libraries of all kinds. The shelving will be arranged to make the maximum use of space and this will usually mean double-sided stacks, with single-sided stacks along walls. Because the distance, however small, by which stack-widths can be reduced will add to stack capacity (in theory at any rate), between-stack distances will be as narrow as possible, the deciding factor probably being access by book trolley. The minimum between-stack width is probably 600 mm (24 in) but this makes access difficult and, particularly where oversize books are shelved on lower portions of the stacks, 685 mm (27 in) is the minimum practicable figure.

Shelves can be fitted close to the floor, leaving only a very small space to keep the books clear of dust; the bottom space should be filled in to facilitate cleaning. The shelves may run close to the ceiling but shelving to an overall height of more than 2·3 m (7 ft 6 in) will mean that the highest book-holding shelf is about 1·9 m (6 ft 3 in) from the floor, therefore some members of the staff will need step-stools in order to reach these books. In theory this is no great inconvenience; in practice such stools get misplaced around the stack, block trolley routes and waste time. Tiers of eight shelves are therefore seldom convenient; moreover, deliberately to install a higher ceiling in order to allow increased shelving height may add to structural, heating and ventilating costs. Stack lighting is a crucial matter when shelving is to run close to the ceiling and is considered separately in chapter 15, on pages 144–6.

Because staff only are to have access to the shelving, provision of cross-aisles is less important than it is for readers. Each cross-aisle will, of course, reduce the amount of shelving available but too few aisles will waste staff time in walking around long unbroken stacks. A reasonable compromise is to have one cross-aisle for every other grid square; with a 5·5 m (18 ft) grid this will reduce the potential stacking by one-twelfth. With an 8·25 m (27 ft) square the reduction will be only one-eighteenth, but there will be a 16·5 m (54 ft) run of unbroken stack to be negotiated.

Within each size of grid there is a limited number of possible combinations of shelving (A and B facing); knowing the between-stack widths and the shelving requirements, the suitable one can be chosen. The plans are based on the recommended grid size of 6·9 m (22 ft 6 in); the following points have been assumed:

shelving 7 shelves high at 18 books per 900 mm shelf (6 books per foot because the books will usually be of a more "serious" nature, also to allow for insertions);

columns not more than 500 mm (18 in) square;

stacks (double-sided) 500 mm (18 in) deep.

Closed stack:
Imperial sizes

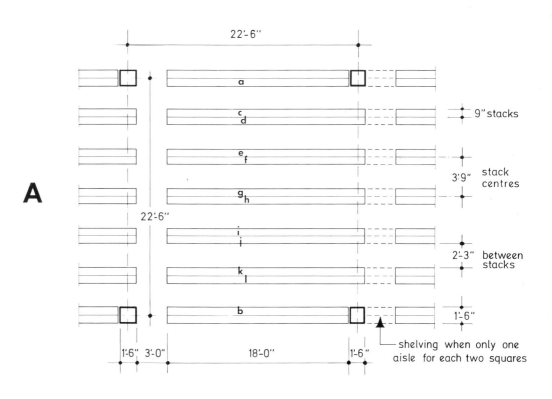

A **Example based on a grid of 6·9 m (22 ft 6 in)**
One 3 ft cross-aisle per grid square

2 single-sided stacks (a and b) each 18ft long = 36 ft ⎫
10 single-sided stacks (c to 1) each 19 ft 6 in ⎬ = 231 ft
 long = 195 ft ⎭

231 ft 7 shelves high = 1617 linear ft
1617 linear ft at 6 books per ft = 9702 books = 19 books/ft².

One 3 ft cross-aisle every other grid square
Extra shelving = 12 × 3 ft = 36 ft

36 ft 7 shelves high = 252 linear ft
252 linear ft at 6 books per ft = 1512 books every other square
= 756 books per square
9702 + 756 = 10 458 books
= 20½ books/ft².

B **Example based on a grid of 6·9 m (22 ft 6 in)**
One 3 ft cross-aisle per grid square

2 single-sided stacks (a and b) each 18 ft long = 36 ft ⎫
8 single-sided stacks (c to j) each 19 ft 6 in long = 156 ft ⎬ = 192 ft
⎭

192 ft 7 shelves high = 1344 linear ft
1344 linear ft at 6 books per ft = 8064 books = 16 books/ft².

One 3 ft cross-aisle every other grid square
Extra shelves = 10 × 3 ft = 30 ft

30 ft 7 shelves high = 210 linear ft
210 linear ft at 6 books per ft = 1260 books every other square
630 books per square
8064 + 630 = 8694 books
= 17 books/ft².

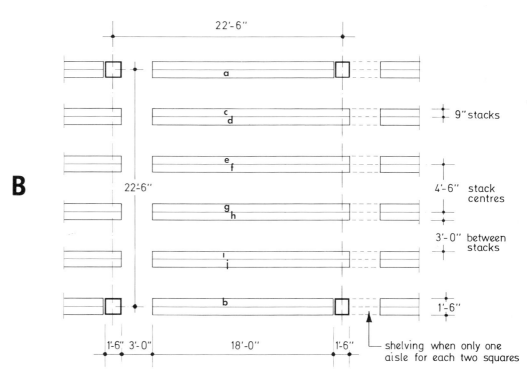

**Closed stack:
metric sizes**

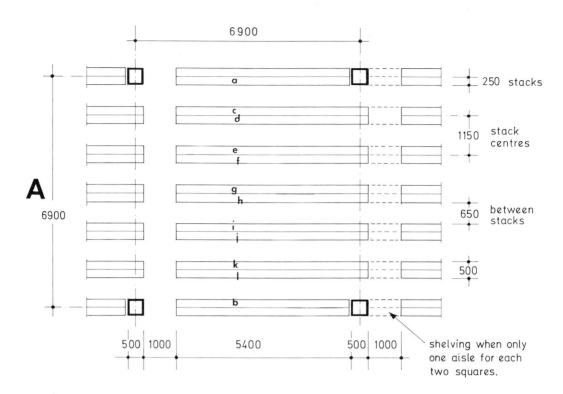

A Metric sizes based on a grid of 6·9 m (22 ft 6 in)
One 1 m cross-aisle per grid square

2 single-sided stacks (a and b) each 5·4 m long	= 10·8 m	
10 single-sided stacks (c to 1) each 5·9 m long	= 59 m	= 69·8 m

69·8 m 7 shelves high = 488·6 linear m
488·6 linear m at 20 books per m = 9772 books
= 204 books/m².

One 1 m cross-aisle every other grid square

Extra shelving = 12 × 1 m = 12 m
12 m 7 shelves high = 84 linear m
84 linear m at 20 books per m = 1 680 books every other square
= 840 books per square
9772 + 840 = 10 612 books
= 221 books/m².

B Metric sizes based on a grid of 6·9 m (22 ft 6 in)
One 1 m cross-aisle per grid square

2 single-sided stacks (a and b) each 5·4 m long	= 10·8 m	
8 single-sided stacks (c to j) each 5·9 m long	= 47·2 m	= 58 m

58 m 7 shelves high = 406 linear m
406 linear m at 20 books per m = 8 120 books
= 169 books/m².

One 1 m cross-aisle every other grid square

Extra shelving 10 × 1 m = 10 m
10 m 7 shelves high = 70 linear m
70 linear m at 20 books per m = 1 400 books every other square
= 700 books per square
8 120 + 700 = 8 820 books
= 184 books/m²

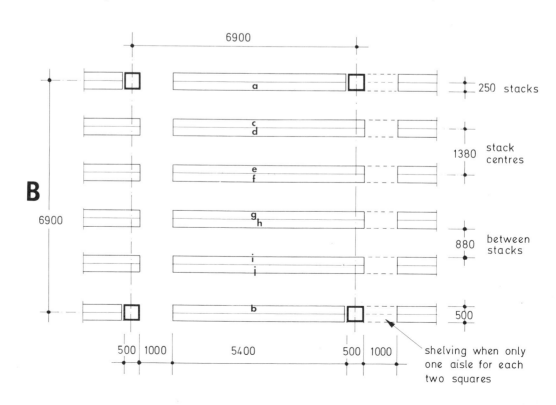

All possible grid sizes are not equally hospitable in this respect: the following are possible alternatives and their respective capacities:

Imperial sizes

Grid size (ft in)	Stack centres (ft in)	No of double-sided stacks*	Books per grid square		Books per ft²	
			One aisle per square	One aisle every other square	One aisle per square	One aisle every other square
18	3 7†	4	6174	6804	19	21
20	4	4	7014	7644	17½	19
24	4	5	10 458	11 214	18	19½
25	3 7†	6	12 810	13 692	20½	22
25	4 2	5	10 962	11 718	17½	19
25 6	3 8†	6	13 104	13 986	20	21½
27	3 10	6	13 986	14 868	18	20½

* Freestanding—includes the equivalent of the two single-sided stacks between the columns which form part of the same square for calculations.
† Almost—more acceptable with stacks only 405 mm (16 in) deep.

Metric sizes

Grid size (m)	Stack centres (m)	No of double-sided stacks	Books per grid square		Books per m² rule	
			One aisle per square	One aisle every other square	One aisle per square	One aisle every other square
6·5	1·1	4	6160	6860	204	226
6	1·2	4	6860	7560	191	210
7·2	1·2	5	10 276	11 116	198	214
7·5	1·25	5	10 780	11 620	192	207
7·7	1·1	6	12 992	13 972	219	237
8·4	1·2	6	14 364	15 344	204	217

Before making use of these figures the following important qualifications must be accepted.

The figures refer to the great bulk of bookstocks which can be housed on stacks seven shelves high, and this usually means with shelves at not more than 300 mm (12in) centres at the most.

Special spatial calculations have to be made for books too large or too deep to be shelved in this way.

If narrower stack centres are used, it will be necessary for some main aisles to be provided at 1375 mm (4 ft 6 in) minimum.

On the other hand it may be possible to fit more than the twenty books per linear metre (6 books per linear foot) which has been allowed for here; in little used stacks, or where additions to stock are rare or do not have to be inserted in a systematic sequence, the allowance could be twenty-three or twenty-four books per linear metre (eight books per linear foot), giving an increase of one third above these capacities.

The questions of shelving oversize books in both closed and open stack needs careful thought. If three sequences are tolerable it is possible to allow for certain tiers to have four shelves rather than seven, and for other tiers to be devoted to very large books. For the latter it is impossible to generalise; in Guildhall Library there is one book nearly 2 m (6 ft) high. Any book more than 500 mm (20 in) high should be housed flat; cases for such books will need a space allowance, usually against walls where the slightly increased depth will be hardly noticeable.

Shelf depth allowances for large books complicate the planning of large and regular stack areas. Poole, referring to shelf depths, says[10]: "... 80 per cent 200 mm (8 in) shelves, 15 per cent 250 mm (10 in) shelves and 5 per cent 300 mm (12 in) shelves." The 255 mm (10 in) books might be accommodated in backless 450 mm (18 in) double-sided stacks by overlapping onto the other side where books will, by the law of averages, be narrower, leaving only 5 per cent to be housed on 300 mm (12 in) depth shelving. It would save space to have the latter on the single-sided stacks which will almost certainly be installed against walls somewhere in the store

and where an additional small increase in depth from the wall will have little effect on space planning.

On the alternative spacings used in both open and closed stack examples, certain figures of books per m² or ft² have emerged, but because these stacks do not hold oversize books, to this extent the figures must necessarily be false for overall application. For this reason these examples cannot be quickly used to deduce the total stack floor area required from a given total bookstock. Perhaps the best method for doing that is the one almost forty years old now, proposed by Henderson[11] and known as the "cubook" formula. This has been more often quoted than understood:

"In estimating capacity then, the unit is a *hypothetical* book. It is important to bear constantly in mind the abstract nature of the unit, and not to confuse it with the actual book ... A cubook is the volume of space required to shelve the average book in a typical library." He took a "typical" reference library as one with 85 per cent of books under 290 mm (11½ in) high, 13 per cent between 290 mm (11½ in) and 480 mm (19 in) high and 2 per cent over 480 mm (19 in) high (shelved flat); he allowed 10 per cent of each shelf empty for ease of book-handling and produce a formula: "100 cubooks will occupy a standard 900 mm (3 ft) section or will run 33⅓ per foot of single-faced tier." To obtain the number of 900 mm (3 ft) tiers theoretically required to house the stock, therefore, it was necessary only to divide the total stock number by 100. By applying this formula to a stack shelving area with a 2300 mm (7 ft 6 in) ceiling and taking into account reasonable aisle widths 1325 mm (52 in), cross-aisles and an allowance for a section of the service core, he stated[12] that cubooks could be reduced to cubic feet by multiplying by 0·676 and to square feet by multiplying by 0·090. It is not convenient to translate his calculations into metric units but the result can be obtained by multiplying the "books per square foot" result by 10·76 to obtain the figure of "books per square metre".

These figures applied only in a "typical reference library" but

**Open stack:
metric sizes**

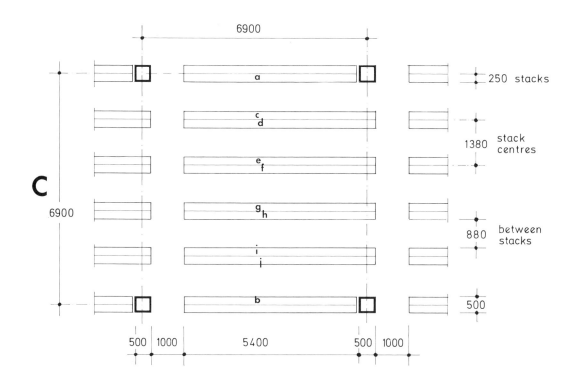

C Metric sizes based on a grid of 6·9 m (22 ft 6 in)

2 stacks (a and b) each 5·4 m long = 10·8 m ⎫
8 stacks (c to j)   each 5·9 m long = 47·2 m ⎬ = 58 m
⎭

58 m 7 shelves high = 406 linear m
406 linear m at 20 books per m = 8120 books
                          = 169 books/m²

D Metric sizes based on a grid of 6·9 m (22 ft 6 in)

2 stacks (a and b) each 5·4 m long = 10·8 m ⎫
6 stacks (c to h)   each 5·9 m long = 35·4 m ⎬ = 46 m
⎭

46 m 7 shelves high = 322 linear m
322 linear m at 20 books per m = 6440 books
                          = 134 books/m²

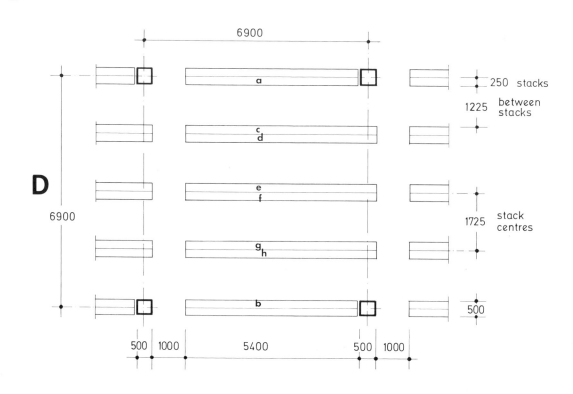

Open stack:
Imperial sizes

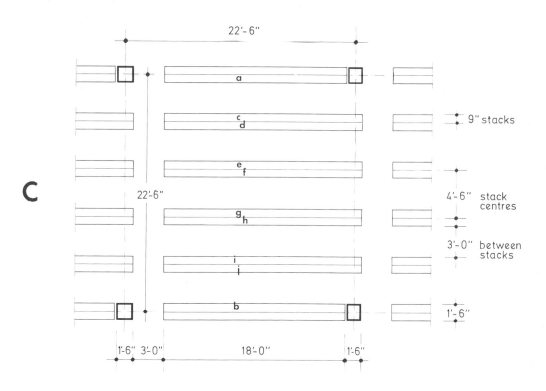

C **C** Example based on a grid of 6·9 m (22 ft 6 in)

2 stacks (a and b) × 18 ft each = 36 ft ⎫
8 stacks (c to j) × 19 ft 6 in each = 156 ft ⎬ = 192 ft

192 ft 7 shelves high = 1344 linear feet
1344 linear feet at 6 books per ft = 8064 books
= about 16 books/ft².

D Example based on a grid of 6·9 m (22 ft 6 in)

2 stacks (a and b) each 18 ft long = 36 ft ⎫
6 stacks (c to h) each 19 ft 6 in long = 117 ft ⎬ = 153 ft

153 ft 7 shelves high = 1071 linear feet
1071 linear ft at 6 books per ft = 6426 books
= about 12·7 books/ft².

D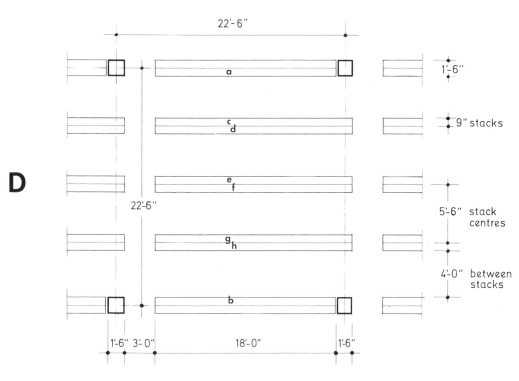

other formulae were provided for establishments which had higher or lower proportions of large books. The thesis is worth considering even now.

"For a rough estimate of the space in a normal stack to house a 'typical reference library' stock:

ascertain the number of 'standard' volumes to be housed [in a typical library no action, in an 'untypical' one by using one of the formulae];

reduce to cubooks;

for stack volume in cubic feet, multiply by 0·676;

for deck [ie stack floor] area in square feet multiply by 0·09."

Put at its crudest this states that a reasonable stack in a typical reference library can house 119·4 books/m² or 16·14 books/m³ (11·1 books/ft² or 1·5 books/ft³). Although this refers to cubooks, it also applies to actual books in a closely filled stack.

OPEN STACK

This is the most common form of shelving in university, and in growing use in college, libraries. It takes up more space than closed stack because more room must be left between stacks for readers to choose their books and for others to pass by. The minimum between-stack distance is 900 mm (3 ft)—ie 1375 mm (4 ft 6 in) centres—and where heavy use is to be expected 1225 mm (4 ft) between stacks—1680 mm (5 ft 6 in) stack centres—would be better.

Because the use is purposive rather than casual it is possible to shelve close to the floor, although one reader crouched low will block the passage-way; again the height of the top shelf must not exceed the comfortable reach of a short reader and step-stools are certainly not advisable. Because most of the readers are young students who will have little difficulty with high and low shelving it is usual to have seven shelves to a tier to a top height of 2300 mm

Imperial sizes

Grid size (ft in)	Stack centres (ft in)	No of double-sided stacks	Books per grid square (one aisle per square)*	Books per ft² (one aisle per square)
18	4 6	3	4914	15
20	5	3	5586	14
24	4 9	4	8694	15
25	5	4	9114	14½
25 6	5 1	4	9324	14
25 6	4 3†	5	11 214	17
27	5 5	4	9954	13½
27	4 6	5	11 970	16½

* Freestanding—includes the equivalent of the two single-sided stacks between columns which form part of the same square for calculations.
† If stacks are only 16 in deep the between-stack distance would be 2 ft 11 in.

Metric sizes

Grid size (m)	Stack centres (m)	No of sided sided stacks	Books per grid square (one aisle per square)	Books per m² (one aisle per square)
5·6	1·4	3	5012	160
6	1·5	3	5460	152
7·25	1·45	4	8610	164
7	1·55	4	9310	155
7·8	1·56	4	9380	154
	1·3	5	11 290	186
8·4	1·68	4	10 220	145
	1·4	5	12 292	174

Note These figures apply only when the following two qualifications are accepted:
They deal only with books which can be shelved seven shelves high and twenty to a metre and six to a foot and a separate space allocation must be made for taller or deeper books.
Main aisles may be necessary if very heavy use if expected or if the stack area is large. Such aisles should be 1500 mm wide (5 ft).

Metric sizes with approximate equivalent in feet and inches

Grid size (m)	(ft in)	No of double-sided stacks	Stack centres (m)	(ft in)	Aisle widths (mm)	(ft in)
5·5	18 1	4	1·1	3 7+	600	2 0−
5·6	18 4+	3	1·4	4 7+	900	3 0−
6	19 9	3	1·5	4 11+	1000	3 3+
		4	1·2	3 11+	700	2 4−
6·9	22 8−	3	1·725	5 8−	1225	4 0+
		4	1·38	4 6+	880	2 11−
		5	1·15	3 9+	650	2 2−
7·2	23 7½	5	1·2	3 11+	700	2 4−
7·25	23 9+	4	1·45	4 9+	950	3 1+
7·5	24 8	5	1·25	4 1+	750	2 5+
7·7	25 3	6	1·1	3 7	600	2 0−
7·75	25 5+	4	1·55	5 1+	1050	3 5+
7·8	25 7+	4	1·56	5 1+	1060	3 6−
		5	1·3	4 3+	800	2 8−
8·4	27 7−	4	1·68	5 6+	1130	3 8+
		5	1·4	4 7+	900	3 0−
		6	1·2	3 11+	700	2 4

(7 ft 6 in) with a bottom shelf 150 mm (6 in) from the floor. Because of heavy use, it is preferable to have one cross-aisle for each grid square, the loss from the gross figure being, in a 5·5 m (18 ft) grid square, one-sixth and in an 8·25 m square, one-ninth. On the recommended grid of 6·86 m (22 ft 6 in) square the two most appropriate layouts and resultant capacities are given opposite:

Again all possible grid sizes are not equally hospitable: the following are possible alternatives and their capacities:

(In open stack conditions, calculations of book capacity for whole floors is complicated by the need for wider main aisles; how many will depend on the shape of the room. In the examples above a cross-aisle of 1 m (3 ft 3 in) has been allowed for each grid square, but a main aisle every, say, four squares will make a small reduction in the overall capacity. The shelving of materials in college and research library stacks is discussed in great detail by Metcalf[13] and this is essential reading).

Edinburgh University Library

Periodicals shelving within stack

Bound periodicals are treated as books. The various methods of shelving unbound periodicals are dealt with in chapter 9, but if they are to be kept in piles, bundles or boxes on stack shelves, there should be a greater distance between stacks because a shelf of periodicals is more frequently used than a shelf of books and because readers take longer to find an issue than a book. A 1200 mm (4 ft) between-stack distance (1675 mm (5 ft 6 in) stack centres) is the very least that should be allowed.

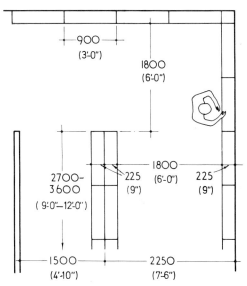

Recommended minimum plan dimensions in open access book stack area

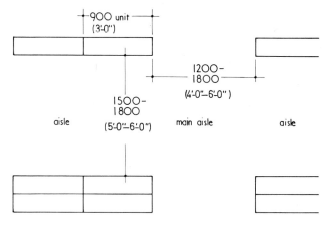

Recommended minimum plan dimensions in open access book stack area with shelving arranged in alcoves

OPEN ACCESS

This method, in which books are spread out widely, attracting readers to browse round them, often in great numbers, is the most space-consuming of all but it must form a large part of public lending, school and hospital libraries, and will be used to some extent in all libraries. The shelving here is not only a practical way of housing books but is itself one of the most important elements in the interior design of a room. The architect will therefore have strong feelings about the height, layout and material of the shelves; he will visualise them filled with brightly coloured books

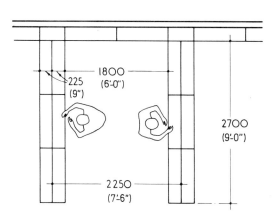

Minimum clearances in reading rooms

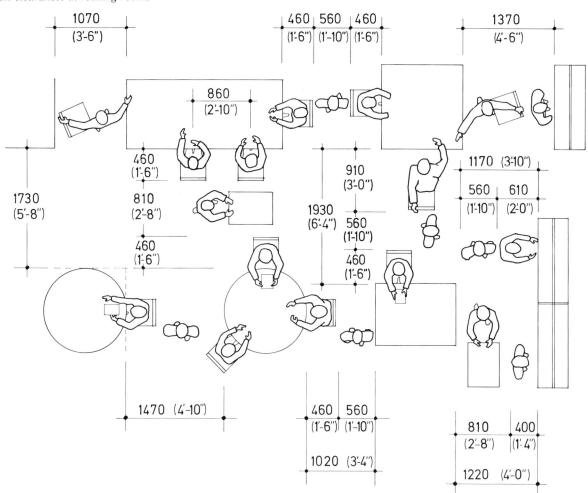

in plastic jackets. The shelving will be arranged informally and its relationship with the reading areas will be very much a matter of individual design. The shelving in British libraries is usually dispersed throughout the room with browsing areas left between groups of bookcases, whereas in Scandinavia (and even more in the US) the practice is to have areas of semi-formal shelving separate from larger reading areas.

The space left around bookcases will naturally vary widely according to the intensity of expected use. The diagrams below show the minimum that should be allowed.

Island book cases cause less congestion than alcoves in busy libraries but they require more space around them. In less formal reading areas, space will have to be allowed for readers to consult books on nearby shelves, and also for trolleys to be pushed between tables. This drawing shows a typical layout in a combined study and browsing area.

The Danish State Library Inspectorate recommends[14] a "browsing space" of about 900 mm (3 ft) in front of all shelving and a "passage space" of about 760 mm (2 ft 6 in) beyond that. This implies a minimum space between facing bookshelves of 2560 mm (8 ft 6 in); with 440 mm (1 ft 6 in) deep double-sided stacks it makes up the 3 m (10 ft) "layout module".

The inspectorate refers to a "standard shelf unit", a bay with a total height of 1600 mm to 1850 mm (5 ft to 6 ft), with a shelf 20 mm ($1\frac{3}{4}$ in) thick. The bottom shelf is 400 mm (16 in) from the floor. The adult shelving has five shelves to a height of 1850 mm (6 ft) and the children's shelving four shelves to a height of 1600 mm (5 ft 6 in): the between-shelf distance is given as 270 mm ($10\frac{1}{2}$ in). On such a tier 1 m wide, the capacity (allowing 20 per cent of unoccupied space) is given as 165 volumes per five-shelf tier. If such a

range of shelving is at 3 m (10 ft) centres, then a space 3 m (10 ft × 1 m (3 ft 3 in) will include two such single-faced tiers and the distance between will accommodate 330 volumes; this gives a capacity of 110 volumes/m² (10 volumes/ft²).

Later in the report[15] the inspectorate says:

"Sample surveys have shown that in libraries of the size under consideration (serving populations from about 5 000 to about 25 000) the practical factors of daylight, traffic, and furniture other than shelving, account for about 40 per cent of the floor space in a well designed library area. A working measure of the capacity in the lending library can thus be reckoned as follows:

"110 volumes/m² less 40 per cent = about 65 volumes/m² [6 volumes/ft²] of floor space."

REFERENCES

[1] REED, J. B. Handbook of special librarianship and information work. Edited by W. Ashworth. ASLIB, London, 1962, 2nd editions, pp 237–264

[2] Metcalf. Op cit, pp 151–157

[3] POOLE, FRAZER G. The selection and evaluation of library bookstacks. *In Library Trends*, April 1965, p 419

[4] Plovgaard. Op cit, p 39

[5] LIBRARY ASSOCIATION. School library resource centres: recommended standards for policy and provision. The Association, London, 1970

[6] ANTHONY, L. J. Library planning. *In Handbook of special librarianship and information work*. ASLIB, London, 1967, 3rd edition, pp 309–364

[7] Poole. Op cit, p 420

[8] LIBRARY ASSOCIATION, COUNTY LIBRARIES SECTION County branch libraries: report and recommended standards. The Association, London, 1958

[9] Plovgaard. Op cit, pp 58–64

[10] Poole. Op cit, p 419

[11] HENDERSON, ROBERT W. Tiers, books and stacks. *In Library Journal*, v 59, 1934, pp 382–383

[12] Ibid. Bookstack planning with the cubook. *In Library Journal*, v 61, 1936, pp 52–54

[13] Metcalf. Op cit, chapter 8

[14] Plovgaard. Op cit, p 41

[15] Ibid, p 43

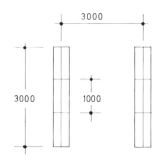

Recommended minimum space between facing bookshelves

9 Layouts and critical sizes: compact shelving

SHELVING BOOKS

Desperate measures

The demand for more space to house books is ubiquitous, eternal and evergrowing. The high cost of building, the shortage of space, with the virtual certainty of demand increasing year by year, force the librarian to take very seriously indeed any method which seems to offer space economies in shelving. He will therefore be most attracted by proprietary systems which offer space savings of the order of 100 per cent to 150 per cent. Even those which make more modest claims will still appeal, but he must first take a look at the overall situation.

Space savings in housing large quantities of books can be made in various ways but always at a price. The simplest and most quoted example is reducing aisle widths from 900 mm (36 in) to 550 mm (22 in); this produces a saving of nearly 40 per cent and leaves a "practicable" aisle. The price to be paid for this is inconvenience to users over the life of the library—no small matter. Many other examples of this kind were made familiar by the work of Rider[1], and there is a copious literature on the subject[2,3].

Where the situation in an existing library is really desperate the librarian has it within his power to rearrange his books so that they take up less space than they do when housed upright on shelves in the normal way. Before turning to the more elaborate methods, mention should be made of the simple ones:

Shelving from floor to ceiling. In an existing library where ceiling height allows this means fittings extensions onto uprights so that more shelves can be arranged above existing shelves.

Eliminating the space allowed on each shelf for book movement: this is possible only with a static book stock, or at the expense of trouble for the staff.

Shelving a second row of books behind the first. Very inconvenient and possibly calling for deeper shelving, but it can be done in a desperate situation where the shelves are deep enough, or the aisles wide enough for deeper shelves to be installed.

Shelving books on the fore-edge so that more shelves can be fitted into a tier. Again a certain minimum shelf and aisle depth are required and the inconvenience to users is obvious.

Sizing (see page 27).

These are desperate measures and it is unlikely that a new library will be planned around any such methods.

In the past ingenious ideas for space-saving shelving equipment have ranged from rotary cases suspended on overhead tracks to shelving books on endless bands. The compact-shelving methods described below are examples of recent proprietary products. Other, improved, ideas may already have replaced them but they have in common the advantage of space saving in different degrees and the following disadvantages:

they cost much more than ordinary shelving;

they may call for extra floor loading to accommodate the weight;

they are less easy and quick to use than standard shelving units;

unless special safeguards are incorporated, books may be damaged.

For these reasons such shelving is usually confined to specially designed stack areas accessible only to staff: in this capacity some types have been widely installed in libraries of all kinds.

Compact shelving units

In a detailed (and perhaps over-elaborate) survey of compact shelving Gawrecki[4] distinguishes between:

revolving shelves (better known in the UK as hinged shelf units);

sliding drawers;

sliding shelves (more usually known as rolling stacks).

The first two methods are chiefly seen in America: the third is universal.

Gawrecki's book contains sections by other authorities on compact shelving which show that such fittings have been devised and installed in libraries for very many years with varying success. Tracing the history of these experiments leads one to believe that human ingenuity and engineering skill will produce improved versions and that there is much to be gained by studying the problem. It is therefore not enough for the librarian to survey only what can be obtained today from equipment manufacturers; it may be that, in special circumstances, ingenuity can devise a specific design that will produce really worth-while space savings. Each year that passes makes this matter more urgent: each rise in the cost of library space alters the economic balance of equipment cost and space saving.

Hinged shelf units

The simplest forms are:

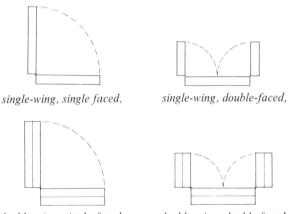

single-wing, single faced,　　*single-wing, double-faced,*

double-wing, single-faced,　　*double-wing, double faced.*

Many variants of these basic principles are possible, and an even greater variation of claims for space saving have been made from them. Without careful comparison of all factors involved it is impossible to dogmatise, but Gawrecki believes that of all these methods the greatest space saving is obtainable by the use of double-wing, double-faced methods.

Various systems have been marketed in recent years, including the "Com-Pac-Case" made by Art Metal Inc which used the double-wing method. Perhaps the system most often quoted is that produced by Snead & Co for the Center for Research Libraries in Chicago.

Another Snead system consists of four rows of bookshelf units with the two outer rows hinged to swing out from the centre shelves, which are fixed. The hinging mechanism is so designed that when a hinged unit is fully open it projects only 400 mm (1 ft 4 in) into the aisle, and with a recommended aisle dimension of

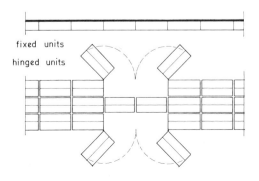

fixed units

hinged units

Four rows of shelf units with outer two hinged to swing open

1 m (3 ft 3 in) there is space for people to pass while the bookshelves are being used. Compared with ordinary book stacks with 200 mm (8 in) shelves and 900 mm (3 ft) wide aisles, capacity is increased by 66 per cent.

Sliding drawers
The best known examples of these are from American manufacturers and there are two basic divisions:
The first, with "single-headed" shelving, consists of drawers which pull outwards into aisles, each drawer holding two rows of books, foredge to foredge, and a shorter front-facing shelf which is accessible from outside the stack when the drawer is recessed.

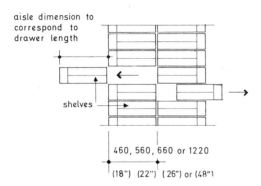

Drawer type book shelf units

This system is made by the Hamilto Manufacturing Co under the name Hamilto Compo Stack. Another such system but with variants comes from C. S. Brown & Co.
The second, the "double-headed' type, is used in the Stor-mor system from W. R. Ames. Here the two foredge to foredge rows of books are shelved in a long drawer which can be withdrawn from either side of its stack. There is no shelf forming a front.

Drawer type shelving withdrawable from either side

If installations such as these are used for large book stocks their very success must cause considerable engineering problems. The mass of closely-shelved books must be placed either at the lowest level of the building or directly above the loadbearing columns or girders; this in itself will limit planning freedom. In addition to the extra floor loading there will be special lighting requirements because of the change of angle constantly presented by the movable stacks.
This equipment is necessarily of very heavy construction and fairly complex, ball-bearing slides being essential. The systems are not common outside the us but their space-saving potential is not negligible. They have other advantages in that it may be possible for such space-saving fittings to be installed within existing bookcase frames, provided that they are strong enough and of the right design.
At their best sliding drawer methods have a less impressive space-saving ratio than hinged units. So many other considerations are involved however that this comparison should not be pressed.

Sliding and rolling cases
A sliding cabinet was used in the Iron Library of the British Museum many years ago and the system then used is similar to one which is still offered today. The cases slid on overhead rails parallel to the range of fixed shelving in front of which they were placed.

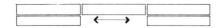

Single-sided sliding shelves

In a similar way the Conserv-a-file system developed by Supreme Equipment and Systems Corporation uses a set of shelves along the face of existing shelving, the front set being one unit shorter than the rear. The front set can slide from side to side exposing a back shelf when needed; the back shelf can slide forward for easy access. This method will give a large increase in shelving without increasing aisle widths, but at the expense of somewhat elaborate equipment. Naturally, its use in large stack installations is limited. The two most commonly used types of rolling stacks are those which roll parallel to their length, and those which roll at right angles to it.

Parallel rollers These have been provided in a large number of libraries for many years, the cases being either suspended from rails or running on tracks. A simple one is the Rolstore system produced by Acrow (Engineering) Ltd. Single-sided shelf units slide on rails in the floor and may be freestanding up to 2200 mm (7 ft 3 in) high, after which a steadying guide rail is required at the top. The units are a standard 900 mm (3 ft) long and arranged up to three units deep. The back row is continuous and fixed while the two sliding rows must omit one unit each to allow access. The units are propelled by hand.

Rolstore compact shelving

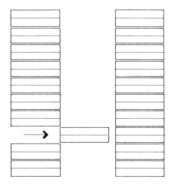

Parallel roller cases

This principle is more effectively used in closely packed stacks where one of a row of cases can be pulled out for access, from either side. Luxfer Ltd offers steel cases of this kind; the cases are mounted on wide treads with ball-bearing rollers and when closed form a solid block.
One outstanding advantage of this system is that it may be used in any library area with a single floor level as it requires neither tracks nor overhead support.

Right-angle rollers This is the principle now in most common use for compact shelving. The stacks run at right angles to their length, leaving a gap in the solid rank of cases; the cases are rolled (by hand or by power) so that the "adjustable" gap allows access to the required shelves. These are made by several firms including Acrow, Glover, Luxfer, Norwood Steel, Bruynzeel.

The various proprietary units move by means of wheels fixed to the chassis, running on rails either embedded in the floor screed or mounted upon the floor surface. To obtain savings of the proportions referred to above, the number of gangways in proportion to the number of stacks must be low and the stacks themselves must be long: this will usually mean that the stacks must be power-operated or, at least power-assisted. This can be done either by pneumatic rams at the base of the units or by built-in electric motors with chain or cable drive. These power-operated stacks include safety devices which halt the movement when any obstacle is encountered. The more recent introduction of cases with ratchets in their bases keying into floor tracks, operated by star-wheel handles on case ends has altered the balance between hand and power operation. The drive is so low-geared that they can be moved with very little effort.

Because all the units running at right angles to their length will fit closely together they may have rubber strips along the stack uprights so that books which protrude slightly from the shelves will not be damaged; other advantages offered by this fitment are exclusion of dust and fire resistance.

Hand-operated stacks, with or without hand levers, will naturally be restricted to shorter length because of the inertia factor, but they can be surprisingly easy to move; their advantage is that they are cheaper and less liable to mechanical breakdown.

Such systems obviously have a great deal to offer and they are already in general use. They will normally be confined to storage areas and attention will have to be paid to the very heavy loading; each manufacturer will be able to supply weight figures. An obvious solution is to install rolling stacks in basement areas. Once again size and positioning of columns are critical if the full advantage of the system is to be obtained.

The savings offered are very well illustrated by the example shown in the advertisement issued by J. Glover & Sons: their Stormor system (type 1), which has been available for over thirty years, gives an increase in these circumstances of nearly 50 per cent, while their Ingold-Compatus system (type 2) which they brought to this country in 1954, increases storage capacity in these circumstances by 131 per cent. The firm claims that this method offers savings from 90 per cent to 150 per cent in ordinary library storage.

The following examples taken at random of an area, say 7·3 × 3·65 m (24 ft × 12 ft) show how the amount of storage is increased by the use of their mobile storage systems.

Acron automatic rolling stacks

1	2	3	4	5	6	7	8
GANGWAY							
9	10	11	12	13	14	15	
16	17	18	19	20	21	22	
23	24	25	26	27	28	29	30

1	2	3	4	5	6	7	8
9	10	11	12	13	14	15→	
16	17	18	19	20	21	22→	
GANGWAY							
23	24	25	26	27	28	29→	
30	31	32	33	34	35	36→	
37	38	39	40	41	42	43	44

In this store ordinary static shelving is employed which requires a gangway to each row. This method is uneconomic as much valuable space is wasted in corridors. 30 bays of shelving 900 × 450 mm (36 in × 18 in) are recommended.

Consider also the energy expended by operators in walking to and from and the cost of building space per bay.

The Stormor Mobile Storage System requires one central gangway on each side of which are placed two or more rows of mobile units in front of fixed shelving. In this case 44 bays of shelving are provided each 900 × 450 mm (36 in × 18 in) which gives an increase of nearly 50 per cent. Access is quicker and energy expended is reduced while building cost per bay is also reduced.

Gloverax bookstacks mobilised by Ingold Compactus, Chichester County Library

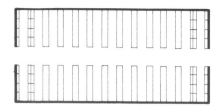

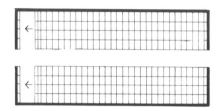

Diagrams show first the layout of fixed racks and then the same space after conversion to motorised Ingold-Compactus and giving an increase of 131 per cent thus avoiding the necessity to extend the building by 237 m² (2 550 ft²).

Horizontal shelving with sliding shelves for large books, Libraco Ltd

Where the area is not designed specifically to accommodate special compact storage devices the gain cannot be as great but Bruynzeel claim that their rolling stack Storage Equipment will fit 35 000 books—624 volumes/m² (fifty-eight volumes/ft²), a gain of "over 50 per cent".

The overall savings, and their effect upon economic considerations, are less easy to compute; Muller[5] and Hill[6] both discuss this question. Compact shelving is always more expensive than conventional shelving and it may be that real cost savings are possible only with a large installation in a building of regular shape with open floors.

See also chapter 14 which includes methods of mechanical retrieval of books; such systems can be used effectively only if the stack is designed specifically for the purpose. The question of the design of shelving is considered in chapter 12, page 123.

SHELVING OTHER MATERIALS

In every library there will be materials other than the normal run of printed books; in research libraries these may form a high proportion of the stock and their shelving problems must be considered according to their different forms:

Very large books
Bound newspapers, atlases, "elephant folios" and so on are best shelved flat because of the great strain on their bindings when they stand upright. A very few may be so large as to call for special accommodation, but generally shelves can be 900 mm (3 ft) long, and so form part of normal shelving stacks, or 600 mm (2 ft) long, thus saving space. The shelves must be at least 450 mm (18 in) deep); it is better if each large volume can have a shelf to itself, the shelves being arranged at from 75 mm to 100 mm (3 in to 4½ in) centres, according to the depth of the book; here adjustable shelving is essential. Because of the wear on the covers of such heavy books when they are slid out of fixed shelves it is preferable to have, either pull-out trays (with stops to prevent them coming right out), or rollers so that the books can be moved out easily.

Because of the great weight of such books it is difficult for these shelves to be used above 1 250 mm (4 ft) from the floor, and rather than waste stack shelving it is better for special low cases to be built. These can have sloping tops so that the books can be consulted *in situ*; the slopes should run 1 m to 1 150 mm (3 ft 3 in to 3 ft 9 in) from the floor and should have upstands along the front edges

Horizontal shelving for large books, the American School in London (Library Design and Engineering Ltd)

to prevent the volumes sliding off. Such heavy volumes, if in constant use, will soon wear the surface of the case tops so it is advisable to use steel or good plastic laminates for the top surfaces.

Very small books
Those less than 75 mm (3 in) square are best kept in boxes of normal book size; the boxes are shelved as books.

Paperbacks
Some libraries, particularly college libraries which cater for students who are not "bookish" may find it tactically valuable to keep stocks of paperback books in order to encourage reading among those for whom this is the only familiar book form. If the paperbacks have been laminated into stiff covers they present little problem, but if they are used in their limp form, special shelving arrangements may be needed. Display cases have been designed so that the books may be shown face forwards so that the most can be made of the attraction of the pictorial covers.

Newspaper readers' slopes, City Business Library, City of London

Newspaper file within reading table, the American School in London (Library Design and Engineering Ltd)

Current use of newspapers

Because newspapers are large and limp the best method is to have each issue held in its own transparent stiff cover but few libraries can afford the very large amount of space this method needs. There is still much to be said for the old-fashioned newspaper slope, each paper being spread out and held under a centre clip or clamping rod. Crude and space consuming as this may seem, it has the advantage of confining users to a limited space and is acceptable except where current issues of newspapers are used for continuous study. Other methods include placing the folded paper in a special shelving rack or the suspended filing system where a stick is placed in the centre of the paper, serving as a stop on its filing rack. All these methods have been in use for many years; none successfully combines convenience in use with efficiency in shelving. The field is open for an inventive designer.

Current issues of periodicals

These form a large and very important part of the stock of many types of library; all libraries feature them prominently, and the major problem is not of housing, but of eye-catching display of thousands of journals for immediate use. The first step must be selection according to frequency of use.

Redcar Library

Most-used titles will be displayed (preferably with individual transparent covers) in reading areas; this is of course extremely space-consuming. They can be housed on special display shelves of which there are numerous designs or on tilted shelves within runs of systems shelving units. More space-saving are units which hold magazines face forward on slopes at an angle to the reader.

An enterprising designer can create such a fitting as part of another piece of library furniture. More conventional cases can have the advantage of providing storage space behind each issue for immediate back numbers, the "home space" of each journal being indicated by having the title lettered on the face of the slopes where it will be covered by the issue itself when it is shelved.

Bromsgrove College of Further Education

University of Bath Library, Library Design and Engineering Ltd

Combined display and file unit for periodicals, Keele's of Hadleigh

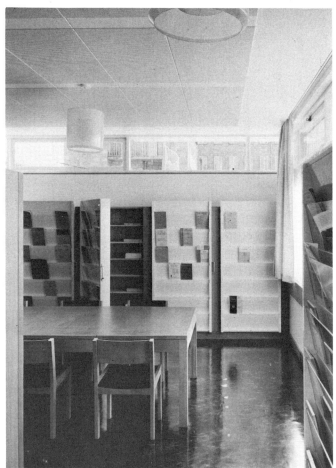

University of Aberdeen Science Library

Horizontal Periodical File, Serota Ltd

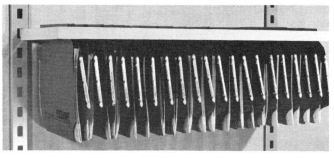

Lateral pamphlet file in systems shelving, Library Design and Engineering Ltd

Architects have tackled the problem imaginatively, a solution for both finding space for the periodicals and spreading out their users, has been to place current issues on single shelves running around otherwise unusable areas, under windows or around guard rails. Less used titles can be housed in individual holders shelved either vertically as if they were very narrow books, or horizontally. These take up much less space but the self-advertising feature of the colourful cover is lost.

Back numbers of periodicals
These are difficult to house effectively because of their ambivalent character; the same title can be in urgent and intense demand as it arrives hot from the press and subject to intermittent recall over a number of years, by which time it has been joined by thousands of its fellows. Because of the growing need for delivery of the required issue, not to the requesting reader but to the photocopying centre, where the needed article will be copied (the issue being returned direct to the shelves) there is a tendency to leave more periodicals unbound. Bound volumes, the traditional method of retaining long runs of periodicals, are less convenient to photocopy. This matter is very much affected by the ever-increasing availability of back runs of periodicals in microform with its great advantages

in reproduction.
Unbound issues can be kept in open-sided boxes, which can be very cheap, or tied up in bundles, which are awkward for access; if loose issues are left unenclosed and piled loosely on the shelves they tend to stray.

Bound volumes
Because these are in book form they present little problem for shelving. The length of the runs may lead the librarian to allow fixed shelving for them, but note should be taken of the tendency of periodicals, even long-established ones, to change their format with disconcerting frequency. The main decision is whether bound volumes of a periodical shall be available close to the current issues in a reading area, or whether it is practicable to use the more economical plan of putting all bound volumes in stack.
It can at least be assumed in most libraries that runs of bound periodicals will seldom be required for browsing—except perhaps in art or history departments.

Where should indexes and periodicals be shelved?
Only experience of relative use and judgment of space priorities can decide this question. General periodical indexes will certainly

be housed in the main bibliographical areas; some specialist libraries also keep index volumes to individual periodicals there: for full efficiency these should duplicate the indexes which must be bound in with the periodicals themselves.

Pamphlets and reports
These are particularly difficult to handle: any of individual importance may be fitted into a case with transparent covers and shelved in its subject sequence as a book. The chief difficulty with this method is that the spine is thin and they may be hard to find. If pamphlets form a finite series they can of course be bound and shelved as books. Perhaps the most usual method of shelving is in special pamphlet boxes made to the appropriate size and shelved as books. Vertical files, sometimes arranged at right angles to the reader rather than facing him, are used to hold pamphlets but present a separate subject sequence for readers to search; such files, when freely used by readers, soon get out of order. Suspended filing within the cases is of course much more satisfactory than files standing upright because of the pamphlets' propensity to slither down; moreover, except for holding numbers of fairly small items and keeping limp files without damage, normal vertical file cases are extremely inefficient in their use of space. A normal vertical file case 450 mm × 700 mm × 1200 mm (1 ft 6 in × 2 ft 4 in × 4 ft) will occupy little over half of the possibly 2300 mm (7 ft 6 in) of usable vertical space; lateral files, with dimensions similar to a double-sided bookcase 900 mm × 450 mm × 2200 mm (3 ft × 1 ft 6 in × 7 ft), will hold up to three times the number of pamphlets or reports which vertical file cases would hold and are just as easily accessible.

For pamphlets in heavy demand, various office-equipment firms have produced display files while lateral filing can be incorporated in systems shelving units. When the immediate pressure has passed, the pamphlets can revert to storage by one of the less space consuming methods.

Picture collections
These are a growing feature in libraries. If framed, pictures can be stored vertically on the floor in areas with close vertical divisions; if unframed, they can be filed horizontally in solander boxes of suitable size. The great difficulty is to arrange for display so that the pictures can be selected ready framed for borrowing; where many readers will attend to choose there is little alternative to individual wall hanging, expensive of space as it is; hinged or sliding accommodation offers much greater economy with some freedom to inspect and choose.

Sliding frames for picture storage, **Sculthorps Art-Utilities Ltd**

Films
Reels are stored in cardboard or metal containers and should be kept in metal drawers or cases, partitioned to hold each reel neatly.

Microforms
This is by far the fastest growing of all methods of storing information. Numerous different organisations are issuing material in this way and there is a great variety of sizes and forms. The basic division is between transparencies and opaques.

Transparencies Reel microfilm in libraries is usually either 16 mm or 35 mm, the latter being much the more common. Both come in 100 ft reels and each roll is normally kept in a cardboard box. These boxes can be filed as books on narrow shelves 105 mm apart, in pigeon holes, or in vertical file drawers. A cabinet 660 mm × 760 mm (2 ft 2 in wide × 2 ft 6 in deep) of normal vertical file height will hold 675 rolls of 35 mm or 125 rolls of 16 mm film. The 70 mm, 105 mm and larger sizes are used chiefly for engineering drawings and similar large documents and are not normally library material.

Short lengths of microfilm can be put in envelopes, particularly in transparent envelopes 125 mm × 205 mm (5 in × 8 in) which offer both protection and speed of inspection; these will be filed upright in drawers. Microfilm frames are also found as parts of aperture cards whose sizes vary widely but which can be filed like catalogue cards.

Microfiche is in stiff rectangular form although transparent. The most usual sizes are 90 mm × 120 mm ($3\frac{1}{2}$ in × $4\frac{3}{4}$ in) 75 mm × 125 mm (3 in × 5 in), and 100 mm × 150 mm (4 in × 6 in). All can be filed as cards in drawers of the appropriate size but should be placed within individual protective envelopes. A recent invention is the desk-top microfiche holder with separate slots to hold thirty-two, sixty-four or 100 fiche of 100 mm × 150 mm) (4 in × 6 in) size. This holder is in fact a collection of viewing units on rotating bases and it has obvious advantages for the quick identification of a fairly small collection of fiche. Some libraries with large stocks store their 100 mm × 150 mm (4 in × 6 in) fiche in an electro-mechanical unit which offers high speed retrieval and will hold as many as 274 000 such fiche in a single piece of equipment.

Ultrafiche is microfiche with a much greater reduction ratio. These again are either 125 mm × 75 mm (5 in × 3 in) or 150 mm × 100 mm (6 in × 4 in) and can be filed as cards. The standard bibliography *Books in English* is issued on 150 mm × 100 mm (6 in × 4 in) microfiche: each transparency contains 2380 frames of information below a title strip readable by the naked eye.

Opaques The term Microcard is loosely, and wrongly, used to refer to all micro-opaques, but it is, in fact, covered by an American patent. Microcards are single-sided and their size is 125 mm × 75 mm (5 in × 3 in). Other micro-opaques include Microprint 225 mm × 150 mm (9 in × 6 in) and Microlex (double-sided) 215 mm × 165 mm ($8\frac{1}{4}$ in × $6\frac{1}{2}$ in). Microprint tape presents no difficulty as it may be attached to cards of any size. As all these forms appear as rigid cards they will be filed in drawers of the appropriate dimensions.

The housing of microforms cannot be considered separately from the positioning of the reading machines. Are these machines and the appropriate microforms to be on open access or issued only by staff? Are the machines to be used by readers without supervision? Are reader-printers to be installed, free or coin-operated? For the best general discussion of all microform questions, see Verry[7].

Photographs, clippings and other illustrations
These are best attached to standard mounts and filed vertically in boxes either 325 mm × 260 mm × 75 mm ($12\frac{3}{4}$ in × $10\frac{1}{4}$ in × 3 in), or 350 mm × 290 mm × 75 mm ($13\frac{3}{4}$ × $11\frac{1}{2}$ in × 3 in), each holding

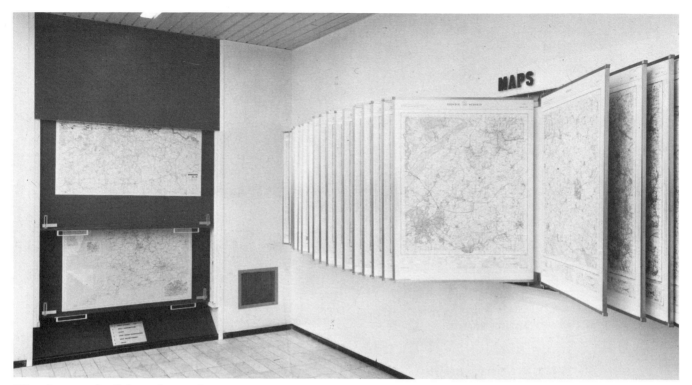

Hinged maps and pull-down fitment for maps in greatest demand, City Business Library, City of London

Horizontal tray file for loose maps, Ranplan

between seventy and ninety mounts. The boxes can be stored on normal adjustable shelving sequences. Larger clippings, tipped to standard mounts, and other items, such as broadsides and prints, can be held flat in solander boxes 700 mm × 550 mm × 60 mm (27 in × 21¼ in × 2¼ in), or 1 m × 750 mm × 60 mm (38¾ in × 29 in × 2¼ in) and shelved horizontally in fixed shelving cases deep enough for the purpose. For such large items it is an advantage to have low cases with sloping tops for immediate consultations.

Slides

Slides (ie transparencies) are usually 2 in × 2 in and use 35 mm film. They can be mounted under glass for permanent storage or slipped into pockets within transparent sheets which can be suspended in vertical file drawers. A sheet can be removed and placed in a viewer so that the required slide can be identified without being

handled, and then removed when needed. Film strips will be kept in their own holders preferably lined with paper to prevent scratching and filed in drawers with close divisions.

Maps

Bound volumes of maps, because of their great size, are best treated as very large books. Loose maps may be shelved horizontally in special cases or suspended in various types of vertical files; with these methods the architect will be very familiar because they are a common feature of planning offices. Individual maps (such as the Ordnance Survey series) may be mounted on linen, folded, reinforced and shelved as narrow books.

Maps in constant use, should be displayed permanently open, either in a pull-down fitment, or on wall panels like wallpaper samples.

Rolled maps will be stored either in very deep pigeon holes (involving a vast use of space) or horizontally on very narrow supporters along a wall.

Music

Sheet music may be bound and stored as books or stored unbound horizontally in drawers or in 4-drawer vertical file cabinets about 1200 mm (4 ft) high, 400 mm (15¾ in) wide and 300 mm (12 in) deep. Scores will normally be bound as books; the only problem lies in making the correct shelf allocation for volumes of such varying height and thickness.

Gramophone records

These are comparatively new to libraries; twenty years ago the discs were usually left in their cardboard covers in closed access cases, and shelved upright and edge on; if they are fairly tightly packed, no harm comes to the disc. Open access methods are more common now because staff time is saved by reader self-service and because of the attractiveness of the coloured sleeves now universally supplied. The discs are best held in open-topped troughs; a "browser box" 350 mm (14 in) long, 75 mm (3 in) deep and 150 mm (6 in) high, mounted on short legs, is convenient and flexible. For larger numbers of records a case 1500 mm (5 ft) high can have three rows of troughs vertically,

Records in drawers and turntables, Libraco Ltd

Record troughs, West Norwood Library, London Borough of Lambeth

Scores shelved above discs, Grimsby Central Library (Terrapin Reska Ltd)

each 350 mm (14 in) long and holding between twenty and forty records in each section; this case will accommodate between sixty and 120 records in each running 350 mm (14 in); a double-sided case of this size 2150 mm (7 ft) long can hold between 700 and 1400 records in conditions enabling the user to make his choice in comfort. Where pressure on space is less acute, lower troughs may be preferred. In theory it is said not to be advisable to store records leaning against each other in this way; in practice it seems to work perfectly well.

When planning such cases for records it may be convenient to keep the disc storage lower and to incorporate shelving above the records for holding miniature scores which are so often used in conjunction with the records.

Tape cassettes and cartridges

These (and video-tape cassettes) are very small and present a security rather than a shelving problem; their sizes still vary alarmingly and the answer so far has usually been to file them in drawers or pigeon-holes and to make them available only on request to the staff. Because of growing use of these forms manufacturers now offer open shelving cases with shelves fixed at the appropriate intervals, and incorporating a security bar across the frame of each shelf so that the cassettes can be on open display but are secured unless the bars are unlocked by staff.

REFERENCES

1   RIDER, FREEMONT Compact book storage. Hadham Press, Middletown, Conn. 1949
2   VAN HOESON, HENRY B., and NORMAN L. KILPATRICK Height of books in relation to heights of stack tiers. *In Library Quarterly*, v 4, 1934, pp 352–357
3   ELLSWORTH, RALPH E. The economy of book storage in college and university libraries. Association of Research Libraries and Scarecrow Press, New Jersey 1969
4   GAWRECKI, DRAHOSLAV Compact library shelving. Library Technology Program, American Library Association, 1968.
5   MULLER, ROBERT H. Economics of compact book shelving. *In Library Trends*, April 1965
6   HILL, F. J. The compact storage of books. *In* Gawrecki, op cit, p 61
7   VERRY, H.R. Microcopying methods. Focal Press, London, 1963

10 Reading areas

Although reading is a basic activity in libraries of all kinds, there is a fundamental difference between serious study and casual browsing: entirely different space allowances have to be made for the two activities, the proportions depending on the aims of the library. Academic libraries will concentrate on serious study but they will not neglect to use the appeal of books in an informal setting to catch the students' interest and widen their horizons. Conversely "popular" libraries will cater for the originally less-committed reader who may decide to settle down and concentrate on continuous reading.

STUDY AREAS

These will form the major part of university, college and public reference libraries. Overall space allowances will have already been determined from the product of the number of readers to be catered for (from the brief) and the space allocation per reader. The layouts that give the most economical use of space are those of study tables in the centre of a room with shelving along the walls, or freestanding stacks in the centre of a room with seats by the windows (see also Metcalf[1]). A great drawback is the limited

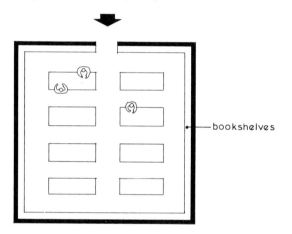

Reference library with shelving round wall

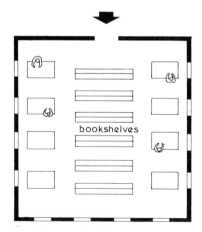

Reference library with shelving in centre

number of books which can thus be made immediately accessible but these are the most suitable layouts for small reference libraries and possibly for undergraduate libraries where the proportion of readers to bookstock is comparatively high.

The traditional relationship between reading-room and books is discussed by Thompson[2] and Brawne[3]. In public reference libraries the usual arrangement was as shown in the top diagram above. In university libraries the two main variants now are stacks separated from large reading-rooms—or, much more common,

reading areas round the outside of the stacks on all subject floors. In the latter case, seats are often placed within as well as outside the stacks.

Tables

Sizes of tables required for serious study have been quoted by many experts and once again the space needs seem to rise decade by decade. At present an acceptable figure seems to be 600 mm × 900 mm (2 ft × 3 ft); common sense and personal testing agree with this. The reader will need room to sit in a chair and to move into position; this space is given by Havard-Williams[4] as 900 mm × 750 mm (3 ft × 2 ft 6 in), but where individual tables are arranged in rows, a figure of 900 mm × 900 mm (3 ft × 3 ft) would be better. To this must be added space for all readers to move about; a reasonable space allowance for a reader at a table might therefore be 1·35 m^2 (15 ft^2). Where individual tables are placed against walls or where multiple tables are used this figure can be reduced to 1·25 m^2 (13$\frac{1}{2}$ ft^2) and 1·4 m^2 (10$\frac{1}{2}$ ft^2) respectively. This of course is not the whole picture; each reader will take up a share of the main access aisles and passage spaces within the room and these make up the normal allowance of 2·3 m^2 (25 ft^2) per reader.

These figures are based on the requirements of the "average reader" or the undergraduate. There will be many cases where large numbers of readers need more table space (universities often allow research workers larger table space, while users of maps and prints need a great deal more room); in an extreme example special areas may be provided, for example for visiting professors (these will be referred to later when carrels are discussed).

There are different ways of providing tables:

Individual table

This has psychological advantages but takes up most space and the stability of the table is limited.

This type of table is very acceptable at right angles to a wall but in serried ranks in an open room they can produce a feeling of regimentation said to disturb concentration.

Readers' reaction to arrangements of single tables seems to vary widely. The new library of the College of Librarianship, Wales, at Aberystwyth has used an informal, almost haphazard, grouping of tables which might appear to embody all the disadvantages

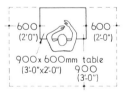

Recommended minimum dimensions for one-person reading table

but has apparently proved very popular with students. Complications can arise if individual table lighting is to be provided in such a situation. Floor sockets will be needed, and if flexibility is also required this will mean a network of electric supply conduits in the floor with sockets perhaps at intervals as frequent as 1400 mm (4 ft 6 in)—a very expensive provision. If the floor is carpeted carpet plugs will also be needed to block sockets that are not in use. This arrangement is to be used in the new Birmingham Central Library on a very large scale and the experience there will be watched with interest.

Dual tables

If without a centre division such tables appear to have little to offer except the freedom of one reader to expand into the space

Sheffield University Library

Warwick University Library

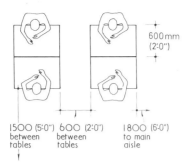

Minimum dimensions for dual reading tables

not occupied by the other reader; this can lead to friction when the second reader arrives.

A centre division prevents this overlap, for good or ill, but it gives some feeling of privacy and may also provide a built-in bookrest. Although this idea has been out of fashion for some years it has optical advantages in that a book on a flat surface is more tiring to read than one at an appropriate angle. Dunne[5] says, *inter alia*, "For a reader sitting upright a range of book-rest angles from $50°$ to $61\frac{1}{2}°$ is needed, positioned so that the height of the bottom of the book can be varied from 260 mm to 400 mm ($10\frac{1}{4}$ in to $15\frac{3}{4}$ in) below the level of the reader's eye, say between 255 mm and 410 mm (10 in and 16 in) below".

On a dual table with a centre division local lighting can be more conveniently provided than on a single table, and each reader can even be shielded with low screens; on the whole, however, dual tables are no more successful than most such compromises.

Long tables

These are certainly the most economical in use of space, but not outstandingly so because access aisles need to be wider. They have

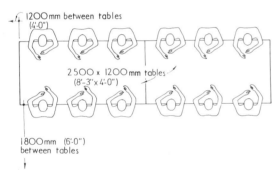

Minimum dimensions for six-person reading tables

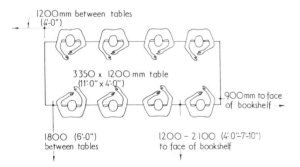

Minimum dimensions for eight-person reading tables

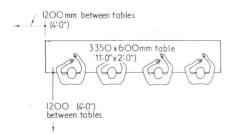

Minimum dimensions for single-sided table for four persons

St Marylebone Reference Library, City of Westminster, remodelled 1967

the advantage that, when the tables are not fully occupied, readers may spread their books into unused spaces. Long tables can be more solidly constructed and are consequently steadier. These gains have to be balanced against readers' reluctance to sit in rows in what they may think of as school conditions; certainly it is noticeable that readers prefer separate seating where it is available. Long-table seating also has the disadvantage that the arrival and departure of readers seriously disturbs other readers' concentration.

Long tables can accommodate from four to twelve readers. The width should not be less than 1200 mm (4 ft) and the lateral space allowance between readers never less than 900 mm (3 ft). Space between parallel tables should not be less than 1800 mm (6 ft) but it is possible to have 1500 mm (5 ft) spacing when shorter tables are used. Seating should never be allowed at the ends of such tables. Long tables can have centre divisions which again will accommodate individual lighting fittings effectively as well as providing jack points for audio-visual equipment. In such cases it would be better to have individual side divisions also in order to give some separation.

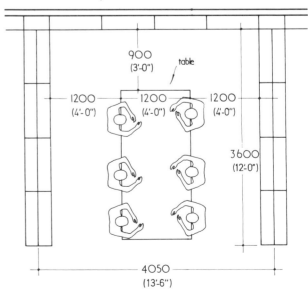

Minimum dimensions for six-person reading tables in alcove

York University Library

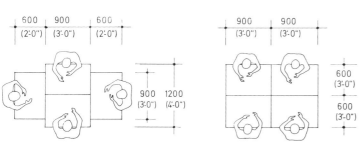

Table space requirements for readers

Special tables

Almost inevitably some tables will have to be designed to meet special circumstances, eg the map-tracing table which has a square of clouded glass let into the surface and lit from below.

Clearances

The following two diagrams show minimum clearances necessary between tables, furniture and bookcases in informal reading areas. Because readers will choose books from the shelves and because trolley access will be needed, the layout of both study tables and casual seating needs careful consideration if congestion is to be avoided at peak times.

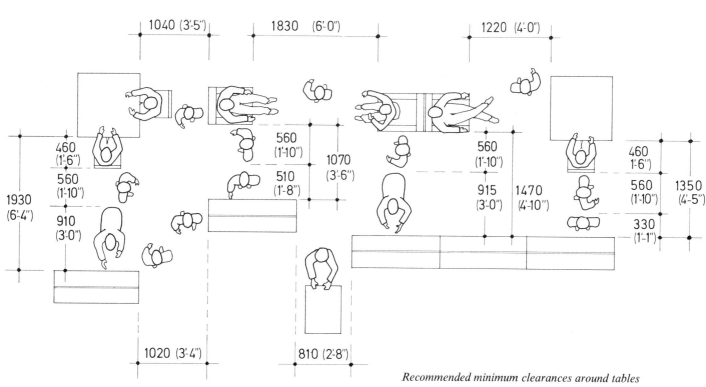

Recommended minimum clearances around tables

Warwick University Library

Warwick University Library

Other types of table

The librarian of the new Central Library of Newcastle upon Tyne writes[6]: "The tables are made up in threes, ie two tables linked by a table top. This reduces the number of table legs and also makes it possible to echelon (ie stagger) the table tops, thus hindering the lateral spread of books and other material being used by readers and achieving the effect of partitions without the expense."

Large tables can be placed in bookcase alcoves, again with the disadvantage that readers wishing to use the books will disturb those writing. Recommended minimum distances are given below. Round tables, sometimes attractive in browsing areas, should never be provided for serious study.

Carrels

These individual study rooms are necessary where serious workers need to be undisturbed and where they require the uninterrupted use of certain books for long periods. "Long" is a relative term; such rooms may be reserved for readers for periods ranging from a day to a term. They may be provided with typewriters or T.V. receivers, or readers may bring their own machines, including tape recorders. Certainly power points for such machines will be needed.

The carrel will have a cupboard (possibly lockable) in which books can be kept in safety when they are not in use, but the library staff must have a record of the books and the right (and a

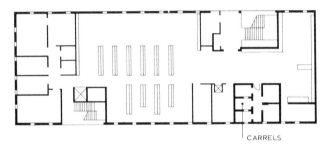

Carrels off separate corridor, Hatfield Polytechnic

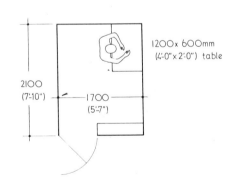

Recommended single-person carrel

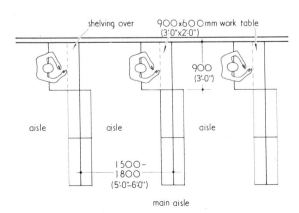

Suggested arrangement for open carrels in bookshelf area

key) to take them away if they are needed elsewhere. A coat-hanging fitment will be provided, and even a washbasin (if, for example, manuscript searches takes place there); an inspection window or a glass door is desirable so that staff can check on the occupant's activities. Carrels must be soundproofed of course because the whole point is to provide study spaces away from the noise and bustle of other areas; in Hatfield Polytechnic a group of carrels is isolated from other reading areas and approached from a separate corridor; this, although space-consuming, has advantages. The size of carrels will vary, according to type of use, from 1500 mm × 1225 mm (5 ft × 4 ft) to 2450 mm × 3650 mm (8 ft × 12 ft)—the latter are virtually private offices.

The carrel has great psychological advantages for readers and the demand is invariably greater than the supply. To meet this demand various compromises have been devised:

individual tables with low screens, possibly located against a wall or window: these give some privacy plus space economy and ease of supervision;

individual tables in book-lined alcoves: the reader is, of course, likely to be disturbed when other readers consult books there;

individual tables, shielded or not, against windows or walls and attached to shelving rows: users of these will be disturbed less than those at tables in bookcase alcoves;

double or quadruple carrels, staggered so that the users are separated. Carrels such as these are also offered by manufacturers of library systems and because they can be dismantled and moved—some can even be stored flat when not in use—they are a valuable aid to flexibility.

Naturally these compromises call for different space allocations: Havard-Williams suggests[7] that a table of 1225 mm × 600 mm (4 ft × 2 ft) with a total cubicle area of 1525 mm × 1225 mm (5 ft × 4 ft) is acceptable. This, with a 50 per cent allowance for aisle space, is the equivalent of Metcalf's suggested 2·8 m² (30 ft²) overall allocation. For a full discussion of reader seating and especially carrel alternatives, see Metcalf[8].

Other rooms

Colleges, universities and some schools will need group reading-rooms, seminar rooms and even talking-rooms. These can be furnished flexibly with groups of standard-sized (600 mm × 900 mm, 2 ft × 3 ft) tables placed together to form larger units according to need. Walls of these rooms can also be shelved.

Study table heights

BS 3893:1965 on office furniture[9]* recommends a table-top height of between 700 mm and 760 mm (28 in and 30 in): Van Buren[10] says 686 mm (27 in), Havard-Williams[11] 762 mm (30 in) with a kneehole height of not less than 635 mm (25 in). Alternative dimensions are given here for adults and children's reading tables and for those in open carrels. Table legs should be a maximum of 150 mm (6 in) from ends of tables.

Chair heights

These need little comment because they are a common factor in public buildings and the architect will have his own source of standards. Van Buren[12] says they should be 430 mm (17 in) high, Havard-Williams[13] says 460 mm (18 in); naturally there will be different requirements in school libraries according to the age groups using them.

BROWSING AREAS

Almost every type of library will need at least one area where readers can sit in relaxing and informal surroundings. In public, hospital and welfare libraries this will be a major requirement; the necessary amount of such provision in academic libraries will be indicated in the statement of aims. A college librarian

* BSS 3044:1958, 3079:1959 and 3404:1961 deal with anatomical, physiological and anthropometric considerations in the design of office furniture, including desks and chairs for machine operators.

Bourne Hall Library, Borough of Epsom and Ewell

Lancaster University Library

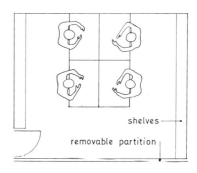

Recommended minimum dimensions for four-person carrel room

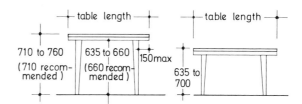

Reading table heights for adults (left) and children (right)

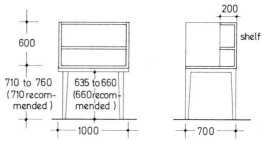

Typical open carrel

Children's reading pit, West Norwood Library, London Borough of Lambeth

Counter, the American School in London (Library Design and Engineering Ltd)

may wish to attract students by having a lounge with reclining chairs where popular periodicals can be read; other librarians may feel that these activities are the province of the students' union and that the library's need is for formal study conditions with only a few soft-seated chairs in a colourful area which can be used as a contrast to, and a break from, study in more spartan conditions.

In a public lending library the requirement will probably be for those users who have made a preliminary choice of books from the shelves and who then wish to sit in comfort for a short time while they evaluate their selection. It could also be that the local community needs a place where people can spend an hour or two in comfort "having a quiet read". These are really two different needs; it is certainly possible for the architect to design one area for both purposes, but he should know that there are two purposes. It is only by analysing the problem that layout, decoration and furniture can be used to produce a good solution; too often a square of carpet and a few low soft chairs covered in a bright fabric, placed in a space that was otherwise unusable, has been regarded as the answer.

Questions to be asked are: for how long is a reader expected to stay in the chairs? What is he to do there—read, write, relax, sleep? These questions will help the designer to know for what he is providing and for what he is not; if students are to be discouraged from working in this area, then tables can be designed at a height inconvenient for that purpose eg "coffee" tables. If readers must not sleep there, why provide deep upholstered lounge chairs which are so soporific? Is the intention really to reproduce a "home" atmosphere? If not, then the need for body-support in comfort does not always have to be met by providing lounge chairs. If the intention is to have a somewhat less relaxed atmosphere, then chairs can have tablet fittings so that note-taking can accompany reading.

The browsing area of a public library will be close to the books and preferably in an oasis of quiet. A school library may make a notational division by using low bookcases as a visual break between areas, and by change of decoration and floor covering. If small discussion groups have to be arranged, it is better to have a separate room for the purpose than to have the library acquire the air of a seminar room.

The layout of chairs in an academic library's informal reading area is more important than it may seem. Is conversation to be encouraged, tolerated or banned? If chairs are grouped in circles (or can be moved to form circles) talk sessions will inevitably result. If this is unwelcome, the chairs can be fixed into a less hospitable relationship, or be built into fitments. If total informality, including uninhibited conversation, is the aim there need be no chairs at all: children and students are very happy with carpeted or cushioned steps round an area of sunken floor—the average reader might even take to the idea.

READER SERVICE AREAS

All libraries need prominently situated centres from which staff can give certain essential services. In multi-storey or sectionalised libraries such a centre may be required for each major division. The centres will have three main functions:
control of the issue and return of books;
bibliographical assistance to readers;
supervision of user activities and security control.

Issue and return of books
In school, hospital, welfare and small public libraries, the main bibliographical functions will all be carried out from the same counter or desk, but in larger libraries the issue and return counter will provide some security control and will be quite separate from the readers' adviser's desk. In very large libraries the counter may be placed in an entrance lobby so that the inevitable noise of reader traffic will be isolated from quieter reading areas. If such a counter dominates the reader's only entrance to and exit

Counter, Edinburgh University Library

from the building it can give him, once inside, the freedom to roam between departments. Virtually the only disadvantages of this arrangement are that it does not give a welcoming air to the main entrance, and that the counter staff are committed to that work only; in slack periods this can be expensive in staff time; on the other hand it obviates the need for divisional control counters. In a large library a centrally positioned counter will be inevitable and the considerable space which such a counter requires will dictate its position. The counter's size depends largely on the issue system in use; where university and some college libraries need elaborate issue records, the space required will be large. This applies to a lesser extent to all libraries using card-and-ticket systems (such as Browne), but when estimating space for the counter the librarian should allow for a future change to a less space-consuming system, such as photo or computer charging. For this reason counters should wherever possible be sectional and freestanding.

The two functions of the counter, issue and return, require two separate traffic routes and it is obviously more efficient if the two routes can be kept apart. An island counter which stands between the two streams offers staffing economy and is the only possible answer in small but busy libraries, but it has psychological disadvantages for the staff; only severe discipline can keep it looking tidy.

In a busy library the receipt and issue of books will take place at separate desks, the issue desk, no more than a simple top to hold the issue recording machinery, serving also as a security control. The return counter will be more elaborate; it needs:

space for the staff to receive books, do the necessary recording and perhaps receive fines;
space for loan records; for modern methods this can be small but for the old ticket-and-card methods it can require as much as 6 m (20 ft) of counter space;
shelving for books to be retained at the counter.
room for housing and movement of trolleys, if used to return books to the library;
stationery cupboards and drawers—there may be space for these under the counter-top;
room for the maximum number of staff required at peak times, and for stools so that they do not have to stand for hours.

With ticket-and-card methods, in which the transaction is completed when the reader has received his ticket, books have to be inspected for physical conditions before return to the shelves. Books requested by other readers may also have to be put aside. In some "delayed-discharge" systems, but not in computer-based ones, all books have to be laid aside for checking against readers' requests before they are ready for return to the shelves. This calls for either a very large shelving allowance behind the counter or a behind-the-scenes sorting area nearby—see "Shelving rooms" below.)

In small single-room libraries the counter will be the only manned service point, so its position and shape will be of particular importance. The County Libraries Section of the Library Association[14] recommends three shapes for small branch libraries:

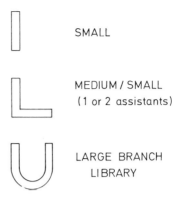

SMALL

MEDIUM / SMALL
(1 or 2 assistants)

LARGE BRANCH LIBRARY

In the single-room library the all-purpose counter was traditionally placed to create a bottleneck for security reasons. For staffing economy it was an island placed to allow supervision of the whole room.

This method dominated public lending library design for many years. When pressure of readers increased and more staff became available, it gave way to a division of functions, with separate issue and return counters, the centre area being used for readers' inquiries.

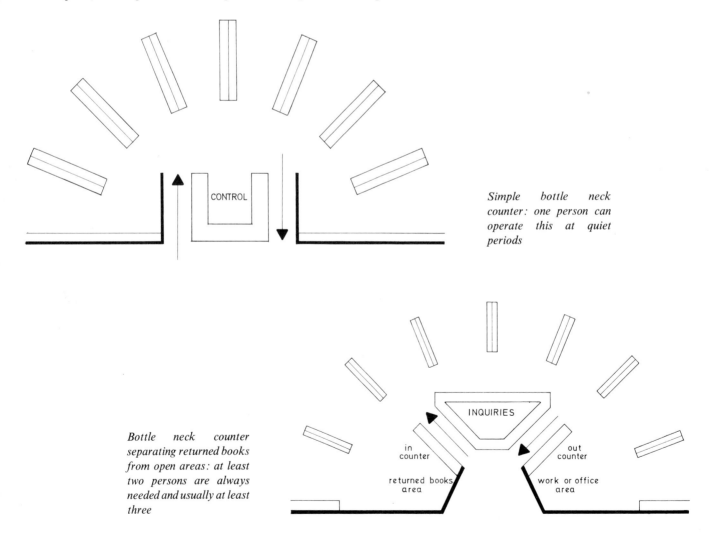

Simple bottle neck counter: one person can operate this at quiet periods

Bottle neck counter separating returned books from open areas: at least two persons are always needed and usually at least three

Both these layouts developed from "safeguarded open access" and made it possible to place lockable wicket gates across entrance and exit for greater security, but they produced a forbidding atmosphere and have given way to the freer layout of an unguarded entrance with counters placed deep within the room. The diagram below shows a very common layout for a small library but the inevitable crossing of traffic routes can be troublesome at peak times.

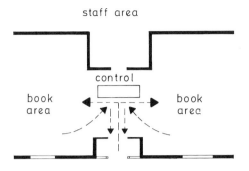

In a larger library crossing of traffic routes can be a major disadvantage. The greater emphasis on a welcoming atmosphere

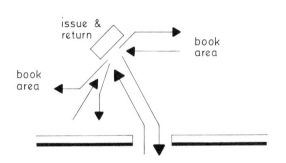

has produced the following layout which offers more security control and fewer traffic problems, but an extra member of staff will be necessary at all times to operate it.

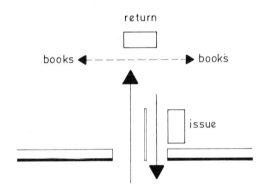

The relative emphasis on security on the one hand and an atmosphere of freedom and welcome on the other are for the librarian to assess. In some libraries, because of heavy book losses, it has become necessary to return to fully safeguarded exits, involving in many cases the installation of lockable wickets or theft-detection devices (see chapter 16).

When planning layouts the basic considerations will be security, economy of staffing and expected reader traffic routes. In making preliminary sketches particular attention will be paid also to the placing of inquiry desks, catalogues and collections of bibliographies. The access routes to any areas which may be under the supervision of the main control, eg children's libraries or reading-rooms, will need special consideration. In larger libraries these will be separate rooms, each with its own layout problem.

Examples of typical control layouts are to be seen in many books; Wheeler and Githens[15] in particular carried out an elaborate survey of American public library buildings, distinguishing a large number of various types and their relative advantages and disadvantages. Mevissen[16] gives examples of simple alternatives and also compares in detail four common counter placings.

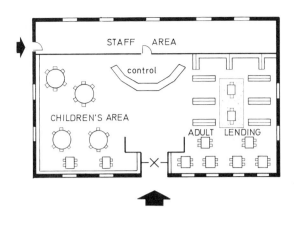

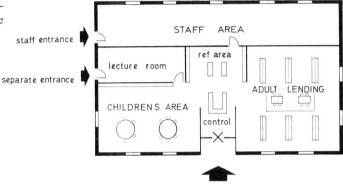

Different counter positions in two single-room branch libraries

Counter design

The detailed design of the counter is of great importance to the library because of the critical operations which take place there. The range of tasks is small but because they will be repeated hundreds of thousands (perhaps millions) of times annually a full method study of these operations must be made before counter design is begun. Such an operation should be carried out by a method study officer in close co-operation with the librarian, rather than by the librarian himself.

If all the different control operations for a small library are to be the work of a single member of the staff the counter must be planned so that minimum movement is needed between operations. The drawing below shows the maximum counter size which can be controlled by one person without unnecessary, and therefore tiring, movements.

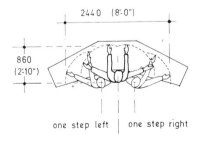

Maximum counter area usable by one person

Counters with special labour-saving fitments—sliding trays, circular revolving tray-holders, and so on—were common in the 1930s and are still offered by manufacturers specialising in library furniture. Most of these gadgets have long been abandoned because they were too inflexible to meet changing demands, but bright ideas are still needed.

When drawings are prepared, the librarian must study them with great care because errors in planning counters and desks can effect the efficiency (and the comfort) of staff who will spend many thousands of working hours there. Seating heights, kneehole space, drawer clearances, positioning of handles and many other details must be checked. Operations should be simulated on existing equipment to make sure that the counter is efficient in human engineering terms. Time spent on this study will be repaid many times over.

Library equipment manufacturers offer complete counters. Some of these can be constructed from unit components similar to those used for the rest of the library equipment and will therefore fit well into the general appearance of the room.

Librarians will have their own views about the need for special fitments such as rails or shelves to hold shopping bags, but one essential is a hard working surface. The wearing of books sliding across the top many thousands of times is greater than some architects can be induced to believe. Hard plastic laminates are certainly the best material here: to use vinyls and linos is not reasonable; no other attribute than durability is required and laminates are obtainable in attractive patterns and colours. Similarly attention should be paid to other parts of the counter which are liable to be handled constantly by users: light wood soon turns dark in these conditions unless it really can be wiped clean.

The greatest weakness in counter design has been the lack of attention to ways of handling expeditiously the very large number of books which come in at peak times. Books can be loaded at once onto shelving trolleys if staff are at hand to take them away quickly, but at peak periods this is a disturbing and time-consuming operation. In very small libraries it is common for the trolleys themselves to act as display shelves, so that readers in fact do some of the book dispersal, but in a library of any size this is a step towards chaos.

In this connection Keele of Hadleigh offers an ingenious arrangement of trolleys which form behind-counter shelving; books can be roughly sorted on to this shelving and when any section is full it can be hooked onto a trolley and rolled out to the appropriate shelving bay where it is latched in to form display shelving of returned books appropriate to that sequence.

Whatever method is used, the operation of receiving books and placing them somewhere for disposal without disturbing the basic task of serving the next reader must be performed thousands of times a day. Two ideas which have been used are described below.

The book box A large box (say 750 mm (2 ft 6 in) square) stands close to the receiving position. Its top is a spring loaded platform on which books are placed; under the growing load the platform sinks to make space for more. As the books are removed the platform rises so that the load is always at a height convenient for lifting. This method will be used only in small libraries where sudden peaks of use occur and where lulls can be used to clear the accumulated books, for example when classes visit a school library.

A conveyor belt can be used to take books to an adjoining sorting room. Early examples of this idea involved a travelling belt behind the assistant and parallel to the counter, so that the assistant had to turn round to place books on the belt. A later development placed the belt at right angles to the assistant (in the photograph below, between two assistants) so that books are dispatched without unnecessary effort and the area is kept uncluttered. Of course this can be arranged only where the in-counter has no other function.

This system is at its simplest when space can be allowed for a sorting room immediately behind the counter but in other circumstances (and particularly when the counter is in a main entrance area) the conveyor belt can take the books to another floor, preferably the one on which they will eventually be shelved. To place

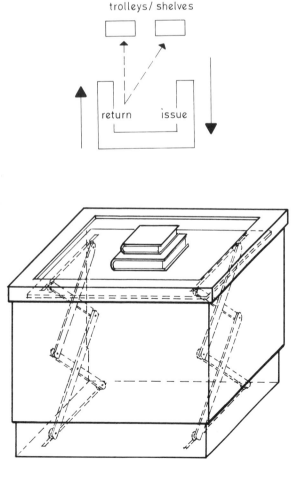

Book box designed by Library Design and Engineering Ltd for the American School in London

In counter with conveyor belt to shelving room, Cannon Street District Library, City of London

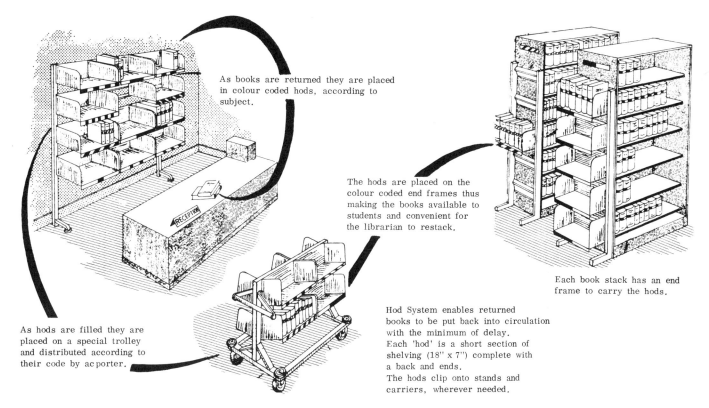

As books are returned they are placed in colour coded hods, according to subject.

The hods are placed on the colour coded end frames thus making the books available to students and convenient for the librarian to restack.

Each book stack has an end frame to carry the hods.

As hods are filled they are placed on a special trolley and distributed according to their code by ac porter.

Hod System enables returned books to be put back into circulation with the minimum of delay. Each 'hod' is a short section of shelving (18" x 7") complete with a back and ends. The hods clip onto stands and carriers, wherever needed.

Hod system of trolleys holding shelving units, Keele's of Hadleigh

the sorting area in a basement and send the books down on a chute may be neat and labour-saving for the counter staff, but it will cause extra work in sending the books back from the basement to the eventual shelving area. If the counter is an island books can be sent on a belt to another area by using an underfloor conveyor, as in both the recent Bradford Central Library and the Washington DC downtown central library.

Unless a sorting room is used there will inevitably be the problem of disposing of large numbers of books which, either on trolleys or carried by assistants, will continually cross the traffic flow of readers. This is a major, and too little considered, operational hazard which reduces the efficiency of some recent libraries with centrally placed return counters.

Plan of counter and sorting room illustrated opposite

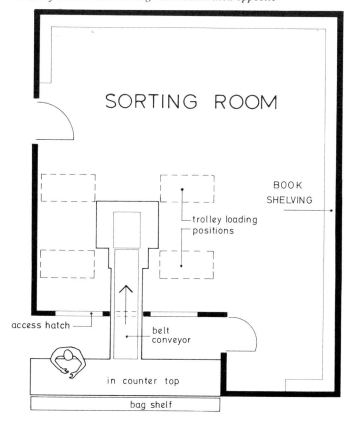

SORTING ROOM

BOOK SHELVING

trolley loading positions

access hatch

belt conveyor

in counter top

bag shelf

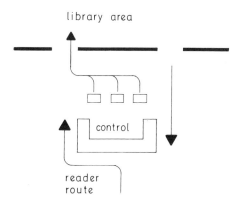

library area

control

reader route

Some university and college libraries have to retain at the counter many books which are in very great demand and can be loaned for only very short periods, sometimes as little as two or three hours; to provide shelving for these books at the counter itself can be an embarrassment. One ingenious expedient has been to place two counters in tandem in a bottleneck area.

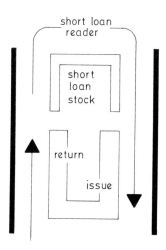

LIBRARY AREA

short loan reader

short loan stock

return

issue

Assistance to readers

Inquiry desk

In all except the smallest libraries there will be a separate desk manned by professional staff to give bibliographical assistance in response to readers' requests. The design of the desk may seem simple enough but it will benefit from a method study of the operations which are to take place there. Certain essential books must be close at hand and the physical relationship with the reader is important: if readers usually stand, at what height should the adviser sit? If the reader is to be seated too (at any rate during lengthy inquiries) is it better for the adviser to face him across a desk or would the relationship be easier if they sat side by side?

An obvious development of the growth of demand is that more readers' advisers will be needed, so the area should be planned to allow space for the maximum numbers of both staff and readers who will meet there.

The position of the desk will differ according to the type of library but it should always be close to the catalogue and to the main bibliographical tools; in a single-room library it will be in a position which allows a control view complementary to that of the counter.

In large libraries the placing of the desk will be a much more complex matter. Before deciding on the layout the librarian should try to put himself in the place of the potential user of the bibliographical services. This user must be led to the area by clear signs and must find before him visual guides to the catalogue and other tools. He will consult the bibliographies and catalogue and then go to the shelves. If he cannot find the book he wants he will go to the assistance centre, the readers' adviser's desk.

This desk may have to accommodate the following operations in addition to that of giving bibliographical advice:

reserving books which are out on loan, and handing them over when they have arrived back: this necessitates space for books to be held (and possibly locked up) while awaiting collection by the reader;

retrieving books from closed stacks and returning them to the stacks after use;

photocopying service, which in research libraries can be a very large undertaking. This can mean sending a book, which the reader has obtained, to a photocopying point, receiving the book back with the copy and delivering the copy to the reader. Filling in forms may be involved, for copyright reasons, as well as the receipt of money in payment. If a photocopy has to be provided from a book in closed stack the procedure involves also having the book traced and transferred to the photocopy centre.

These activities alone show that the placing of such a point for efficient service can mean a relationship with a document delivering system, a stack retrieval system and a book transfer system. Even if do-it-yourself photocopying machines are at hand, there will be many items which cannot be reproduced on these machines so that the book will have to go to a photographic section.

All these operations will take up space; again a method study and a well-thought-out traffic diagram are most valuable, not only for the layout and space allocation but also for the design of the often complex fitments.

The planning of such a central bibliographical service does not necessarily end the problem of assistance to readers. Subject departments, particularly on other floors, may need their own subject catalogues and the library may be able to afford reader service points in such departments. This will involve requests and delivery of books from stack to different departments—a very complicated and possibly expensive matter. The architect may wish to impress on the librarian the advantages of a centralised service, even at the cost of some inconvenience to readers.

Catalogues

The catalogue is a most important piece of equipment; at its smallest it is merely the record of the titles of books in the library, but if that library forms part of a system, the catalogue may record the holdings of the whole system; in a research library dealing with information rather than books as such, it will be a major bibliographical tool. In a library with a large closed stack, the catalogue may become so bulky as to dominate its area and if only for this reason librarians have sought for many years for a less space-consuming alternative to the card or sheaf form. Some libraries have already replaced these with a computer print-out in book form; they are expensive to produce but potentially economical in staff time: they are as yet most unattractive in appearance but the space saving and opportunity for revision offer such advantages that the trend will certainly continue. If there is any likelihood of such a change in a library which is being planned, the architect should provide freestanding catalogue cabinets which can be removed later, rather than built-in units.

Sheaf catalogues are less used than card, chiefly because they take up more space and because revision is slower, but they have the great advantage that readers can remove the separate binders and use them at nearby tables, reducing congestion. The size of the slips in the binder can be 75 mm × 160 mm (3 in × 6¼ in) or 125 mm × 200 mm (5 in × 8 in). The smaller size is more often used in libraries, the binders being housed on shelves 100 mm (4 in) apart.

The traditional card catalogue is either single or double-sided: cabinets with alternate rows of drawers facing in opposite directions can give a saving in depth of cabinet at the expense of doubling the length. Because of the way in which readers consult the cards there are strict limits on the top and bottom height of the cabinet and thus on the number of drawers accommodated. Six drawers high is usually the maximum, and allowing 1 000 cards per drawer and three cards per average book, one vertical row of drawers will represent only two thousand titles.

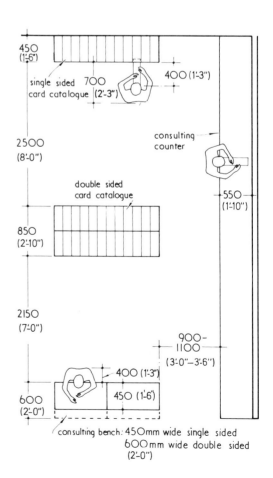

Recommended minimum plan dimensions in card catalogue area

Synagogue library, Mayfair

Recommended drawer heights in catalogue area

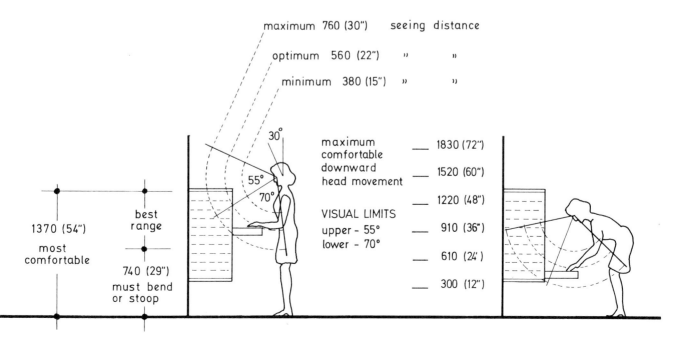

maximum 760 (30")   seeing distance

optimum 560 (22")   "   "

minimum 380 (15")   "   "

30°

55°

70°

1370 (54")

most comfortable

best range

740 (29")

must bend or stoop

maximum comfortable downward head movement

VISUAL LIMITS
upper - 55°
lower - 70°

___ 1830 (72")

___ 1520 (60")

___ 1220 (48")

___ 910 (36")

___ 610 (24')

___ 300 (12")

Catalogue and bibliographer's room, Reading University (Terrapin Reska)

It is obviously an advantage if more drawers can be accommodated without inconveniencing readers. This drawing demonstrates that a seven-drawer unit is acceptable and even a ten-drawer unit, although in the latter case the reader will have to bend to consult the lower drawers.

As catalogues and bibliographies are tools used for similar purposes they will normally be kept together and it can be convenient to house runs of bibliographies, which are always large volumes, below the runs of catalogue drawers. Proprietary catalogue cabinets can be incorporated in units that will hold quite long runs of the necessary bibliographies.

In a large library the catalogue will occupy a great deal of floor space—indeed some large libraries are being eaten up by their catalogues. A saving of open floor space can be achieved by having a single catalogue set against a wall, with the drawers designed to be removed and searched at special tables nearby. In such a case the drawers can start lower and continue higher, giving a vertical row of twelve rows and, as readers do not have to stand immediately in front of the cabinets while using the catalogue, congestion is eased. The only disadvantages of such a scheme are that quick consultation for a single title is made more cumbersome and the great mass of the catalogue cabinet looks formidable.

Alternatively the drawers can be spread thinly along walls with books shelved above and below them, or as occasional tiers between tiers of books, but in a large library this is inflexible (except with some systems shelving methods: see page 125) and will use up long wall runs; the method is better suited to small catalogues in separate subject rooms or to special libraries. On the Continent separate catalogue rooms are often found, but these have not been generally adopted in the UK, partly because readers seem not to like them and partly because they will be separated from the staff who offer bibliographical assistance.

Apart from these alternatives there is little choice in layout. The catalogues will be placed along walls or grouped in an area which they will entirely dominate.

Before any catalogue area can be planned or any size of catalogue units specified it is necessary for the librarian to take a hard look at the whole problem—the purpose the catalogue is to serve, the possible reaction of readers, the probable usage and the relative efficiency of the many alternatives now available. Because the librarian himself finds the catalogue, as it now exists, an indispensable tool it does not necessarily follow that his readers have the same reaction. Research has been done[17] on catalogue use in libraries of various types and the librarian must be familiar with the findings.

A large catalogue placed close to the bibliographies in research libraries (a collection of several hundred large volumes) produces a small library in itself. Because it must be used by readers of all subjects it is often associated with a collection of general reference books which are equally all-pervasive. The problem becomes one of planning a room that is conveniently placed *en route* to all departments and will hold perhaps 5 000 books, most of them above normal size, with perhaps 18 m² (200 ft²) of catalogues, with an effective reader's advisory service nearby and with space for very heavy use by readers. Little seating is required but shelves or narrow tables may have to be installed so that heavy bibliographies may be consulted. Because the dimensions of card catalogues are limiting and bibliographies are usually tall books, there is little freedom in planning such a room.

SECURITY CONTROL

In very small single-room libraries there will be one general-purposes counter to control the entrance and exit. In larger libraries the various elements of the service counter will serve the same purpose, but in very large libraries which have several departments opening off a general entrance hall the space required around the counter to allow for the large number of readers will make the counter useless as a security control: a separate control point will then be needed. Where it is essential to protect the book stock against theft it will be necessary to have a member of staff (usually an attendant) with this specific duty. Such an arrangement can seldom be 100 per cent effective but the very attention paid to the matter has a good psychological effect in deterring potential book thieves; this matter is discussed in detail in chapter 16. If a control is established across the entrance-exit it is important to provide a special cubicle for the purpose, so as to give both reasonable working conditions and a sense of dignity to an attendant employed on such a dreary task.

REFERENCES

[1] Metcalf. Op cit, p 105

[2] Thompson. Op cit, pp 13–15

[3] Brawne. Op cit, pp 12–20

[4] Havard-Williams. Op cit

[5] DUNNE, MICHAEL The optimum values and range needed for the angle and height of book rests. *In The Book Trolley*, v 2 no 10, June 1970

[6] WALLACE, A. Newcastle-upon-Tyne Central Library. *In Library World*, June 1971, pp 332–334

[7] Havard-Williams. Op cit

[8] Metcalf. Op cit, pp 119–128

[9] BRITISH STANDARDS INSTITUTION, BS 3893: 1965. Office desks, tables and seating

[10] VAN BUREN, MARTIN Design of library furniture. *In Library Trends*, April 1965, pp 392–393

[11] Havard-Williams. Op cit

[12] Van Buren. Op cit

[13] Havard-Williams. Op cit

[14] Library Association, County Libraries Section. Op cit

[15] Wheeler and Githens. Op cit, pp 97–99

[16] MEVISSEN, WERNER Public library building. Heyer. Essen, 1958, pp 45 and 58

[17] LIPETZ, BEN-AMI Catalog use in a large research library. *In Library Quarterly*, v 42 no 1, January 1972

11 Other areas

ANCILLARY PUBLIC AMENITIES

Book display

The librarian will always wish to draw readers' attention to special, changeable, groups of books. Neither the book form nor ways of displaying it are new: originality is hard to find in this field. In the past book jackets were pinned on boards; now that these jackets are sealed onto books, only the books themselves can be used. Display equipment has to be attractive, eye-catching and possess some degree of originality. To produce it will be the sort of challenge for which an architect is well qualified and he will certainly not want advice from the librarian in matters of design. A measure of disagreement may however develop on this subject: the architect, seeing a blank space, wants to use it for an "interesting feature" such as sculpture, mural or flowers; the librarian wants to display books and yet more books. Apart from the use of shop windows and flexible display cases, braced, like museum exhibit cases, from floor or ceiling, the only permanent provision needed is a supply of power points throughout the library.

Exhibition areas

The architect may wish to associate exhibition areas with decorative features in the building—murals, fixed sculpture and so on. To provide the framework for changeable displays will be simple for him if he knows what the librarian has in mind. If these displays are to be incorporated in corridors and entrance halls he must know the potential size of the displays so that clear passages can be allowed. In small libraries space can best be utilised by having open-backed display units which can serve as space dividers without the need for a separate area. Each display item the librarian needs must be indicated in the primary brief and elaborated in the secondary brief. Even the requirement of a board for public notices (many libraries, alas, suffer from the statutory need to house such dreary documents), should be recorded; to add a board to a wall which the architect had visualised as unblemished is to interfere with the overall design.

Lecture rooms

Many libraries of all kinds need rooms for meetings, lectures, play-readings and similar community activities, often in the late evenings when the main library services have ceased for the day. The rooms may need separate approaches from outside the building and special arrangement must be made for security and public safety. Public lavatories may have to be associated with these rooms and in some cases cloakrooms, manned or unmanned. In the latter case the possibility of key-operated lockers should be explored (see chapter 17). The County Libraries Section of the Library Association[1] says, "Lecture rooms [in public libraries] as such, are not recommended for communities of under 25 000 population" and goes on to recommend flexibility in the fittings of main rooms of small libraries so that these can be adapted for lectures after library hours. Many librarians will disagree strongly with this idea.

The brief will say how many seats are needed and whether a stage, special lighting and changing-rooms are to be provided. It is fair to say that there is more muddled, or at least inconclusive, thinking on this subject than on most other library questions, and that it is usually the librarian who is at fault.

To provide a room with adequate seating, a simple stage, some spotlights, a basic proscenium and a public address system is easy enough, but if the librarian has in mind the escalation of activities at some future date and the possibility of amateur stage performances in costume, then the matter is very different. To attempt to house these performances in a room not designed for the purpose and without proper acoustic treatment, changing-rooms, washing and make-up facilities will mean failure or very expensive alterations. Public safety regulations for "theatres" are very different from those for meeting rooms; lengthy plays need intervals and intervals call for kitchens, refreshment rooms, box office arrangements and facilities for handling money, often in large quantities. Such a transformation is not to be attempted lightly. Clear identification of future possible needs before the brief is written is essential.

Theatres

Because of the obvious connection between the written and the spoken word, more libraries are becoming more closely associated with theatres. The association is simple enough in the large educational campus where the theatre will be a companion to the library in its service to the community, but in the public library field the library and the theatre are often planned within the same building and sometimes run within the same staff framework. A recent one is in the Borough of Thurrock where the two services share the same building but are not in other ways integrated. A pioneer example at the Manchester Central Library, which now has two separate theatres in different parts of the city, is under the management of the city librarian and has a lounge and refreshment area serving both theatre and library patrons. The common use of these facilities has the great advantage of publicising each service to those familiar only with the other.

The design of theatres is a matter so complicated and so technically involved that it cannot be dealt with here; in general, because of problems of crowding and noise, it is better if the two services are planned back-to-back, the only elements which might be shared being staff rest facilities. If large theatre companies are to be involved even this arrangement is better avoided, because the rest times and requirements of the two professions are so utterly different. An excellent book for any librarian who may be even indirectly concerned with the subject is Roderick Ham's *Theatre planning*[2].

Recreational facilities for readers

Many libraries will have no call for this fairly recent development, particularly those which are small or are part of an institution which is already adequately served. University libraries will certainly need restaurants, or at least cafeterias, for students who can be expected to spend many hours on the premises, but the campus may already have facilities near enough to serve the purpose. There is a growing tendency for libraries of all kinds to have coffee bars, or food-and-drink-vending machines, in open areas as an encouragement to readers to regard the library as a hospitable centre.

Much will depend on the authority's policy; the coffee bar may be near the entrance as an attraction to passers-by, or it may be deliberately isolated so that it will serve mainly those using a long term facility such as a study area, lecture room or theatre. A coffee bar can be incorporated into the general library area but if heavy use is expected it is better sited separately. Its furniture will be chosen to achieve the intended atmosphere.

Libraries used by long-term readers may need a room or rooms where smoking is allowed: the trend towards allowing smoking within general reading areas, common abroad, has made little impact in the UK, except in some special libraries. This is more a matter of inertia than a deliberate policy based on either fire safety or insurance regulations. If smoking is ever to be allowed in reading areas, then there should be at least one reading area catering for non-smokers who find the habit offensive: perhaps the

Coffee bar off entrance hall, Stockton District Library, Teesside CB

Flexible exhibition area off entrance hall, Edinburgh University Library

Display as room divider, Belle Isle Branch Library, Leeds CB

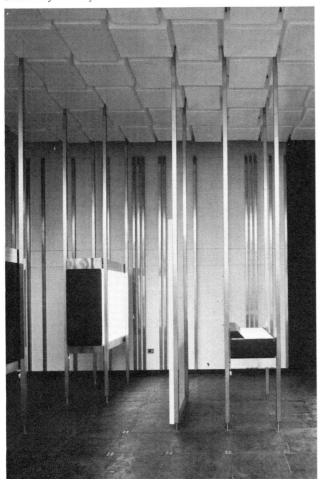

trend today is against special provision for smokers. It is possible to allow smoking in exhibition areas, where displays of art or of library treasures can be an added attraction. Comfortable seating should be available otherwise the whole point of the venture will be lost.

STAFF AREAS

Staff work areas

Metcalf[3] has said, "If experience over the last fifty years applies today (and there is no reason to believe that it does not), it seems fair to say that in most library buildings accommodations for the staff tend to become inadequate before those for books or for readers."

There is a fundamental difference between local work areas in public service sectors where immediate needs are met (the handling of new books, minor repairs etc) and workrooms for the centralised operations common to the whole library or the whole system. In the smallest libraries all action will take place in the one workroom; in branch libraries the centralised operations may have already been carried out for the whole system in another building. The layout of work areas and the design of their furniture and equipment can usefully be discussed only with a knowledge of the requirements of the individual case. The following points are intended simply as a reminder of some of the actions for which allowance has to be made.

Arrival of materials

Van access should preferably be under cover with a ramp to facilitate loading and unloading without lifting heavy packages: if a ramp is not possible, a pulley should be fitted. Tables for unpacking will have to be provided and, particularly where satellite libraries have to be served and transfers of book stock organised, areas of immediate shelving (industrial shelving will be adequate). Space for storing packing cases which may have to be reused, for disposal of rubbish, and access, direct or by hoist, to the accessioning area will be important.

Accessioning

A large amount of shelving space will be necessary and the librarian must be careful not to underestimate this need if future expansion is predicted. Because the operations are largely routine it will be possible to design the layout as a production line. Easy access will be required by hand, trolley, hoist, or (best of all) conveyor belt, to the cataloguing section.

The receipt of periodicals is a much larger undertaking than an outsider would believe. The arrival of hundreds of current journals, the checking-off, which is a critical operation particularly in a scholarly library, and their distribution to different subject areas, all call for careful planning.

Cataloguing and classifying

The layout of these sections will depend on whether the two processes are to be carried out together or separately. It is difficult to generalise because the attention paid to an individual book will vary so enormously in different types of library, particularly in special libraries where abstracting may be involved. There will be great variations between the types of book handled within a single large library: fiction and children's books almost always follow a flow-line different from that for more bibliographically complex books. Where possible however, the arrangement should be in the form of a production line with a single direction of movement. The largest single item of furniture will be the staff catalogue (or its equivalent) and the traffic routes of each cataloguer should be carefully worked out. The architect will know about the recommended allocation of space per office worker but it must be emphasised that cataloguers need space not only to work on the books in hand but also for the large number of bibliographical tools they use in their craft: 14 m² (150 ft²) per cataloguer is a reasonable overall figure.

The strategic placing of those bibliographical tools which are too expensive and too bulky to duplicate is a critical matter: interruptions to the working time of specialist staff are expensive. The growing tendency towards the production of these tools in microform (and especially in ultra-microfiche) will offer immediate space savings, but the positioning of the necessary reading machine, or machines, will become critical.

In planning the layout and furniture for such working areas it is important to use the best possible source of information—those who do the work. The cataloguers should be very much involved in the layout proposals, but the ideas which can come from asking each of them how he would like his own immediate working areas to be planned can be even more valuable. Unless the library is tied to contract furniture, or is very short of funds, each desk and its book holding fitments should be built as each cataloguer himself wishes, complete with freestanding bookcases at the appropriate angle, swivel fitments to hold copies of the most used bibliographical tools, and built-in stationery containers. The result will cost a little more than the standard desk; this is seldom a vital matter in the cost of a new building. Cataloguers leave and are replaced, but the result can be higher productivity; it will certainly make for a happier staff.

Copy typing will have a place in the flow line, as will the reproduction of catalogue cards by machine duplicators, tape typewriters and so on. A recent complication is the placing of computer input machinery; as its use develops this machinery will have a drastic effect upon flow lines. If there is any possibility that it may be introduced in the future, then area planning must be flexible enough to accommodate it.

All the present tendencies are towards a reduction of the attention paid in any single library to the tasks of cataloguing and classification because centralised information can now be supplied through computers in tape form. For this reason alone flexibility in planning becomes more important, as does the siting of accessions, cataloguing and classification in a single large area where space saved on one process can be used for another.

Processing

All library materials need some form of treatment before they are ready for use by readers. At the very least books have to be labelled and lettered, and although in very small libraries this can be done in the general workroom, in most cases there will need to be a special place in the flow line for this work. Books may have to be jacketed, laminated or strengthened, and this may call for fairly heavy (and therefore static) machinery. In the largest libraries there will be a bindery; this will require very heavy equipment and will be laid out on the lines of a small factory.

Office staff

When new books have been checked in the arrival or accessioning areas, invoices will be passed to clerical staff who will deal with the financial procedures. Communication between the sections, either direct or by document conveyor, must therefore be close. If readers have to make payments for certain services it can be an advantage if the clerical/financial section can be sited where readers can get to it. This may be a difficult planning requirement but its successful solution can remove the need for handling of cash by library staff who are busy on professional tasks.

Under the Offices, Shops, and Railway Premises Act 1963, persons habitually occupying a room are entitled to a minimum of 3·72 m² (40 ft²) each or 11·32 m³ (400 ft³) if the ceiling is lower than 3 m (10 ft). The working space per head of staff in general work areas should generally be between 7 m² and 9·3 m² (75 ft² and 100 ft²); staff largely occupied at single desks (eg typists) will need only 7 m² to 8 m² (75 ft² to 85 ft²), but other specialists need 9·3 m² to 11·6 m² (100 ft² to 125 ft²), with more for senior staff because they will be consulted by their colleagues. Individual offices will be from 9·3 m² to 28 m² (100 ft² to 300 ft²) according to function.

Even where large clerical offices are open plan for greater flexibility, furniture, and particularly bookcases, can be arranged to give each member of the office staff some feeling of privacy and diminish both visual and aural distraction.

Senior staff

Larger offices will be needed, often with adjoining secretarial offices; in small libraries the chief librarian may also be the supervisor of public services and wish to be placed where he can exercise this function directly, but in large ones this duty will be delegated to departmental heads and the chief librarian can be accommodated on an upper floor where space is less precious. He may wish to be close to the clerical office or the accessions department: this will depend on the procedures and his personal assessment of his role.

Dispatch

The arrivals areas will usually accommodate this function as well but a special area may be needed where books are assembled for dispatch to satellites or where books requiring extra protection can be gathered to await dispatch to an outside bindery.

Another 'dispatch' area, growing in importance, is where books on interchange with other libraries, or photocopies supplied to other libraries, are handled. In small libraries these will be dealt with by the postal section of the clerical office but in large ones it may be a complicated operation involving several staff.

In all these sections careful consideration is needed to plan an effective flow of work and materials; if a series of such charts has been drawn up in the brief the architect will be able to plan an effective layout; the duty of checking this against a simulated operation rests with the librarian.

Photographic department

The range of work in this field can vary from the dry-copier, which requires little except the space on which it stands (plus an electric power point), to a full photographic laboratory complex employing many staff. Any library holding large and/or fragile material which may have to be photocopied will find that no single machine will economically do the whole range of work. Camera machines need professional photographers and if one of these is to be employed then his work must be scheduled so that his time is used most economically. Unless he is given non-professional assistance he will necessarily spend valuable time on tasks below his capability (and salary level). A large library therefore may need a full photographic department; the tasks to be carried out have to be scheduled, and operation movements visualised (preferably with the assistance of a professional photographer). This information will be handed to the architect who will plan the appropriate area.

This is the theory; in practice I believe that there are three areas for which the architect is not the best person to produce a layout— photographic department, the library bindery and printing department. In each case it is better to have the layout designed by the professional concerned, preferably the one who is to run the department.

Printing department

The variations of work and equipment here are so wide that it is impossible to generalise.

Maintenance staff

In large establishments there will be a workshop for those who have to maintain the elaborate service machinery, but in a small library if there is a caretaker-handyman who has to "make-and-mend" then he should be provided with the space and the equipment to do his work properly. Benches, tool housing and storage for materials will be needed, as well as space for the inevitable chairs awaiting repair. In many libraries broken chairs are piled in odd corners where they are a hindrance and may be a fire hazard.

Cleaners will need space for storing materials as well as for vacuum cleaners and brushes (which can be tall). There should be a sink where buckets can be filled and dirty water poured away: washbasins should never be used for either purpose. These provisions should be made in each major area; cleaners too often have to haul buckets of water and cleaning materials for long distances because these operations had not been thought out at the planning stage.

Staff training section

In a large library a room will be needed for informal lectures given as part of an in-service training programme. Such a room, if placed near the main staff rest areas, could also be made available to the staff for occasional social functions. Blackboards, pinboards, projectors and screens can be freestanding.

Committee rooms

A requirement often met with is a committee or board room for occasional use by the authority. Although this will increase the overall allocation it can hardly be grudged by the authority and moreover, if the room contains shelves it can also become a "special collections" room or be used for seminars or as an occasional office. It is very useful to have at least one room which has no specific function at the outset; a need will certainly arise, even before the opening takes place.

Staff entrance

This is always necessary. It should be approachable by a well paved path; there should be facilities for staff car, motor-cycle and bicycle parking, preferably separate from the public provision, and under cover.

STAFF TOILET AND REST AREAS

Rest areas

The requirements for rest areas will differ widely among libraries, chiefly because of the working times of the staff. If shifts are worked, or if the library is in a place without easily accessible canteens or restaurants, fairly elaborate kitchens and dining facilities will be needed. Some libraries will have a small combined kitchen and staffroom divided notionally between dining and lounge areas by furniture or by contrasting flooring materials. In others, only an electric kettle, a small heater, storage cupboards and washing-up facilities may be needed, either within, or separate from, the staff lounge. This seems a simple stipulation but it is worth forming a small staff subcommittee to find out what is really needed. Too many uneasy compromises are to be found in this field.

A provision too seldom made, even in large libraries, is a small private rest area for women staff. This should be quite separate from the usual staff restrooms and possibly associated with the women's lavatory. Libraries with a large staff should include a first-aid room; a bindery will certainly need one. Whether such a room can be sited so as to serve readers in emergencies is a decision to be made by the librarian and intimated in the brief.

There is nothing unusual in the rest or lavatory requirements for library staffs; architects know about modern standards of comfort and there is no reason for the librarian to take any part in the planning and design of these areas. His only involvement is to give in brief the numbers of each sex to be catered for and to examine carefully the sketch plans to see that they meet the requirements.

The positioning of the restrooms is of some importance because of the potential waste of staff time in getting to those rooms from working areas. In a multi-storey building the architect will wish to group such areas vertically so as to simplify plumbing services within a service core and this will largely determine the position; nevertheless the librarian should notionally "time" the approach to each room by the staff who are to use it, taking into account lifts and stairways. In other countries one finds washbasins in workrooms and offices, seemingly a very civilised provision, but in British libraries they are seldom seen. Are they not asked for in the brief or do architects find them difficult to provide?

Lavatories

Experience has shown that it is as well for the architect's plans to be examined carefully and especially for the arrangements for women's lavatories to be scrutinised by a woman member of the staff. In these matters, as well as provision of lockers, architects have often underestimated staff needs.

In small buildings lavatories and lockers will be centralised but in large ones they will be needed on each floor, partly because this saves staff time. It seems obvious that there should be ample space for staff to get at their lockers but the architect may forget that access to all the lockers may be needed at one time (eg opening and closing times). Locker designs often annoy staff because some proprietary types allow too little space for coats to be hung without crushing; the result is that garments are hung on doors or across chairs throughout staff areas. In addition to lockers, drawers will be needed in all work areas for women's handbags.

In long-stay institutions, especially colleges and universities, it may be necessary to include lavatories for readers, but most public libraries oppose the provision of public lavatories (par-ticularly on the ground floor) because the library then becomes a calling-place for passers-by in that part of the town. If public lavatories are necessary it is better to put them close to long-stay departments rather than near the main entrance. In very small public libraries, which double as community lecture and film centres outside library hours, such provision may be essential; if for reasons of economy staff lavatories have to be made available to the public after library hours, access must not be through the staff restroom. In any case this is a disagreeable expedient, and the librarian should require separate public lavatories if at all possible.

Floor plans alone will not give the librarian all the information needed to check the suitability of provision: lists of equipment must also be scrutinised in detail. It should not be necessary? It is.

REFERENCES

[1] Library Association, County Libraries Section. Op. cit.

[2] HAM. RODERICK Theatre planning. The Architectural Press, London, 1972

[3] METCALF Op. cit., p 129

12 Furniture and fittings

In both sketch designs and financial estimating a distinction is usually drawn between fixtures and fittings and loose furniture. The former are stipulated in the brief, allowed for by the architect and shown on the sketch plans. Loose furniture, on the other hand, because it has little practical influence on the building design (although it will obviously affect the internal appearance), will be left until late in the programme and the choice will be a matter for consultation between architect and librarian. The distinction between the two categories is not entirely straightforward: formal book shelving, for example, is usually regarded as a "fitting", even though it may in fact be freestanding. The items discussed in this chapter therefore may fall into either category. Critical sizes and recommended layouts were considered in chapters 8 and 9; it is now necessary to look at the materials, designs and relative costs of the more important items.

The librarian should always choose the shelving, catalogues and technical equipment; the architect should choose the chairs and tables, because they are elements with which he is concerned throughout his professional life. Close consultation is perhaps even more important than the decision as to who makes the choice: the architect chooses tables, but the librarian is vitally interested in their stability, wearing quality of the tops and so on: similarly the librarian chooses the catalogue cabinets but the architect is very much concerned with the shape, material and colour because of their effect on the interior design, and the cost. If, for reasons of economy or of design, the architect recommends the purchase of furnishings from a single proprietary range, the librarian must inspect every item in that range before agreeing. As furniture and equipment commonly account for between 10 per cent and 15 per cent of the total cost of a library project, this is obviously not a matter to be treated lightly.

SHELVING

Factors for the librarian to bear in mind are appearance, durability, suitability for purpose, and cost; in practice there are other factors, such as weight, stability, public safety and so on, which the architect will certainly take into account but which will already have been given due attention by the highly efficient library furniture industry.

The relative importance of the qualities of bookshelving will vary, not only according to the type of library but also in different sections of each library. Almost every library will make a saving by having cheaper shelving in closed stack areas where appearance is less important; an exception perhaps is the large library where the very size of the contract can produce economy by using the same proprietary shelving throughout. Except in the case of some special hardwood bookcases with glass fronts, the architect today is less likely to have shelving constructed to his own designs; unless he has access to especially favourable labour conditions, he will find that manufacturers can offer library shelving more versatile and at a lower cost than any that can be specially made. There are many advantages in having shelving supplied by library equipment specialists; their wide experience over very many years and many countries, and the benefits of mass production, can outweigh the limitations which they place on the architect's freedom to design.

Many systems furniture suppliers offer a consultancy service in the planning and layout of shelving areas which can add much to the design teams expertise. If the contract is eventually given to that firm, the costs of the consultancy will be "free" (ie included in the total costs); if not, there may be a charge for the consultancy service but this could be worth while for the ideas it might produce. It is like employing a specialist consultant on a specific task. The architect will, of course, retain overall design control because the finished product must fit in with his concept. It is unfortunate that no independent testing institution inspects and reports on what is commercially available in the UK as is done under the Library Technology Programme of the American Library Association. As a guide to the strength and durability of the products, the architect has to rely on the manufacturer's word and reputation and his own experience. Here the value of visits to other libraries becomes apparent. Another very valuable exercise is to ask shelving suppliers to lend a unit of their shelving and to put this into use in the old library: after a few months' experience the librarian and architect will have much more knowledge of the unit's suitability than could have been gained by reading hundreds of leaflets.

The first consideration is the choice of materials—wood or metal; plastic shelving is not yet a feasible proposition (although plastic coverings are now offered) but its time may come. Moulded glass fibre has been seen but not much is yet known about its properties.

Softwood

This can be the cheapest of all materials for shelves. Easily assembled softwood units, a by-product of the materials storage industry, were at one time suitable only for the roughest stack conditions, but they are now obtainable in designs previously to be found only in hardwood at a much higher cost. In areas of high humidity, softwood shelving may tend to absorb moisture and become distorted when drying out unless it has been carefully prepared. Nevertheless when cost is critical and atmospheric conditions are suitable, this material should not be discounted, especially in non-public areas. All examples must be carefully examined to see that they are not subject to splintering and surface roughness.

Softwood or pressed board shelves on metal racks are also offered by materials handling firms, and give even greater freedom in dismantling and re-erection and a high cost saving. The librarian must consider carefully the loadbearing properties of the shelves; experience has shown that rows of heavy books have caused softwood shelves to bow, even in only 900 mm (3 ft) lengths.

Some librarians have stipulated painted softwood shelving for public use, or it may have been forced on them for reasons of economy. It is certainly cheap and has the advantage of complete freedom in colour choice, both of which may be important in small conversions, but it must not be forgotten that the constant movement of books soon marks painted shelves and that regular repainting is neither cheap nor convenient.

Hardwood

This was for centuries the only material in use in libraries and may still be preferred for its warm, mature, appearance, and its quietness. It can be cut to fit corners more easily than metal but is usually dearer. Poole[1] says it "may run to 20 per cent to 30 per cent more than steel". In the UK conditions the ratio may be higher. During the last thirty years a greater range of hardwoods has come on the market, particularly from tropical countries. How the cost relationship will change in the future is still uncertain: hardwoods may be priced out of the library market completely within a few years. Veneered plywood is a valuable compromise: it is strong, cheaper than true hardwood and can be attractive.

Wooden shelving is made in a "bookcase", backed or backless; in the latter case, cross-bracing may be needed to ensure rigidity. Adjustable shelving can be held by shelf supports, such as the familiar Tonks fittings, or by pegs in holes let into the sides of the uprights. Metal cases with brackets can be fitted with wooden shelves and decorative end panels; these are discussed under metal shelving below.

In some libraries hardwood shelving is essential because it gives a mellow atmosphere and this may be needed in law libraries for example, or in special collection rooms or research libraries; its appearance in such places is unrivalled.

In theory wooden shelving presents a greater fire hazard than metal but in practice this has seldom to be taken seriously: fire detection equipment will have been alerted and fire control action taken long before the intensity of heat is high enough to ignite wood.

Metal

Metal shelving is much the most common for tall stacks in large libraries where vast stocks of books have to be housed. The stacks are usually of steel although some pillars and brackets are now made of lighter materials. The stacks are of considerable strength and the shelves, particularly with u-type construction, can now be provided up to 1400 mm (4 ft 6 in) long without intermediate supports. On the other hand metal shelves of this kind are thicker than wood, so there is a loss of vertical space—which can be important.

Products of the materials handling industry can be used for shelving where cheapness is the only consideration but there will usually be some reduction in adjustability. Some firms offer prefabricated strips which are cheap and can be bolted together and used with either metal or wood (or even pressed-board) shelves in storage areas.

Such methods can be acceptable provided that the shelf surfaces, and particularly the edges, do not damage the books; it is also important to see that no bolt heads or shanks protrude. The body of the bolt should be located within the shelf thickness, not below it. Where possible, clips are better than bolts for this purpose.

Metal shelving, constructed specially for library use, is always better but of course more expensive. This shelving will have enamelled or plastic-coated surfaces and it comes in a wide range of colours. The two main types are the "case", in which the shelves slide (and possibly lock) into slots in the upright sides, and the "brackets", in which shelf brackets fit into slots in the upright columns.

The variations in style and method of construction offered by various manufacturers is so large that it is perhaps better to say merely that the case type is enclosed, and the bracket type open. Most other generalisations can be proved wrong by examples. Similarly the distinction between the bracket type and the systems shelving method (which will be referred to later) is becoming ever more blurred.

Poole[1] gives performance tests for bracket-type steel bookcases and also for their finishes: such tests with official backing would be most helpful in this country.

Adjustability is usually based on lines of slots or holes at 25 mm (1 in) intervals but another method is to have the brackets gripping the uprights by a fitment which can quickly be released, thus giving infinite adjustability. The latter costs more, and it must be seldom indeed that such a critical adjustment is necessary.

Rigidity can be obtained by cross-bracing but in many examples today the top and bottom members alone are sufficiently strong to hold stacks rigid; such bracing can prevent books being shelved to their full depth in open-backed stacks.

Stability is a matter of some importance because of possible "card-castle" collapses which can be very dangerous indeed. The safest ways are certainly to anchor the stacks to the floor or to fasten the uprights to the ceilings by collars, but these obviously limit flexibility. In the past, stacks were often linked by rods fastened to the walls; these are seldom seen today but they could be used as a safeguard in closed stacks. Case-type shelving is normally rigid enough in itself, but bracket-type often has wider feet for stability; the size and angle of these feet must be examined with care to see that they do not protrude into passageways. Many librarians consider that these feet give an unpleasing appearance in open access rooms but this is a subjective judgment. Because library floors are not always perfectly even, level adjusters under the feet can be a great asset.

Canopies can be supplied to bracket-type stacks to keep out dust or to serve as lighting holders; in stack conditions there seems little need for them, particularly in well-lit and air-conditioned buildings.

Systems metal shelving

Manufacturers now offer a very wide range of units which can be assembled to make both freestanding and wall-fixed shelving. They are planned around a range of uprights, brackets and shelves, many different sizes and finishes being available. There are apertures in the uprights, and into these either shelf-supporting brackets or brackets with integral shelves are inserted. A less common variant is to have brackets integral with the shelves which fold away for neat storing when they are kept in reserve.

Decorative panels, of wood, laminated plastic or plastic covered metal can be supplied and it is therefore possible to change the appearance of a library merely by changing the colour, design and shape of these end panels. Another great advantage is the very wide range of accessories made to fit into the unit systems: sloping shelves, display racks, catalogues, single study tables, seats—the number is constantly growing and offers the opportunity for internal flexibility at very low cost.

Perhaps the greatest extra facility is that of forming wall-shelving without the need for uprights. Vertical wall strips, with the usual line of openings to take the brackets, can be fastened to, or let into, the wall. In the latter case, only a vertical strip 8 mm ($\frac{5}{16}$ in)* wide will show when the wall is not being used for shelving, and decorative panels can be fitted to the walls between the strips. By this system, true flexibility of shelving can be obtained because a whole wall can be either used for shelving, or left unshelved, but decorated; in extreme examples, all walls of the building could be treated like this with even greater flexibility, but the cost would be high.

Although shelves normally fit the distance between fixed uprights, it is possible with wall strips to have very long, unbroken runs of metal shelf (or wood if the jointing is done carefully), supported by brackets at the wall strips. This will not be needed in many libraries but in some circumstances the architect might welcome the opportunity to provide a long, straight run without vertical divisions. Special book supports will be needed; see page 127.

Summarising then, metal shelving is cheaper, stronger and can be more colourful than wood, but its great disadvantages are that it can feel "cold and hard" and that it is noisy, books "clanging" as they are placed on the shelves.

CATALOGUE CABINETS

The size of the drawers is related to the size of the guide cards which are naturally larger than catalogue cards. The details of dimensions and fittings will not be discussed here because there is no substitute for the examination of examples of catalogues (this term is preferred to "catalogue cabinets") offered by specialist firms. Steel catalogues are noisy: softwood and plastic are nearly always unsatisfactory. Hardwood is expensive but almost inevitable. Proprietary catalogues, with label holders, card-locking rods, safety catches and so on, are the result of many years' experience; the production of catalogues, designed by the architect and made specially for the occasion by joiners, is fraught with difficulty and expense. Most library equipment firms offer standard carcasses for which special fronts may be produced to meet the architect's design requirements. If higher vertical rows of drawers are decreed, despite the greater difficulty which the reader will find on consultation, these can be supplied. Some catalogues incorporate consultation shelves below or between the drawers.

***

* If brackets are to hold shelves running in both directions, a double strip will be needed, so the amount showing will be 13·6 mm ($\frac{1}{2}$ in) wide.

Closed shelving area created from systems shelving units, Library Design and Engineering Ltd

Reader's seat in systems shelving, Library Design and Engineering Ltd

Manufacturers of library systems offer catalogues cantilevered off wall strips and thus completely interchangeable with wall shelving. This makes it possible for a subject catalogue to be dispersed, the cards for each subject being housed among the appropriate subject book tiers.

CHAIRS AND TABLES

Chairs

There is little special about the chairs needed for libraries. The librarian's contribution is confined to providing information about the use to be expected, the categories of readers who will use them, and the atmosphere of the room: for example he may object to plastic chairs in a very dignified ambience. Otherwise the material of which they are made concerns him little so long as the chairs are suitable for the predicted use, preferably untippable (leaning a chair backwards weakens the joints), durable and easy to clean: their cover material must not make readers uncomfortable, not make their clothes shine: they must neither damage the floor nor be noisy when moved. He should inspect samples of all the chairs proposed, preferably on the type of floor on which they will be used.

Tables

Tables suitable for all categories of readers are the common currency of the architect's world. The librarian will be concerned with rigidity and with the possible effect which the feet may have on floor surfaces; in extreme cases castors or glides may be necessary. He should test a suggested table by piling books on one end of it; this test fails some very attractive tables, offered at low prices by makers of office furnishings, because they are not designed for library conditions. The position of the table legs in relation to readers' seating positions needs thought.

The material of the table tops is certainly of concern to every librarian. Leather is particularly attractive to use but is easily marked; linoleum and rexine are harder; vinyl very much harder and available in a wider range of colours and patterns. When considering the relative resistance of these materials to the wear they will receive from books (particularly heavy manuscripts with metal clasps), it should be noted that there is usually a strip of wood about 40 mm ($1\frac{1}{2}$ in) wide around the resilient material on the table-top, and that this wood will also be vulnerable. If linoleum, for example, is chosen for the top because of its pleasant feel, accepting that it will have to be replaced at intervals, then the wood edging strip may need attention too and this is a much more expensive matter. A compromise could be a lino top with plastic laminate edging but many people still dislike plastic laminates on table tops.

A wooden table can be very attractive to the user; it marks less easily than leather or linoleum but if marks do appear, they are more difficult to remove. To renew a complete surface is a major undertaking. New developments in polyester coatings may make wood more feasible in the future; if veneered wood is to be used it is important to protect the edges against chipping by finishing them with a wooden strip or by bevelling.

The most durable materials are enamelled metal and plastic laminates but they feel cold and "unfriendly": it may be that

Shelf guiding, Library Design and Engineering Ltd

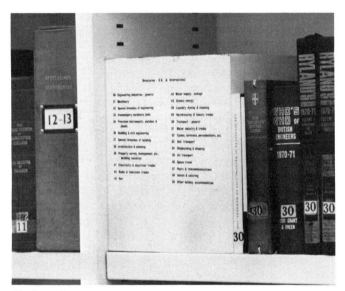

Block guides to contents of shelves, City Business Library, City of London

Guiding—stack end, fascia and shelf, University of Bath (Library Design and Engineering Ltd)

this is old-fashioned prejudice that will pass, and that future students will accept melamine as a normal writing surface. A very wide range of colours and patterns is available in these materials, (including imitation wood if prejudice can be overcome). It is important to test a surface in normal use conditions. If one tries to write with a ball-tip pen on a single sheet of paper laid on various table tops it will be found that some coverings are too soft (leather), some too uneven (oak or teak unless coated), some so hard that ink will not flow in the pen (glass and plastic laminates): but does the reader ever write like this on a single piece of paper? Questions of colour contrast and reflectance will be considered in chapter 15.

GUIDES

Guides to the contents of the individual cases, ties or even shelves will be needed and an infinite variety of these is available. In closed stack areas guides are less important because only the staff will have to locate books. Flat or tilted guides on ends of stacks plus, possibly, slip-on shelf guides are normally sufficient. When readers have to be guided to the required shelf, the matter is much more complicated.

General guides

In a prominent position near the reader entrance there should be a plan of the shelf layout of the entire library; another will be needed for each separate room. Ingenious systems have been devised, ranging from a layout map with coloured symbols (the colours being associated with the guides to individual shelving areas) to press-button systems which light up the required area on map.

Guide to tiers

Book cases usually have a fascia guide strip at the top of each tier but this is not possible when the top shelves have been left open, to accommodate larger books, or for a preferred "bookshop" appearance. Because the position of books on the shelves changes fairly rapidly in popular libraries, fascia tier guides must be easily changeable. Individual letters of cork or plastic can be fastened to fascias, by glue or pins. Cork lettering is available in a very wide range of founts for the purist, is comparatively cheap and can be coloured easily to particular requirements: plastic comes in a good range of colours and is stronger. These offer great advantages in flexibility but cork particularly can be easily tampered with and removed. All these single-letter guiding systems tend to mark wooden fascias and this can limit theoretical flexibility. Lettered strips offer rather less flexibility but are interchangeable within tiers, and even reversible, and they can be slid and locked into grooves on the fascias. If desired the lettering, either permanent or stuck on, can be on translucent material so that the guides can be back-lit. They can also be installed behind transparent material for protection.

Guides to shelves

Because of the greater thickness of steel shelves there is often provision for lettered strips to be slid along the front edges of the shelves, either letter by letter, or in made-up words; in some systems springing is incorporated to clip the guides into place. Where such provision is not made, sliding shelf clips can be used but these have the disadvantage of protruding slightly onto the top of the shelf. Lettering can be fastened to the edges of wooden shelves but this is a poor expedient. Individual shelf blocks can be made as guides to a shelf or to the whole tier. Where space can be spared on the shelves it is very helpful to the reader to have a block, perhaps 150 mm (6 in) cube, bearing on its face a guide to the contents of the shelf or tier. When neatly lettered such blocks can be attractive and most readers seem to like them. They also serve as book supports.

Book supports

As shelves will seldom be completely full in open access conditions, rows of books will tend to fall sideways, so some form of support is valuable, particularly for large books. On wooden shelves such supports can take the form of reversed U-shapes of rounded section rod, screwed onto the shelves but on both wood and metal shelves movable supports are more usual. These can be of metal or plastic and can stand independently on the shelves, being moved along as books are inserted or removed; systems shelving methods offer supports which can be clipped into the shelf above or slotted into the uprights. The latter is particularly useful where unbroken shelves beyond standard lengths are to be used. A more elaborate support can be spring loaded and fixed to a rail mounted on the wall behind wall shelving. Whatever method is used, it is as well for the support to be at least 15 mm ($\frac{1}{2}$ in) thick, and rounded; wire or very narrow metal supports, tend to get between pages of books when they are placed on the shelves in a hurry.

Tiers of oversized books, or awkwardly thin volumes, such as music scores or picture books, will need taller supports at closer intervals because larger books exert considerable pressure when falling sideways: because of the weight of these books the support should be permanently fastened to the shelves, top and bottom, or consist of sets of long rods which extend from top to bottom

Book supports, top and from wall strip by Interlink

shelf of a whole tier, passing through holes in each shelf. These are offered by some manufacturers of systems shelving but presumably could be organised in any type of shelving, with some loss of flexibility. Spring loaded rods have been offered for this purpose but are seldom very satisfactory. The best way is to have divisions running from front to back of each shelf to support the whole depth of the book.

A useful piece of shelf equipment is the narrow block of wood or plastic, roughly the size of a book, which is substituted for a particular volume that has been removed from a reference shelf. Space is available on the "spine" of the block for the book's title, while on the side can be a notice to the effect that the book is available elsewhere—usually on application to the staff. If the block has a built-in flange at the base it can also serve as a book support.

EQUIPMENT

In the brief the librarian will have indicated that he requires certain equipment—cameras, photocopiers, presses, guillotines, typewriters, duplicators and so on. The choice of this machinery is entirely his own; because so many different fields of activity are involved no attempt is made here to deal with the choice of models. The only matters that concern the team, and the architect in particular, are the space needed, weight for floor loading, electrical

Push-button guide to subject location, Central Library, Luton BC (Conran & Co Ltd)

outlets and cost (if these items are to be included in the contract). The latter point is one for the authority to decide. If the cost is to be included, the librarian informs the architect how much money is to be allowed for each specific item, including installation and transport costs if relevant. In most cases these items will not be included in order to save the cost of the contractor's percentage on all items on the contract.

Microform production and reading

This is a highly specialised field in which new equipment is constantly being marketed. At intervals *The Architects' Journal* publishes an information sheet on the subject, but much new equipment is produced between issues. The librarian must keep up to date with the latest articles on the subject and with manufacturers' catalogues. A decision must be made at an early stage so that the architect can make space, weight and electrical arrangements, but it is almost inevitable that during the planning and building process the librarian will become aware of equipment that will suit his needs better than that originally evisaged.

Manuscript storage

The librarian has indicated the method of storage he wishes to use and the size of document containers to be provided, but the architect should not choose them without the librarian's specific approval because much damage can be done if containers made of material with a high acid content are allowed to come into contact with manuscripts (or other materials) for long periods. This is the librarian's province and close consultation is needed.

REFERENCE

[1] POOLE, FRAZER G. The selection and evaluation of library bookstacks. *In Library Trends,* April 1965, p 425

13 Floors

The wear to which floors in libraries are subjected is similar to that in other public buildings—theatres, shops, town halls and so on. With these and their problems the architect will be familiar. He will know all about the range of covering materials available, their various properties and relative costs. The librarian's contribution will be to indicate the expected use, section by section, and his priorities with regard to such qualities as durability, quietness and ease of maintenance; later in the programme he will check the architect's recommendation against his own experience. In general, initial cost will dominate the choice of floor covering; it is unfortunate that because the cost of flooring is such a large element in the building there is always a temptation to economise in order to reduce the overall price, with the result that appearance and readers' comfort suffer, and maintenance costs are increased (see Berkeley[1])—a very serious matter as floors are the biggest single item in library maintenance.

Standards in commercial buildings seem to be usually higher—a sad comment on the community's attitude to public buildings. On the whole it is true that you get what you pay for. In each group of materials there is a cheap and an expensive grade and to expect one to give the same service as the other is unreasonable. In many cases the better, more expensive grade, has a lower maintenance cost. To work out the balance of advantages, each library's peculiar problem must be studied. No library will use the same materials everywhere; in practice it is the choice of combinations that matter. In areas exposed to the weather, or where noise is not an important consideration, terrazzo would give long-term savings but it is too seldom seen in libraries.

For each separate use the librarian must assess properties in terms of: cost—initial and long term, durability, maintenance, quietness, comfort, safety (non-slip), thermal conductivity, reflectance (shine), appearance.

For each of these qualities there is a "best choice"; but in order to make the correct overall decision it is necessary to know something of the properties of the different materials.

QUALITIES REQUIRED

Cost

Costs can be compared only when materials are directly comparable; for example, poured concrete is cheaper than carpet, but they are unlikely to be alternatives for a particular floor area. For each type of material there will be wide differences in cost, according to thickness and quality, and this complicates comparison between types: some vinyl is dearer than some carpet, but generally carpet is much dearer than vinyl. Rolls are usually cheaper over a given area than square tiles of the same material but not necessarily in a large contract: the question of whether tiles are to be stuck down is also a relevant cost factor.

At the lower end of the price scale come concrete, asphalt, vinyl asbestos and linoleum; then rubber, cork, hardwood block and the better thermoplastics; towards the top come nylon carpet, polyesters and polyurethanes. Even higher are wool carpet and the best of the very hard surfaces—terrazzo and marble. These are initial costs; a truer comparison is the total cost, including maintenance, over the expected life of the flooring. Such comparisons are very difficult to obtain except from manufacturers, whose claims are seldom acceptable as evidence. As a very wide generalisation it can be said that the initial extra cost of good quality carpet will be between a quarter and twice the price of the resilient material which are its main competitors. It is widely stated that the higher initial cost will be offset by the much lower maintenance costs of carpeting; this seems likely, but after some experience of carpets the writer is a little uneasy about such a claim, never having heard of controlled experiments which prove it.

Even Berkeley's figures are inconclusive on the matter.

Durability

The very hard materials are unchallengable in this respect; marble, terrazzo, brick, wood block (in that order). Carpet, especially that with a proportion of man-made fibres, can be quite good but the appearance suffers after a time. Rubber is much better than most vinyls and linoleum. If the chief source of wear is grit on shoes off wet roads, cork can be a disaster. Stiletto heels (if they every return) ruin linoleum, vinyl and rubber. Different materials vary widely in their resistance to stains such as those made by cigarettes, tea, coffee and ink, but hard non-porous surfaces are obviously much the best.

Maintenance

Carpet is quickly cleaned by vacuum cleaner but this is not the end of the story; in heavily used areas, particularly near entrances, a pattern of dirt will develop and the carpet will have to be shampooed—by no means a simple task. Carpet is also vulnerable to cigarette burns and stains of many kinds: it is not as hygienic as the non-porous surfaces. Marble, tile and similar stone materials are very easily washed; hardwood blocks need more attention but the work is fairly simple. Other surfaces can be less easy to maintain: linoleum needs both polishing and regular resealing but requires less attention than cork. Vinyl is unsatisfactory both because of the regular cleaning it requires and because it is marked so easily, particularly by rubber heels. The way the material is laid—rolls or tiles—affects the issue: see below.

Quietness

This is not so easy to assess as it might appear: carpet is so good as a sound insulator that it is usually the most important piece of acoustic treatment for its area, but if other absorbent materials are present the result can be too "dead" and inhuman. See Saunders[2] and Koderas[3]. Rubber, cork and linoleum are fairly good for quietness; vinyl is less good but better than wood. In general all the very hard floors are noisy, but even this generalisation should not be accepted too easily: in the City Business Library, London, a marble floor, usually considered impossibly noisy, has proved very acceptable in an area where absolute quiet is not required.

Comfort

This is largely a matter of opinion. Carpet with a good backing gives a luxurious feeling but even sheet linoleum can be very soft to the feet if it has a rubber underlay. Is softness underfoot a desirable quality? Staff who have to be on their feet for long periods, in counter areas for example, may find that too soft a flooring can be tiring. On the other hand staff should never be expected to spend long periods standing on the harder floors which soon make ankles and feet very painful. If a counter area is set into the middle of a hard floor, the counter should be fitted with a resilient surface. If this is not done initially it will certainly have to be done later under pressure of staff complaints: and the pieces of softer material then used will, because they are not built-in, be a possible cause of accidents.

In general carpet is outstanding, rubber and linoleum good, cork and vinyl quite good.

Safety

Highly polished marble and vinyl (but not embossed vinyl) can be particularly dangerous but for most materials correct maintenance according to the manufacturer's instructions will give safe conditions. Carpet is excellent and cork good.

Central Library, Bebington BC

Thermal conductivity

The ability to conduct heat affects the decision as to choice of flooring materials in two opposite ways: where heat inside the building is to be conserved, low conductivity is desirable; conversely when underfloor heating is installed, as much heat as possible has to pass upwards into the library, so high conductivity is desirable. Some of the harder materials have high conductivity—concrete, marble, and asphalt; vinyl and rubber have a higher conductivity than linoleum, cork very much less; carpet, of course, has least of all.

Generally, carpet is best for keeping a library warm and cosy but it is worst for the efficient operation of under-floor heating.

Reflectance

Brock Arms[4] has said, "For study conditions where reading tasks require a long attention span, it is desirable to use only materials and colours within the field of vision which reflect percentages of light within the allowable contrast ration of 1 to 10." Vinyl in particular can offend here.

Appearance

Perhaps this should be left entirely to the architect, but it is legitimate to note that there are infinite varieties of colour and pattern available in vinyl. Where this material is laid in tiles rather than rolls, bright patterns are easily made; some librarians feel that the temptation to create jazzy patterns has been too much for some modern architects. Many librarians feel that wood block and cork offer the best "mature" appearance in a library.

UNDERFLOORS

The architect will deal with the important matter of the under-flooring. It must be smooth, or its irregularities may work through the flooring material; unless it is laid over ventilated space it must be waterproof. Concrete is most usual (but can concrete ever be completely waterproof?): wood may be used in certain situations. Where damp is to be expected a separate waterproof underlay may be essential.

SPECIAL AREAS

For entrance areas the librarian's priorities will be durability and ease of maintenance. Durability is important for two reasons: cost of renewal and because replacement of the entrance floor can bring the whole library to a standstill. The librarian may therefore place the highest priority on the need to have uninterrupted use of the area for many years, and might in this case favour marble, terrazzo or a poured floor. Alternatively he may prefer thick rubber which is quiet and can be replaced very easily. For general public service areas the librarian will have to be sure that the architect fully understands the tremendous wear which certain traffic lanes in a library may undergo. The IN and OUT lanes beside lending library counters suffer very heavily, particularly if readers come to the IN counter direct from outside the building with grit on damp shoe soles. Here it is reasonable to have marble or terrazzo tiles or strips of thick rubber rather than replace sections of carpet, linoleum or vinyl as they wear out. Naturally this reduces flexibility and the change of flooring is difficult to provide in open plan libraries. The use of dirt-attracting mats at entrances, supplied on a contract basis, can be a great economy but for safety they should be fitted in mat wells.

For corridors, closed stack rooms, and staff working areas the architect will use a suitable "public building" material: cork, vinyl or linoleum. Even here carpet, usually of a cheap grade, is becoming common; to use throughout a large building will mean a very large order and consequently an advantageous price.

MATERIALS AND THEIR QUALITIES

Carpet

Carpets are unrivalled in their range of colours and their power to create a welcoming and luxurious atmosphere. The emphasis on "luxury" may seem academic but it can have practical advantages in that children are said to be more restrained in carpeted rooms (it may be that the effect wears off with familiarity).

Carpet should have a pile density of 100 tufts per 625 mm^2/(in^2) and pile height of 15 mm to 18 mm. It can be composed of 100 per cent wool or 100 per cent man-made fibres; mixtures are common, perhaps the most popular proportion at present is 80 per cent wool–20 per cent nylon. The differences between these types of carpets are important: advantages and disadvantages being present in each type in varying degrees[5]. It will be necessary to balance price, stain resistance, wearing qualities, anti-static qualities, and so on: this subject is worth studying by the librarian before he commits his library to heavy expenditure on this material. A good quality sponge rubber underlay will help to produce an even softer feel and a longer life. This underlay can either be laid as a roll, pre-fixed to a roll of carpet or pre-fixed to each carpet tile. More common are backings of polypropylene, polyvinyl-chloride or bitumen and these are normally stuck to the subfloor. Many developments have recently taken place with the use of man-made fibre and animal bristles for non-woven carpets, such as Heugafloor and Heugafelt. These are often of very short pile, closely packed; the surface is resistant to dirt, but does not offer the same attractive appearance, or sense of luxury, as woven carpeting. Non-woven carpets have great advantages for areas such as stairs, where quietness, safety, hard wear and economy are needed. Manufacturers' ranges and claims must be studied carefully: this is the architect's business.

Ten years ago carpet was usually specified only as a luxury for areas where hard use was not expected, but it is now found in most libraries which can afford it; a survey of newly-built public libraries in the US shows that 80 per cent of those built in 1969, 86 per cent of those built in 1970 and 1971 and 89 per cent of those built in 1972 were carpeted[6].

Vinyl

For some years this has been the most used floor covering in British libraries. When bonded to its own soft backing, vinyl can be comfortable but without this it can feel hard. Many variations in plastics have been made, including vinyl asbestos, and cork covered with a transparent vinyl. On the whole such floor coverings are cheap, fairly durable and available in a wide range of patterns and colours, but they are not particularly quiet, they are easily scratched and marked and their shine may reflect overhead lights to the annoyance of users. Some consider that a large expanse of shining vinyl gives an institutional feeling: perhaps this is just a matter of taste.

Linoleum

This was once almost universal in libraries, usually of "battleship" quality—3·2 mm gauge: it is cheap and good to walk on but the colours are less attractive than those of vinyl and it takes time and energy to maintain its appearance.

Rubber

This varies immensely, particularly in thickness. Thick rubber, now usually synthetic, has proved surprisingly long-lasting and comfortable in use. While it can not create an air of welcoming luxury, it is useful for quietness and durability in a very heavily used area. It tends to deteriorate in continuous direct sunlight.

Cork

When well maintained cork can look most attractive, but its maintenance is a serious problem in areas of heavy use. The grit carried in on readers' shoes can soon break down the surface seal, and resealing can be carried out only when the room is not in use. Cork is not particularly durable and after a time there will be a noticeable difference in colour between tiles which have received the heaviest wear, and have therefore been cleaned most often, and those close to furniture.

Wood

Hardwood blocks, parquet and softwoods of various kinds were widely used in the past but are seen less frequently today in reading and traffic areas. They are all noisy; wood block and parquet are expensive but look very ttractive indeed. Certain newer composition floors contain finely ground wood among other elements; these are fairly cheap and are quieter than very hard floors but as yet it is difficult to obtain reliable information about wearing qualities. Like all composition floors, these tend to look drab.

ROLL OR TILES

Some materials may be laid either in roll or in square tiles; each has its advantages and disadvantages. As the question arises most often in the field of carpeting, comment will be restricted to that field, but it applies to flexible flooring in general.

Rolls of material are easier, and in some circumstances can be cheaper, to lay. Their appearance is even, there are no spaces in which dirt can accumulate and micro-organisms breed. When sections show signs of wear, patching can be difficult, although some rolls with bonded underlay can be cut easily and the edges do not fray.

In small quantities carpet tiles can turn out to be dearer than rolls of the same material, partly because of the labour cost of sticking them down, but bulk purchase may reverse this difference. However well tiles are laid, the joints will show. Some designers see this as an advantage over plain carpet and point out that in roll carpet the seams will show as long runs and may be less acceptable visually. Tiles are less hygienic than roll, and if they do not fit closely they may trip people up. As loaded trolleys can force up the edges of tiles, it may be necessary to have the trolleys fitted with specially wide castors, but if tiles are well stuck down this should not apply. The great advantage of tiles is said to be that worn ones can be interchanged with others from a less worn area, but the writer has not found this acceptable in practice, if only because wear is usually gradual over a number of tiles. Alternatively worn tiles may be replaced by new ones; if this is the intention it is advisable to buy extras when the floor is laid as colours vary in different batches.

Carpet tiles are usually 500 mm (20 in) square; when laid on a sound base they do knit together, but because they are affected by moisture in the air and can expand by between 2 per cent and 6 per cent an appropriate allowance may have to be made when they are first fitted. If they are to be stuck down—much the better policy in most situations—this allowance cannot be made.

REFERENCES

[1] BERKELEY, BERNARD Floors: selection and maintenance. Library Technology Program, American Library Association, Chicago, 1968 (Useful citation of articles on different flooring materials in the bibliography)

[2] SAUNDERS, D. J. Sound insulation and use of carpets *In Flooring and carpet specifier*, May 1970, pp 2–7

[3] KODERAS, M. J. Sound absorbative properties of carpeting. *In Interiors*, June 1969, pp 130–131

[4] ARMS, BROCK Principles of illumination for libraries. *In The library environment: aspects of interior planning.* American Library Association, Chicago, 1965, pp 32–33

[5] KREUTZBERG, H. The right answers on carpeting. *In Architect*, October 1971, pp 83–87 and November 1971, pp 83–86

[6] *Library Journal* December 1 1972

14 Circulation

Horizontal circulation of people, whether readers or staff, will be taken into account by the architect when he is designing the overall layout. He will see the quantities involved from "activities and users", the direction from the circulation and traffic diagrams. He will already be familiar with the standard space allowances for a person moving within a building and with doorway and corridor widths.

The positioning of stairways, particularly in their effects on access and security, have already been mentioned, but the librarian will also be concerned with the possible aural and visual distraction of readers, especially in open-plan libraries. This has been an unfortunate feature of the design of some modern university libraries: readers must be protected from such distraction.

The number and size of lifts can be assessed from the statistics provided, but other questions must be answered:

Will "staff only" lifts be needed, eg for use with book trolleys? Is access to certain floors to be restricted to staff? It so, will locks and keys be necessary?

Will "staff only" lifts be needed, eg for use with book trolleys? operation at peak times or at all times?

Is special provision to be made for the disabled, even on mezzanines?

If continuous lifts, such as paternosters, are to be used what provision will be made for the disabled or the elderly?

It may be an advantage to have escalators instead of lifts and the librarian will be less familiar with their qualities than he will with those of lifts. Escalators can deal with very large numbers indeed and they can be reversible, taking readers up only during most of the day but bringing a great many down quickly at closing time. Alternatively, an upward escalator only may be provided, leaving readers to use stairs for downward journeys. Escalators can be efficient but they have some drawbacks (apart from high cost): they will need far more horizontal space than lifts and will therefore be a major factor in the design. The example here from the plans for the new Birmingham Central Library show how complex such a system can be.

If only because of fire regulations, stairways will have to be provided as well as either lifts or escalators. The relationship between these facilities affects both reader traffic routes and planning considerations.

Fire regulations will also cause emergency exits to appear in the sketch plans. These are the despair of librarians because they so often make nonsense of the proposed security arrangements. A simple push-bar door is an open invitation to readers to walk

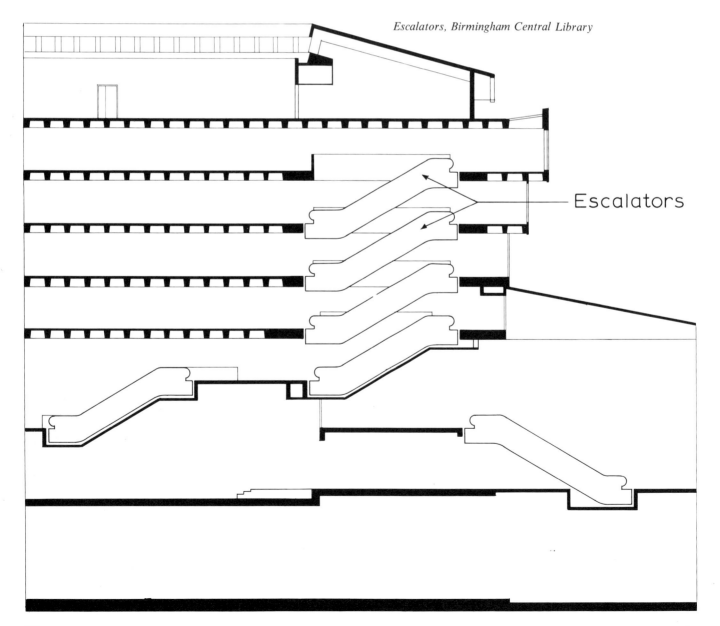

Escalators, Birmingham Central Library

Escalators

out with books. One common solution, putting a bell on the door, is helpful only in telling the librarian that he has lost another book. But break-glass systems may be acceptable to the fire authorities and these have a value as a psychological deterrent although they are far from perfect. Such doors will also need conventional locks if staff are to use them during the course of their work and this means that many duplicate keys will be needed. Main entrance and exit doors deserve particularly careful study. Will there be a lobby to prevent draughts affecting staff on duty at a counter just inside the entrance? This is essential unless doors are revolving. A heat curtain may be expensive but perhaps it will be justified.

If revolving doors are proposed, is there provision for a by-pass at peak times and can the doors be swung aside to allow furniture and similar items to enter the building?

MATERIALS CIRCULATION

Because "materials" in a library consist largely of books, and because the librarian will be very experienced in handling books, his special knowledge will be invaluable. "Books are different" and they cannot be treated merely as objects of a certain size and weight; whatever methods are used to move them must allow variations in handling according to the value and the fragility of different volumes.

Books in a library present three entirely different handling problems:

distribution after arrival, through the preparation processes and then to open or closed shelves;

replacement on shelves after readers have removed them;

retrieval of books from closed stack and their return after use.

Distribution of books after arrival
The progress of books through the processing section has received too little attention. The number to be handled hourly may be small but over months and years multiple handling can represent a very expensive use of staff time. In many libraries, day after day, staff manhandle parcels from delivery, up steps, onto book trolleys (which were designed for quite a different purpose), along corridors and into passenger lifts, crossing public access routes and wasting an incredible amount of time. A little thought at the planning stage can make a great deal of difference.

Loading and unloading
The main feature of a loading bay should be a ramp or platform so that transfer to and from a van can be made without a change of level.

The delivery route to the unpacking point should have been given its degree of priority in the "activities and users" section of the brief so that the architect will have made the route direct, unimpeded and clear of other routes.

Horizontal conveying
In most libraries members of the staff carry the books: the greatest concession to automation is the book trolley. If trolleys are to be used for this purpose—and in small libraries it will be the obvious method—they should be chosen from the products of the materials handling industry, not from library suppliers.

Where large numbers of books are involved and there are changes of level in their progress from section to section, thought should be given (by the architect at the request of the librarian) to provide more labour-saving methods. Few libraries are likely to need tracked trolley systems or powered rollers but some may. On the other hand gravity roller tracking, possibly telescopic and removable, would be a boon in many existing libraries' preparation departments. A good example of planning book movement can be seen in the National Lending Library for Science and Technology at Boston Spa: an overhead conveyor system with (page 133) sophisticated control features and other devices, both horizontal and vertical.

Carrier on overhead chain conveyor (Crown copyright)

Three-level conveyor system in packing area (Crown copyright)

Feed and discharge conveyors connecting automatic lift to packing conveyors (Crown copyright)

Box loading on to Lamson selective vertical conveyor

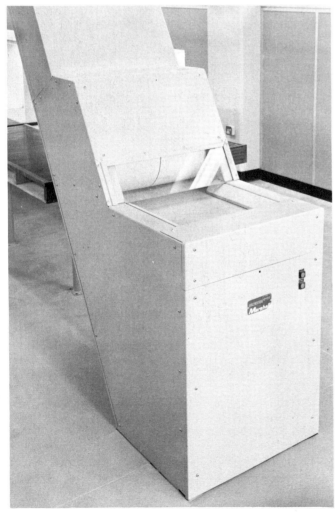

Document lift at NLL

In less advanced systems some form of closed container will have to be employed. Containers may also be needed where automatic book hoists are used, or to assemble books in bulk for transport to different parts of the building or to branch libraries. Too little attention has been paid to the design of these containers; factors to be considered are:

size relative to the channels or positions in to which the containers will have to fit, particularly if they are to be stacked when not in use;

weight and size should be related to the reasonable lifting capability of those who have to handle them;

material—both its durability and its effect upon books. Wicker boxes have often been used because they are light and cheap but after heavy use they tend to splinter and damage the books. Plastic and fibreboard are the best materials today, but if containers made of these are to be regularly loaded onto vans they may have to be bound with metal or framed in wood.

handles and method of labelling to show contents and/or destination: small points perhaps, but such matters should be thought out at the beginning, not after the need has been discovered.

Vertical conveying

Alternatives for this purpose include:

trolley into passenger lift; obviously inconvenient in staff time and in interference with other services;

special trolley lift—better: a signal system will be required to tell staff to take the trolley out at the appropriate floor;

book hoist: this will of course take smaller numbers but it should be large enough 635 mm × 455 mm (24 in × 18 in) to take bound newspapers. Again, light or sound signals (or both) will be needed to indicate arrival. Firm discipline for immediate clearance of hoists will be needed or chaos will result.

Improvements on the old book hoist are available, including semi-automatic loading and unloading and automatic selection of floor for delivery. One type uses a platform, counter-balanced by a spring so that it remains still when holding an empty container; when a loaded container is placed on the platform it swings towards the centre of the elevator and the container is picked from the loading platform automatically by pegs on the elevator chain. When the chosen floor is reached the container is automatically discharged; the floor is indicated by a simple sliding tab on the container.

Such requirements must be thought out by the librarian at a very early stage and incorporated in the primary brief. Almost all these installations will have spatial as well as structural implications; some book hoists can be freestanding but even these will have to be near other core elements and the architect must know what is needed in this field before he proceeds to his feasibility study. When books are moved in quantity (for example when new books arrive in parcels, a service lift system may be needed).

Books are not the only items that have to be moved about the library but most others—documents, microforms, tapes, records—are much less bulky and present fewer problems. The item causing most frequent movement is probably the photocopy. Photocopies can be placed in containers in book delivery systems; alternatively provision can be made for special conveyors that have their own route and their own priority (see p. 133).

Distribution to shelves

This activity involves careful thought about the design of book trolleys.

Book trolleys

Proprietary trolleys are available. Attention must be paid to their stability and to the ease with which they can be pushed, particularly over carpets; the size and type of castors is critical. As always, the exact function must be identified before a decision is made.

For books in boxes and, to a lesser extent, large books (such as bound periodicals) piled in heaps, the transport trolley is used.

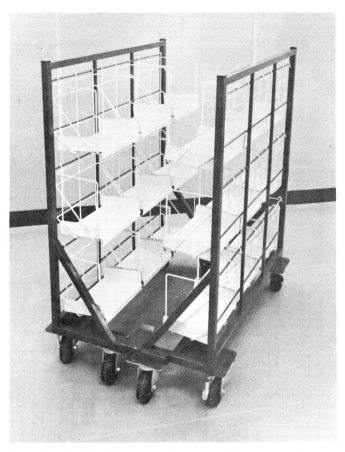

Pair of trolleys locked together for moving (Crown copyright)

Shelving hods suspended from wire mesh panels (Crown copyright)

A flat and wide shelf is an obvious priority. If the load on one shelf is as much as the staff can push, why have the usual two shelves? (Perhaps the second is essential for the trolley's stability.) For conveying books to a position from which they can be shelved by hand, the usual library trolley will be used. These are generally made with a slight slope on each side so that titles can be sorted easily into order; they serve a dual purpose in housing a ready-made display of books which have been newly returned to the library. While stationary this trolley can have a foot-operated lock applied to the wheels. It is a common feature in small lending libraries but as a shelving unit it is inconveniently low for most readers. It saves staff time in that readers take books from it and so reduce the number which have to be shelved but it is really a lazy expedient.

For special circumstances (for example where a trolley cannot be taken close to the shelves because there are stairs on the route) there is a trolley with integral removable troughs with a handle at each end. Because of the weight of a whole row of books, the length of this unit has been kept down to 600 mm (2 ft). The Hod system described on page 113 should also be considered as should the ingenious system at the National Lending Library which uses similar hods on trolleys and on shelving stacks. For hospital wards where bed-ridden patients should be able to choose from a selection of titles, a special trolley is necessary. It must be light enough to be handled for long periods, stand stable and be narrow enough to pass between beds.

For the use of mothers accompanied by small children in a lending library there is a trolley which includes space for both books and a child and this enables the mother to carry books around in comfort while keeping the child out of harm's way.

Future developments include a motorised trolley for use in large libraries and large hospitals where distances between wards can be considerable. The Hospitals and Handicapped Readers' Group of the Library Association has done good work on this project: the *Unesco Bulletin*[1] illustrates an electric trolley with two small revolving bookcases on a low carriage which enables bedridden patients to choose without having to stretch.

Trolley with removable shelves, Warwick Production Co Ltd

Retrieval from stack

Closed stack is certainly the method most economical of space but to provide the reader quickly with the book he needs becomes a most expensive operation and one requiring careful study.

In the simplest case the reader will enter the call number of the required book on a slip which he hands to a member of the staff

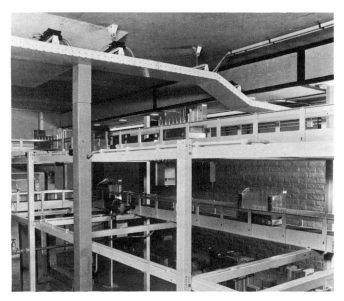

Randtriever conveyor showing containers in transit

Control station showing book container arriving

who will check it for accuracy and fetch the book. In a large library this process will not be feasible because the stack is likely to extend over several floors. Such a stack will be divided notionally into sectors, each with its own staff. Because of the long opening hours of libraries, a large number of staff will be needed for this operation, so any method which can reduce that number deserves careful consideration.

The operation can be broken down into the following parts:

Receiving and checking the call slip prepared by the reader. Because readers can so easily misunderstand location information it is never advisable to allow slips to be dispatched unchecked to the stack. A preliminary glance by the librarian on duty may save much fruitless searching.

Transmission of the call-slip information to the appropriate stack sector. This will start from the inquiry desk, but in a large system with inquiry points throughout the library it will be necessary to have a distribution centre for routing the slips, or the information on them, to the appropriate sector of the stack.

Searching for and delivering the book to the reader. In practice, delivery will usually be to the staff point within the reading area and from here the inquiry staff or attendants will take over distribution to the reader, the number of the seat where he may be found being shown on the slip. Alternatively, an illuminated panel near the staff desk may indicate that the book is ready for collection.

Returning the book to stack—from reader to staff desk, to stack centre, to stack sector and so to the shelf place.

BOOK RETRIEVAL COMMUNICATIONS

To transmit the identifying information about a required book from reader service point to access area of closed stack, the following methods are possible:

Telephone—cheap in installation but expensive in staff time in that two people take part. There is also risk of mishearing.

Telex (Teletype) This calls for more expensive equipment, particularly if there are many reader service points, but takes only one staff member's time in sending the information because the recorded message can wait at the receiving machine until staff are available to deal with it.

Fascimile transmission This system copies the call slip and reproduces it at the stack point. It is necessary only to insert the slip in the machine; no other staff time is needed. To the cost of the transmitter and receiver (or a more expensive combined transmitter/receiver permits two-way communication) is added only a pair of ordinary telephone wires and a negligible use of electricity. The only drawback is that the scanning system involves

a slight delay while it is operating and the next slip cannot be inserted until the previous one has been completed.

Pneumatic tube This is much the most common method and it has been in use for very many years. Modern systems use plastic conveyors with outside measurements only 60 mm ($2\frac{3}{8}$ in) in diameter running in plastic tubes, with comparatively small power plants. The old noise problem has been largely overcome but the system can never be absolutely silent. The setting of a control on the carrier can, by tripping levers, direct it to the appropriate sector point. This system appeals most in a new building where plans can be made in good time to accommodate the system of tubes.

Gravity tube This is the cheapest and quietest system, the slip needing no enclosed carrier, but it is possible only where there is a vertical free fall.

Document carrier There are several varieties (page 133)—document lift, drag-band or travelling double-belt: all have their advantages. Much depends on the angles round which the flexible belts have to travel and the space available for the width of the belt.

AUTOMATED BOOK RETRIEVAL

Any method which could reduce staff involvement in the time-wasting and laborious business of fetching books from stock would be a boon. Several methods of varying complexity have been devised. Brawne[2] describes the Bibliofoon system which has been installed for some years in the Technological Institute at Delft, Holland.

Here the reader dials the call number of the required book on one of several phones situated in the public areas near the catalogues. The call is monitored electronically to see that the book is not already on issue; if it is not, a switching system causes direction lights to appear in the stacks guiding the attendant to the appropriate tier. The call number of the book appears on a digit indicator tube close to the appropriate stack: the attendant removes the book and dispatches it by a system of spiral chutes and conveyor belts to the issue point. He also presses a button which causes the call number of the book to be automatically recorded at the issue point. If the book is not on the shelf the attendant presses a different button which records the number of the wanted book at the loan centre, so informing the staff that the book cannot be found. The loan centre therefore knows about the transaction, whether it is completed or not.

This scheme has certain sophisticated advantages over earlier methods and it could presumably be developed further by the use of computers and by a mechanical book return system, but it still requires the time of an attendant who has to find and dispatch

Conserv-a-trieve selection machinery

Conserv-a-trieve system

the book and, more important, both his time and his judgment in reshelving it.

A great step forward was made by the Randtriever produced by Sperry-Rand Inc. Essentially this is a method of storing file boxes in stacks where they can be packed closely (and therefore economically of space) because they are to be retrieved entirely by machine and no space for human access is required (other than a minimum for maintenance engineers): in fact, stacks can be as high as 7264 mm (23 ft 10 in).

When this installation is included in the plans for a new library, therefore, the maximum height can be used by eliminating the floors needed for access to conventional-height stacks. This in itself produces a saving in structural costs.

Requests in the form of call numbers are typed manually or transmitted by punched cards from a control desk in the reader area. This information passes electronically to a "head" which then moves both laterally and vertically to locate the desired file container. The head latches onto the container, pulls it from its rack and brings it to the control centre by a system of conveyor belts and hoists. All these actions—selection of head, guidance of head to container and transport of container—are carried out entirely automatically.

When the file container is to be returned it is put in its holder at the control desk, buttons are again pressed (or punched cards inserted) and the container will find its way back to its appointed place in the stacks.

This is an extremely simplified description of a very complicated system which can store files very compactly, and select, deliver and return them swiftly with a minimum of human interference. There are many special features which allow calls to be stored during busy periods and dealt with in their turn, "shunting" arrangements so that file retrieval can take precedence over file return, and other answers to the objections which at once spring to a librarian's mind. In all it is a highly effective answer to mass filing and retrieval arrangements.

The system was designed to retrieve box files but has since been applied to library stacks, the unit being a "file box" full of boxes. The box could hold a single large book of course, but it would normally hold a number that will vary with their sizes. A specification quoted by Schriefer and Mostecky[3] gives the average contents of the file box as 8.33 books. The whole box will be transported to the control point; the required book will be withdrawn and the file box will return swiftly to its place (a spring arrangement can easily keep the other books from moving within the box). On return the box will again be sent for, the issued book inserted, and the full box will again find its way back to the proper place on the shelf. Books in the stacks can be in any order provided that their location is recorded; it is of course a fixed location system in that new books cannot economically be inserted into the shelf order, but as they can never be consulted except through the retrieval machinery this is no disadvantage, indeed it saves space by making shelving by sizes practicable. Stack areas can be sealed to simplify cleaning and fire problems.

The immediate reaction of most librarians is to deplore the loss of the opportunity to handle several books in order to settle one inquiry. This difficulty can be overcome once it is realised that any number of books can be fetched swiftly, although shelving in a completely random sequence may make answering a subject inquiry a lengthy operation. Given that the books are "handled" gently and that the machine is durable, it opens a new era in book retrieval. After detailed investigations the writer found the only drawback to be the cost of the machinery and its inability to handle really enormous books. The cost has to be considered against space and staff savings, which, over the whole life of the building can be considerable.

Figures supplied by Sperry-Rand Inc[4] refer to installations 7264 mm (23 ft 10 in) high, 20066 mm (65 ft 10 in) wide and 15824 mm (51 ft 11 in) long; claiming that these dimensions accommodate 209 475 average volumes. The floor of this area must be designed to carry a uniformly distributed load of 25·5 kN/m² (536 lb/ft²);

this would normally imply that the stack was on the bottom floor of the building. To offset the cost of the installation would be the saving of one entire floor of the building. (If a smaller installation were put in an existing building this particular saving could not of course be made.)

A somewhat similar system is available in the UK under the trade name Conserv-a-trieve, marketed by Roneo-Vickers. Here again an electronically controlled head locates and withdraws a specific metal file or book container from its storage position on instructions from a control desk and brings it to the desk at a speed of 1270 mm (50 in) per second, returning it to its own stack position in the same way. The entire retrieve and return operation can therefore take place smoothly within a few seconds, certainly well under a minute even in the largest installation. The savings in space are enormous and for staffing the system requires only a seated operator who translates the inquiry into push-button terms. To gain the full advantage from such a system the stack must of course be designed for the purpose, but it can be installed in an older library with some loss of efficiency.

REFERENCES

[1] Unesco Bulletin, March/April 1969, pp 84–85

[2] Brawne Op cit, pp 141–143

[3] SCHRIFFER, KENT and IVA MOSTECKY Compact book storage: mechanized systems. *In Library Trends*, January 1971, pp 362–378

[4] SPERRY-RAND CORPORATION *In* Schriefer and Mostecky. Op cit, p 375

15 Lighting

Choosing the best lighting for a library is a particularly complex problem because the lighting has to do several entirely different things: to allow reading to take place in comfort, to contribute to the internal appearance of the building and, to a lesser extent, to the external impact upon the passer-by. For each of these there will be available artificial light, which is entirely controllable, and natural light which is very much less controllable. Because the human response to light is largely subjective, or at any rate conditioned, there are no absolute standards by which success can be judged and the librarian's experience can be as sound a guide as the architect's. Even a specialist lighting consultant will be expert on the best methods rather than the most acceptable results.

Even in the most easily definable aspect of lighting, the intensity, standards differ so widely, and so wildly, that we are not justified in presuming that the librarian will present the problem and the architect provide the solution. Certainly in matters of aesthetics and the means of providing light the architect is master, but for the satisfaction of a reader's lighting needs there is no authoritative technical solution, only numerous opinions.

The standard authority in this field is The Illuminating Engineering Society (IES), but by this we mean the British society whereas American references are to the American society with the same title and initials. To add to the confusion there is very little conformity between the codes and technical reports of the two bodies.

Intensity of light is the most obvious of the questions to be considered but by no means the most important; in using light to contribute to the overall design the architect will employ variations, not only of intensity but also of quality, colour, direction, shape (as created by the fittings) and contrast to contribute to both operational efficiency and interior design. These variations will enable the architect to indicate change of mood in different parts of the building, and to produce interest, quietness, sparkle or whatever effect he wants to achieve. In doing so he must take care that reading conditions are not impaired and must assess what levels of glare and contrast are acceptable.

The librarian will also be concerned about the lighting's effect upon the materials in his care. All paper, vellum and parchment, as well as the words or other marks upon them, can be damaged by light, as can other sensitive materials which the library may hold. While he will be most concerned about old and valuable material, the librarian will not forget that paper of the mechanical wood period (late nineteenth century) is particularly vulnerable. The damage is chiefly but not entirely, caused by ultra-violet (uv) radiation emitted by all white light sources, daylight being the most dangerous. The rate of damage will depend on the intensity of the light and the length of exposure; in general it will accord with the product of these elements—the higher the intensity, the greater the damage; the longer the exposure the greater the damage. These matters will seldom be of any consequence when materials are being studied by readers but when items are displayed for long periods the results can be very serious.

Sensitive materials should not be exposed continuously to a level of more then 50 lux (for lighting measurements, see next column). As daylight of this level would be too low to be acceptable for a public exhibition, an artificial light source must be used. As it would obviously be inconvenient to withdraw an exhibit every few hours, a common answer is to arrange for displays of the most sensitive materials (old manuscripts, water-colours etc) to be covered with curtains which can be easily drawn aside by viewers. Where this cannot be done it will be necessary to control the uv radiation from both natural and some artificial light sources. Tungsten incandescent lamps emit very little uv but many fluorescent light tubes do and some quartz iodide lamps are particularly

dangerous. (These comments are generalisations: the architect may be aware of recent developments which invalidate them.)

The most effective method of preventing uv damage, and the only one in the case of natural light coming through glass, is to interpose a screen of transparent uv-absorbing film between the light source and the object. This can be a varnish or a plastic sheet; their relative efficiency, and cost, will need to be studied.[2]

NATURAL LIGHTING

Any plan for natural lighting depends upon the architect's ideas on fenestration. Natural light is free, but it has three great disadvantages:

whether through wall or roof, it imposes severe restrictions upon the flexible and economic use of floor and wall space;

protection has to be provided against the concomitant heat, cold and glare: this can be extremely expensive;

enormous variations in intensity: a clear summer day can be twenty-five times brighter than a cloudy winter day, and as the human eye is very sensitive to change, variation of a tenth of this amount is unacceptable in continuous reading conditions. Also the continuous change in the angle of the light, although predictable, is often disturbing to the serious reader.

Very sophisticated equipment whereby photo-electric cells automatically **vary** the level of artificial lighting to compensate for variations in the level of natural lighting can be used but they are expensive and are found chiefly in art galleries where constant lighting is considered essential.

From the sole viewpoint of functional efficiency it would be much better to use only artificial, and therefore controllable, light; library rooms without natural light have been provided in many parts of the world and are physically acceptable, but the architect may decide that natural light is desirable for psychological and aesthetic reasons. His problem will be to control the natural light, and to bear in mind its various and changing effects when he plans an artificial lighting system suited to the needs of the different users of the library.

ARTIFICIAL LIGHTING

Intensity

Standards of intensity are based upon the light-emitting power of a candle, and the intensity is expressed in candelas. The illumination is the spread of light over a surface and is expressed in lux (or lumens/m^2). The former unit was the lumen/ft^2, known in American as the foot-candle. To plan a lighting scheme in full, it would be necessary to use the factor of luminance (brightness) which can be expressed either in fundamental units (candelas/ft^2 or m^2) or in terms of the equivalent illumination related through reflectance (the foot-lambert or its metric equivalent, the apostilb). Although the British lighting industry has not got fully used to metric conversions the metric term lux is used here because the *Code*[2] and other recommendations of the (British) Illuminating Engineering Society use that standard. The numerical relationship between the comparable units is one of direct metric conversion, one lux being equal to 0.0929 lumens/ft^2; one lumen/ft^2 equals 10·764 lux. For a full explanation of these matters see Hopkinson and Collins[3].

Librarians should generally confine their observations to levels directly related to the IES recommendations. If a librarian does decide to use a light meter himself he should be sure that readings are taken at the horizontal plane at 850 mm (2 ft 9 in) above floor level or at the normal working height, but it should be noted that light from any source decreases with the square of the distance from the source and that the illumination on a surface varies as the cosine of the angle at which it reaches the surface. To know the light power of a source therefore is not in itself very helpful. Reference has already been made to the wide divergence between the views of the various experts in this field. The intensities (and glare limits) recommended in the (British) IES *Report*[4] are:

Recommended lighting intensities

	Recommended illumination (lux)	Limiting glare* index
Reading rooms (newspapers and magazines)	200	19
Reading tables (lending libraries)	400	19
Reading tables (reference libraries)	600	16
Counters	600	19
Closed book stores	100 (on vertical surface)	—
Binding	600	22
Cataloguing, sorting, stock rooms	400	22

*These figures represent the maximum acceptable degree of glare for the room in which each activity is to take place. The IES *Glare index* is widely used for comparison purposes throughout industry and its levels are stipulated in lighting contracts.

These recommendations are of course very general and should not be applied uncritically; for example the wide variation between the lighting of reading rooms and for reading tables will apply only in particular circumstances. There is also a great difference between the needs of younger and older readers.

It should be noted that the levels given here refer to the "maintained" intensity, that is the operating level when the lamps are well used and have normal accretion of dust and dirt, not the level of a brand new lamp. The former may have only two-thirds the intensity of the latter.

These recommendations are dated 1968; a few years earlier the figures were very much lower; no doubt in a few years' time they will be much higher. The steady escalation of lighting levels in libraries (in America they are usually higher than in this country) is an intriguing phenomenon and Metcalf[5] writes about this with humour. There is strong medical evidence that the human eye has not changed in the last few decades and that no present-day reader's eyesight would be strained by reading in the conditions familiar to our fathers, even though such conditions would today be regarded as intolerably gloomy. We tend to forget that to read black print on white paper is not difficult visually. The eye will not be damaged by bad lighting, but "information collection" may be less efficient.

A conclusion from research that is of particular interest is that people who have the same standard of visual acuity (sharpness of vision) do not necessarily perform visually with the same ease. Further experiments led to the conclusion[6] that an increase in the intensity of light on the task material considerably improved its readability for the average person up to a level of 300 lux (approximately 28 lumens/ft[2]) but that the improvement after this point is much less dramatic even though it does continue. On the other hand people with poor sight benefit more from increased levels of lighting than do people with normal sight. It is also important to note that visual comfort (a very important matter) appears to be more affected by increased luminance of the surrounding area than is the actual task of reading. An increase in the surrounding luminance to about thirty times* that of the

*This is a complicated question. Variations in the level of natural light in the UK show only thirteen times more between a summer noon and a winter afternoon (DSIR *Technical Paper 17*, 1935 HMSO), but American investigations (IES *Lighting Handbook*, New York, Chapter 7) show variations of forty-eight times at 46° latitude. These are natural light intensity levels; obviously shade conditions within the building have also to be taken into account. Thomson says that an object in a daylit gallery may receive 100 times more light on a sunny day than on a gloomy one.

reading matter impairs the reading performance and increases discomfort. Uncomfortable conditions of luminance of the surrounding area are therefore more likely to give rise to complaints of glare, while the effect on reading performance may not be great. It may be that the high intensity of general lighting in libraries today can be put down to the effects of fashion and the lighting industry's propaganda.

Normal reading—and in serious working conditions reading includes note-taking—can take place perfectly adequately with a general lighting intensity of 150 lux (14 lumens/ft[2]), but few librarians today dare offer such a low level. Investigations by Blackwell[8] produce interesting conclusions:

"The light intensity we require depends drastically upon the task we are to perform. This conclusion supports the idea of localised lighting for areas where the *most* difficult tasks are performed .... The data certainly suggest that more light is needed for many tasks than is needed for well-printed books."

Tests by the (American) Illuminating Engineering Society led them to recommend 70 foot-candles (753 lux) because the lighting needed for reading medium-hard pencil marks on white paper was used as a basis. Is this a fair assessment of study use?

Tests leading to this recommendation (quoted by Blackwell[9]) suggest that by the same reasoning the level required for comfortable reading of 8-point printed type need be only 15 foot-candles (164 lux). The whole question obviously needs further scientific study before categorical statements can be justified.

A psychological factor to be taken into account is that the reader will be happy to work in a bright area within sight of other areas which are less brightly lit, but he will suffer a sense of frustration if he can see areas brighter than the one in which he is working. This must be allowed for in the layout by isolating from any brighter areas rooms where intensive study is to take place.

Reading is not the only activity which concerns the librarian; in matters of general display the best guide is the IES *Report*[10] on the lighting of art galleries and museums which gives many examples of the problems and recommends solutions.

Contrast

Eye fatigue is caused mainly by glare and excessive contrast. The romantic picture of a reader in a dark room working with a pool of light on his book shows an unhealthy situation. Extensive investigation of the best lighting for comfortable working shows that the aim should be smooth graduation in brightness from the book itself to the immediate surround (the table top) and finally to the general background. A ratio of luminance (photometric brightness) of about 3:1 between page and table top is probably best and more than 5:1 is bad for continuous reading. If the page must be white, the table top should not be too dark; certainly it should not be black. The general background should be less bright than the table top, but not excessively so.

Books are normally printed on white paper of a reflectance of 0·7 to 0·8. If the table top has a reflectance of about 0·2 to 0·3 (Munsell values 5 to 6)* and is illuminated more or less uniformly, the recommended luminance ratio will have been achieved. To give acceptable conditions the colour and material of the table top and the surrounding areas will have to be balanced, so lighting cannot be considered in isolation from interior decoration and choice of furniture.

The luminance of the background will naturally vary enormously; there will usually be bookshelves close to the reader, and their luminance is less than that of the table top, but light-coloured walls and ceilings as well as open spaces, also form part of the background and have to be taken into account. A great deal depends on the reflectance factors of the various colours and materials in the room: figures for these are available and the interior decoration consultant will take them into account in his designs. Unless the walls are panelled, and provided that some

*For a definition of Munsell values, see IES *Technical Report 14*.

light is cast upwards to a light ceiling, the background is not likely to appear too dark.

In libraries there is usually a fair amount of light shining upwards from bookstack lighting, but where there is none, it is desirable to direct some light towards the ceiling; this may not be necessary if the floor is of a very light colour (Munsell value 6 or more) in which case there may be adequate reflection from the general lighting. Where bookcases are close together this may not be the case, since they will obstruct a large proportion of reflected light. To avoid distraction it is important to avoid too much upward light, while the use of totally indirect lighting is especially to be deprecated: the present fashion for totally diffused lighting spread absolutely evenly over a large white ceiling area (except by multi-layer polarising panels) is uninteresting, expensive and probably ineffective in a library. Blackwell[12] says, "The best material (multi-layer polarising panels) permit use of three times as many foot-candles without discomfort as the worst materials (perfectly diffusing panels)."

The human eye responds more directly to change than to intensity itself and much depends on the "adaptation level", the level to which the eye has become adapted in the previous few minutes. Because the eye's response to change is proportional to the existing light, an increase in level from 20 to 30 lux will produce the same benefit as an increase from 100 to 150 lux. Brock Arms says[13]: "One group of readers was subjected to 30 foot-candles (323 lux), another group to 50 foot-candles (538 lux) and another to 70 foot-candles (753 lux). At the end of thirty minutes of general reading tasks, the three groups were exposed to a series of progressively higher levels of illumination. Each individual in the experiment was then asked to mark the level at which he found the light most comfortable for reading. The majority of people who had adjusted previously to 30 foot-candles indicated a level near 30 foot-candles. The group which had adjusted to 50 foot-candles marked a level near 50 foot-candles. The group which had adjusted to 70 foot-candles marked a level near 70 foot-candles."

Glare

This depends on various factors: the brightness itself, both from the source and by reflection, size and position of the source and number of sources in view. It follows that there is more danger of glare in open areas because of the greater number of sources in view. Blackwell[14] shows that the angle at which the light source is visible is absolutely critical and that the best results are obtained when light is obtained from as large a percentage of the ceiling area as possible. After a scientific analysis he says, "Thus we can say categorically that the best lighting installations can provide the visibility criterion with less than one-fourth of the light level required with the worst lighting installation."

The most obvious control of glare is by directing all light sources downwards, shading them from horizontal emission, but this will certainly be ineffective in lighting horizontal bookcase surfaces. Large shades around incandescent lights are commonly used to control glare but there will be a consequent loss of efficiency and limits on interior design.

Efficiency of lighting installations

Fluorescent tubes	Light output (lumens)
80 watt	3 100 to 4 850
65 watt	2 700 to 4 400
40 watt	1 700 to 2 600

Filament bulbs	Light output (lumens)
25 watt	200
40 watt*	390
60 watt*	665
100 watt*	1 260
200 watt	2 720
500 watt	7 700

*Coiled coil

Cost

To step up the lighting intensity can be expensive, not only in the cost of current but also in more fittings and heavier maintenance and cleaning bills. As lighting can account for as much as 10 per cent of the construction costs (in extreme cases) and 25 per cent of the cleaning and maintenance costs, this is very serious.

The efficiency of a lighting installation can be measured and expressed in lumens per watt. Examples of typical installations are given by Hopkinson and Collins[15]:

Of the usual alternatives, fluorescent lighting has been found to be cheaper than filament bulb lighting if it is used for more than $\frac{3}{4}$-hour a day (180 hours a year), but a true costing can be computed only after taking into account the costs of the initial installation, periodic cleaning and later replacement, as well as length of life of tubes and bulbs. Formulae have been worked out for this purpose and the architect, or at any rate his lighting consultant, will be familiar with them.

In his feasibility study the architect will make a rough estimate of these costs (taking into account the number of hours when lighting will be in use, the cleaning and replacement schedules and the likely labour costs). These estimates should be considered carefully; where the library forms part of a large complex (universities, colleges, schools for example) the authority may call for comment from its own officers who can compare the levels and the costs with those in other parts of the institution. If the costs are deemed to be too high, the architect may have to amend his proposals. In making his plans the architect may draw upon the expertise of a lighting consultant but it is rare for this expert to report direct to the authority: because lighting is so vital a part of the aesthetic effect he intends to produce, the architect will usually decide to reserve the final decisions to himself.

Colour

Colour of lighting affects one's response to the visual environment but it has no effect upon the eye's efficiency. The human appreciation of the colour of lighting does not correspond with any scientific measurement, but neither is it truly subjective, being influenced by human experience as well as the relation to other colours within view at the same time. To obtain a suitable colour rendering by using "cold" or "warm" fluorescent lights is therefore no answer on its own because an area with a certain lighting colour can look warm in a very white room and cold in a yellow one. Daylight and tungsten incandescent lamps are, on the whole, neutral in tone (but not when filtered through uv absorbent materials); the influence of different reflecting surfaces too will completely alter this neutrality.

METHODS OF ARTIFICIAL LIGHTING

At present the most usual form of general lighting for reading areas consists of fluorescent lights recessed into a false ceiling and covered by diffusers. The effect is bright, efficient, cold and rather soulless. Among the advantages are flexibility, comparative cleanliness (and therefore economy of maintenance) absence of shadows and low consumption of current.

The architect will certainly wish to vary the lighting conditions in different parts of the building in order to indicate changes of environment and to add sparkle and interest. Combinations of lighting will be an important part of his aesthetic concept and he will break up regular and rather flat functional lighting by spots and chandeliers. In doing so he must consider carefully the effect which these lights may have upon serious readers and must design and position them to avoid glare. Lighting fittings exist to provide adequate visibility and to add to the attraction of the building, but only in exceptional cases should they draw attention to themselves.

Flexibility

Obtaining complete freedom appears to involve having an absolutely even system of lighting throughout the building and

Spot lighting over counter, Burngreen Branch Library, Kilsyth, Stirling County. This photograph also illustrates how fixed heaters (if they are essential) may be concealed within the counter (see page 151)

this the architect will be unhappy to provide for aesthetic reasons. A compromise is likely to be the provision of numerous electric points so that fittings may be altered when a change of use is required. Because certain areas will require high intensity it follows that each point must be able to take the highest possible level. In practice this will be limited by common sense; entrance halls, lobbies, corridors and so on will never be converted into reading rooms.

A very convenient means of providing lighting from above is to have a demountable ceiling with tiles approximately 600 mm (2 ft) square, of which any can be replaced by a fluorescent fitting. Several proprietary ceilings of this kind are on the market and lighting fittings are available to fit the same suspension members; a further advantage is that air ducting can also be allied to these interchangeable fittings. For ease of alteration it is desirable to provide one 5-amp three-pin socket outlet either above each ceiling tile or one to every two, three or four tiles. The layout can

therefore be altered completely by interchanging the lighting fittings with blank tiles. All fittings should be provided with short leads and fused plugs so that they can simply be plugged into the nearest socket.

Although this method involves a comparatively large number of sockets, only a few are likely to be in use at any one time and the cost can therefore be reduced by grouping them into a few circuits each controlled by a miniature circuit breaker combining the function of fuse and switch. Change can be achieved by plugging a fitting into either an A or a B socket. Each fitting should be protected locally with a fused terminal block or a fused plug top.

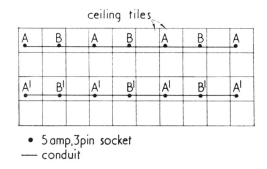

• 5 amp, 3 pin socket
— conduit

Sockets can be grouped into circuits

Such methods of recessing fluorescent lighting in the ceiling are widely used in single-storey open-plan libraries, the counter area being distinguished (and lit more intensely) by hanging incandescent lamps in eye-catching shades. Unless such lamps are hung from the same trunking system and its replaceable tiles there will be an immediate bar to flexibility.

For reference library study areas the IES *Code*[16] calls for levels of 600 lux (56 lumens/ft^2) and this is certainly necessary for concentrated reading and, in particular, for the library's own typists and office workers. Carrels and other areas of intense study will need this level, as will desks where maps, documents of little

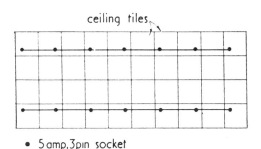

• 5 amp, 3 pin socket
— conduit

Pattern of socket outlets in a suspended ceiling

contrast, or prints requiring critical colour discrimination, are to be studied. For general reading areas the figure is perhaps unnecessarily high.

To provide everywhere the highest level of lighting that may be required in any single instance is very expensive. The other extreme is to have a fairly low level of overall lighting with direct individual lighting to reading desks and to bookcases. From the point of view of the serious reader and searcher for books (and this, after all, is what really matters) this is a most attractive proposal, particularly if the desk lights can be fitted with individual controls to vary the intensity of each light, but it requires very expensive and elaborate planning if flexibility is to be retained. The scheme proposed for the new Central Library at Birmingham is to relieve the low general lighting level with a change of ceiling height (by the use of voids through ceilings, staggered on alternate floors) and with floor electric points on every 1375 mm (4 ft 6 in) grid square throughout reading areas. This achieves good flexibility at the cost of a most elaborate wiring network in the flooring; as the floors are to be carpeted it also means that holes must be made to allow the wires through, and there must be carpet plugs to fill in the holes over any points no longer in use owing to a change in layout.

A reasonable compromise is to have a medium level of overall lighting with the facility to plug in a table lamp wherever higher levels are particularly required; certain tables can be specified for this purpose.

Illumination of bookshelves is difficult to arrange satisfactorily if full adaptability is to be retained. The IES Code[17] recommends a minimum illumination level of 50 to 100 lux (4·7 to 9 lumens ft²) on the vertical surfaces of bookcases and it is clearly important that no light should shine into the eyes of people who are choosing books. In open-access or heavily used open-stack conditions illumination can be provided either by general room lighting (such as fluorescent tubes set into coffered ceiling panels with removable plastic shields), by direct shelf lighting or by a combination of the two.

General lighting has the advantage of giving complete flexibility in the positioning of stacks and reading areas; plug-in points for use in local displays or reading positions can be provided. Illumination for stacks is conditioned by their closeness together and by the need for flexibility in any future rearrangement. For

Lighting fitted to stand off from stacks, West Norwood Library, London Borough of Lambeth

General lighting for flexibility of use, Edinburgh University Library

these reasons the fluorescent lighting fittings (preferably recessed) should run across the direction of the stacks at 900 mm (6 ft) intervals, but if the tops of the stacks are less than 250 mm (10 in) from the light source it may be necessary, because of shadows, and possibly of heat problems (even with fluorescent tubes) to return to the usual expedient of having the tubes running between the stacks and in the same direction, although this method is less efficient. In this case the gaps between ends of tubes should not be more than 600 mm (2 ft) because the light does not spread well along the line of the tubes.

Direct shelf lighting can be mounted on each case with a pelmet, or for each row by stand-off fitments. The farther the stand-off the better; up to 450 mm (18 in) is desirable, 230 mm (9 in) being the minimum. By such means it is easy to light the upper shelves adequately but lighting on the lower shelves falls away drastically (by the square of the distance from the light source). An expedient used in open-access libraries is to tilt the lower shelves upwards to catch the light but this has the disadvantage of increasing the depth of shelving as well as looking untidy. Its use in close stacking would be most uneconomical of space. To increase the light falling on the lower shelves it is desirable to have a light coloured floor, or at least a strip of floor about 300 mm (10 ft) wide in front of each bookstack with a reflectance of about 0·4 (Munsell value 7).

The combination of general lighting and individual case lighting is chiefly met when a low level of illumination is provided between stacks as a safety measure, individual incandescent lights for each stack being switched on when required, and possibly turned off by a time switch. This will never be done when fluorescent tubes are used because frequent switching on can be more expensive in tube replacement than the cost of current when tubes are left on.

In areas with high ceilings where bookshelves form alcoves against walls and where each alcove has a reading table in the centre, fittings hanging from, or mounted on, the ceiling can give enough light on the tables and in the room generally, but it seldom lights the bookshelves adequately. It is difficult in these cases to provide pelmets or spotlights on the shelves themselves because they conflict aesthetically with the high ceiling and the alcoves. Lamps with large translucent shades on each table are often useful, not so much to light the tables as to cast light on the bookshelves.

There are two principal means of direct bookcase lighting, as shown below.

In the first diagram each bookcase is provided with a pelmet behind which is mounted a reflector type fluorescent tube. The tops of the pelmets can be closed in or left partly open to throw light onto the ceiling. Some upward lighting is usually preferred,

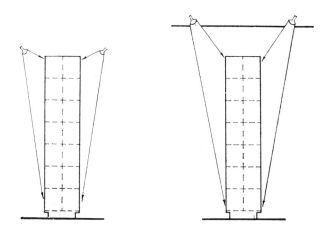

Spotlights can give more evenly distributed light and may be recessed if ceiling is low

can be directed downwards and so diminish the contrast between the illumination of the upper and lower shelves.

On the other hand, the life of spotlight lamps is limited, maintenance costs are high and it is very difficult to prevent glare from some angles. Each spotlight has to be directed individually and there is always a tendency for small spotlights of neat design to work loose owing to cyclic heating and cooling as the lamps are switched on and off. Where accessible to the public, lamps are also vulnerable to interference.

Adjustable spotlights recessed into the ceiling can be used where siting of bookcases can be accurately determined in advance and the ceiling is low. Change can be obtained if the system of removable ceiling tiles referred to earlier is used.

In areas used for bulk storage of books in stacks it frequently happens that when the library is first opened the stacks are spaced quite far apart. As the stock builds up more racks are added and the spacing is reduced. If incandescent or fluorescent fittings are to be ceiling mounted between each pair of stacks it should be possible to move them as stack positions are altered.

One way of doing this is to mount the lighting fittings on a simple trunking system on which they can slide. The space between the fittings is closed by a blanking piece and as racks are added it is necessary only to shorten the blanking pieces, slide the fitting along and add the extra fittings at one end. There are several proprietary trunking systems, some for flush and some for surface mounting,

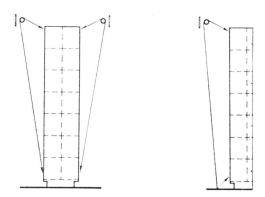

Fluorescent tubes lighting bookcases, light reflected from the floor can improve the lighting of lower shelves

but screening may be necessary to prevent unsightly shadows.

If required the pelmet can be cut away and provided with holders for translucent frames carrying subject titles. It may be convenient to mount the fluorescent gear on top of the bookcase with small leads only running to the tubes.

An alternative method is to use incandescent spotlights carried on a frame or pelmet fixed to the top of the bookcase. Spotlights

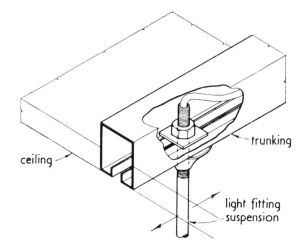

Trunking channels at right angles to the bookcases will enable lighting fittings to be moved to suit different shelving layouts

which enable this to be done economically with the minimum of disturbance.

The easiest way to permit movement of bookcases is to provide each case with built-in lighting which can be moved with it. This can be achieved by bringing all wiring to a junction box at the

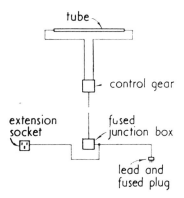

tube

control gear

extension socket

fused junction box

lead and fused plug

Wiring diagram for bookcases. Control gear can usually be concealed on top of the unit

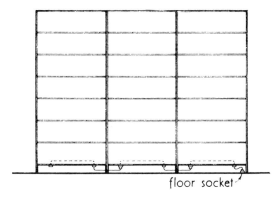

floor socket

Adjacent book cases can usually be connected to each other thus reducing the number of floor outlets required.

bottom of the bookcase with a lead and socket. Each bookcase can then be connected either to a floor socket or to an adjacent bookcase.

Floor sockets can be installed in a simple grid system for complete flexibility. Each socket can serve a row of cases and therefore the grid of sockets need not be very dense; 1·2 m to 2m (4 ft to 6 ft 6 in) centres should be enough. In any floor trunking system the junction boxes constitute the most expensive item so it is desirable to adopt a fishbone layout which reduces the number of boxes—fig *a* is cheaper than fig *b*.

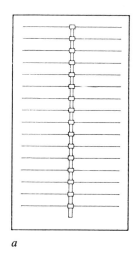

a

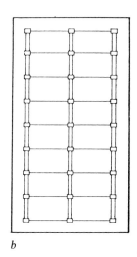

b

Alternative patterns for floor trunking. The fishbone layout (left) is cheaper

Comparison of environmental conditions—lighting

	Edinburgh	Essex	Lancaster	Warwick
Lighting levels*	*Readers* 377–430 lux at table top *Stack* 129–161 lux on vertical surface	*Readers* 377 lux at table top *Stack* 108 lux on vertical surface	*Readers* 430 lux at table top *Stack* 108 lux on vertical surface	*Readers* 473 lux at table top *Stack* 54 lux on vertical surface of bottom shelf
Ceiling height	2450 mm (8 ft)	Second to fifth floor 3200 mm (10 ft 6 in)	Ground floor 3650 mm (12 ft) first and second 2750 mm (9 ft)	2750 mm (9 ft)
Artificial lighting (present layout)	Fixed continuous recessed fluorescent lighting strip at 1375 mm (4 ft 6 in) centres along bookstack aisles, across width of building	Suspended fluorescent fittings along bookstack aisles across width of building	Recessed fluorescent panels at 2450 mm (8 ft) centres parallel to outside faces of building. Fittings in continuous strips at right angles to book stacks; non-continuous in reader areas	Fixed continuous semi-recessed fluorescent strips at 3050 mm (10 ft) centres, at right angles to book stacks along length of building
Natural lighting	Continuous full height glazing; fixed horizontal louvres on east and west faces; south face with tinted glass shielded by projecting floor structure	Continuous sill to ceiling-height windows with vertical adjustable blinds on all faces	High level windows and 1200 mm (4 ft) viewing windows at 5500 mm (18 ft) centres on external wall; continuous full height windows with overhanging projection forms wall onto internal courtyard	Continuous double-glazed windows above sill height, with adjustable blinds in cavity
Comment	Good overall even lighting. There is the minimum of lighting contrast on the ceilings; in reading areas polished desk surfaces and polished linoleum reflects dazzle. In spite of tinted glass, the large window area on south side creates a certain amount of glare and dazzle, particularly in winter	Amount of light at table top is satisfactory but there is an extreme contrast between the suspended fittings and the dark fairfaced concrete ceiling. Readers find that the blinds do not adequately control glare from the sun	Good overall even lighting except in perimeter areas adjacent to external walls. The combination of high level and viewing windows produces strong contrast of light in perimeter reading areas	Good overall even lighting. There is the minimum of lighting contrast on the ceiling. The colour and even tone of all finishes contribute to a good quality of light. Readers find that the adjustable blinds do not adequately control glare from the sun
Adaptability	Bookstacks are restricted to the 1375 mm (4ft 6 in) module in the direction and position they are now in, so as to maintain an even distribution of light. Lighting conditions are suitable for readers over the entire floor area. Bookstacks cannot be placed within 1825 mm (6 ft) of windows on south face	There is a two-way lighting grid from which detachable lighting fittings can be suspended. This adaptable lighting layout makes restrictions on bookstack or reader arrangements unnecessary. Bookstacks cannot be placed within 2750 mm (9 ft) of windows	Lighting panels are interchangeable with the standard 600 × 600 mm (2 ft × 2 ft) heated ceiling panels but require a specialist contractor for the work. The adaptable lighting layout makes restrictions on bookstack or reader arrangements unnecessary. Bookstacks cannot be placed within 2750 mm (9 ft) of viewing windows or 1825 mm (6 ft) of courtyard windows	Bookstacks can be placed at any centres in the direction they are now in but at 3050 mm (10 ft) centres only if placed parallel to lighting layout so as to maintain an even distribution of light. Lighting conditions are suitable for readers over the entire floor area. Bookstacks cannot be placed within 2750 mm (9 ft) of windows

*1 lumen/ft² = 1 foot-candle = 10·76 lux.

In most cases absolute interchangeability will not be needed since certain areas (walls for example) will always be used for shelving and other areas (in front of windows perhaps) will always be used for tables. Floor trunking and ceiling sockets need be provided only in those areas where the layout may be changed. By these means reasonable flexibility can be obtained at comparatively small cost. Such identification of reasonable limits can achieve a great saving.

MAINTENANCE

Because of high labour costs fluorescent tubes are now usually replaced periodically in bulk, rather than piecemeal as one tube fails. This can result in lower lighting levels in certain areas while replacement is awaited. To overcome this by having higher lighting levels than are needed, to allow for failure, is wrong; a better method (at a higher initial cost) is to have two, or even three, tubes in a fitting, one to come into operation automatically if another should fail. Easy access to fittings is also an item of economic importance in maintenance; ornamental clusters in high ceiling areas which require scaffolding so that lights can be cleaned or replaced are a librarian's nightmare.

In open areas the switches which control lighting should be placed where they are entirely under staff control, the **whole area** being lit or unlit as one unit. Local control may be needed for areas near windows where lights will be needed less often but these again should be controlled only by the staff. Individual carrels will have their own switches, but staff time will be saved if all these can be overridden by a master switch so that staff do not have to check that each light is out at the end of the day. A similar arrangement is economical for closed stacks: switches for each stack ensure that lights can be put on when needed but all lights should be controllable by a central cut-off at closing time. Main aisle lighting can be exempted from this central control so that patrol and cleaning can take place at night.

Local switches for stack lighting were essential for saving current when incandescent lamps were universally used; with fluorescent lamps the emphasis has changed and it is usually cheaper to leave tubes switched on than to switch them on and off at frequent intervals. Possible measures worth examining are the **switching** on of one tube in a set of three for minimal use (aisle lighting at night for example), with time switches to control this. On the other hand, extra switching arrangements add heavily to installation costs: the architect must balance all these factors.

THE LIBRARIAN'S TASKS

With regard to lighting the librarian's chief tasks are to indicate in the brief the purposes of the different functional areas and say where special circumstances call for different levels of lighting.

He will be ill-advised to venture too far into the technicalities of lighting levels, quality and so on, but he may wish to draw the architect's attention to an existing library which has the kind of conditions he would like to achieve. When he receives the sketch plans he should study carefully the possible effect of glare and contrast on readers seated in the different areas; this is certainly the architect's business, but mistakes have been made and the librarian has had to live with them. The librarian will be more directly concerned with the cleaning and maintenance problems and these he should visualise from a study of the plans.

Lighting is a major factor in the successful operation of a library and the librarian cannot play his part as a member of the team unless he can visualise this, as every other element of the final plan.

The table shows the lighting conditions provided in the four recent British university libraries, with comments upon both the degree of adaptability and the environmental effect (page 145).

REFERENCES

[1] THOMSON, GARRY Conservation and museum lighting. Museums Association Information Sheet. Museums Association, London, May, 1970, p 2
[2] ILLUMINATING ENGINEERING SOCIETY IES Code. London, undated
[3] HOPKINSON, R. G. and COLLINS, J. B. The ergonomics of lighting. Macdonald Technical & Scientific, London, 1970, p 41
[4] ILLUMINATING ENGINEERING SOCIETY Technical Report 8. Lighting of libraries. London, 1966, p5
[5] Metcalf. Op cit, p 181
[6] BLACKWELL, H. RICHARD Lighting the library: standards for illumination. *In the library environment: aspects of interior planning.* American Library Association, Chicago, 1965, pp 26–27
[7] Thomson. Op cit, p 3
[8] Blackwell. Op cit, p 26
[9] Ibid, p 24
[10] ILLUMINATING ENGINEERING SOCIETY Technical Report 14. Lighting of art galleries and museums. London, 1970
[11] Ibid, glossary, p 29
[12] Blackwell. Op cit, pp 29–30
[13] Arms. Op cit, p 32
[14] Blackwell. Op cit, p 29
[15] Hopkinson and Collins. Op cit, p 39
[16] Lighting of libraries. Op cit, p 5
[17] Ibid

16 Security and protection

The degree of security required and the priority to be accorded to it were indicated in the brief; the librarian made his decision knowing that all security measures will diminish, to a greater or lesser extent, readers' freedom to enjoy the library.

There are two categories of hazard: natural forces (fire, flood and "acts of God") and, much more damaging, readers.

FIRE

All libraries—the buildings, the people inside them and the materials—must be protected against certain hazards. Of these, by far the greatest is fire, and the damage which often accompanies it, caused chiefly by smoke and water.

To what extent is it justifiable to incur considerable expense and inconvenience to readers where there is little danger and the materials are not difficult to replace? As part of the Library Technology Project, Gage-Babcock & Associates Inc[1] made a survey of fires in libraries in the US and related it to similar occurrences in other public buildings as well as to the main causes of the fires. One of their first findings was that libraries are among the institutions in the category of lowest fire risk, chiefly by reason of the range of activities taking place in them. Nevertheless, the researchers point out that the data make it clear that libraries in themselves are no safer from harm than other buildings.

"The idea that books do not burn easily is a dangerous halftruth. When they are tightly packed on the shelves, they do burn at a slow rate. However in a situation of multi-tier stacks with unrestricted passageways and openings in the floors permitting vertical drafts, intense fires can build up in the stacks very quickly."[2]

The librarian will play his part by ensuring careful discipline in operation, and particularly in the organising of materials so that loose papers, packing materials and so on are never left near possible (even remotely possible) fire hazards. It is perhaps significant that most fires begin in basements. With one important exception, the greatest of these hazards are heating and lighting systems, principally electrical ones. The exception referred to is smoking; the American investigations show this to be by far the greatest single cause of library fires: staff and reader discipline is, in the end, the only answer[3,4].

In every aspect of planning attention will be paid to the effect upon the safety of the building. Even the choice of furniture is affected: some paints allow flames to spread along a surface much more quickly than others and wood is in general more flammable than metal. If a fire does start its progress through the building must be delayed as much as possible and this depends not only on the material on which it can feed (books, paper, furniture and equipment) but also on its passage through walls and doors, and on the supply of air. A door that is easily consumed by flames, a lift shaft or stair well which allows air to be funnelled upwards, a weak wall—all these are hazards to be guarded against in designing for protection against fire.

This is the world of the architect and of the fire prevention officer, but the librarian should be aware of the prevention and suppression factors to be used so that he can drill his staff to know them clearly and to make full use of them almost instinctively. The architect will deal with:

Inspection He may use complicated systems for this, including closed-circuit television or he may rely on a planned isolation of danger points (eg smoking areas) and on staff discipline.

Localising For this he will stipulate materials for walls, floors and doors which have a built-in "time-delay" factor. Obviously thick concrete will delay a fire longer than wood, but there are innumerable variations among the different materials available and he must balance the likelihood of danger against the structural and cost implications. His choice will be limited by the very stringent fire regulations he must satisfy when obtaining permissions.

Detection Again there are sophisticated devices which can give early warning of a fire developing, both locally (usually placed on the underside of ceilings) and in general areas (such as air-conditioning ducts). These devices usually detect either rises in temperature or the presence of smoke.

Suppression When a fire is found an alarm is sounded to warn staff and, where possible, to alert the fire brigade directly. Because speed is essential, action may be triggered automatically to suppress the fire. This action has in the past been mainly the operating of a sprinkler and librarians have always viewed such installations with concern, knowing that water is often far more damaging to books than the fire itself. Whether this is true with the coming of "mist-sprinkler" systems is questionable, but the carbon-dioxide systems which can kill a fire in a matter of seconds in confined areas is obviously better. This expedient is space consuming (in the storage of bulky CO_2 cylinders), expensive and is a possible risk to human life in certain circumstances. The advice of fire prevention officers is called for here, as it is in the choice of portable fire extinguishers for operation by the staff. Whatever system is chosen there should be an efficient early-warning system alerting a nearby fire station: a warning to an intermediary, such as a caretaker, is not an adequate substitute.

The architect will be alert to the danger of fire from adjoining properties and will plan fire-isolating spaces or walls with this in mind.

FLOOD

Water has probably damaged more libraries than fire and the architect will be aware of the possible danger from water pipes within the building (and even water mains near basement stacks). The few inches below the first shelf of books will give protection for a time but detection of a flood is seldom automatic and it may be necessary, in underground areas, for water breaks to be formed to isolate and limit any danger. In certain circumstances it may also be expedient to build special walls to protect underground storage areas from possible external flooding, but this need will have been indicated at an early stage in the report of the geological survey.

READER HAZARDS

Book theft

To protect the library against this common and, alas, growing habit there are two "weapons": supervision of exits and compulsory depositing of cases and bags in a cloakroom.

Supervision of exits
The obvious protection against theft is to have some form of inspection at exit points, although such supervision will create a bottleneck.

During the last century the attitude to inspection in public libraries has suffered a series of changes. For many years all public libraries were entirely closed-access, readers being separated from the books by a barrier, each book requested being fetched by a member of the staff and issued to the reader. Later, indicators were installed, machines which showed which books were in and which were out but no reader was allowed to handle a book until it had been checked out to him.

Towards the end of the nineteenth century (in the UK) came the move to "safeguarded open access"; it is difficult now to understand the furore the proposals caused, but at the time there was bitter controversy between those for and against the new method.

Security turnstiles permitting examination of bags, Hull University Library

Open access won, at first gradually, and then in a landslide; readers were admitted to the shelves. The exit counter in this system was fitted with a locking wicket which was released by a staff member and the reader allowed to leave only when the book had been checked out. For years these wickets were in widespread use, but many librarians remember that they were often permanently locked open, partly because they irritated honest readers and partly because the greatly increased use of the library was not matched by an increase in staff or in space, so the system became unworkable. During the last thirty years more and more libraries moved away

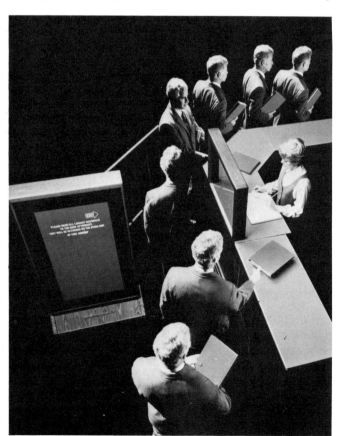

Electronic security control system, by Checkpoint

from both the lockable wicket and the bottleneck counter which dominated entrance and exit routes; counters were placed further and further from the entrance to make the library's atmosphere more welcoming. It is for the authority (through the librarian) to decide how much control is to be sacrificed in order to produce an attractive and cheerful library; certainly the architect would welcome the disappearance of the island enclosure grimly guarding the entrance doors.

Sadly, book losses have became so high, in college and university, as well as public, libraries, that the atmosphere of freedom has reluctantly been abandoned. Safeguards have returned and, consequently, bottlenecks. Books in most demand are often issued to readers only after direct request to the staff; the wheel has turned full circle.

In small libraries, control will have to be exercised from the counter and the readers' advisory desk within a single room, but in large libraries, particularly multi-storey university libraries, control will be carried out at a special position dominating the entrance and exit to the building. This will usually be a glass-sided cubicle manned by security staff who have no other task, and who have positive control over exits, and facilities as well as authority for examination of readers' cases. Turnstiles, after a long period of discredit, are to be seen again. Modern versions can appear less forbidding than the old types but are just as effective. Fire exit regulations must be carefully watched and it will be necessary for turnstiles to have fast and complete release mechanisms.

A comparatively recent development is the detection system which operates a locking wicket and sounds an alarm whenever an attempt at unauthorised removal is made. In these systems each reader passes out of the library (or out of a single room) through a bottleneck across which is an invisible magnetic or electronic field. A "trigger" within the book affects this field, causing the alarm and locking device to operate. The trigger differs in the various proprietary systems: it can be a strip of material hidden in a binding (Diver Detection Ltd or Tattle-tape) or a larger piece which can serve as a bookplate pasted onto the cover (Checkpoint). In reference libraries where no books are issued for use outside the library, the system is fairly simple; similarly it can be used for "reference only" books in other libraries. But in lending libraries it will be necessary to have each book which is authorised for issue neutralised so that it can pass through the screen; alternatively the book can be taken out only when a member of the staff has handled it and by-passed the field. In the former systems, each book has to be reactivated on its return to the library.

Further electronic systems are undoubtedly being developed and the drawbacks to the present ones will be overcome, but at the moment there undoubtedly are drawbacks, including:

high cost of the detection machinery and the need for special control furniture;

narrowness of the field; 900 mm (3 ft) is the usual maximum;

cost, especially in staff time of inserting the trigger in many thousands of books;

time consumed in operating the system (although not much in some methods);

false alarms caused by metallic objects in readers' possession, or by nearby electrical installations (more likely to occur in some systems than in others);

possible need (in some systems) to reactivate the trigger which may lose its effectiveness;

the challenge to the inventive student to find a way of beating the machine.

Against these disadvantages must be set these systems' undoubted success in reducing book losses. No manufacturer claims that his system is foolproof but the moral effect is certainly good; it has been found that it is not necessary to protect all books, as the knowledge that the scheme is in operation acts as a deterrent to potential thieves.

If such a system is to be installed the architect will be required to plan for a bottleneck exit and for special equipment including a screen and electrical machinery; he will also have to arrange for an adequate by-pass route to satisfy fire regulations. He may find it distasteful to incorporate this large and alien element within his interior design.

Obviously there can be no control over the stock if readers are able to leave the building unobserved. It is therefore essential to consider, in the context of security, the provision for fire exits. Adequate alternative methods of escape for large numbers of people is a matter on which the fire authority has strong powers, and it exerts them. If it is decreed that there shall be (say) three exits other than the main, controlled, one and that each shall have an outward-pushable action, then supervision becomes a farce. The answer lies in negotiations between the architect and the fire authorities in order to work out an acceptable compromise: one is to use the psychological deterrent of the break-glass system, perhaps fitted with a loud alarm to operate when the glass is broken. The architect can also help by ensuring that fire exit doors are sited where staff can keep an eye on them.

Banning of cases from book areas

Another solution is to require all cases to be deposited in a control section just inside the entrance hall. To be without a case can be a considerable inconvenience to a serious worker but he can adapt himself to this rule.

Bags can be handed over to attendants on duty and a token receipt given, but before embarking on such a plan the librarian will do well to assess the total peak use, the very large amount of space required to house the bags, and the high cost in man hours of operating this system during the long opening hours of a modern library.

An alternative is to provide lockers with removable keys and make their use compulsory; again it will be necessary to check that the large amount of space needed can be made available. For extra security, and to avoid having clothes, particularly wet coats, inside reading areas, it can be decreed that coats must also be deposited. To avoid heavy staffing costs it may be possible to use a locking hanger system for clothes.

Both bag and clothes lockers are usual in libraries on the Continent, but they are less often seen in the UK, perhaps because the very large numbers of readers in the small available space makes lockers impracticable. It will be necessary to display a notice disclaiming responsibility for loss of or damage to any items left in deposit areas. If deposit is compulsory this seems iniquitous but there appears to be no alternative.

Convexed mirror, B. H. Blackwell Ltd, Oxford Bookshop (John Little Associates)

In some universities and colleges it is the practice to demand that all cases and bags be opened for inspection. This, though a sound solution, may cause congestion at busy periods and understandably irritates readers. A possible alternative is to check certain bags at random, say one in five, but this too can cause personal problems. The writer has a vivid recollection of acrimonious interviews with readers who resented being chosen for such a search after other readers had passed unchallenged; it may be difficult to persuade a reader that he is not being victimised. The only reasonable solution is for the rule about random search to be very clearly advertised in the entrance hall and on membership cards.

The searching of bags is not foolproof as books can be hidden in clothing (and in women's handbags) but it has the advantage, if a book is detected, of demolishing the excuse that the reader had not really intended to take the book out of the library.

All such controls must of course be so placed that no alternative exit from the building can be reached, and there should always be a positive check to restrain the reader until the inspection has taken place. When contemplating any such methods the librarian will be wise to take the advice of his authority's legal expert and to see that all staff are aware of the legal position.

Mutilation of books

Where books particularly vulnerable to mutilation are issued for use outside the library a system of checking before acceptance back can be arranged, a record of the book's borrower and its physical condition before it is issued being kept inside the book itself. This prevents the reader from claiming that the book was mutilated when he received it. The staff member inspecting on its return will sign to indicate that it has been returned in good condition; as the reader's name has been recorded, the inspection can be done at off-peak time. The system is of course very time-consuming.

Books can be protected against misuse by readers while inside the library only by adequate supervision, but this is often a counsel of perfection. Even if attendants are employed specifically for this purpose it is very difficult for them to see everything; to expect staff to carry out this supervision in addition to their professional duties is hopeless. Alert staff and attendants can do a great deal, the psychological results of their obvious alertness probably being more effective than any actual detection they do. The architect may be able to help in specified areas by positioning a control desk so that it overlooks certain tables at which users of valuable books can be required to work. The use of strip-silvered (Venetian) glass in doors of staff rooms has a deterrent value; in Manchester Central Library the grilles between stack and reader areas have a similar effect in that the reader can never be sure that he is not being watched. The use of convex mirrors or closed circuit television to keep readers under supervision can have a great psychological value, even if it is not possible for surveillance to be maintained at all times. A drawback with CCTV is that even with wide-angle lenses on the cameras, the field of vision is seldom sufficient for full protection and more cameras will usually be needed than was at first envisaged. This will involve either a bank of screens to be kept under supervision, or a switching device (controlled or automatic) to a single screen: this is expensive and cannot provide continuous control.

To protect rare and valuable items an allocation of special security accommodation will have been indicated in the brief. The provision could be a strongroom that is both "fire, flood and and thief resistant"; within it could be a "burglar-proof" safe. The degree of protection given will depend very much on the price the library is prepared to pay. When planning such an installation, the architect will bear in mind its position relevant to external walls and the thickness of those walls.

Break-in
The protection of the building from possible break-in while the library is closed is a matter which requires the attention of a security consultant but the librarian should be aware of the protection devices available. Apart from solid doors and walls and good locks on windows, much depends on whether the building is to be patrolled after closing time. If not, and if the value of the contents warrants it, a system of either sonic rays or light rays flooding invisibly the interior of a key area can be most effective in giving immediate notification of an intruder's presence. A cheaper alternative is to have windows with wiring incorporated in the panes, so that if the window is disturbed or the glass broken a circuit contact is completed and an alarm sounded. Security consultants recommend a combination of good break-proof fittings with an effective alarm system, but such systems are only as good as their weakest point.

Windows in quiet corners of the library should be capable of being secured by key; it is not unknown for a reader to open a window from the inside and hand out books to an accomplice. A good security consultant is worth his fee if only for his ability to look at a proposed scheme and to point out how it can be circumvented. If such expert advice cannot be obtained, the librarian should at least read a book written by such a consultant.[5]

REFERENCES

[1] Protecting the library and its resources: a guide to physical protection and insurance; report on a study conducted by Gage-Babcock & Associates Inc. Library Technology Project, American Library Association, Chicago, 1963

[2] Ibid

[3] FIRE PROTECTION ASSOCIATION Fire protection design guide. FPA, London, 1970

[4] LEEDHAM, JOHN Live safely with fire. Longmans for the FPA, London, 1969

[5] WRIGHT, K. G. Cost-effective security. London, McGraw-Hill, 1972

17 Physical conditions

HEATING AND COOLING

Acceptable thermal conditions for people are those in which body heat is retained at not less than 27° C (80° F); as body heat is almost always higher than that of the air in the library, the aim is to stop excessive loss of body heat, loss caused chiefly by convection. If air is still and its temperature between 20° and 22° C (68° and 72° F), readers (in the UK) will normally be content. Much depends on their clothing and on their personal preferences; experience has shown that readers notice, and dislike, *change* of temperature more than conditions which are either a few degrees too hot or too cold. If readers are moving about, choosing and carrying books for instance, the acceptable temperature can be as low as 13° C (55° F) in lending departments, where visits may be short and outdoor clothing is normally worn; the comfort of the staff who work at desks for long periods is the critical factor. In small libraries staff comfort may be achieved by providing local heating at inquiry counters and in workrooms and the essential here is a system that can quickly be varied to compensate for a fall in temperature without making readers in outdoor clothing feel uncomfortably warm. Heat curtains at doorways obviously conserve the heat which has been produced and can be most effective. Books keep better at lower temperatures, so that in general the lowest acceptable level for humans is satisfactory for book preservation. In little visited rare-book storage rooms a much lower temperature is suitable, with consequent fuel savings.

In theory the correct relationship of air temperature and surface temperature within a library can be obtained by a 25 per cent radiation heat and 75 per cent convection heat. For comfort of readers seated for long periods, feet should be warmer than heads and this is best achieved by underfloor heating, either electric or by hot water coils. This method has the additional advantage of not taking up space which could be used for bookcases or tables. It used to be said that staff who are on their feet all day dislike underfloor heating because it "draws the feet" but this objection seems to have been dropped. Ceiling heating panels offer similar space saving qualities but heating the air above readers' heads results in a feeling of stuffiness; low wall panels are a possible compromise if wall space can be allowed, but they tend to create dust patterns on the walls. The use of heating panels in the lower part of full-length clear windows can serve also as a safety measure. Heating can be combined with ventilation by bringing in heated air at low level, through walls or hollow columns, and extracting it at a high level; heating arrangements often do the opposite. There are advantages and disadvantages in each method and this is a matter to be discussed with the heating consultant. The abomination of high level gas radiators should never be tolerated; long hours worked with these inevitably produces headaches.

The placing of radiators and convector heaters is a matter of much concern. Wall radiators not only prevent the wall from being used for shelving but also waste space by creating "dead" areas along side the radiators. Much worse are freestanding radiators and convectors, which can be both hindrances and dangers; the only possible solution is to have the heaters built into library fittings but even there they are not particularly efficient and are a bar to flexibility.

The choice of heating fuels will not normally lie with the librarian; the alternatives are (roughly in increasing order of cost), solid fuels, oil, gas and electricity. Faber and Kell[1] give a table showing relative fuel and labour costs, but it would be a bold man who would today predict the relative price and availability of these fuels throughout the life of a newly erected library. Solid fuels are dropping out of use, chiefly perhaps because labour is no longer available to work the boilers; of the others, the cost ratio is being upset by recent off-peak storage rates for electricity which are un-

deniably cheap. On the other hand it requires a meteorologist with uncanny powers to predict the next day's weather in the British climate.

Libraries in the UK are free from the problems caused by excessive natural heat which apply in the tropics, so cooling is necessary mainly to dissipate heat produced by people themselves, by solar gain from south-facing windows in the summer, and by very high lighting levels. Where full air-conditioning cannot be installed, adequate mechanical ventilation can provide generally satisfactory conditions for readers but less definitely for fragile books.

In certain crowded areas with low ceilings, mechanical air cooling can be better than forced ventilation which may produce an uncomfortable draught. Free circulation of air is essential for all these conditions and here the open-plan system shows its advantages. In heavily shelved stack areas, particularly if the stacks are closely fitted to floor and ceiling, there is a distinct gain in having open centres to double-sided stacks so that air can circulate more freely.

An expanse of glass windows will produce heat gains and losses which can be very expensive to counter; in some modern buildings this is the largest single service cost—far higher than heating or lighting. Librarians who have not experienced this problem would do well to read a recent account[2] of the alterations and adaptations needed to make one of the earliest and most famous all glass buildings in London suitable for general office use without discomfort—and to find out what it had cost. An architectural solution common abroad is to have an overhanging section of masonry to provide shade, but in this country this is seldom justified solely to exclude sunlight.

Special heat-reflecting glass, often combined with double glazing, is a possible solution but at a high initial cost, and it might be difficult to clean. Double glazing may be inevitable if very low outdoor temperatures are expected. If venetian blinds or curtains are proposed the librarian will again need to consider the cleaning and maintenance problems. If glass roofing is to be used, motorised horizontal blinds may be needed, if possible controlled automatically by light-sensitive cells.

Air should be changed at least three times an hour—more in summer—to avoid stuffiness; there are eight changes an hour in some modern British universities and thirty changes an hour in a recent art gallery, but suitable provision depends on the cubic capacity and the number of people in the area. If smoking is allowed anywhere in the building the polluted air should not be recirculated without filtering.

Air-conditioning

The advantages of full air-conditioning should not be taken lightly: the *Parry Report*[3] says:

"Firstly, solid particles of dirt, and liquid and gaseous forms of acids suspended in the atmosphere have a seriously deleterious effect on books and manuscripts resulting under the worst conditions in complete destruction of bindings, paper and vellum. Secondly, even in Britain, excessive changes of temperature and humidity accentuate this deterioration and can also lead to additional destruction as a result of the growth of moulds, fungi and bacteria which such conditions favour. For these reasons it is essential that for the best conditions for the preservation of books, the atmosphere should be free from dirt and acidity in gas or liquid form and that temperature and humidity should be controlled; in fact these conditions are obtained only by the installation of full air-conditioning plant (water washers to extract liquid or gaseous acids, filters to remove solid dirt, heating plant and refrigerating plant). In areas of highly-polluted air it is our view that library stocks, housed both in reading-rooms and stacks, can be preserved only in a fully air-conditioned atmosphere."

Despite these strong and clear recommendations of an official government committee, only a minority of British librarians will have the freedom to insist on air-conditioning for their libraries. Full air-conditioning, is of course, very expensive, its costs being in many cases approximately double that of the total of other forms of heating and ventilating. A more economical compromise, the plenum system described by Thompson[4], is seldom seen in libraries today.

An air-conditioning system calls for an adequate water supply and usually for supervisory labour; it can be noisy, but its greatest drawback is the vast amount of space required for the ducts and the machinery. In large buildings these have to be seen to be believed. Nevertheless it can be the complete answer: the standard authority on the subject is Faber and Kell[5]. Cheap air-conditioning has a deservedly bad reputation.

Although the building will be virtually sealed, it will be necessary for some windows to open, preferably key operated, in case the air-conditioning fails or for use in a power cut. If air-conditioning is to be installed only in certain parts of the building, lobbies or air traps will be needed so that the effect will not be lost by access to the outside air.

A few years ago to propose full air-conditioning would have seemed a counsel of perfection but the last annual survey of new public libraries[6] built in the US shows that in 1969 80 per cent were air-conditioned, in 1970 86 per cent and in 1971 92 per cent. This is obviously the trend and it is far more economical and efficient to install air-conditioning in a building as it is erected than to add it later.

HUMIDITY

Humidity is a factor often disregarded in popular libraries but it is of vital importance in those containing older books and manuscripts. Artificial heat dries out paper and skins (parchment and vellum) and can cause irreparable damage to paper made of mechanical wood pulp, which includes many newspapers and journals of the late nineteenth century. It is therefore essential to ensure that the relative humidity of the air around such books is from 45 per cent to 55 per cent, the latter being the recommended figure. In the UK, control is most needed in winter months when heating is switched on, and the cold air suffers a drop in humidity. To obtain an exact humidity level in all parts of a large building is an expensive stipulation: if books of a nature likely to be affected are all stored in special rooms then it is more economical for humidifying apparatus to be installed only in those rooms. (The air passes through a humidifier where water is atomised, absorbs moisture to the required level and passes back into the room.) Intermittent use of the books in general reading-rooms will not damage them. If the required humidity is to be provided throughout all reading rooms there may be trouble with condensation on windows and the only generally satisfactory way of dealing with this is to install double glazing. A consultant may find a cheaper expedient: he should make tests in the conditions to be expected. The converse, excess humidity, is caused by very hot air increasing in humidity on entering the cooler building; a high outside level of humidity accentuates the problem, but this condition does not often occur in the UK. Direct reduction of humidity is obtained by passing the air through dehumidifiers which include a refrigerant circuit; air from a room, at normal atmospheric pressure, is cooled to below its dew-point by passing it over evaporator coils where excess moisture is condensed out. Heat is also extracted and this is absorbed by the refrigerant, which in turn gives it back to the air as it re-enters the room. Troughs and tubing are installed to take the water discharge to drains.

Both humidifiers and dehumidifiers can be easily installed in air ducts but their effectiveness is reduced unless windows are kept closed to retain the treated air. Filters to remove impurities in the air can be used in a similar way, but for economy all these are used only in the air supply to special rooms where such conditions are necessary. Even cheaper is the method of providing "spot"

humidifiers and dehumidifiers within the room itself.

An unusual condition is where materials exhibit signs of mould even though the temperature and humidity levels appear to be correct. This may be caused by materials coming to the library from a place where humidity was high and where they acquired the spores which developed when a warmer temperature was experienced. The only remedy is thorough cleaning; the problem should not recur.

General atmospheric control

Whatever the methods proposed by the architect for correct atmospheric condition control, the librarian should watch the following points:

demands on space and limits on flexibility caused by the various installations;

possible noise caused by air-conditioning, forced air circulation or cooling plants;

need for central thermostatic control of heating equipment to avoid wasting staff time in attending to individual switches (the latter will be needed in rooms where special conditions are required so that central controls can be overridden);

location of all controls and thermostats where staff only may operate them;

fixing overall heating and ventilating levels on those suitable for reader service areas and not for staff workrooms where local controls can operate and windows be opened;

special ventilation requirements, of areas where fumes can be produced: fumigation equipment in repair rooms and binderies is a good example.

A table comparing the heating and ventilation provision in the four recent British university libraries is given opposite.

NOISE

The best account of this highly technical subject is given by Thompson[7].

External noise

Some libraries will inevitably be close to sources of external noise, ranging from aircraft overhead and road traffic to students in corridors and typing in nearby offices. These the architect will deal with by using enclosing walls and windows which attenuate the noise to a suitable degree; there is no need for the librarian to enter into the world of decibels and the sound-reducing qualities of different walls. This may seem inconsistent with his involvement in measurements in lux in the section on lighting (chapter 16). The reason is that while lighting can be affected by his own actions when the library is operating (placing tables, switching on lights at certain times, drawing venetian blinds and so on) there is nothing he can do about external noise (except close doors and windows).

Internal noise

An environment acceptable to readers includes a noise level that is never obtrusive. The acoustic expert has at his disposal a much wider range of noise-absorbing surfaces than was available a few years ago. Control will in fact be exercised by choice, not only of wall, floor and partitioning surfaces but also of curtains and any other soft surfaces which tend to absorb sound. In an open-plan library the spaces themselves, if surrounded by soft surfaces, will do this, if to a limited extent.

Space alone can complicate the issue; the hard high domes of old-fashioned reading-rooms sometimes produce echoes of surprisingly long duration—Manchester Central Reference Library is a striking example and a warning. The greatest single step forward has been the installation of carpets; these with the sound-absorbing quality of books in quantity, will make book-lined

Comparison of environmental conditions— heating/ventilating

Services	Edinburgh	Essex	Lancaster	Warwick
Mechanical	Full air-conditioning	Plenum ventilation system	Plenum ventilation system. Heated ceiling to offset fabric losses	Plenum ventilation to central area of each floor Air-conditioning in special collection room only
Temperature	20°C (68°F)	20°C ± 1·7°C (68°F ± 3°F)	20°C ± 1·7°C (68°F ± 3°F)	18·3°C (65°F)
Relative humidity	55 per cent	Minimum limit 50 per cent	No control	No control
Air changes per hour	Five	Four in winter, ten in summer	Three	Six
Filtration	To 5 micron size. Air washer	To 5 micron size No washer	To 5 micron size No washer	To 5 micron size No washer
Heat gain	Projecting floors Double glazing Heat-absorbing glass on south face. Fixed louvres on east and west faces	Internal vertical adjustable blinds .	Horizontal internal blinds Projecting floors on courtyard elevations	Double glazing. Adjustable blinds within double-glazed units
Additional heating	Perimeter heating under windows	Perimeter heating below windows	Heated gilled pipes under windows	Convectors under windows
Zoning	Two zones on each side of building on each floor	None	Thermostat at each column on each floor	Two zones (primary) on each floor, collectively controlled
Comment	Air-conditioning was given priority by both librarian and architect. Although each floor is about 76 × 45 m (250 ft × 150 ft), conditions are generally excellent and readers could be placed anywhere on any floor. On each floor average occupancy in any one bay is taken as thirty-four readers. The large window areas cause considerable variation in temperature, between south- and north-facing reading positions in spite of double glazing, projecting floors and heat-absorbing glass	Air-conditioning, asked for by librarian, was rejected on grounds of cost. Readers find it necessary to complement the mechanical ventilation system by opening windows	General conditions are satisfactory. Absence of humidity control results in a very low humidity level in winter Data for mechanical services refer to phase 1. It is hoped to maintain the same standard in phases 2 and 3 if cost permits	Air-conditioning, asked for by librarian, was rejected on grounds of cost, except the special collection room. Perimeter areas rely on natural ventilation. The large 1800 × 1200 mm (6 ft × 4 ft) windows make it difficult to control ventilation, particularly in winter, as draughts occur when windows are opened. Absence of humidity control results in a very low humidity level in winter

Comparison of disturbance levels

	Edinburgh	Essex	Lancaster	Warwick
Visual disturbance	Segregation: the entrance and circulation desk area is separated from all other areas. A lift lobby within the central core is closed off from the two undergraduate reading floors by a glazed partition. Groups of readers are isolated from the core and from each other by stacks	Segregation: entrance, circulation desk and primary vertical movement are all contained in one core with a central light well, separated from main library wing by a glazed partition	Segregation: entrance and circulation desk areas are closed off from rest of library. Vertical movement is by staircase within service cores	Segregation: the entrance area is closed off from the library, only the circulation desk is set back off the main library floor. Lifts and main staircase are within the central core. On each stack floor the two main reader groups are isolated from each other by the stacks
Aural disturbance	Sound absorbing materials: acoustic ceiling tiles are used throughout. Carpet is used throughout the two undergraduate reading floors, but reading areas only on stack floors. Fixed double glazing	Sound absorbing materials: no acoustic treatment of any surface in main service core. No acoustic ceiling treatment in bookstack area. Carpet is laid throughout main library wing. Fixed single glazing: small slit opening windows	Sound absorbing materials: acoustic ceiling tiles are used throughout. Carpet is laid throughout. Windows open onto internal courtyard	Sound absorbing materials: acoustic ceiling tiles are used throughout. Carpet is laid throughout, except ground floor. Opening double glazed windows
Comment	Excellent conditions. Although it is a large building with many occupants, there is minimum disturbance to each individual. Double glazing reduces normal urban external noise	In spite of carpet on stack floors the noise level is high, because of the high ceilings and lack of acoustic treatment. Noise from the service core penetrates into quiet areas	Excellent conditions. Readers broken into small isolated groups	Excellent conditions. Carpet and acoustic tiles control disturbance from noise, although each group of readers is large. There is no external noise on the rural site
Noise criteria level*	25	45	40	30 to 35

*The noise criteria levels from equipment are the common levels for equal sound pressure over the eight octave bands (IHVE *Guide*, 1965).

L

alcoves tolerable except for high levels of sound from outside the alcove.

Noise inside a library consists mainly of conversation, frictional noise (chairs scraping the floor and the impact of heels on hard surfaces), and mechanical noises (from book-hoists and type-writers). Staff discipline can eliminate a good deal of noise—librarians on duty are often less inhibited in their conversation than readers and a high-pitched voice speaking into the telephone can carry a long way. Acoustic hoods are seldom popular with busy staff but their use over telephones may have to be enforced.

The architect will make the major contribution by using acoustic tiles or other prepared surfaces on ceilings and by breaking up open areas by partitions or bookcases; in libraries used by large numbers of young students it may help to provide outlets for conversation in the form of group discussion rooms, or isolated areas where talking is not discouraged. It may also be possible to provide, in extreme cases, a level of low frequency hum; it will be unnoticed but will cover the sound of conversation that is in-evitable in study areas. It is assumed that the architect will not add to the problem by installing fluorescent tubes which buzz, or air control machinery which hums. In entrance halls and corridors, where noise will not distract readers, the architect may plan for a level of lively sound.

The table below shows the noise level and both the aural and visual disturbance factors in the four university libraries.

York University library, built at the same time as the other four, is much less satisfactory in these respects. A survey[8] reports:

"Most readers are disturbed, both visually and aurally, by move-ment of other readers round the library, as the noise is carried from one floor to another via the light wells, and readers are constantly aware of the movement of people. Rain on the roof-light causes considerable noise."

A shield has been added above the counter to protect readers on upper floors from the noise and an inner skin added beneath the roof. See plans, page 31 and photos, pages 105 and 154.

Reading and open stack areas around void over counter, York University Library

REFERENCES

[1] FABER, OSCAR and J. R. KELL Heating and air-conditioning of buildings, 5th edition, revised by J. R. Kell and P. L. Martin. Architectural Press, London, 1972

[2] Building revisited, New Zealand House. *In Architects' Journal*, 10 March 1971, pp 531–542

[3] Parry Report. Op cit, p 92

[4] THOMPSON. Op cit, p 35

[5] FABER and KELL. Op cit

[6] *Library Journal.* 1 December 1971, p 3968

[7] THOMPSON. Op cit, pp 28–30

[8] *Architects' Journal*, 6 March 1968, p 573

18 Enclosing elements and finishes

EXTERNAL CLADDING

Some libraries may be built with the load-bearing walls   earlier days but the majority will have steel or reinforced concrete framing with slabs of material hung from, or fastened to the frames. Obviously there will be fundamentally different approaches according to the scale and solidity of the building: a small single-storey library can be of much lighter construction than a multi-storey one.

It may be bewildering to a layman that the Auditor-General's *Report* (1966–67), quoted by Derrick Oxley in the *Spectator* (4 March 1972), stated, "Industrialised building is more expensive than traditional." Without doubt there is more to this question than the cladding material but it can be fairly stated, with considerable relevance to recent libraries, that glass walls are very dear, and irregular glass walls even dearer. Old-fashioned brick walls are, by comparison, very cheap.

The cladding will have a great effect upon the appearance of the building, and thus on its appeal to potential users; it will also be an important item in the cost, but it is entirely the architect's business, subject to planning approval, and no comment is called for from the librarian. If he does strongly object to the appearance of the building, as shown in the sketches submitted by the architect, he will have to make his views known to his authority when the feasibility report is being considered. In such a case the authority might ask the architect to make an alternative suggestion: happily this is a most unlikely occurrence.

If commemorative murals or a civic crest are to form part of the façade, this will have been indicated in the brief and the architect will allow an appropriate sum in the estimate. If he himself wishes to propose such an adornment he will make the proposal as part of the feasibility report.

INTERNAL WALLS

A high proportion of the walls of most libraries will be covered by shelving, either in cases or on brackets. Above the shelving and on blank walls, the architect will plan colour and texture as part of his design. The librarian will have two legitimate points of interest with regard to these walls—their acoustic quality and, more important, their maintenance cost.

Wall surfaces, particularly those which can be touched by readers, will soon need cleaning; this raises two questions: the cost of cleaning, and the effect of regular cleaning on the durability of the wall covering. High gloss paint is certainly the best from this point of view but it is often considered institutional in appearance and it has disadvantages in high reflectance of both light and sound. These disadvantages are not unsurmountable; sound absorption can be provided in other ways, by floor or ceiling, and light reflection can be controlled by careful siting of light sources.

The current fashion among architects for rough, hammered and pitted concrete surfaces causes particular problems of maintenance; the surfaces hold dust—indeed pitted concrete seems to produce dust—and they are not easy to keep clean. To a librarian it seems better not to use such surfaces inside a building unless they are efficiently sealed.

In most cases it is a counsel of perfection to say that all internal surfaces should be permanent and never require renewal. This would be an enormous advantage throughout the life of the building and it could be done, by the use of concrete, Formica on internal walls, durable materials on floors and polyurethane-coated furniture. The initial cost would be high, the running costs low. An experienced librarian may have strong feelings on this subject. When he studies the list of proposed finishes he will ask the architect whether they will comply with the stipulated requirements of acoustic quality, ease of maintenance and so on: if he is assured that they will, there the matter ends, unless he is prepared to ask his authority to support his objection and require the proposals to be altered.

Partitions

The flexibility requested by the librarian may result in some internal walls being removable so that space allocations can be altered at some future date. The brief must state clearly how

Accoustically-acceptable flexible partitioning, University College, Dublin, Faculty of Arts (Brockhouse ModernFold Ltd)

"temporary" such partition walls are to be; it would be a serious error if a flimsy demountable partition with low noise insulating qualities were installed, when changes were known not to be needed for some years. In such a case a brickwork partition wall could have been provided, as the cost and trouble of alteration would form an acceptable part of a future major change. The exact opposite applies when partitioning is to be demounted at weekly or monthly intervals.

Lettering

Whether or not it is strictly within the architect's province to design lettering for all the library notices, it is nevertheless an advantage to make use of his professional expertise. Time and again one visits a recently opened library to find it disfigured by notices of a quality, fount, style and colour which clash with the internal design. In a fine new library people will expect lettering in impeccable taste. If possible, the architect should choose the lettering to be used throughout, including shelf guiding, and the librarian should always keep to that style.

Similarly all notice boards, inside and outside the building, should be part of the overall design. The librarian must provide the wording and information they will carry, which will include times of opening and lists of associated activities. He will say whether the boards are to be illuminated after dark and whether a general illuminated (even neon) sign will be needed to advertise the building, but he has nothing to do with its design.

The librarian should also check the type of door furniture to be provided. It may be objected that this again is entirely the architect's responsibility: true, but the librarian will have to live with any difficulties caused by lack of forethought. Doors which are much used by the public should be heavy and well enough sprung to enable them to close without catches; these always wear out under heavy use. "Push" and "pull" notices should be generously provided on heavily used doors; their absence causes much frustration and readers have been known to break a wrist by pushing too hard at the wrong half-door. All-plate-glass doors should be marked clearly so that near-sighted readers are in no danger of bumping into them.

MAINTENANCE

A librarian must never forget that during the expected life of a building operational costs will be very much greater than the initial cost. Of the operational costs, maintenance of the fabric will be a major element. On the whole the time and money spent on maintaining public buildings such as libraries is very much lower than in comparable commercial buildings, consequently many libraries have a run-down appearance after a few years of service. Governing bodies find it expedient to defer redecoration as an economy; wood surfaces and seat coverings become worn in ways that would not be acceptable to firms conscious of the importance of their image. Perhaps the fault lies as much with librarians as with their masters, but in any case the architect must plan to keep to a minimum the need for cleaning, replacement of worn-out items, redecorating and attention to mechanical fittings. This is unfortunate but it is a fact of public service life.

The times and conditions under which cleaning, maintenance and redecorating can be carried out will already be known to the architect (probably from the secondary brief). Major maintenance in a school may have to be confined to school holiday times but in a public library, open fifty-two weeks each year, all maintenance may have to take place while people are using the library (the cost of nightwork being prohibitive). The architect will need to bear these facts in mind when choosing materials, finishes and methods of construction.

When the architect's proposals are received, in the form of plans and specifications, the librarian must understand them well enough to satisfy himself that they are practicable in view of the operational requirements of the service. He will be particularly concerned with:

Doors Is the machinery of main entrance doors sound enough for the very heavy use they will receive; if they jam or break down, how will readers enter the library while repairs are in progress?

Windows Is the control machinery (if any) easy to operate or does it require special equipment and ladders? How are the windows to be cleaned? Will the cleaning be particularly expensive?

Light fittings and large windows Will they need special scaffolding in order to clean them and can it be built into the structure? Can they be cleaned by one person or will a team be needed? Can fittings be changed as a routine every few months, rather than piecemeal as they break down or wear out? If they are to be changed as a whole at specified intervals, will there be adequate lighting if some bulbs or tubes fail before the time for renewal arrives?

Roof glazing—if any How is it to be cleaned, and how often? Would it not be worth fitting glass pyramids, steeply sloped so as to be as far as possible self-cleaning?

Power points and water taps Will there be enough of these within a reasonable distance of every area where a cleaner is to operate? Are there adequate and well-sited cupboards for cleaning materials and have cloakrooms been provided for cleaning staff?

*Redecoration—*interior and exterior. How often should it take place? How long are the fabric or other coverings of chair seats expected to last?

Floor coverings Are worn areas to be replaced in sections or must the whole area be renewed? If in sections, is there any guarantee that matching pieces will be obtainable in the future? How often must floors be cleaned and how often resealed? How long will the operation take?

Heating and ventilating machinery What happens if it breaks down? Is there to be a maintenance contract; if so, what will it cost? How long will the library be without services when a breakdown occurs? Is there any emergency provision in case the lighting system should fail? In a building where hundreds of people can be trapped in the dark this needs serious consideration.

Not all the 'items listed above' are strictly maintenance questions but they might place the librarian in difficulties after the architect has left the scene. It is ideal if the authority has its own buildings or maintenance officer who can be a member of the team from the beginning. Otherwise the architect should record recommendations as to the cleaning and maintenance schedules for all areas. It might be possible (at a price) for the architect to take part in the supervision of maintenance for a limited number of years after the opening.

The architect will certainly be expected to adjudicate on any disputes with the contractor about troubles which occur during a stipulated period after completion of the contract. This is entirely the architect's business but he should be asked to put the librarian in the picture in order to avoid misunderstandings. An example, perhaps a petty one, from personal experience; not long after opening day a large number of fluorescent light tubes failed. The contractor successfully pleaded that the tubes had been heavily used by library staff for several weeks in moving books and preparing areas for service before the building had been handed over. This matter had not been foreseen; it should have been.

19 Detail design

Earlier in this book the design programme was left at the scheme design stage while attention was paid to layouts, critical sizes, materials, and matters for which the librarian's peculiar requirements forced the architect to make special studies. Now that the latter has mastered these subjects he can apply the results to his plans, including the implication of any changes which might have arisen from submission of the scheme report. Once more he will reassess his proposals and discuss with the specialist consultants and the quantity surveyor any necessary alterations and developments.

The project then moves on to its next phase—producing the full details required for making the working drawings, schedules and specifications to be used by the building contractors when they come to construct the library.

WORKING DRAWINGS AND SPECIFICATIONS

Producing the mass of working drawings will take time; accompanying the drawings will be schedules and specifications, detailed statements of materials to be used, methods of construction, and required standards and tolerances. These documents will be too numerous and too complicated for the librarian to handle but he should see the ones with which he is concerned, however technical. For example, he must examine the joinery detail drawings for construction of an issue counter, if only because he has been so meticulous in deciding on its ideal method of operation. It is here that the full value of a library consultant is obtained: he will have the specialist knowledge, and the time to study the drawings and schedules in detail and to interpret them in the light of the library's functional needs.

In the case of very large and complicated projects detailed specifications for the whole building may not be produced but the architect and quantity surveyor may together prepare, for incorporation into the bills of quantity, specification clauses covering the work: the working drawings themselves will have many specification notes on them. On certain aspects of the building there may be separate specifications, for example on structural reinforced concrete and on service installations. In a large project the complexity of the building makes preparation of a specification for every operation an enormously complicated task out of line with modern building practice, which tends more to elemental drawings and production information.

For small projects today, as in the past, specifications are produced, trade by trade, in great detail as to quality, workmanship and method. When read in conjunction with the drawings they should define exactly how a building is to be constructed. Specifications are the architect's responsibility, but because both quantities and prices are involved a large part in preparing them must be played by the quantity surveyor. For special work he will have had to prepare special bills in advance so that they can form the basis of prime cost sums to be allowed within the tender. Specifications must be highly detailed and precise, with reference (in the UK) to British Standards and Codes of Practice. Any looseness here may be the cause of dispute later which can be very expensive, not only for the client but also for the architect, as he can be held liable for instructions which allow of more than one interpretation. The recommendations of the various specialist consultants—heating, sound, ventilating, electrical, structural— were included in reports submitted when each stage was completed. The details of these requirements will now be embodied in a complete specification in which all possible elements will be included.

From the specifications and the working drawings, the quantity surveyor will now draw up bills of quantity.

BILLS OF QUANTITIES

These documents are exact and very detailed statements of the quality and quantity of all materials to be used, and are accompanied by a specific pricing. This pricing is a highly skilled operation which is the basis of the quantity surveyor's profession; it involves a very full knowledge of every detail of each operation to take place during the construction, and an absolutely up-to-date knowledge of the current prices for every class of material as well as the time-cost of each operation. The figures produced in the bills will be gathered into subtotals, then into a grand total. From these total figures the architect will be able to see how his apportioned cost allocations have been followed and where his running estimates have proved incorrect. He will have many discussions with his technical team members and will revise and reconsider in order to produce the desired result.

The final figure will be critical in the architect's scheme; to it he will add the other costs involved—fees, consent costs, and so on— and those which may already have been incurred, for example site bore hole tests, and he will arrive at a grand total which should correspond to the estimate agreed earlier by the authority. Naturally the amounts will seldom correspond exactly and the architect will consult with his team to see whether it is feasible to bring the figure down to the original estimate (it could be that the final figure is lower than the original estimate, but it seems never to be so). If he finds that the increase is unavoidable, he has no alternative but to report yet again to the authority, asking whether the increased figure is acceptable. If cuts are judged to be necessary then much work has to be done in deciding what features have to be omitted and where lower standards can be accepted.

Although this total is referred to here as the "final" figure, it is still in effect an estimate. It is the cost for which the architect believes it will be possible for the building to be completed. If the "casting off" of quantities and costs has not been done with absolute accuracy or with correct judgment of current prices, then tenders received will be different from the total and again he has either to recast and replan or return to the authority with a request for an amendment of the total sum available.

TENDERS

Where a library is to form part of a larger construction the contractor already working will study the drawings and specifications and submit his own costings, which again may not correspond with the architect's and more discussions will be necessary. If the operation is separate, it is usual at this stage to invite tenders. Tenders may be advertised openly, or selected contractors (known to be capable of carrying out this class of work) may be invited to tender. In the case of a building which is to be erected from public funds the former may seem the most open and honest method but it has some disadvantages. The authority has the right to know that the contractor has the necessary financial soundness for such a large undertaking and may decide to appoint only a firm which has already had practical experience in the field of library building. If the authority has such preconceptions it would be wrong to encourage firms without the requisite qualifications to spend the large amount of time and money needed to submit a tender.

When the tenders are received (usually under legal stipulations of secrecy and strictly controlled delivery) they will be considered by the authority along with a report from the architect on any factor which, from his expert knowledge, he might wish to bring to their attention. This could include his own assessment of the particular contractor, a report on other buildings recently carried out by him and so on. The architect has an important task in commenting upon a particular tender and he may not recommend acceptance of the lowest tender if, for example, he judges that the large margin between the lowest and the next tender casts doubt upon the soundness of the estimating by the firm offering the lowest one. Acceptance of an abnormally low tender can land the client in serious trouble if the contractor has underpriced to such an extent that he cannot meet his financial commitments. The authority may disregard the architect's advice—the decision is their responsibility and the lowest tender might be accepted against the architect's recommendations.

Tenders may be invited for several different parts of the project or a single overall tender may be called for, prime cost sums being included within the global sum for special contract work, such as heating, machinery or loose furniture. Alternatively some of these, particularly loose furniture, may be excluded to save the contractor's percentage charge. Contractors for these special sections may be nominated, or the sections themselves may be subject to tender. It will be clearly indicated in the main contract what responsibilities lie upon the contractor for the work of the various subcontractors or specialist suppliers. The main contractor will normally be responsible for seeing that subcontractor's work is entirely acceptable.

This method of fixed price tendering is the most usual one but in recent years of continuously rising costs it has proved difficult to apply to very large projects. A firm tendering for work which may take months or even years to complete will be unwilling to commit itself to a figure when cost increases, over which it has no control, can arise. Even if the total figure is projected ahead with percentage increases to allow for estimated rises in costs over the period of the contract, the tenderer will still be at the mercy of such uncontrollable forces as labour difficulties, shortages of materials and rapid inflation. For these he will wish to claim additional costs which cannot be estimated at the outset but he knows that the authority will be unwilling to agree to them.

To resolve this difficulty there are various alternative methods of tendering. One is to enter into a contract on a fluctuating basis. Here the current prices of materials and labour are included for all aspects of the work, and increases in the costs of these, as ascertained by the quantity surveyor, are added to the contract sum as they arise. The advantage of this method is that the contractor is not expected to gamble on possible variations in the rates that he will have to pay for materials and labour, and knows that he will be paid a fair sum to cover such increases. If the contractor has to allow for unknown future increases he will naturally price above the highest level of increase that he can anticipate in order to cover himself for the risks involved. Another danger is that he will underestimate the possible rises and, being bound by contract, have to face unpleasant surprises caused by circumstances beyond his control. This in turn can lead to genuine financial embarrassment or even **bankruptcy**, which is certainly not in the client's interest. The disadvantage of accepting a "fluctuating" price is that the authority will not know its total commitment until it is too late to make savings if the cost comes out above what it is prepared to spend.

Another alternative is to deal with the tender in two stages: in stage 1 firms are invited to tender on the basis of the priced bill of quantities prepared by the quantity surveyor. From these tenders a firm is chosen and then, at stage 2, that firm is brought into consultation and co-operates with the architect in completing a firm bill of quantities from which a target price is produced, including a set percentage for management and profit. A contract is then drawn up, acceptable to both sides, which apportions between them the sum of money, either above or below the target figure, which the project will finally cost. This system is very complex and places upon the architect a greater responsibility in checking true actual costs for goods and labour than if he had only to certify that the work was carried out correctly.

This is a highly specialised business, particularly in the case of

projects which may take several years to build. The work of drawing up the contract itself takes time and inevitably involves the legal departments of the authority as well as the architect and the contracting firms. From this point the team is enlarged by the addition of the representatives of the various contractors and subcontractors. The architect will have already been busy planning the construction project and much depends upon the efficiency of his plans.

SITE WORK

At the appropriate time the contractor will be given access to the site under exactly stipulated conditions, and work can begin. During the whole period of construction the architect will visit the site; he is paid, however, not for constant, but for general supervision and is not normally expected to be constantly on site. In large jobs constant supervision will be provided by a clerk of works, who inspects the work under the architect's instructions but is appointed by the client. His job is to ensure that the architect's intentions are fully realised and to keep records of progress, to warn the architect of difficulties and anomalies in the information and record time spent by the contractor on works measured at daywork rates.

The contractor has accepted a price for a job on certain strict conditions, and if these conditions are not met he will have the right to claim extra payment. Conversely if the contractor does not meet his exact obligations, he will cause delay and extra costs through the effect which the variation will have upon others. For all this the architect and clerk of works will be responsible.

The architect may feel, therefore, that at least he should be spared the librarian's attention but, unfortunately, this cannot be. Throughout the entire period of the construction there should be constant contact between members of the team, including the librarian. It is not enough for the architect to meet him at intervals to assure him that all goes well; there should be regular meetings on site, and joint inspection of the work. This may seem wasteful because, at least in the earlier stages, the librarian will not understand what is going on, or be able to visualise the completed library. Nevertheless it is important, particularly as the librarian's specialist knowledge, and his understanding of the detailed function of every section, will enable him to see where expensive errors are likely to arise from possible earlier misunderstandings. It is at least as important that the librarian should understand that any alteration he might wish to have made at this stage will cost a great deal of money. By accepting on behalf of his authority the architect's proposals he has committed himself to those proposals (hence the great importance of his understanding them); if he now has second thoughts and wishes to make alterations, they will be extra to the scheme for which the architect has received full acceptance, and extras must be paid for, both their individual costs and those of any delays they may cause and effects they may have on the whole job. It is most important also that any changes, or even comments, which the librarian wishes to make should be communicated only to the architect. If the librarian asks the contractor to make alterations, even in such a small matter as the position of door fittings, he is likely to cause chaos, and to commit his authority to extra expenditure. This is particularly important in the penalty clauses: these parts of a contract place financial penalties on the contractor, should he fail to complete work by a stipulated time. When the contractor accepts such a clause he does so on the condition that he shall be uninterrupted in his work as prescribed.

The application of penalty clauses is fraught with legal difficulties: the contractor will accept responsibility for the delay only where he is undeniably at fault. If he feels that the prescribed conditions have been violated he will resist them and a legal battle will take place. The legal position is not simple and it may be necessary for the authority to prove that it has been caused actual financial loss by the delay—not always easy in the case of a non-profit making body such as a library. One of the claims which a contractor may make in defence of his own timetable is that it was disrupted by requests from the librarian. This is not as far-fetched as it sounds: if a librarian has been so ill-advised as to go direct to the contractor and ask for a small alteration, the contractor may claim that a representative of the authority has enforced changes outside the contract.

An even more petty matter can cause trouble: the librarian may wish to use part of the building which appears to be completed in order to move in some of his stock or equipment to save time at the end of the project; unless he does this with the full consent of the contractor, through the architect, the contractor can later claim that this was not in the contract and that it caused delays. Even if legal action against a contractor is successful it is an unhappy and expensive state of affairs.

Because the architect is retained by the authority he is responsible to it for all aspects of the project, but he is not entirely its employee in his dealings with the contractor. As a professional man he has an ethical responsibility for the relationship between the authority and its legally contracted construction firm; he holds here something of the position of referee and this responsibility must be fully accepted by both sides. The architect also has responsibilities to nominated subcontractors to see fair play in their relationship with the main contractor.

While construction is in progress, seeing that work goes according to schedule will not be the architect's only preoccupation: he will also be engaged in analysing the management and progress of the job, feeding back progress reports to his technical team and constantly reconsidering the methods and timetables in the interests of greater efficiency. Few jobs proceed exactly as they have been visualised and after each site inspection he will expect to receive comments (and probably complaints) from the various people involved—contractors, subcontractors, engineering specialists and so on—which call for continuous adjustment to the programme. In such a complicated operation these people's interests may often conflict and the architect will act as judge on the different claims and counter-claims. He will have the task of assessing the work as it progresses and (with the clerk of works and the quantity surveyor) certifying for payment the sums claimed by the different contractors which become due as certain agreed portions of their task are completed. He must keep his eye on the overall programme and timetable; if delay is inevitable, he must report at the earliest opportunity so that adjustments can be made. Some delays, such as those resulting from exceptionally bad weather or strikes, are inevitable, but they are always unpopular. Trouble may arise as a result of the architect's own specifications. If for instance the stipulated plaster fails to dry in the period allowed, there may be delay before paint can be applied and this can set off a chain-reaction of delay throughout the finishing. He has to report this fact and accept financial liability on behalf of the authority. On the other hand the contractor may have laid a screed which does not meet the architect's specifications and he will require it to be taken up and relaid; this will involve delays and extra costs which he will certify as being due to breach of conditions by the contractor, recommending that the extra cost be charged him. This may seem a gloomy picture but the complicated process of erecting a large building can seldom be expected to run exactly according to plan.

20 Conversions

A variation of library planning which may face architect and librarian is the less glamorous, but often more challenging, task of converting an out-of-date building into a modern library. Because so many more new buildings have been put up in the field of formal education in the last two decades, most of the conversions have been public library projects. Some colleges and schools (particularly independent schools) may convert rather than build afresh, and hospital libraries (as the need is recognised more widely) may find that conversion is the only way of acquiring satisfactory premises within an existing building complex. The variants are:

conversion of a non-library (be it shop, garage, barn or house) into a library;
creation of a new library within the walls of an existing one;
building an extension to an existing library, linking up to form a single service unit.

Conversion of a non-library building
This presents far more difficulties to the architect than designing a new building. On the other hand the building to be converted may have an atmosphere and charm that would be difficult to achieve in a modern structure.

The procedure is exactly the same as for a new one: a brief from the librarian, site investigation, planning consents (which may be more involved than usual because of the fire requirements of the Building Regulations) and so on, the whole programme to be carried out by a design team. Because the range of buildings which could be converted into libraries is so wide it is difficult to generalise; perhaps the most common single problem is the strength of the structure and the limits on floor loading which a change may produce.

Conversion is much more likely to concern a public library than any other type because of the importance in public library siting of a position in the heart of the shopping or civic section of town; as most such desirable sites will already be in use, conversion is a fairly common occurrence. Houses and shops have been converted in their hundreds: many very successful examples may be visited, and there immediately spring to mind Greenhills Branch, Sheffield (an old and very dignified house) and Cannon Street Branch in the City of London, where three small business areas which had been linked up for use as a bank have been converted as a busy lending library.

Modernising an old library
Making a modern library within the shell of an old one has been a familiar task of architects to public library authorities for many years. The existence of large numbers of Carnegie-type branch and central libraries on desirable sites, and the shortage of funds for public libraries has led many authorities to choose this, often short-sighted scheme. The façades of such buildings are seldom altered (apart from modern signs) and although the result may be most attractive inside and a credit to the architect, the building will usually fail in one of its chief tasks—that of attracting the casual reader to sample the service. Nevertheless, this scheme is often adopted; the chief aims are:

Change of emphasis
Many of the older libraries, particularly the Carnegie-type libraries of half a century ago, gave a great deal of space to the reading room, which was a newspaper and periodical reading area provided partly as a social, rather than a cultural, amenity. This space can be used for, or used to extend, the lending service, the aspect on which the greatest emphasis is now placed. This

could mean simply a switch of activities between the two areas, but usually more effective is the breaking down of divisions and creation of an open-plan library. The greatest difficulty is usually the ceiling heights, but false ceilings can be installed or the height can be put to good use for a mezzanine or half-floor catering for new services (gramophone record section, coffee bar or microform area). Similarly universities or colleges may be able to let overcrowded sections overflow into areas which have proved too lavish—exhibition rooms and display areas for example.

Expansion
Adjoining buildings may be taken over or alien sections, such as museums, may be removed to other quarters. If it is possible to make a single open-plan library, existing separate rooms which cannot be included may be used as lecture and exhibition spaces, or to provide study-rooms for Open University students, linking corridors being contrived. In some cases it has proved possible to remove the administration areas of the library to separate premises and to use the erstwhile office space for carrels, audio-visual rooms and so on.

Inquiry desk—before and after, Central Library, Borough of Dudley

Lending Library—before and after, Central Library, Borough of Dudley

Children's library—before and after, Govanhill District Library,
City of Glasgow

Functional efficiency

Advances in the techniques of book issue and return, and a changing attitude to security, may reduce the need for the vast control counters of the past and so permit the entrance to become more welcoming. The merging of separate rooms (such as children's libraries and reference rooms) into a single open-plan area can give a feeling of space as well as require fewer supervisory staff.

Change of internal environment

This is the heart of the matter, where a good architect can have an enormous influence. Some factors have already been mentioned; others include:

lowering the height of, and resiting, bookcases: in the past these were often arranged in patterns radiating from the counter for good supervision; they can be rearranged so that the vista invites the reader deeper into the library;
greater emphasis on wall shelving to open out the room;
replacement of old-fashioned, dark coloured metal bookcases by modern wood or metal cases in lighter colours;
use of more hospitable materials, particularly carpets, to make the atmosphere welcoming and brighter lighting to comply with the (often unnecessarily high) fashionable standards;
introduction of "fringe" activities such as coffee bars and listening rooms to make the library a place where people will find it a pleasure to spend an hour.

In all such conversions the librarian has to accept that the new library may have open shelf space for fewer books than the old one. This can mean that more books have to be kept in store, using staff time to fetch them when needed. As always it is up to the librarian to think out his priorities at an early stage and to state them clearly in the brief.

Because such conversions are usually more economically budgeted than new buildings, the need for constant discussion within the design team will be greater than in the case of a completely new project. If the librarian decides that a service of some sort must be carried on while the conversion is in progress (and this may be a reasonable tactical decision) the work of both architect and contractor will be made more difficult. Nevertheless this decision lies with the librarian, representing his authority, and any consequent difficulties and extra costs will be included by the architect in his feasibility study.

Appendix I Published standards

PUBLIC LIBRARY STANDARDS

This subject is well documented in the UK because the matter has been given government attention in various ways since 1957 when the Roberts Committee was set up. The official statements are contained in the Working Party Report[1] (one for England and Wales, one for Scotland). Standards issued in 1959 by the International Federation of Library Associations[2] (IFLA) were summarised in the reports, and comments made about their application to the UK. Since 1962 pronouncements have been made by the Department of Education and Science (DES) and by the Library Advisory Council[3]: IFLA Standards are in process of revision, but the Working Party Report remains the relevant official statement.

The Working Party prescribed no standards of size of building nor of total book stock but laid down, first, a minimum number of books and periodicals which needed to be added annually to a library system in order to provide a "basic library service" (which it defined loosely) and, second, the minimum annual additions to stock which should be acquired by a library giving more than the basic service. These figures alone are not very helpful in deciding what size a library should be unless more is known of bookstock before additions are made, but it should be remembered that the purpose of the Standards was to provide a reference basis for deciding the size of the smallest area whose local government council could be considered as a viable library authority.

To provide a library both effective and economically acceptable for a small community, be it school, hospital, or village, is always difficult. The Library Advisory Councils say[4]:

"In even the smallest community a wide range of tastes and interests can be expected, and it should be the function of the library to foster these rather than to restrict choice to a narrow range of popular material. For this reason, in even the smallest fixed service point the shelf stock should preferably be not less than 5000 volumes, and in some isolated communities a much larger shelf stock may be justified. This represents a larger stock per head of population than would normally be considered necessary, and suggests that a community of 1500 the total stock should be 5500–6000 volumes."

Size of service unit

Under the heading 'premises', the Working Party said[5]:

"... it is ... economical ... if urban populations are served in units of not less than 15 000 .... In urban areas no person should normally have to travel more than one mile to a library; the distance should be less in heavily built-up areas."

Working backwards from a given site, therefore, we can estimate the population likely to be within reasonable range of the service point; knowing that the percentage of active users to population is normally between 25 per cent and 30 per cent, a basic figure for readership can be assumed. To this must be added, where appropriate, a figure for those who live further away but may be expected to use the library because they have no alternative service, because public transport is convenient, because they work or receive education nearby, because they will shop in the area, and so on.

Basing planning on the criterion that no reader in an urban area should have to travel more than a mile to a library will inevitably produce many branch libraries, and for financial reasons they will be small. In fact the Library Advisory Councils say[6]:

"We do not consider it unreasonable that even in an urban area some readers should have to travel more than a mile in order to have the advantage of a full range of library services, including reference facilities, the assistance of professional staff and a level of stock which adequately reflects the tastes and interests of the community served. Good public transport, increased car ownership and adequate parking facilities are conditions that help to make a longer journey to the library acceptable."

The Library Association says[7]:

"... maximum economy and efficiency are secured when a branch offers the maximum book stock to the maximum number of users. Thus the most economical unit is theoretically one with a shelf stock of between 15 000 and 20 000 serving a population of between 20 000 and 30 000. But for geographical and other reasons, it won't usually work out that way."

In the same booklet it says, "On average one branch library will serve about 12 000 people": this cannot be of much help when a librarian has to plan to serve an isolated community of half that number.

In a document published in 1958, the County Library Section of the Library Association stated[8]:

"Every community of 5000 population or more should be served by a branch library open not less than thirty hours a week, and controlled by a qualified branch librarian. Every community of 1000–4000 population requires a part-time branch library."

This statement takes no account of mobile library services: neither does this book.

In the long run the librarian has to depend on his professional judgment and knowledge of the peculiar requirements of a certain area in producing estimates of the size of service appropriate to a small community, and in persuading his authority to accept them. Reader use surveys[9] can offer general guidance but the pattern of use can vary enormously between apparently similar areas; the variation will be even greater between, on the one hand, sections of a vast conurbation and on the other, sparsely populated rural area. Research into the reasons behind these great variations is still needed and the DES has a team working on the problem. In comparable situations, for example when a new branch library is envisaged for an area in a town which has branches serving similar areas, a readership survey, plotting the home and employment locations of readers, can be a most useful guide.

Book stock

The Working Party[10] suggested that a library serving a population of 40 000 will normally be expected to add about 10 000 volumes a year if giving more than a basic service; libraries serving between 30 000 and 100 000 population should add (in addition to the basic figures quoted above) about 500 non-fiction titles for every 10 000 population served up to 100 000. No figures whatever are quoted for populations larger than 100 000. Full-time branches serving a population of under 30 000 should aim to add to their stock annually 250 volumes (including ninety non-fiction) per 1000 population. These branches will be expected to receive full support (including the supply of less popular material on request) from the system of which they are part. In 1965 the DES[11] added the useful recommendation:

"A book stock of not less than $1\frac{1}{2}$ currently useful books per head of population may be considered reasonable for an authority of under 40 000 population."

According to the Library Advisory Councils[12]: "The minimum shelf stock on display in a branch library open for thirty hours a week or more should be about 6000 volumes. If it is assumed that the number of volumes on loan at any one time is equivalent to about one per head for 50 per cent of the population, this implies a total branch stock of some 8000 volumes in a population of 4000."

IFLA Standards[13] in the 1972 revision say:

"The number of volumes displayed on open shelves in any adult lending library serving a population of 3000 or more should never be less than 4000. [There should be] a minimum stock of 9000 volumes, of which one-third might be for children."

Withers[15], summarising the standards of fourteen different countries says:

"In general it may be said that the recommended figures for bookstocks per inhabitant—which naturally are higher for small populations than large ones—range from about three volumes to one volume per inhabitant (sometimes less than one where populations exceeds one million)."

This may be compared with Galvin and Van Buren[15] who, in 1959, suggested $1\frac{1}{2}$ to three books per head of population, and said that the minimum useful size of a library is 3000 adult books and 500 to 1000 children's books.

Mevissen[16] makes a most valuable statement:

"Supposing that 20 per cent of the community goes regularly to the public library and that every registered reader borrows a yearly average of twenty volumes. Supposing also that the book stock is turned over about four times a year, then the result in a community of about 3000 inhabitants will show 600 registered readers borrowing 12 000 volumes a year. For this a book stock of 3000 is needed, coming to one volume per head of the population."

Although Mevissen's figures may not be appropriate to all countries they show a method which, by applying relevant statistics, can be used to compute acceptable figures.

Space allowances
The Working Party quoted and commented upon the table space allowances in the standards of IFLA and the (British) Library Association; the figures are given below, with the Working Party's comments[17]:

Space allowances by population

Population served	Allowance per 1000 of population
10 000 to 20 000	42 m² (450 ft²)
20 000 to 35 000	39 m² (420 ft²)
35 000 to 65 000	35 m² (375 ft²)
65 000 to 100 000	31 m² (335 ft²)
over 100 000	28 m² (300 ft²)

British Working Party's comment:

"We do not think that the overall scale of provision can be reduced to the extent indicated as the population to be served increases. While the scale of provision in lending libraries may be reduced in relation to population, there is need for space to house larger reserve stocks, larger reference and local history collections and often also a commercial and technical library and other special departments and auxiliary services.
"We doubt whether any standards of general applicability can usefully be laid down, except perhaps strictly as minimum standards, for libraries serving populations over, say, 65 000."

In their study of the American public library, Wheeler and Githens[18] produced a formula which can be used to determine the appropriate size of a public library from knowing the population eventually to be served. They called this the VSC formula; V being the total number of volumes (in both open shelf and stack), s the number of seats required for readers and c the circulation in volumes per year. In applying this formula the authors use certain conclusions of their own which the architect may not be willing to accept: that 1 m² is sufficient for housing 110 volumes (1 ft² is sufficient for housing ten volumes) whether on stack or open shelf: that one reader seat requires 3·72 m² (40 ft²); and that 1 m² may be regarded as sufficient for a circulation of 430 volumes 1 year. (1 ft² of library space for a circulation of forty volumes a year).

With these figures in mind the VSC formula states that the required area in m² for a public library building is:

$$\frac{\text{No of books}}{10} + (\text{seats} \times 3\cdot7) + (\text{circulation} \div 3\cdot7)$$

The imperial equivalent of this would be:

$$\frac{\text{No of books}}{10} + (\text{seats} \times 40) + (\text{circulation} \div 40).$$

Note that the VSC formula had assumed an overall space allowance per seated reader of 3·72 m² (40 ft²).

In itself this formula cannot be very helpful for a future building, where the number of books, readers and circulation are all unknown quantities. If however the formula is used in conjunction with standards issued by an authoritative body, then helpful area figures for the new library can be deduced and these will at least be a starting point for study and discussion. Anyone attempting to use this formula must certainly consult *the American public library building* as this summary represents only the outline of the method defined and amended more precisely in that book.

Mevissen[19] suggests space allocations for the main reader service areas for public libraries: 200 m² for those with stocks of 3000 volumes to 4808 m² for those with 200 000 volumes. In these allocations he estimates that most public libraries with fewer than 25 000 volumes will house 32·5 volumes/m², those with up to 200 000 volumes will house 70 volumes/m². He also suggests that libraries with over 200 000 volumes will have a further 100 000 volumes stored systematically at 150 volumes/m².

In themselves these figures will be of little help to the architect in making an overall space assessment. Wheeler and Githens[20] say:

"The familiar allowances of 12, 15 or 20 volumes/ft² (112, 140, 185/m²) in stack construction and 20 ft², 25 ft² or 30 ft² (1·85 m², 2·30 m² or 2·80 m²) (per reader) in reading-rooms are insufficient because they refer to floor areas of individual rooms within surrounding walls. The values ... must each be sufficiently large to include its proportionate share of the space required for general administration, heating service, stairs, corridors, toilets, wall thicknesses, pier masses etc."

Floor areas of various departments
The following is from the IFLA standards[21]:

"The proportion of the total area occupied by adult lending departments, reference and reading-rooms and children's departments will vary considerably, according to size, from as much as 90 to 95 per cent in the small one-room branch to as little as 25 per cent in the very large central library with special departments, offices, storage stacks, etc. The library in the medium group (ie serving between 35 000 and 65 000) should offer a minimum 9·3 m² (100 ft²) per 1000 population for the adult lending library and 7 m² (75 ft²) for reference and reading-rooms.
"In a medium sized library an allocation of 4·6 m² (50 ft²) per 1000 population for the children's department will be reasonable but it should be remembered, on the one hand, that it is most desirable that the children's library should be big enough to hold a school class and to secure this in a smaller place will require a higher allocation per thousand and, on the other hand, as children should not be required to go long distances to the library, it is seldom in a larger urban area that a children's library will have to serve the children from a population of more than 30000; consequently even in the central library of a large city a room of 140 m² (1500 ft²) will be sufficient."

On this the Working Party comments:

"1 We consider that, even excluding the space occupied by special subject departments, the proportion of 25 per cent of the total floor space to be devoted to adult lending departments, reference and reading-rooms and children's departments in large libraries is too low. Except for the largest city libraries, it is doubtful whether the proportion should fall below 40 per cent. Variations in local conditions, such as the level of service required from the reference library, make it difficult to give any figure for general application.
"2 As the population to be served increases, the lending library normally becomes proportionately smaller than the reference library, but the exact sizes needed for the two departments will depend on local conditions. Our inquiries have shown that in some areas the suggested allowance of 9·3 m² (100 ft²) per 1000 population for the adult lending department in libraries serving 35 000–65 000 population is inadequate.
"3 It is becoming increasingly necessary to provide space where children can do their homework and other forms of study with access to a good range of books. The suggested maximum size for a children's library 140 m² (1500 ft²) should be considerably increased to allow for this type of provision. In large cities the main provision for children may not be in the central library.
"4 Since there is a limited number of worthwhile children's books available and since there is no reason to display large numbers of duplicate copies, we think that the optimum capacity for all children's libraries, except the smallest, might be between 4000 and 6000 volumes. If allowance is made for the lower bookcases necessary this will give a children's department of 1000 to 1500 ft² with additional study space provided for the larger populations and to allow for class use."

The standards for small public libraries issued in 1967 by the Danish State Library Inspectorate were specifically concerned only with public libraries serving populations between 5000 and 25 000 but in its space recommendations it is more categorical and helpful than other official bodies. The Inspectorate[22] reports that the space requirements for libraries serving populations of around 5000 (the lowest population figure for which full-time staff will be employed) will be somewhat under 600 m² (6400 ft²) and that for libraries serving populations of 25 000 will be 1600 m² (17 075 ft²). Within this range the requirements rise steadily with rise of population to be served. The Inspectorate's standards deal also with such matters as categories of rooms to be provided, readers' seats, numbers of staff and book stock provision.

Withers[23] gives details of space allocations in the countries whose standards he surveys: although many of these figures are most helpful, differences of local clientèle, conditions, and practice make it impossible to summarise them.

Bassenet[24] has studied a large number of central public libraries in the US and the UK finding the average *overall* capacity to be 53·8 volumes/m² (five volumes/ft²). He also arrived at figures for "ideal" space and seating allowances for central public libraries serving population ranges of around 150 000, 300 000, 550 000, and 800 000. Although such recommendations are based entirely on personal judgments, they are of great value as guides (top two tables facing).

The 1972 revision of the IFLA Standards[25] contains much more detail of space allocations for different departments and because they are both specific and current they are worth quoting at length:

"In all larger libraries [larger than small branch libraries] allow 15 m² (161 ft²) for every 1000 volumes on open shelves. This assumes that shelf units for adults will be five shelves high. Provision on this scale will allow for circulations of readers within the area, accommodation for staff counters and catalogues, informal seating without table space on the scale of one seat per 1000 population and a moderate amount of display equipment. If access to any part of the book stack is permitted, this should not result in any reduction in the number of volumes accommodated on freely accessible open shelves on the scale indicated below.

Adult lending facilities

Population served	Open shelf accommodation		Floor area at 15 m² per 1000 volumes (minimum 100 m²)	
	Volumes per 1000 population	Total capacity (volumes)		
			m²	ft²
3000	1333	4000	100	(1076)
5000	800	4000	100	(1076)
10 000	600	6000	100	(1076)
20 000	600	12 000	180	(1938)
40 000	600	24 000	360	(3875)
60 000	600	36 000	540	(5813)
80 000	550	44 000	660	(7104)
100 000	500	50 000	750	(8073)

[Additional space requirements relevant to adult lending areas are discussed later in the document].

For adult reference facilities the IFLA Standards say:

"Although reference books may require on average more shelf space per volume than books for loan, space for the circulation of readers in open-shelf areas does not need to be so generous as that described for lending areas and it has been considered sufficient to allow 10 m² (108 ft²) per 1000 volumes on open shelves. The lowest facing table shows, for libraries serving populations of different sizes, the open-shelf reference stocks which are considered likely in most cases to be necessary and adequate as basic working collections, together with the space required for their accommodation, and the additional areas likely to be needed for seating. Together, these will allow sufficient space to accommodate any staff desks which are needed in the public area."

The Standards emphasise[26] that space required for housing and consulting periodicals and storage and use of audio-visual materials must be added to the areas recommended.

For children's libraries, the Standards recommend a space allowance of 15 m² (161 ft²) for every 1000 volumes on open shelves —the same as for the adult lending library, even though the shelf units for children are to be four shelves high. "Provision on this scale will allow—as in the adult lending area—for circulation of readers, accommodation for staff counters and catalogues, informal seating without table space and a moderate amount of display equipment. In libraries serving a total population of up to 10 000 the area needed for the above purposes will commonly be 75 m² to 100 m² (807 ft² to 1076 ft²). Between 10 000 and 20 000 population an area of 100 m² to 150 m² (1076 ft² to 1615 ft²) will usually be needed. Libraries serving larger populations will need more accommodation than this, depending upon local patterns of use. In all cases there should be sufficient space to accommodate a class of schoolchildren without seriously disturbing other users. The Standards go on to say that space in addition to the above will be needs for study as well as for activities such as talks and story hours.

The Library Association issued standards[27] for reference departments in public libraries, indicating that libraries need to provide one reference seat for each 500 population served (confirming the Working Party Standard); and that the floor area for each seat should be 2·32 m² (25 ft²). The amount of open-shelf reference stock should not be fewer than 200 volumes per 1000 population served, with a floor area of 8·36 m² (90 ft²) per 1000 volumes. The remaining reference stock housed in stack requires a floor area of 4·18 m² (45 ft²) per 1000 volumes. Periodicals should be at the rate of 0·09 m² (1 ft²) of floor space per periodical for current periodicals on open access, 7 m² (75 ft²) per 1000 volumes in stack when bound.

Summary of recommendations: areas

Population group	Gross area ft² per capita*	Percentage of gross area						
		First floor	Readers' service	Stacks	Staff	Extension activities	Environmental features	Mechanical features
Group 1 100 000 to 200 000	0·5 to 0·6	30	52	14	20	6	3	5
Group 2 200 000 to 400 000	0·45 to 0·5	20	47	20	21	5	3	4
Group 3 400 000 to 700 000	0·4 to 0·5	15	(38) 37†	31	23	(3) 4†	2	3
Group 4 700 000 and above	0·25 to 0·4	15	34	35	23	3	2	3

* To stop unlimited increase of areas, subtract 10 per cent of total for every 500 000 population over 2 000 000.
†P. J. Bassenet has pointed out in correspondence with the writer that the figures in brackets are probably the more correct statistically. He does say however that as large libraries of this kind tend to diversify their extension activities into branch libraries it may be that one city may need central extension activity areas greater than another city in a higher population bracket.

Summary of recommendations: seating

Population group	No of seats per 1000 population	Private carrel seats	Study seats	Lounge seats	Auditorium seats	Lecture and meeting room seats
		percentage				
Group 1 100 000 to 200 000	3 to 4	5	75	20	200 to 300	50 to 100
Group 2 200 000 to 400 000	2 to 3	5	80	15	250 to 500	100 to 200
Group 3 400 000 to 700 000	2 to 2½	5	80	15	300 to 600	200 to 300
Group 4 700 000 and above	1½ to 2	5	80	15	400 to 600	200 to 600

*Subtract 10 per cent of readers' seats for every 500 000 population over 2 000 000.

Reference stock and seating requirements

Population served	Minimum total working stock of library		Adult reference facilities			
			Open-shelf bookstock		Seating accommodation	
	Per head of population	Total number of volumes	Number of volumes (percentage of total stock in brackets)	Area required at 10 m² per 1000 volumes	No of places at 1.5 per 1000 population	Area required at 3 m² per place
3000	3	9000	100 (1)	1 m² (11 ft²)	5	15 m² (161 ft²)
5000	3	15 000	300 (2)	3 m² (32 ft²)	8	24 m² (258 ft²)
10 000	3	30 000	900 (3)	9 m² (97 ft²)	15	45 m² (484 ft²)
20 000	3	60 000	3 000 (5)	30 m² (323 ft²)	30	90 m² (969 ft²)
40 000	2½	100 000	7 000 (7)	70 m² (753 ft²)	60	180 m² (1938 ft²)
60 000	2	120 000	12 000 (10)	120 m² (1292 ft²)	75	225 m² (2422 ft²)
80 000	2	160 000	16 000 (10)	160 m² (1722 ft²)	120	360 m² (3875 ft²)
100 000	2	200 000	20 000 (10)	200 m² (2153 ft²)	150	450 m² (4844 ft²)

UNIVERSITY LIBRARIES

The difficulty of studying international standards for university libraries is intensified by the different types of institutions to which the term is applied. Withers says[28]:

"[The university] covers a very wide range of libraries and this must be constantly borne in mind when considering the question of standards . . . the nature and extent of the collections and other facilities vary from the universities with a very high, and sometimes almost exclusive, load of postgraduate (particularly doctoral) work and other research work to the universities whose role is mainly that of preparing students for first degrees. From the top to the bottom of the scale the differences in the collections of materials, staffing and other requirements are enormous."

In his paper *Standards in university libraries* Humphreys[20] discusses this problem and quotes from standards from many different countries, clearly illustrating how figures vary, and says,

". . . almost all the standards I have quoted have little or no validity outside the environment for which they were invented."

Two examples will make this clear: Humphreys quotes from the Association of College and Research Libraries Joint Committee on University Library Standards which based its finding on current practices of fifty leading university libraries in the US and Canada; this committee proposed that the total stock of a university library should be 2 000 000 volumes with an annual acquisition rate of 100 000 volumes; the average holding to be 100 volumes and one current periodical per student, the total number of periodicals currently received to be 15 000.

His second quotation is from the University Standards Committee of the Canadian Association of College and University Libraries which suggests that "a minimum collection of 100 000 volumes is desirable" and above that size "75 volumes per full-time student". Both these examples differ considerably from general European practice (or even recommendation) and are of little help unless the financial authorities are prepared to accept the expenditure which these recommendations imply. As the financial allocation is so critical, and indeed is the main deciding factor, the basic element seems to be the percentage of total university funds which may be allocated to the library. To attempt, therefore, to provide detailed standards of size of building is an unprofitable exercise.

In the UK all universities cover the complete range of activities from undergraduate teaching to research, but they differ widely in other ways. The university libraries of Oxford and Cambridge are copyright libraries with vast collections; the University of London has colleges located in many parts of the metropolis while other older universities have special subject libraries associated with different schools. The newer, particularly the post-second-war, universities have more in common with each other although they differ widely in their type of environment and in their specialities. Little relevant comment can be made about a standard common to all. Such comment as exists has come from SCONUL (Standing Conference of National and University Libraries) and from the Parry *Report* of 1967. Indeed the most useful information is to be found in the evidence which SCONUL[30] submitted to the Parry Committee, although this too stresses the great difficulty of generalising where so many differences exist.

In planning a library for a new university there can be little conscious choice of a "total bookstock"; the range of subjects and the depth of research will affect selection, the money available will decide numbers to be purchased. In an institution of this kind the flow of new acquisitions is the life blood, and, as there will be comparatively little discarding of older material, there is theoretically no limit to the optimum size. Withers[31] quotes quantitative book stock standards of both the American and the Canadian Library Associations; both suggest a figure of around 300 000 volumes as a minimum for a university with 4000 students, but these are specifically stated to be minima. The ALA says:

". . . stronger institutions will demand considerably larger and richer collections".

The Parry *Report*[32] referred to a medium sized university with a stock of half a million volumes. Saunders says[33]:

"There should be no question of standardising or restricting the size of a library which is supposed to support research . . . It is economic and educational common sense, and not empire building or wild extravagance, for any university library to aspire towards its first million volumes as rapidly as possible."

The funds to support this bookstock and in fact regulate its growth come in the UK (almost entirely) from the University Grants Committee, a permanent body which assesses the claims of the whole of the British university world; for this reason the question of a final bookstock total will lie between the university authority and the UGC, not with the librarian.

Housing of readers

The proportion of the future readers who can be expected to occupy seats at peak times will be affected by various factors. There may be departmental reading-rooms, and in residential establishments study-bedrooms will cater for a fair number of readers. The study habits of postgraduate and research workers will almost certainly differ from those of undergraduates. Almost all educational libraries will have peak seating demands in the periods immediately preceding examination, but to base seating provision on these periodic explosions would mean half-empty rooms at other times; it may be preferable to open nearby class or tutorial rooms as overflow reading areas rather than cater for an artificial peak.

According to the American Library Association, in *Standards for college libraries*[35]: "Accommodation for at least one-third of the student body will be essential. The changing concept of the role of the library in the academic community may lead to an upward revision of this figure." The Canadian Library Association says[35]: "It is suggested that 25 per cent to 40 per cent of total student enrolment should be taken as the number of seats to be provided for students . . . A new and small institution would normally use the higher figure." The subject has been given more attention in America and something can be learned from American experience if due allowance is made for differences in the size and organisation of the universities in the two countries. Metcalf[36] suggests that, in general, library seating provision should be made for 20 per cent to 60 per cent of students at any one time. He also declares that far greater use is made of the library by workers in the fields of the humanities and the social sciences than by others and that, although in general there are five times as many undergraduates as workers for advanced degrees, the steadily growing emphasis on research rather than teaching means a much greater use of the library by the faculty.

The question of how many seats should be provided by the library for every hundred students is complicated by the possible provision of "reading halls" in residential blocks. This is of course a very wide field of study but there is much to be said for allowing the library to cater for all reading and study needs; if a large library with an expensive stock has to be provided it is more cost efficient when it is heavily used; moreover it need be no more expensive to provide extra seats in libraries than in residential reading halls.

POLYTECHNIC LIBRARIES

From the planning point of view British polytechnics can best be thought of as universities; the practical difference at present is that they are usually being formed out of groupings of existing colleges and a library service may have to be planned, at any rate in the immediate future, for a group of separate buildings, rather than for a settled campus. This may call for a network of linked college libraries rather than one dominant central library, which will certainly complicate any attempt to apply such standards as have been published.

Recently issued (1971) standards for polytechnic libraries issued by the DES state:

"The appropriate usable area for polytechnic libraries is dependent on the pattern of studies and the physical location of departments in a particular establishment. This area may be up to 1·29 m² [14 ft²] per FTE [Further Technical Education] student, comprising a basic allowance of 0·8 m² [8½ ft²] per FTE student, supplemented as necessary by an addition from the non-specialised teaching accommodation. The maximum area would permit the provision of readers' seats on a scale of one to every four FTE students, display and storage space for books and periodicals, audio-visual aids, counter and catalogue areas, a librarian's office, a workroom, seminar and tutorial rooms and carols [sic] for private study attached to the library suite and facilities for photocopying and a darkroom. The department approves the provision of a 'calculated balance area', that is an allowance for corridors, stairs, foyers, toilets and so on, of 25 per cent of the library accommodation."

The Library Association issued standards for polytechnic libraries in 1968[38], recommending a basic stock of 150 000 volumes and 3000 periodical titles; it also recommends that 80 per cent of the stock should be on open access at 8·36 m² (90 ft²) per 1000 volumes and 20 per cent in limited access at 4·18 m² (45 ft²) per 1000 volumes. For display of current periodicals it recommends a space allowance of 0·09 m² (1 ft²) per periodical title. Space allowance for readers is to be calculated according to discipline, one place for every four students of scientific and technological disciplines, one place for every three students of other disciplines and one place for every ten part-time students, irrespective of discipline. Seating space allowances recommended are: 2·3 m² (25 ft²) for undergraduates generally and 3·2 m² (35 ft²) for postgraduate students, and students of art, architecture and other similar disciplines.

Space allowances for library functions are given in some detail and are worth quoting:
Library staff—cataloguing, 9·3 m² (100 ft²) per person; stock selection, 7·43 m² (80 ft²) per person; clerical staff, 3·72 m² (40 ft²) per person. As some staff are on duty in public areas and others have split duties, only 70 per cent of staff may need space allocation. Some members of staff require more space than others for interview and discussion. Thus librarian, deputy librarian and chief information officer, 13·94 m² (150 ft²) minimum each. (Administrative offices should incorporate data processing equipment, which may need special environmental consideration.)
Committee room—18·58 m² (200 ft²) minimum.
Staff room—0·93 m² (10 ft²) per person (minimum 13·94 m² (150 ft²). (Kitchen facilities may be required, but these could be incorporated with a small self-service snack bar available to library users—an important feature of evening and weekend openings.)
Lecture, seminar and tutorial rooms should be incorporated in the library suite. Lecture rooms should accommodate the maximum number of students likely to attend first-year degree courses (forty minimum), and there should be seminar rooms for a similar number—eg five seating eight students each. Tutorial rooms should be provided as generously as possible, particularly in polytechnics with courses in social sciences, law and the humanities. All rooms should be equipped with visual and audio aids.
Audio and visual equipment requires special facilities. Records and tapes may need a central control area, though listening booths or facilities for listening at study tables may be sited separately. Additionally, the technician may require a maintenance area—37 m² (400 ft²) minimum, excluding storage of records and tapes.
Repairs and preparation for binding—37 m² (400 ft²) minimum.
Micro-storage—a large collection needs to be housed under controlled humidity and temperature conditions. Some storage units which house large collections of a quarter of a million may need special floor loading.
Reprographic facilities These have special space requirements—

eg electrostatic copiers, 5·57 m² (60 ft²); offset printing and plate making, 28 m² (300 ft²) minimum; cameras, 9·29 m² (100 ft²) each minimum; processors, 9·29 m² (100 ft²) minimum.
Research and development—depending on staff, but 14 m² (150 ft²) minimum.
Issue, readers' and advisory points and catalogue space (dependent on the possible requirements for branch libraries, computerised catalogues and other features), 93 m² (1 000 ft²) minimum.
Communication If the building is on more than one floor, book conveyors, lifts and pneumatic dispatch systems will require additional space. Space will also be required for internal and external communicational devices, eg Telex links with computers, and closed circuit television when installed."
The Library Association recommendations end with the italicised comment: "*Add the usual 40 per cent balance area.*"
As polytechnics are not strictly comparable with any foreign equivalent, no alternative standards are quoted by Withers.

COLLEGE LIBRARIES

Because their role in education has expanded, and will continue to expand, so enormously, college authorities need to rethink drastically the function and size standards of their libraries. There is a very wide disparity in size, scope and function among colleges; for example the ALA *Standards for college libraries*[39] apply to a limited range of American colleges which are in many ways akin to British universities. Standards therefore need to be considered for each major type of college separately. The best guidance is given by the publications of the Library Association and the work of its specialist groups.
The DES[40] said in 1971:

"The appropriate usable area for a college library is dependent not only on the number of students but also on the level of courses offered. It follows that more space is required for colleges with a high proportion of advanced work than for other colleges. For that reason there is a higher allowance for colleges where work at the advanced level is at least 30 per cent of the whole.
"The allowances are as follows:
Colleges with at least 30 per cent advanced work:
390 m² [4200 ft²] for the first 500 FTE students, then
0·44 m² [475 ft²] for each additional FTE student.
Colleges with less than 30 per cent advanced work:
300 m² [3230 ft²] for the first 500 FTE students, then
0·38 m² [409 ft²] for each additional student.
"The allowances are intended to permit the provision of readers' seats on a scale of one to every eight FTE [Further Technical Education] students, display and storage space for books and periodicals, counter and catalogue areas, a librarian's office, a workroom, seminar and tutorial rooms and carols [sic] for private study attached to the library suite and possibly facilities for photocopying and a darkroom. Again a 'calculated balance area' of 25 per cent of the above is recommended."

Published figures for proportions of students to be provided with seats in university libraries will be helpful but the availability of alternative study facilities will be different. Non-residential college libraries in towns may be used by students late into the night while in country areas they may be unused at these times. Again the demand for seats at immediate pre-examination periods cannot be taken as an indication of reasonable needs.

Colleges of Technology and Further Education

In the Library Association's excellent *College libraries*[41] it is stated that the basic stock for a college without degree work should not be fewer than 10 000 book titles, and for a larger college with some degree work and specialised advanced courses not fewer than 25 000 titles. In a college with several degree courses this figure should be considerably exceeded. There are required also, in varying degrees, multiple copies of books, periodicals, pamphlets, audio, visual and other non-book material, and stock, particu-

M

larly for thesis and postgraduate work. The number of periodicals should range from around 100 for a small college to a minimum of 600 for a college with substantial advanced work.

This publication quotes DES building bulletin 5⬤, 1959 *New colleges of further education* and lists the main areas to be included in the plans. For seating space requirements it gives:

one place for every five students of technology and applied science;
one place for every four students of pure science; ·
one place for every three students of other disciplines;
one place for every ten part-time students, irrespective of discipline;
2·32 m² (25 ft²) per undergraduate;
3·25 m² (35 ft²) for postgraduate students.

Seats should be provided for not less than 10 per cent of the total staff; there are advantages in having a staff study or, in higher level colleges, a research room (both of which may contain lockers, individual desks or carrels for staff).

At least one classroom of 42 m² to 56 m² (450 ft² to 600 ft²) opening off the library should be divisible into smaller rooms for practical work or for seminars.

The space requirements are summarised as at 557 m² (6000 ft²) for a small college and 1672 m² (18 000 ft²) for a regional college, based on figures in DES Building Bulletin 5.

Withers quotes the following from the *Notes on procedure for the approval of further education building project* 1967. "The following table shows the total library areas now recommended for different types of colleges. The areas shown are for actual library spaces: 25 per cent should be added for circulation, services etc. |

Maximum student capacity .	Recommended area for library			
	Colleges with at least 30 per cent advanced work		Colleges with less than 30 per cent advanced work	
	(m²)	(ft²)	(m²)	(ft²)
500 or less	273·9	2975	237·8	2560
1000	438·5	4720	349·8	3765
1500	565·3	6085	461·7	4970
2000	695·8	7490	577·3	6215
2500	820·8	8835	685·6	7380
3000	957·8	10 310	797·6	8585
3500	1085·6	11 685	909·5	9790
4000	1222·6	13 160	1023·8	11 020
4500	1368·9	14 735	1138·0	12 250
5000	1505·9	16 210	1252·3	13 480

*"Maximum student capacity" will usually be from 25 per cent to 50 per cent higher than the average day student population to permit some flexibility in the use of classrooms.

The recommended area is intended to provide readers' seats, display and storage space for books and periodicals, counter and catalogue areas and a micro-reader, librarian's office, workroom, seminar and tutorial rooms and carrels for private study attached to the library suite and possibly facilities for photocopying and a darkroom.

Colleges of Education
The changes taking place within schools must be led by those who are now being educated to teach; because of this and other factors, such as the establishment of BED courses and postgraduate research, colleges of education have been expanding their scope, and the range of their resources, at a faster rate even than other types of college. For this reason the existing official standards are probably more out of date than some others.

The DES in 1968 set the following targets: Minimum book stock targets to be reached by 1978.

Student numbers	Volumes
500 or less	30 000
750	40 500
1000	52 500
1250	60 300
1500	68 820

These figures exclude provision for degree work and certain special facilities. In 1967 The Association of Teachers in Colleges of Education and Departments of Education[44] published jointly with the Library Association their own recommended standards and these are rather more generous than those of the DES. They include useful data on estimated use by students and staff: reading areas, for example, are based on the supposition that at least 25 per cent of the staff and students may be in the library at the same time. They

also recommend that at least 20 000 volumes of currently effective stock should be immediately available for consultation and loan, and that a schools service section of at least 7500 volumes should be provided (see minimum figures in table below). Shelving for four-fifths of the library's book stock should be provided on the basis of 7 m² (75 ft²) per 1000 volumes; the remainder should be in stack areas at 5·1 m² (55 ft²) per 1000 volumes.

Minimum stocks for main library and school services library

Student numbers	Main library volumes	School services library volumes	Total volumes
500	31 000	8600	39 000
750	43 000	11 750	54 750
1000	55 000	15 250	70 250

The DES document *The design of libraries in colleges of education* 1969[45], gives the following areas, which include the book store and

No of students	Recommended areas	
	m²	ft²
100	100	1150
200	210	2300
300	320	3450
400	430	4600
500	530	5750
600	620	6675
700	710	7590
800	800	8510
900	880	9430
1000	960	10 350
1100	1040	11 210
1200	1120	12 070

private study places but are net; 25 per cent should be added for circulation, services etc.

The New Zealand Library Association's *Standards for teachers' college libraries*[46] 1967, says:

"Reader accommodation is recommended at 20 per cent of the combined staff and student rolls at 2·8 m² (30 ft²) staff and 2·3 m² (25 ft²) students. Space for books is estimated at 9·3 m² (100 ft²) for each 1000 volumes. A net working area of 1280 m² (13 800 ft²) is suggested for a college of 1000 students."

Again an addition of 25 per cent would need to be made for circulation, services etc.

SCHOOL LIBRARIES

No quantitative standards for book stock are available from British official sources; the only guide figures—by the DES for England and Wales, by the Scottish Education Department and, only semi-officially, by the Association of Education Committees —are expressed in terms of financial grants for book purchase. As all these figures are now several years old, they are of little practical value because of price inflation. It is possible to attempt to update these figures by using an appropriate factor for present-day prices but any exercise of this kind requires the sympathetic support of both head teacher and education authority.

Withers[47], quotes a wide range of standards from different countries, says:

"The three most comprehensive sets of school library standards come from three countries where an approach to education, defined recently as 'a shift from teacher-orientated whole class instruction, where the textbook reigns supreme, to a pupil-orientated situation where the individual child learns actively from an environment rich in learning stimuli' is actively encouraged. These are Australia, Canada and the United States . . ."

The details he quotes of the standards of these three countries should certainly be studied by all who are interested in the changing role of the school library.

Official British recommendations for space allowances for school libraries are to be found only in the two DES Building Bulletins (Nos 2 and 2A) but as these are now so out of date it is better to use the Library Association's booklet[48]; this recognises the wide variation in size, environment and type between schools but gives useful quantitative guidance for two categories:

Primary schools
There should be no fewer than eight books per child; in most primary schools therefore there will be between 2000 and 4000 books. Provision should be made for one-tenth of the pupils to use the library areas at any one time, with an allocation of 1·86 m² (20 ft²) per reader, with a minimum of 23·2 m² (250 ft²).

Middle and secondary schools
There should not be less than ten books per pupil below sixth form level and fifteen books at that level. These figures exclude books which the school may be able to obtain on loan from a school library service operated by the library and education authorities. Again provision should be made for one-tenth of the pupils to use the library areas at any one time but the an allocation of 2·32 m² (25 ft²) per reader and an addition of 28 m² (300 ft²) for administrative accommodation (ie working space for the school librarian).

Total space allocations

	m²	ft²
Upper junior and central library area	2·044	220
Infants library area	14·86	160
Lower junior library area	16·72	180
Total for a seven-class school (280 children)	52·00	560

All library areas should be accessible to all children.

It is here that the full impact of the trend towards the use of non-book media is being felt. Allowance of space must be made not only for storage of and operating areas for audio-visual materials but also for preparing them.

Total space allocations

	m²	ft²
Main library	232·3	2500
Librarian's workroom	13·94	150
Audio-visual workroom	27·87	300
Planning and reprographic area	46·45	500
Facilities for studying material	69·68	750
Total for eight-form entry	390·00	4200

The document goes on to comment on allocation of spaces in more detail but in view of the changes in teaching methods, and so in the orientation of activities within the school, it is perhaps better to use the totals given as a general guide and to leave any further breakdown to the collective decision of the staff of the particular school. Mention must however be made of the fast increasing use of materials other than books; slides, films, tapes, records, television, video-tape and so on need storage and operational space, both for the equipment and for the "software". The school library is the obvious centre for both storing and deploying such media, so the necessary space should be allowed.

SPECIAL LIBRARIES

No standards exist in the UK for the planning of special libraries because so many different types are grouped under that term. In 1964 the (American) Special Libraries Association published *Objectives and standards for special libraries*[49] based on a questionnaire completed by special librarians from a wide range of different institutions; it gives profiles of the operations typical in various fields.

Because generalisation is impossible the special librarian may be able to learn from the type of library to which his is in some ways akin; the guidance given on university and polytechnic libraries will perhaps be appropriate (if on a smaller scale) to the special library which has teaching and research functions. In other cases recommendations for public reference libraries may apply.

Many small special libraries can estimate their space requirements only by making an assessment of the service they hope to give, and the number of readers who will use it, and then applying "standards" for the spatial needs of each item by using information derived from libraries for which published recommendations exist —college libraries, for example.

An alternative method is for the librarian to plan his future library as a functional unit by allocating the necessary furniture, equipment, tables, seats and so on arbitrarily and using a formula to deduce the total space necessary to house them efficiently. Using this method, Reed says[50]:

"A full schedule of tables, desks, chairs, filing units, cupboards, display racks, shelving etc should be made, including in this the respective floor projection areas of the items. These areas should then be totalled and if a multiplying factor of 3 to 3·5 is applied to this the result will be a gross floor area that will accept everything with reasonable clearances."

Naturally the projection made will include the allowance for future expansion which has been presumed and the result can be a rough but acceptable estimate of the area of a single service room. This can be used as an assessment which must in its turn form the basis of a brief and to it must be added all the other necessary spaces, both operational and architectural.

Another expedient would be to find a library which is giving a satisfactory service in a similar situation and copy its space allowances.

HOSPITAL LIBRARIES

In 1969 IFLA published standards[51] for libraries in hospitals. Because of the immense variation in conditions between different countries, the standards cannot be applied in every case, but many features are common. The basic necessities are a room solely for use as a library which patients can visit, and a ward trolley service. Two nations are recorded as having made recommendations for the size of the room:

Federal Republic of Germany: 30 m² minimum and

$$\frac{4 \times \text{book stock}}{1000} \times 25 \text{ m}^2.$$

United Kingdom: 37 m² (400 ft²) minimum for the general library with an additional 47 m² (500 ft²) for the medical library, plus 20 m² (215 ft²) for storage and work space.
Size of library room according to number of beds:
200 to 400 beds,   56 m² (600 ft²)
401 to 600 beds,   65 m² (700 ft²)
over 600 beds,   75 m² (800 ft²)
Book stocks recommended in national standards are:
Czechoslavakia: Four books per bed in short-term institutions; eight books per bed in long term institutions.
Federal Republic of Germany: Four books per bed; long-stay hospitals (six months) five books per bed; 7 per cent to 10 per cent of the books should be changed annually.
United Kingdom: Up to 50 beds, 1000 books; 51 to 100 beds, 1500 books; 101 to 150 beds, 2000 books; 151 to 200 beds, 2500 books; 201 to 300 beds, 3000 books; 300 to 600 beds, up to 5000 books.
United States: Up to 300 beds, eight books per bed; 301 to 500 beds, seven books per bed; 501 to 800 beds, six books per bed; 801 to 1100 beds, five books per bed; 1101 to 1500 beds, four books per bed. There is an increase of 25 per cent for orthopaedic hospitals, children's hospitals, and 200 to 400-bed mental hospitals; 50 per cent more for tuberculosis patients.
IFLA: 500 beds, eight books per bed; 500 to 1000 beds, six books per bed; over 1000 beds, five books per bed. There is an increase of 40 per cent to 60 per cent for long-stay hospitals.
The publication of the (British) Department of Health and Social Security *Library services in hospitals*[52] makes the following useful comment:

"Physical separation of staff and patients' libraries is desirable but they should be planned close together so that they can be administered as a single library and information service." Dealing with the staff library it says:

"The purpose of the staff library is to serve the needs of the hospital"—medical, dental, nursing and other professional and medical staff; and to provide a service for general practitioners, local authority doctors and other professional people who work in the NHS outside the hospital and who make use of hospital postgraduate training facilities. If the hospital has a nurses' training school a library will be required for that, and consideration should be given to the possibility of its being administered jointly with the main staff library.
The staff library will usually be sited in the postgraduate medical centre, if any: whether or not such a centre is provided the library must be conveniently sited for those who use the staff library and should be accessible at all hours of the day. It should provide reading space which is available at all times, and not used for lectures, discussion groups or other types of activity or as a medical staffroom.

Undergraduates and trainees	1 seat for 4
Student nurses	1 seat for 8
Other students and trainee technicians	1 seat for 8
Graduates, trained staff, consultants and medical staff	1 seat for 6
Trained technicians	1 seat for 10
General practitioners, dentists, nurses	1 seat for 20

Library service for patients

A survey in 1963 showed that 1910 out of 2536 British hospitals provided a service and the position is much improved today.

"An efficient trolley service visiting each ward at sufficiently frequent intervals to enable the service to be used properly is required for patients who cannot leave the ward. Patients who can do so should be encouraged to visit the library and make their own selection from the shelves: this and a readers' advisory service is particularly important in long-stay hospitals."

"An attractive hospital patients' library easily accessible and with a welcoming informal atmosphere can make an effective contribution towards the treatment of patients with mental illness."

"The library service might also include the maintenance of a stock of gramophone records and the provision of sets of plays for play reading and special (often large) books for mentally handicapped readers."[52]

The functions of and differences between the various types of library needed in hospitals have been dealt with in much more detail in the Library Association's *Hospital libraries: recommended standards*[53]. Here the library and information service in the hospital is studied, separate attention being paid to:
the general library (which includes service for patients and staff);
the medical library (other than medical school libraries).
For the general library the space and bookstock standards are similar to those quoted earlier for the UK but more detail is given. When dealing with medical libraries, however, the pamphlet is entering on new ground so far as these standards are concerned; because the nature of regional hospital organisation complicates the issue, it is better to refer readers to the pamphlet itself than to attempt to summarise its findings.

REFERENCES

1 Standards of public library service in England and Wales: report of the working party appointed by the Minister of Education in March 1961. HMSO, London, 1962
2 INTERNATIONAL FEDERATION OF LIBRARY ASSOCIATIONS Standards of public library service. IFLA/FIAB. *In Libri,* v 2 1958, pp 189–199
3 LIBRARY ADVISORY COUNCILS (England and Wales). Public library service points: a report with some notes on staffing. Department of Education and Science, HMSO, 1971
4 Ibid, p 9
5 Standards of public library service in England and Wales. Op cit, p 33
6 Library Advisory Councils. Op cit, p 2
7 LIBRARY ASSOCIATION Public library buildings—the way ahead. Library Association, London, 1960
8 LIBRARY ASSOCIATION, County Libraries Section. Op cit, p 2
9 ATKIN, PAULINE Bibliography of use surveys of public and academic libraries 1950–November 1970. *In Library and Information Bulletin* 14. Library Association, 1971
10 Standards of public library service in England and Wales. Op cit, pp 18–21
11 DEPARTMENT OF EDUCATION AND SCIENCE Circular 4/65, March 1965, p 13
12 Library Advisory Councils. Op cit, p 9

[13] INTERNATIONAL FEDERATION OF LIBRARY ASSOCIATION Standards for public libraries, 1972, para 86

[14] Withers, Op cit, p 12

[15] GALVIN, HOYT R. and MARTIN VAN BUREN The small public library. UNESCO, Paris, 1959

[16] Mevissen. Op cit

[17] Standards of public library service in England and Wales. Op cit, p 120

[18] Wheeler and Githens. Op cit

[19] Mevissen. Op cit

[20] Wheeler and Githens. Op cit

[21] Standards of public library service in England and Wales. Op cit, pp 120–121

[22] Plovgaard. Op cit, p 68

[23] Withers, Op cit

[24] Bassenet. Op cit

[25] IFLA Standards 1972. Op cit, paras 87 and 90

[26] Ibid, paras 105 and 106

[27] LIBRARY ASSOCIATION Standards for reference services in public libraries. *In Library Association Record*, v 72 no 2, February 1970, pp 53–57

[28] Withers. Op cit, p 157

[29] HUMPHREYS, K. W. Standards in University libraries. *In Libri*, v 20, 1970, pp 144–155

[30] STANDING CONFERENCE OF NATIONAL AND UNIVERSITY LIBRARIES Report of the subcommittee of SCONUL on financial standards in university libraries. *In* Parry Report. Op cit, pp 264–279

[31] Withers. Op cit

[32] Parry Report. Op cit

[33] SAUNDERS, W. L. *In Journal of Librarianship*, v 1 no 4, October 1969, P 202

[34] AMERICAN LIBRARY ASSOCIATION Standards for college libraries. *In College and Research Libraries*, v 20 no 4, July 1959

[35] CANADIAN LIBRARY ASSOCIATION Report of University Library Standards Committee of Canadian Association of College and University Libraries: guide to Canadian university library standards 1961–1964. Ottawa, 1967

[36] Metcalf. Op cit, p 391

[37] DEPARTMENT OF EDUCATION AND SCIENCE Notes on procedure for the approval of polytechnic projects. November 1971

[38] LIBRARY ASSOCIATION Libraries in the new polytechnics. *In Library Association Record*, v 70 no 9, September 1968, pp 240 243

[39] American Library Association. Standards for college libraries. Op cit

[40] DEPARTMENT OF EDUCATION AND SCIENCE Notes on procedure for the approval of further education projects (other than polytechnics), 1972

[41] LIBRARY ASSOCIATION Recommended standards of library provision in colleges of further education. 2nd edition. Library Association, 1971

[42] Withers. Op cit, p 180

[43] DEPARTMENT OF EDUCATION AND SCIENCE College letter 2/68, ref R34/65/01 March 1968

[44] ASSOCIATION OF TEACHERS IN COLLEGES OF EDUCATION AND DEPARTMENTS OF EDUCATION and LIBRARY ASSOCIATION Colleges of education libraries: recommended standards for their development. London, 1967

[45] DEPARTMENT OF EDUCATION AND SCIENCE The design of libraries in colleges of education. HMSO, 1969

[46] NEW ZEALAND LIBRARY ASSOCIATION Standards for teachers' college libraries. Wellington, 1967

[47] Withers. Op cit, p 121

[48] Library Association. School library resource centres. Op cit

[49] SPECIAL LIBRARIES ASSOCIATION Objectives and standards for special libraries. *In Special libraries*, v 55 no 10, 1964

[50] Reed. Op cit

[51] INTERNATIONAL FEDERATION OF LIBRARY ASSOCIATIONS Standards for libraries in hospitals (general service) by the IFLA/FIAB Libraries in Hospitals Subsection. *In* UNESCO *Bulletin for libraries*, v 23 no 2, March–April 1969

[52] Library Service in hospitals. Op cit

[53] Library Association. Hospital libraries. Op cit

Appendix II Network analysis for a university

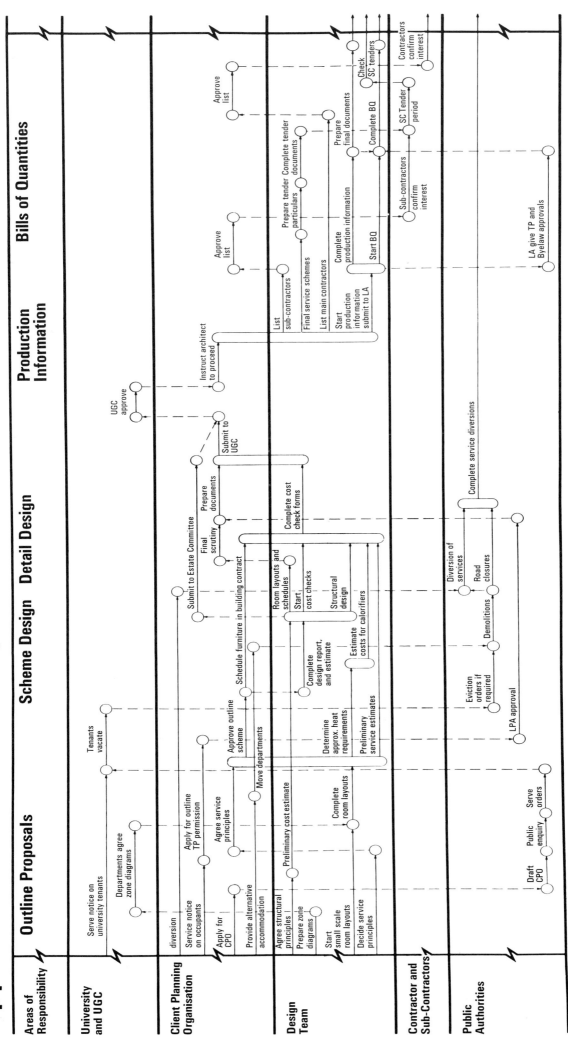

Bibliography

Library planning and design: general

AMERICAN LIBRARY ASSOCIATION. *Library buildings for library service:* papers presented before the Library Institute at the University of Chicago, August 5–10 1946.

AMERICAN LIBRARY ASSOCIATION. *Problems in planning library facilities.* ALA Chicago 1964.

ASSOCIATION OF COLLEGE AND REFERENCE LIBRARIES (ACRL). *The Library Building Plans Institute: Second ... proceedings of the conference ...* Donald C Davidson, ed ... [with] *A College and University Library Buildings bibliography,* 1945–53. ACRL Monographs, No 10 Chicago 1953.

ASSOCIATION OF COLLEGE AND REFERENCE LIBRARIES. *The Library Building Plans Institute: Third ... Proceedings of the conference ...* Howard Ronelstad, ed ... [with] *College and University Library Buildings bibliographies,* 1953–54 and 1939–45. ACRA Monographs, No 11 Chicago 1954.

ASSOCIATION OF COLLEGE AND REFERENCE LIBRARIES. *The Library Building Plans Institute: Fifth and Sixth ... proceedings of the meetings ...* Walter W Wright ed ... [with] *A College and University Library Buildings bibliography,* 1954–55. ACRL Monograph No 15 Chicago 1956.

BANZ, GEORGE. 'Libraries' in *Canadian Architect* 1962 Feb, pp 42–44.

BRAWNE, MICHAEL. *Libraries: Architecture and Equipment,* Pall Mall Press, London 1970.

BRAWNE, MICHAEL. 'Libraries', in *Architectural Review* 1961 Oct, pp 245–56.

COWGILL, C W and PETTENGILL, G E. 'The Library Building', Part 1 *Jnl* AIA 1959 May, pp 55–66. Part 2 *Jnl* AIA 1959 June, pp 103–13.

DONS K and ROVELSTAD H eds. *Guidelines for library planners: proceedings of the library buildings and equipment institute,* ALA Chicago 1960.

EASTLICK, J T. *A library building programme ... The librarian's greatest challenge,* University of the State of New York (1961).

EDUCATIONAL FACILITIES LABORATORIES. *The impact of technology on the library building,* EFL, New York 1967.

FUSSLER, HERMAN H ed. *Library buildings for library service,* ALA Chicago 1947.

FUSSLER, HERMAN H and SIMON, JULIAN L. *Patterns in the use of books in large research libraries.* University of Chicago Press, Chicago 1969.

GALVIN H R and DEVEREAUX K A eds. *Planning a library building: the major steps,* ALA Chicago 1955.

'The Impact of technology on the Library Building', in *Canadian Architect* 1968 July pp 29–34.

KATZ, W A and SWARTZ, R G eds. *Problems in planning library facilities: consultants, architects, plans and critiques,* ALA Chicago 1964.

KAULA, PRITHRI N. *Library buildings: planning and design.* Vikas, Delhi, New York: Oceana New York 1971.

KEMENY, JOHN G. 'A Library for 2000 AD', in *Management and the computer of the future,* ed by Martin Greenberger. MIT Press and Wiley, Cambridge and New York 1962 pp 133–178.

'Libraries: A General Article with examples of recent University and Public Libraries, in Great Britain and Abroad,' *in Architectural Design* 1960 Oct, pp 369–411.

LIBRARY ASSOCIATION. 'New library buildings' 1962–1963 and 1963–1964: articles and reports reprinted from the *Library Association Record* for December 1963 and December 1964, LA London 1963 and 1964.

LIBRARY ASSOCIATION. *Library buildings 1965,* LA 1966.

Library buildings 1966, LA 1967, edited by J D Reynolds.

LIBRARY ASSOCIATION. *Library buildings 1967–8,* ed by S G Berriman, LA 1969

LIBRARY ASSOCIATION: London and Home Counties Branch. *Design in the Library, 1960.*

Library buildings—design and fulfilment, 1967.

Better Library Buildings: architect/librarian co-operation in their design, 1969.

Library technology and architecture: Report of a conference held at the Harvard Graduate School of Education Feb 9th 1967 Library, Graduate School of Education, Harvard University 1968.

LODEWYCKS, K A. *Essentials of library planning,* University of Melbourne Library 1961.

MASON, E. *Writing a Building Program, in* Library Journal, 1966 1 December pp 5838–5844.

ORR, J M. *Designing library buildings for activity,* A Deutsch, London 1972.

PETERSON, HARRY N. 'Developments in the planning of main library buildings,' *in Library Trends* 1972 April, pp 693–741.

PEVSNER, SIR NIKOLAUS. 'Libraries' (Historical survey of libraries from the ninth century AD) *Architectural Review* 1961 Oct, pp 240–4.

ROTH, H L ed. *Planning library buildings for service,* ALA Chicago 1964.

SHAW, RALPH ed. *The state of the library art: Vol 3,* Graduate School of Library Service, Rutgers 1960.

SHAW, ROBERT J ed. *Libraries: building for the future,* ALA Chicago 1967.

THOMPSON, ANTHONY. *Library buildings of Britain and Europe: an international study.* Butterworths, London 1963.

THOMSEN, C. 'The architect and the librarian,' *in Unesco Bulletin for Libraries* 1962 May–June pp 136–40.

WILSON, A ed. *Post-war libraries in the West Midlands: a record of new buildings and adaptations,* LA Birmingham and District Branch 1961.

WITHERS, F N. *Standards for library service,* UNESCO, Paris 1970.

YENAWINE, WAYNE S, ed. *Contemporary Library Design* (Frontiers of Librarianship No 1). Syracuse UP 1958.

ZABEL, K J. 'Problems of the open-access library system,' *in Bauen & Wohnen* (Munich) 1962 No 9, Chronik pp 1–2.

Library planning and design: university libraries

BONSOR, WILFRID. 'University library buildings: university library planning,' *in* ASLIB *Proceedings* 1951 May, pp 59–62.

BROWN, HARRY FAULKNER ed. *Planning the academic library: Metcalf and Ellesworth at York.* Oriel Press, Newcastle upon Tyne 1971.

BURCHARD, J E. *Planning the university library building: a summary of discussions by librarians, architects and engineers.* Princeton University Press, 1949.

BUSH, G C, GALLIHER, H P and MORSE, P M. 'Attendance and use of the science library at MIT' *in American Documentation* 1956 v. VII No 2 pp 87–109.

Campus architecture shaped by master plans,' *in Architectural Record,* 1967 April, pp 185–212

CANADIAN LIBRARY ASSOCIATION. *Report of University Library standards committee of Canadian Association of college and university libraries: guide to Canadian university library standards* 1961–1964, Ottawa 1967.

(BRITISH) DEPARTMENT OF EDUCATION AND SCIENCE. *Notes on procedure for the approval of polytechnic projects,* DES Nov 1971.

ELLSWORTH, R E. *Planning the college and university library building: a book for campus planners and architects,* Pruett Press 1960. Boulder, Colorado.

GELFAND, M A. *University libraries for developing countries* (UNESCO manuals for libraries, 14), UNESCO Paris 1968.

HUMPHREYS, H W. 'Standards in university libraries,' *in Libri* 1970 v 20, pp 144–155.

PLUMBE, WILFRED J. 'Climate as a factor in the planning of university library buildings, *in* UNESCO *Bulletin for Libraries* 1963 Nov–Dec pp 316–325.

LANGMEAD, STEPHEN and BECKMAN, MARGARET. *New Library Design: guide lines to planning academic library buildings*, Wiley, Toronto 1970.

LIBRARY ASSOCIATION. 'Libraries in the new polytechnics,' *in Library Association Record* 1968 Sept v 70 No 9, pp 240–243.

NEAL, K W. *British University Libraries*. Neal, Wilmslow 1970.

PRASECKI, W. 'University library interiors' *in* UNESCO *Bulletin for Libraries*. 1963 Nov–Dec pp 346–50.

UNIVERSITY GRANTS COMMITTEE. *Report of the Committee on Libraries* (The Parry Report). HMSO London 1967.

WILSON, LOUIS ROUND and TAUBER, MAURICE F. *The University Library*, 2nd ed. Columbia University Press, New York 1956, Chapter XIV: 'Buildings and equipment'.

Library planning and design: college libraries

AMERICAN LIBRARY ASSOCIATION. 'Standards for college libraries,' *in College and research libraries* 1959 July v 20 No 4.

ASSOCIATION OF TEACHERS IN COLLEGES OF EDUCATION AND DEPARTMENTS OF EDUCATION and the LIBRARY ASSOCIATION. *Colleges of Education Libraries: recommended standards for their development*, ATCE London 1967.

ASSOCIATION OF TECHNICAL INSTITUTIONS AND ASSOCIATION OF PRINCIPALS OF TECHNICAL INSTITUTIONS, *Technical college buildings:* second interim report. *The college library*, ATI London 1962.

(BRITISH) DEPARTMENT OF EDUCATION AND SCIENCE. *College letter No 2/68*, DES (R34/65/01) 1968.

(BRITISH) DEPARTMENT OF EDUCATION AND SCIENCE. *The design of libraries in colleges of education*, HMSO London 1969.

(BRITISH) DEPARTMENT OF EDUCATION AND SCIENCE. *Notes on procedure for the approval of further education projects (other than polytechnics)* DES 1972.

LIBRARY ASSOCIATION. *Recommended standards of library provision in colleges of further education*, 2nd ed, LA London 1971.

NEAL, K W. *Technical college libraries*, Neal, Wilmslow, 1965.

NEW ZEALAND LIBRARY ASSOCIATION. *Standards for teachers' college libraries*, Wellington 1967.

PLATT, PETER ed. *Libraries in colleges of education* 2nd ed, LA London 1972.

MCCOLVIN E R. 'The technical college library: some suggested standards' *in Technical Education* 1959 May, pp 26–28.

SIMMONS, J. 'Planning, accommodation and furnishing' *in* Furlong, N ed *Library Practice for Colleges of Education*, LA 1966 pp 38–60.

THOMPSON, DONALD E. 'Form v function: architecture and the college library,' *in Library Trends* 1969 July v 18 No 1, p 45.

Library planning and design: public libraries

AMERICAN LIBRARY ASSOCIATION. *Minimum standards for public library services*, ALA Chicago 1966.

ASHBURNER, E H. *Modern public libraries: their planning and design*, Grafton London 1946.

BASSENET, PETER J. *Spatial and administrative relationships in large public libraries: an investigation into the planning of municipal libraries serving populations exceeding one hundred thousand.* Thesis accepted by the Library Association, 1970.

BERRIMAN, S G and HARRISON, K C. *British public library buildings*, Deutsch London 1966.

BRAWNE, MICHAEL. 'Off the shelf': (surveys the development of community library design and appraises the new Redcar Library), *in Architectural Review*, 1971 July, pp 51–4.

CAMPBELL, H C. *Metropolitan public library planning throughout the world*, Pergamon Press, London 1967.

GALVIN, HOYT R and VAN BUREN, MARTIN. *The small public library building* (UNESCO Public Library Manuals No 10) UNESCO Paris 1959.

GARDNER, F M. 'Planning of central libraries,' (Library Association, *Proceedings of the annual conference, Llandudno 1962*).

JOLLIFFE, HAROLD. *Public library extension activities*, 2nd ed., LA London 1968.

LIBRARY ASSOCIATION. *Public library buildings: the way ahead*, LA London 1960.

LIBRARY ASSOCIATION. 'Standards for reference services in public libraries' *in Library Association Record* 1970 Feb v 72 No 2, pp 53–57.

LIBRARY ASSOCIATION, COUNTY LIBRARIES SECTION. *County branch libraries: Recommended standards*, LA London 1958.

LOCK, R NORTHWOOD ed. *James Duff Brown's Manual of Library Economy*, 7th ed. Grafton 1961 ('The public library: siting, planning, building, equipping' pp 85–106).

MEVISSEN, WERNER. *Buchereibau: Public Library Building*, (Text in English and German) English tr. by Sybil Hamilton, Ernst Heyer Essen, 1958.

MYLLER, ROLF. *The design of the small public library*, R R Bowker, New York, 1966.

PLOVGAARD, SVEN. *Public library buildings: standards and type plans for library premises in areas with populations of between 5000 and 25 000.* Originally issued by the Danish State Library Inspectorate's Committee for the Compilation of Standards for Library Buildings in 1967, *trans* Oliver Stallybrass, Library Association, London, 1971.

Public Libraries and Museums Act 1964 Cr. 75 HMSO London

US OFFICE OF EDUCATION, DEPT OF HEALTH, EDUCATION AND WELFARE. *Proposed outline for public library buildings, institutes and workshops*, prepared by H R Galvin 1964.

WESTERN AUSTRALIA LIBRARY BOARD. *Siting and design of library buildings: notes for the guidance of local authorities and architects*, The Board, 1962.

WHEELER, JOSEPH L. *The small library building*. ALA Chicago 1963.

WHEELER, JOSEPH L and GITHENS, ALFRED MORTON. *The American public library building*, Charles Scribner's Sons, New York 1941.

Library planning and design: school libraries

ELLSWORTH, R E AND WAGENER, H D. *The school library: facilities for independent study in secondary school*, Educational Facilities Laboratory, New York, 1963.

LIBRARY ASSOCIATION. *School library resource centres: recommended standards for policy and provision*, LA London 1970.

Library Journal 1969 Nov. 15 p. 4213.

MINISTRY OF EDUCATION *Building Bulletins* Nos 2 (1950) and 2A (1954).

NEW ZEALAND, NATIONAL LIBRARY SERVICE. *School library service: planning the school library*, 2nd ed Wellington 1961.

School Library Journal 1969 Nov. p. 47.

STROHECKER, EDWIN O ed. *Design for progress: a report of the workshop in school library quarters and equipment*, Louisville, Kentucky, Nazareth College, Department of Library Science 1963.

WARRE, H E. *Library service in schools* 2nd ed, Library Association, London 1972

Library planning and design: hospital libraries

(BRITISH) DEPARTMENT OF HEALTH AND SOCIAL SECURITY and the WELSH OFFICE, *Library service in hospitals*, HM(70), HMSO 1970.

GOLDSMITH, S. *Designing for the disabled*, RIBA, London 1967.

'IFLA Standards for Libraries in Hospitals (general service) by the IFLA/FIAB Libraries in hospitals sub-section' *in* UNESCO *Bulletin for Libraries*, 1969 Mar-April, v 23 No 2.

LEWIS, M JOY. *Libraries for the Handicapped*, 1967, Sevensma prize essay (Library Association pamphlet No 33), LA London 1969.

LIBRARY ASSOCIATION. *Hospital libraries: recommended standards for libraries in hospitals*, LA London 1972 (ew standards will follow after the re-organisation of the Health and Local Government services has taken place).

SANDERS, BRENDA MARY. *Library services in hospitals: a survey of their present provision and possible future development in the*

South East Metropolitan region. Library Association pamphlets No 27, Library Association London, 1966.

Library planning and design: special libraries

ANTHONY, L J. 'Library Planning,' *in* Ashworth, W (*ed*) *Handbook of special librarianship and information work*, ASLIB: London 3rd ed, 1967 pp 309–64.

CALDERHEAD, PATRICIA ed. *Libraries for professional practice*, Architectural Press, London 1972.

LEWIS, CHESTER M ed. *Special libraries: how to plan and equip them*, SLA Monograph No 2, Special Libraries Association, New York, 1963.

REED, J B. 'Library Planning' *in* Ashworth, W ed, *Handbook of special librarianship and information work* 2nd ed, ASLIB 1962.

SPECIAL LIBRARIES ASSOCIATION. 'Objectives and standards for special libraries,' *in Special Libraries* 1964 v 55 No 10.

Book storage methods

BAUMANN, C H. *The influence of Angus Snead Macdonald and the Snead bookstack on library architecture*, University of Illinois, 1969.

CASSATA, MARY B ed. 'Book storage' *in Library Trends* 1971, Jan, Vol 19 No 3

COLLEY, DAVID I. 'The storage and retrieval of stack material', *in Library Association Record*, 1965, Feb, v 67, pp 37–42.

COLLISON, R L. *Commercial and industrial record storage*, Benn & John de Graff, London, 1969.

COX, J GRADY. *Optimum storage of library material*, Indiana Purdue University Libraries, Lafayette 1964.

ELLSWORTH, RALPH E. *The economy of book storage in college and university libraries*, Association of Research Libraries and Scarecrow Press, Metuchen NJ 1969.

GAWRECKI, DRAHOSLAV. *Compact library shelving, library technology program*, American Library Association, Chicago 1968.

HEINTZE, I. *Shelving for Periodicals, Bibliotekstjanst:* Lund, Sweden, 1966.

HILL, FRANCIS JOHN. 'Compact storage of books: a study of methods and equipment' *in Journal of Documentation*, 1955 Dec, pp 202–16.

MULLER, ROBERT H. 'Economics of compact book shelving', *in Library Trends* 1965 April v 3 pp 433–47

MUSZEWSKI, J M. 'Contemporary developments in library book storage,' *Architect and Builder* (Cape Town) 1969 July, pp 28–30.

PLUMB, P W. *Central library storage of books*, Library Association, London 1965.

POOLE, FRAZER G. 'The selection and evaluation of library bookstacks,' *in Library Trends* 1965 April p 419.

RIDER, FREEMONT. *Compact book storage*, Hadham Press, 1949.

SCHRIEFER, KENT and MOSTECKY, IVA. Compact book storage: mechanized systems, *in Library Trends* 1971 Jan v 19 No 3 pp 362–378.

VAN HOESON, HENRY B and KILPATRICK, NORMAN L. 'Height of books in relation to heights of stack,' *in Library Quarterly* 1934 v 4 pp 352–357.

Furniture and equipment

BLETON, J. Furnishing small public libraries, *in* UNESCO *Bulletin for Libraries* (Paris) 1962 Nov–Dec pp 273–95.

'Library Furniture and Furnishings,' issue editor Frazer G Poole *Library Trends*, April 1965.

MILLARD, P. *Modern library equipment*, Crosby Lockwood, London, 1966.

'New dimensions in educational technology for multi-media centres' *Library Trends* 1971 April.

Heating, lighting and ventilation

ARMS, BROCK. 'Principles of illumination for libraries,' *in The library environment: aspects of interior planning*, ALA, Chicago, 1965 pp 32–33.

BLACKWELL, H RICHARD. 'Lighting the library: standards for illumination' *in The Library Environment: aspects of interior planning*, ALA, Chicago 1965 pp 26–27.

CECIL, RAYMOND J. 'Libraries: a survey of current lighting practice,' *in Light and Lighting* 1962 August, pp 228–241.

FABER, OSCAR and KELL, J R. *Heating and air-conditioning of buildings*, 5th ed, rev by J R Kell and P L Martin, Architectural Press, London 1972.

'Heating and ventilating for Norwich central library,' *in Heating and Ventilating Engineer*, 1963 Sept, p 145.

HOPKINSON, R G and COLLINS, J B, *The ergonomics of lighting*, Macdonald Technical and Scientific, London, 1970.

ILLUMINATING ENGINEERING SOCIETY. IES *Code*, London n.d., *Lighting of libraries:* IES Technical Report No 8, London 1966, *Lighting of art galleries and museums*, IES Technical Report No 14, London 1970.

LIVINGSTON, F C. 'Specialised demands on heating, ventilating and air-conditioning for libraries and printing works,' *in Heating and Ventilating Engineer* 1969, July pp 27–32.

THOMSON, GARRY. *'Conservation and museum lighting,'* Museums Association, London 1970.

Floors and other materials

BERKELEY, BERNARD. *Floors: Selection and Maintenance, Library Technology Program*, ALA, Chicago, 1968.

KODERAS, M J. 'Sound absorbtive properties of carpeting,' *in Interiors* 1969, June, pp 130–131.

KREUTZBERG, H. 'The right answers on carpeting,' *in Architect* 1971 Oct, pp 83–87 and Nov pp 83–86.

MESSMAN, H H. *Building materials in library construction*, University of Illinois Graduate School of Library Science 1963 (Occasional Papers No 67).

SAUNDERS, D J. 'Sound insulation and use of carpets,' *in Flooring and Carpet Specifier*, 1970 May, pp 2–7.

Security

FIRE PROTECTION ASSOCIATION. *Fire protection design guide*, FPA, London 1970.

LEEDHAM, JOHN. *Live safely with fire*, Longmans for the FPA, London, 1969.

Protecting the library and its resources: a guide to physical protection and insurance; Report on a study conducted by Gage-Babcock and Associates Inc, Library Technology Project, American Library Association, Chicago, 1963.

WRIGHT, K G. *Cost-effective security*, London, McGraw-Hill, 1972.

Description of new libraries: universities and colleges

ABERDEEN: University science library. *In Architectural Review*, 1965 August, pp 130–4. *Concrete Quarterly* No 67 pp 2–3, *Official Architecture and Planning* 1965 Sept, pp 1274–8, *La Maison* (Brussels) 1966 No 2 pp 46–9.

DUBLIN: Trinity college library, *In Architects Journal*, 1967 Oct 11, pp 903–22, *Architect and Building News*, 1967, Oct 11, pp 611–18, *Building* 1967 Oct 20, pp 121–5, *Architectural Design* 1967 October, pp 459–68, *Architectural Review* 1967, Oct, pp 264–77.

DURHAM: University of Durham Library. *In Architectural Review*, 1964 Jan, p 31 *Building*, 1968 Nov 29, pp 73–6.

EDINBURGH. University Postgraduate Library. *In Interior Design* 1968 June, pp 36–41.

ESSEX: University of Essex Library *In Interbuild*, 1965 Oct, p 20, *Builder*, 1965 Oct, p 812, *Architect and Building News*, 1966 17 Aug, p 271.

GLASGOW: The University of Glasgow Reading Room (administered as a separate building by the Glasgow University Library) *In* RIBA *Journal*, 1950 Aug, pp 390–1. *Architect and Building News*, 1950 June 16, p 616. *Architects Journal*, 1950 June 15, p 736.

HARVARD UNIVERSITY: Harvard College Library. *Space for books and scholars (Proposed new underground extensions to the library)* The University Cambridge, Mass (1969?).

HULL: Hull University Library. *In Architectural Review*, 1966 January, 23, *Light and Lighting*, 1969 August, pp 229–31, *Archi-*

tects Journal, 1971 January 27, pp 189–204, *Architectural Design*, 1970 January, pp 26–31, *Library Association Record* 1960 June, pp 185–9.

LEEDS: Brotherton Library, Leeds University. *In Architecture and Building*, 1955 July, pp 275–77.

LEICESTER: University of Leicester Library, *In Architectural Design*, 1968 March, pp 137–40.

LIVERPOOL: Extension to the City College of Commerce, Liverpool; including a library and reading room. *In Architecture and Building News* 1953 Oct 29, pp 504–7.

LONDON: Library block for Queen Elizabeth College, Campden Hill, London; includes a lecture room, assembly hall, stage, laboratory and offices as well as the library. *In Builder* 1954 Jan 15, pp 119–24.

NOTTINGHAM: Electrical Engineering and Department of Architecture tower block and science library, Nottingham University. *In Architectural and Building News*, 1965 Aug 18, pp 299–306.

OXFORD: Proposed new group for Oxford (The group comprises a law library, a library for the English faculty and permanent premises for the Institute of Statistics). *In Architects Journal* 1960 Oct 6, pp 493–6, *Architectural and Building News*, 1960 Oct 5, pp 422–4, *Architectural Design*, 1960 Oct, pp 399–403.

OXFORD: GILLAM, S G. *The Building Accounts of the Radcliffe Camera* (Oxford Historical Society, New Series, Vol XIII) Oxford, Clarendon Press 1958.

OXFORD: New building at Wadham College, Oxford: consisting mainly of a library, common room and twenty-three sets of undergraduates' rooms.
In Building, 1953 Oct, pp 368–74, *Builder*, 1957 July 5, pp 10–11.

SHEFFIELD: University Library, Sheffield.
In Architectural Review, 1959 Dec, pp 307–14, *Architects Journal*, 1959 Dec 31, pp 777–96 (cost analysis), *Builder*, 1960 March 4, pp 447–54, *Architects Journal*, 1965 March 17, pp 673–81, *Architect and Building News*, 1960 March 23, pp 375–86 (cost analysis), *Architectural Design*, 1960 Oct, pp 396–8.

SUSSEX: University of Sussex Library, Brighton.
In Architect and Building News, 1965 Feb 17, pp 311–16. *Library Association Record*, 1965 May, pp 157–62.

SWANSEA: Library extension, University College of Swansea.
In Architect and Building News, 1968 July 10, pp 52–9.

SWANSEA: Swansea Arts Building and Library.
In Building 1966 Dec 23, p 26.

WARWICK: University of Warwick Library.
In Architects Journal, 1966 Nov 23, pp 1271–84, *Architecture and Building News* 1967 April 12, pp 629–38, *Builder*, 1965 April 9, p 810, *Building*, 1966 Oct 28, pp 95–8, *Interbuild* 1966 Oct, pp 28–30, *Interior Design*, 1966 Nov, pp 528–32.

Descriptions of new libraries: public central libraries (municipal)
BIRMINGHAM: Central public library, Paradise Circus.
In Building, 1970 July 10, pp 57–8.

BRADFORD: New Central Library.
In Builder 1964 Nov 27, pp 1180–4, *Building* 1968 Feb 23, pp 77–80, *Official Architecture*, 1964 Oct, pp 1180–4, *Surveyor*, 1964 Sept 12, pp 25–6, 74, *West Yorkshire Society of Architects Journal*, 1964 Oct, pp 6–10.

HAMPSTEAD: Hampstead Public Library.
In Architect and Building News, 1964 Nov 11, pp 923–36, *Architects Journal*, 1964 Nov 25, pp 1245–58, *Architects Journal* 1965 Mar 24, pp 731–4, *Builder*, 1964 Nov 27, pp 1131–5, 1166, *Concrete and Constructional Engineering*, 1965 Feb, pp 63–7, *Concrete Quarterly*, 1964 Oct–Dec, pp 14–18, *Library Association Record* 1964 Dec, pp 502–9, *Official Architecture*, 1964 Dec, pp 1533–9, *Surveyor*, 1964 Nov 14, pp 53–4.

HOLBORN: Holborn Central Library, London.
In Architect and Building News, 1960 Oct 19, pp 493–504, (cost analysis), *Architects Journal*, 1965 Mar 3, pp 549–61, *Builder*, 1960 Oct 14, pp 694–8, *Library Association Record* 1960 Nov, pp 358–61, *Official Architecture*, 1960 Nov, pp 493, 497–50.

HORNSEY: Hornsey Central Library, Haringey, London.

In Library Association Record, 1965 April, pp 117–23.

KENSINGTON: Kensington Central Library, London.
In Official Architecture, 1960 Nov, pp 506–9, *Library Association Record*, 1960 Nov, pp 361–5.

KINGSTON-UPON-HULL: Central Library Extension, Kingston-upon-Hull.
In Official Architecture, 1963 Dec, pp 1210–14.

LUTON: Luton Central Library.
In Architect and Building News, 1964 Nov, pp 871–6, *Official Architecture*, 1962 Dec, pp 801–5

MAIDENHEAD: Maidenhead Central Library.
In Tubular Structure 1971 April, No 18, p 23.

NEWCASTLE UPON TYNE: Central Library, Newcastle upon Tyne.
In Architektur und Wohnform (Stuttgart) 1965 Oct, pp 362–3, *Builder*, 1964 Sep 11, pp 541–5
Building, 1969 August 29, pp 47–9.

NORWICH: Central Library.
The New Central Library Norwich: technical notes, City Architects Department, Norwich 1963, Norwich, Libraries Committee, Norwich 1963.
Also in Official Architect, 1960 Nov, pp 512–6, *Architects Journal*, 1963 May 8, pp 99–102, *International Lighting Review*, 1965 No 1, pp 12–17, *Library Association Record*, 1960 Nov, pp 373–4.

NUNEATON: Public Library Nuneaton.
In Architectural Review, 1963 April, pp 285–6, *Builder*, 1963 May 24, pp 1033–7.

ORPINGTON: Central Public Library, Orpington.
In Official Architecture, 1965 June, pp 821–23.

PORTSMOUTH: Central Library **Portsmouth**.
In Architects Journal, 1971 Dec 22 and 29, pp 1408–9.

ST PANCRAS: St Pancras Library, Shaw Theatre, and office block, Euston Road, London.
In Architects Journal, 1971 June 9, pp 1311–24.

Descriptions of new libraries: public central libraries (county)
BRECON: County Library Headquarters, Brecon
In Interior Design, 1970 Feb, pp 96–7

BUCKINGHAMSHIRE: Buckinghamshire County Council Offices, Aylesbury, (houses the Aylesbury town library, District Register Office, Youth Employment Bureau, and Civil Defence training centre as well as the usual council offices).
In Architect and Building News, 1966 Nov 2, pp 769–82, *Building*, 1966 Nov 25, pp 71–4, *Architects Journal*, 1966 Oct 5, pp 851–66.

KENT: County Library Headquarters, Maidstone.
In Architect and Building News, 1964 Sept 30, pp 633–40, *Official Architecture*, 1964 Dec, pp 1525–31, *Library Association Record,* 1964 Dec. pp 530–8.

WEST RIDING, YORKSHIRE: West Riding County Library Headquarters, Wakefield.
In Library Association Record, 1964 Dec, pp 522–30

Descriptions of new libraries: public branch libraries
ASHINGTON: Branch Library, Ashington, Northumberland.
In Building, 1966 Dec 30, pp 43–6.

BASILDON: Basildon Fryerns Branch Library and Community Centre, Essex.
In Builder, 1962 March 30, p 655.

BEACONSFIELD: Public Library in Reynolds Road, Beaconsfield, Bucks.
In Architects Journal, 1959 July 25, pp 149–58, *Architecture and Building*, 1957 August, pp 323–5, *Architects Journal*, 1965 Mar 10, pp 621–5 (re-appraisal).

BOGNOR REGIS: Branch Library Bognor Regis.
In Builder, 1965 Feb 12, pp 339–40.

BRISTOL: Branch Library, Bristol.
In Builder, 1961 June 2, pp 1036–7.

CHEAM: County Branch Library, Cheam.
In Interbuild, 1962 July, pp 20–2, *Architect and Building News*, 1963 March 6, pp 343–6.

CINDERFORD: Design for a library with laminated timber arches, Cinderford, Glos.
In Wood, 1962 Oct, pp 404–5.
ENFIELD: Bush Hill Public Library London Borough of Enfield.
In Building Specification 1971, September, pp 41–3, 58.
ESSEX: Examples of six Essex County Libraries at Broomfield, Canvey Island, Debden, Wanstead and Woodford, Harlow and Romford.
In Builder, 1962 March 16, pp 542–9.
EWELL: Bourne Hall, Public Library and Community Centre, Ewell, Surrey.
In Surveyor, 1970 Feb 13, pp 48–9, Concrete, 1970 March, pp 101–3. *Architect and Building News*, 1970 March 19, pp 54–5, *Building*, 1970 April 17, pp 63–7.
FINSBURY: Public Library, Finsbury.
In Architect and Building News, 1967 Nov 1, pp 727–9, *Building*, 1967 April 21, pp 95–8.
FINSBURY: St Luke's Branch Library, Finsbury, London.
In Architect and Building News, 1963 March 6, pp 351–4.
GUILDFORD: Library and Exhibition Centre, Guildford.
In Official Architecture, 1963 Feb, pp 119–23.
HACKNEY: Stamford Hill branch Library, Hackney, London.
In Surveyor, 1968 Nov 23, p 38.
HAYLING ISLAND: Branch Library, Hayling Island, Hampshire.
In Brick Bulletin, 1967 July, pp 2–5.
HORLEY: Central Library, Horley Surrey.
In Building, 1966 Dec 16, pp 57–9.
KINGSTON-UPON-HULL: Gipsyville Branch Library, Kingston-upon-Hull.
In Official Architecture and Planning, 1957 May, pp 230–2.
LAMBETH: Library and Public Hall at West Norwood, London.
In Architects Journal, 1969 Sep 17, pp 688–704, *Arup Journal*, 1970 June, pp 17–21.
LANGLEY: Branch Library, Langley, Bucks.
In Architects Journal, 1965 March 10, pp 613–9.
LEEDS: Branch Library, Seacroft, Leeds.
In Builder, 1964 Dec 11, pp 1247–9.
LEWISHAM: Bromley Road Branch Library, Lewisham, London.
In Official Architecture, 1963 Aug, pp 738–42.
MARSKE: Marske Branch Library.
In Builder, 1963 Aug 9, pp 271–2.
MORECAMBE: Branch Library Morecambe.
In Building, 1968 April 19, pp 89–92.

NEWCASTLE: Jesmond Public Library, Newcastle.
In Builder, 1965 March 26, pp 671–4, *Northern Architect*, 1965 March, pp 472–7.
PORTSMOUTH: Project for Branch Library, Drayton.
In Architectural Design, 1969 Jan, p 28.
REDBRIDGE: Branch Public Library, Wanstead, London
In Building, 1970 May 15, pp 79–82.
REDBRIDGE: Covered swimming pool and library, Fullwell Cross, Barkingside, London.
In Architects Journal, 1968 June 12, pp 1331–46.
REDCAR: District Library.
In Architectural Review, 1971 July, pp 43–50.
ST PANCRAS: Regents Park Library, St Pancras, London.
In Architect and Building News, 1962 May 9, pp 679–82.
ST AUSTELL: Branch Library, St Austell, Cornwall.
In Architects Journal, 1961 Aug 16, pp 235–46, *Builder*, 1962 Feb 23, pp 396–8.
SKELMORLIE: Village Centre, Skelmorlie, Ayr.
In Builder, 1962 Sep 14, pp 533–4.
SOUTHEND-ON-SEA: Branch Library at Westcliffe, Southend-on-Sea.
In Architects Journal, 1961 Jan 26, pp 149–58, *Deutsche Bauzeitschrift*, 1961, No 7, pp 931–2.
SUDBURY: Conversion of Corn Exchange to Branch Library.
In ERA, 1969 June, pp 23–6.
SUNBURY-ON-THAMES: Public Library.
In Architects Journal, 1968 Jan 3, pp 37–46, *Architect and Building News*, 1967 Dec 6, pp 909–14. *Interior Design*, 1969 Oct, pp 642–4.
ULVERSTON: Ulverston Branch Library, Lancs.
In Builder, 1965 June 4, pp 1221–3.
WALLSEND: Library, Wallsend.
In Architect and Building News, 1967 Feb 8, pp 233–44.
WEMBLEY: Branch Public Library, Carlton Ave East, Wembley, London.
In Architect and Building News, 1965 Sep 8, pp 457–60.
WEST BYFLEET: Public Library, West Byfleet, Surrey.
In Architect and Building News, 1966 August 24, pp 331–4.
WESTMINSTER: Children's Library, Churchill Gardens, Pimlico, London.
In Architect and Building News, 1960 Oct 12, pp 465–8, *Library Association Record*, 1960 Nov, pp 367–8.
WITNEY: Welch Way Development, Witney.
In Building, 1967 June 9, pp 89–93.

Illustration credits

a = architect   t = top, b = bottom, c = centre
c = copyright   l = left, r = right
m = manufacturer   1, 2, etc = first, second etc
p = photographer   AJ = Architects' Journal
                   LA = Library Association

Page

45t: a, c, Spence, Glover and Ferguson; p A L Hunter
45b: a, c, Russell, Hodgson and Leigh
46t: a York, Rosenberg and Mardall; cp AJ, W J Toomey
46b: a Tom Mellor and Partners; cp AJ
48b: a Williamson, Faulkner Brown and Partners; cp AJ, W J Toomey
49t: cp LA
49b: a Edward Hollamby; p Richard Einzig; c Brecht-Einzig Ltd
61t: cm Terrapin Reska Ltd; p Harrison and Laking Ltd
71b: p LA, p L Maylott
73t: a Castle Park Dean Hook; c, p AJ, W J Toomey
73c: a, c Castle Park Dean Hook
73b: a Williamson, Faulkner Brown and Partners; cp AJ, W J Toomey
76t: ap Dept of Planning and Development, Teesside
76b: c City Librarian, Manchester
79cl: a Ahrends, Burton, Koralek; cp John Donat
79bl::   m Library Design and Engineering Ltd; a Doncaster Borough Architects Department; p John Maltby Ltd
83tl: m Terrapin Reska Ltd; p A C H Kirk
90:      ac Spence, Glover and Ferguson; p Henk Snoek
94:      mc Acrow (Engineering) Ltd
95tr: mc Acrow Automation; p Derek Evans
95br: mc J Glover and Sons; p John Davis Ltd
96tr: mc Libraco Ltd
96cr: a Shaver with Fitzroy Robinson & Partners; mc Library Design and Engineering Ltd
97tr: m Library Design and Engineering Ltd
97tl: cp AJ W J Toomey
97bl: c LA
97cr: a Ahrends, Burton and Koralek; cp John Donat
97br: a Matthew, Johnson Marshall and Partners; cp John Donat
98tl: m Keeles of Hadleigh Ltd; p Keith Gibson
98bl: m Serota Ltd
98tr: a George, Trew, Dunn; p Henk Snoek
98br: m Library Design and Engineering Ltd; p John Maltby
99:      mc Sculthorpe's Art Utilities Ltd
100c: m Ranplan; p Stewart Bale Ltd

100t: cp AJ, W J Toomey
101tl: m Libraco Ltd; p G A Harvey
101tr: a Edward Hollamby; c AJ p Sam Lambert
101cl: m Terrapin Reska Ltd; p A C H Kirk
103t: a Gollins Melvin Ward; cp Henk Snoek
103b: ac Yorke, Rosenberg, Mardall; p Thomas-Photos
104tr: cp Snoek-Westwood
105t: a Matthew, Johnson-Marshall and Partners; c AJ, p Keith Gibson
106:      both: a Yorke, Rosenberg, Mardall; cp AJ, W J Toomey
107tr: cp LA
107cr: ap Tom Mellor and Partners
108t: ac Edward Hallamby (Lambeth Borough); p Eric de Maré
108b: a Shaver with Fitzroy Robinson and Partners; m Library Design and Engineering Ltd
109:      a Spence, Glover and Ferguson; pc Henk Snoek
112:      both: cp AJ, W J Toomey
113t: m Keeles of Hadleigh
115t: a Julian Sofaer; p Colin Westwood
116:      m Terrapin-Reska; cp John Tarlton
119:      acp Department of Planning and Development, Teesside
119bl: ac Spence, Glover and Ferguson; cp Snoek-Westwood
119br: c City Librarian, Leeds
125:      both: m Library Design and Engineering Ltd; p John Maltby
126tl, tr: m Library Design and Engineering Ltd; p John Maltby
126cl: p author
127bl: mcp Conran and Co
127tr: mc Interlink; p Studio Lisa
130:      c LA, p B J Studios
133t: m Geo W King; p Gilchrist Photo Services
134t: Lamson Engineering Co Ltd
134b   m Marshall Handling Equipment Ltd
135tl, tr: Crown copyright
135br: m Warwick Production Co Ltd; p Thomas Photos
136tl, tr: m Sperry-Rand; p Tom Kroeza, Rotterdam
137:      m Roneo-Vickers Ltd
142t: p Cumbernauld News Studio
143t: a Edward Hollamby (Lambeth Borough); pc Brecht-Einzig Ltd
143b: ac Spence, Glover and Ferguson
148t: a Castle Park Dean Hook; cp AJ, W J Toomey
148b: m Checkpoint
149:      m John Little Associates
154:      a Matthew, Johnson-Marshall and Partners; cp AJ, Keith Gibson
155:      m Brockhouse Modernfold Ltd
160, 161:   both: c Borough of Dudley
162: c City of Glasgow Corporation

Index

30735

1994 A

A

A

WITHDRAWN